THIRTY YEARS OF BLUES COMMENTARY

Blues off the Record

PAUL OLIVER

A DA CAPO PAPERBACK

Library of Congress Cataloging in Publication Data

Oliver, Paul.
  Blues off the record: thirty years of blues commentary / Paul Oliver.
  (A Da Capo paperback)
  Reprint. Originally published: Tunbridge Wells, England: Baton Press, 1984.
  Includes index.
  ISBN 0-306-80321-6 (pbk.)
  1. Blues (Music)—History and criticism. I. Title.
[ML3521.O44 1988]
784.5′3′00973—dc19   87-34668
                                                                            CIP

This Da Capo Press paperback edition of *Blues Off the Record* is an unabridged republication
of the edition published in Tunbridge Wells, England in 1984. It is reprinted by
arrangement with the author.

Published by Da Capo Press, Inc.
A Subsidiary of Plenum Publishing Corporation
233 Spring Street, New York, N.Y. 10013

Contents

CHAPTER 3 MOANERS AND SHOUTERS

CHAPTER 4 LET'S GO TO TOWN

CHAPTER 5 STOMP 'EM DOWN

CHAPTER 6 TALKING BLUES

CHAPTER 7 SITTIN' HERE THINKIN'

Stop
and Listen

PAUL OLIVER

Illustration for "Jazz: New Music with Ancient Roots", *Radio Times*, July 27, 1956

An Introduction

Radio station KPFA in Berkeley is fairly typical of the small American station; one or two rooms, a library of tapes stashed in a cupboard and a lot more tape on the floor. Every broadcaster seems to be his own disc jockey, managing the records, putting in a plug or two for local functions, taking calls on the phone. It's quite a juggling act, talking to a listener while the record is playing then switching to the turntable in time as the disc comes to an end. And interviewing visitors who happen to be in town, as I was in February 1981. Tom Mazzolini has a regular blues spot and invited me to the studio for a discussion. It was a long session and the questions were interesting. As far as most such interviews go, they were more probing than usual. The discussion even got round to the kind of interest that people have shown in different parts of the world, and a comparison between interviews in, say, Germany or Australia.

'What are some of the questions you're often asked?' Tom inquired.

'The most boring and repetitive question, "How did you first become interest in the blues?" – that's asked me every time,' I replied, after which he could hardly ask it. Not really fair on my part, but it does arise at every interview and every lecture. 'The most frequent questions are either about me in relation to blues, which is understandable in a lecture situation, a matter of curiosity, or "How come you're British and white and you're talking about a black music, and etc. etc." the same old thing,' I added.

For the most part in my writing I tend to keep myself out of the text, so that there's a focus on the subject of blues or blues singers, without any intrusion. But this collection of essays and articles is a retrospect over three decades, so for a change I am adding a few personal reminiscences that may answer, somewhat obliquely I admit, some of those questions. *How* then, did I get interested in the blues?

It was the summer of 1942 and I, as a young teenager, was expected to work in what was then termed a 'harvest camp'. This was a means of getting farm work done while releasing men for service in the Army. Later I helped run logging camps, where trees were felled and logged up for pit props. The camp I'm speaking of now was at Stoke-by-Clare in Suffolk and the Americans, who had just entered the War, were digging in. As I understood it later, these military camps were supposed not to be segregated, but the only men I ever saw doing the heavy manual work were black. Not that I was aware of them immediately.

I had a friend named Stan who was a little older than me. He knew I was interested in songs and that I used to get a carter named Herbert, who was leading the hay wagon, to sing me the songs he knew. I used to exchange them for sketches I did of Herbert, his horse and the farm, and I remember him saying as he carefully put into the pocket of his corduroy jacket a pencil portrait of himself: 'I'll remember you long after you've forgotten me.' But it's not true, Herbert, if you are still living, which I doubt: I'll always remember the kindliness and simplicity of that farm worker, who never in his life had ventured outside his county. In a way, it was Herbert who influenced me as much as anybody, but Stan had other adventures in mind. 'I'm going to take you to hear something you won't forget,' he said. And that was certainly true.

It very nearly didn't happen, though.

Stan led me out to where the base was being established, strictly 'out of bounds'. On the other side of a hedge a gang of black soldiers were swinging what we called mattocks, digging a trench. 'Listen. They'll be singing in a minute,' Stan whispered, but there was no sound except the sinking of the mattocks in the soil and the grunted exhalations of the men. A few minutes later an NCO stopped them working, called them together and marched them off after a few minutes of barked and indistinct orders. All of them, that is, except two, who were presumably put on 'fatigues' and left to complete the work.

We stayed behind the hedge, getting cold. I was getting impatient too, when suddenly the air seemed split by the most eerie sounds. The two men were singing, swooping, undulating, unintelligible words, and the back of my neck tingled. 'They're singing a *blues*,' Stan hissed at me. It was the strangest, most compelling singing I'd ever heard, and when at last the NCO came back and after a cursory examination of their work, marched them off too, I wanted to know from Stan how he knew what they were singing, and what it was?

Stan, it turned out, had a collection of records which he kept in an orange box. They were blues records, he explained, and when we got back from the camp he played them to me over and over again. A while after he himself went into the Army, under age, and I never saw him again. But I'd started my own collection and soon there were quite a few friends who were doing so too, all of us prepared to cross London in spite of the difficulties of wartime transport and complete blackout, in order to purchase a 78rpm record. Record shops had a quota under wartime restrictions, and only a very few thought that stocking blues or jazz was worth considering when they could so easily dispose of their quota in records of

Bing Crosby, Gracie Fields or Vera Lynn. I learned the merits of the orange box myself; the boxes were in two compartments each just over ten inches in width and strong enough to take as many records as one could lift.

That's how it began, but in a sense, I was already prepared for the blues when I first heard those two soldiers. Since I was about eleven I had been collecting songs in notebooks, first of all from the singing of my mother. She came from Herefordshire on the Welsh border and had an extraordinary repertoire of songs drawn from every kind of source. When there was a radio programme in which American folk songs and, eventually, blues and work songs, were featured (Alan Lomax was responsible for one or two) she would help me take down the words by taking alternate lines. I have those notebooks still. One I bound in oilcloth so that it would stand up to the weather when I was in camp.

I'd started collecting books about that time. They could be bought very cheaply – for a few pence on the Farringdon Road bookstalls. One day I picked up *Roll Jordan Roll* by Julia Peterkin, with photographs by Dorothy Ulmann, published in 1933. The account of life in a Georgia Sea Island community with its praise house, its baptisms, conjure woman and work on the chain gang, and the soft-focus but moving photographs that illustrated it, filled out the background to the records I was buying. Some words were explained, some allusions made clear, and I began seeking other books that would help to create a picture in depth of the music that was taking up so much of my time.

There wasn't much to be gained from any other source, though the one or two jazz magazines usually had occasional features on blues. Max Jones in particular wrote articles and the Jazz Sociological Society published booklets which included a 'tribute to Huddie Ledbetter' and features of interest. Jazz Music Books printed Ernest Borneman's *An Anthropologist Looks at Jazz* and Rudi Blesh's *This Is Jazz* which placed blues in the context of jazz. But the most important book to me was published by the Workers' Music Association, *Background of the Blues* by Iain Lang. He, too, regarded blues as part of jazz but he gave it greater importance. Then in 1946 Albert McCarthy's *PL Year-book of Jazz* was published with a long article 'On Blues' by Max Jones, which I read avidly.

It was still a few years before I felt confident enough to start writing myself, and that was largely prompted by exasperation. But once I did there seemed to be no problem in getting the articles published, only a problem of time in which to write and research them, let alone transcribe the words on the records. One of the nicest aspects of blues collecting, and one that has not changed over all the intervening years, is the friendliness and helpfulness of other collectors. A network of friendships was woven between enthusiasts of many countries, occupations and ages, and the sharing of information was always generous. Many of them helped while I was writing *Blues Fell This Morning* and the initials after the details of cited records are some indication of my indebtedness to them.

Blues Fell This Morning was due to be handed in to the publisher in Spring 1958. After visiting Paris over Easter, my wife, Val, and I took a coach to Grenoble carrying the text, two typewriters and a ream of paper. We found a small hotel in the mountains at Laffrey on the Route Napoleon and settled in to complete the work, with me writing the final chapters while Val typed the finished copy. The idea was to have energetic walks in between sessions but a heavy snowstorm kept us confined to the

hotel. We were the only guests but the patron insisted on serving five-course meals twice a day, with unlimited wine, marvellous, in a way, but it was hard to keep a clear head for writing. Back at last when the snow was cleared from the road, I handed in my manuscript to the publisher. Soon after, a long printers' dispute effectively held up the publishing on the book for nearly two years, during which I wrote and saw published a small book on *Bessie Smith*.

All our small savings went into a trip to the United States in 1960, augmented by a State Department Grant. Out of the interviews I put together some programmes for the BBC and started compiling a book that would be a form of continuous narrative about the blues by the singers themselves. Selecting the passages from the tapes was far from easy and requests for articles, or sleeve notes for long-playing record issues kept on coming in. The Sixties was a very prolific period for me, so far as blues was concerned, but my work in painting and graphics was now almost totally concentrated on record sleeve designs, illustrations and occasional book jackets for jazz and blues issues. It was 1965 before *Conversation with the Blues* came out.

By this time I had been teaching part-time at the Architectural Association; blues and jazz articles hardly paid, and I couldn't make a living solely out of illustration. Then I had a request to teach in Ghana, West Africa, in both the School of Architecture at the University in Kumasi, and at the Music Department of the Institute of African Studies at the University of Ghana, Legon, which was run by the distinguished African music scholar, Kwabena Nketia. It was too good to miss. I'd had a deep interest in African art since my student days and had built up a modest collection – mainly from the junk shops where I was hunting for records. Quite a few African records had come my way as well, so I was well prepared – or so I thought. Africa was more exciting and more influential on me than I had expected, and an opportunity to work in the north of Ghana on the border with Upper Volta in the Savannah region, opened up ideas about African music and its relation to blues, which only the live experience could make possible. It took me five years to synthesize the result of my researches in Africa and the eventual book, *Savannah Syncopators: African Retentions in the Blues*, was, I think, the one I'm most glad to have written, though some found its challenge to the received ideas about the relationship of African music to that of Afro-America hard to accept. The title was a pun on the name of Oliver's Savannah Syncopators orchestra, but no-one noticed.

That was much later; my immediate problem on returning from Ghana and Nigeria was to organize a major exhibition at the American Embassy. During the 1960s the Embassy had an enlightened policy towards cultural activities under the direction of its Cultural Affairs Officer, Francis Mason. When the new Embassy building designed by Eero Saarinen was opened in Grosvenor Square, I was asked to give the opening lecture in the new lecture hall; I gave it on my field recordings in the United States. Afterwards a lady came up to me and referring to the last recording I played, 'Sugar Babe' by Mance Lipscomb, she said: 'I always thought that *something* was going on, on the other side of the tracks. I come from Navasota myself.'

Francis Mason also approached me, but to plan an exhibition on the blues. It took three years to get the photographs, copy them and return them, obtain the copyright releases, write the texts and have the exhibition planned. There were some five hundred items on show and they filled the huge foyer that was then the exhibition space. It was a great pleasure to me to have such singers as Lightnin' Hopkins and Little Walter visit the show, not to mention Langston Hughes, and the whole Alvin Ailey Dance Company. Out of that came *The Story of the Blues* as a book, though between times I wrote a collection of essays on aspects of blues which interested me, or which presented problems that I felt had to be confronted. One of these was the sheer quantity of sexual blues, and one beneficial outcome of the *Lady Chatterley's Lover* trial was that it was possible to deal with the subject without dishonest bowdlerization. *Screening the Blues* came out in 1968 while I was still working with Mack McCormick on a book on blues in Texas. The material we amassed reached Titanic proportions, and unfortunately the work met its own iceberg. I still hope that it will be recovered.

By 1970 I had a lot that I wanted to write on architecture and felt I needed a rest from writing about blues. For one thing, the blues magazines that started with *Blues Unlimited* in 1963 were thriving and there were now many writers on the subject on both sides of the Atlantic. In 1973 Val and I moved down to Dartington in Devon and it made a suitable time to make the break. I had the opportunity to stop writing and listen to my collection afresh. For much of the next ten years I concentrated on the *other* forms of black music which the focus on blues had largely eclipsed. As I write this I am bringing that material together in another book. It wasn't a completely unproductive period so far as the blues was concerned though; I was able to write the entries for *The New Grove Dictionary of Music and Musicians*, and more recently I've been occasionally writing sleeve notes again.

One of the problems of writing is that texts go out of print; this is inconvenient enough with books, which have a life of a few years, but particularly the case with articles and sleeves notes. Not only do they go out of print, the magazines cease to publish and the record companies cut out their issues or go into liquidation. Looking back over thirty years of writing in these more ephemeral media I'm aware of how much has gone beyond any easy recall. This book is a collection of such writings brought together in the form of a personal anthology. I hope there is a lot that will be new to many readers.

There are problems of course. In a field which has expanded like blues there has been much later writing that has added new information on the work of many singers. Sadly, there have been many deaths among blues singers in recent years, and articles based on interviews and current recordings are now republished posthumously. Where it has been necessary to correct such details, or bring the text up to date, I have made an additional note. There are variations in length – from short essays on record sleeves to long studies in magazines like *Jazz Monthly*. But I hope these will give to the reader that variety they gave me in writing them. Because records are sometimes issued of the same artists, there is often an overlap of information, a fact which raises the problem of how much the pieces should be edited. Where there is obvious redundancy I've edited it out and, in a few instances, passages which were apposite at the time but which have no relevance now, have been omitted.

Generally though, the essays have been edited as little as possible which means that some details read 'in period'. Of these the use of the term 'Negro', which was the preferred one in the Sixties and early Seventies, and its replacement in the late Seventies to the present day by 'black', has not been tampered with; they appear as was thought proper at the time the passages were written. There is a problem of function also. Articles

for magazines have a different purpose from those written as sleeve notes. Fortunately, recording companies reissuing blues discs do not pressure sleeve-note writers to say 'good' things about the contents. When I wasn't interested in the issue I declined the invitation to write the notes, but the references to specific artists or titles often reflects the choice of items being issued. In a few instances where a couple of notes have been written on the same subject and complement each other, they've been run together, but I have made it clear where this has been done.

Rather than arrange the articles chronologically, which might have made the changes in style less apparent, I've grouped them according to subject. While most of my books have been thematic, most of my articles and notes have been on individual singers. A thematic section 'Going on Record' opens the book, with examples of some of the forms and functions of rural music that went into or which paralleled the blues, and the factors which influenced the recording of the music. 'Picking the Box', on guitar-playing bluesmen, follows, while 'Moaners and Shouters' groups together pieces on the jazz/blues singers and stage entertainers. The movement from the rural areas to the cities in the South, to the North and to the West is indicated in 'Let's Go to Town'; and some of the urban pianists are the subject of 'Stomp 'Em Down'. Many of these have been articles based largely on the evidence of records, but 'Talking Blues' is specifically devoted to essays arising from interviews with blues singers. The final chapter, 'Sittin' and Thinkin' opens up a few speculations, always for me the most enjoyable aspect of writing.

This being a personal collection I've introduced the sections with a few recollections related to their themes, while the line illustrations are from record-sleeve designs and other drawings done in connection with articles and broadcasts. A few personal photographs fill out the images. From the discs that shaped my musical taste, to the features that were written on the music they contained; from the notes written for the LP sleeves to the drawings designed for their covers; from the material gathered in informal conversations with blues singers to the autobiographical fragments in the introductory passages; this is, in more ways than one, an 'off the record' compilation on the blues.

1
Going on Record

Illustration to "Give Me That Old Time Religion" *Jazz Journal*, Vol 5, No 2, February 1952

Oddly enough, the first article that I published wasn't on blues at all. I wrote it in 1951 and it was published in February 1952 in *Jazz Journal*. To my surprise Tom Cundall and Sinclair Traill made it the lead article; I'd expected it to be tucked away at the back of the magazine. After all, it wasn't on jazz either, but on black religious music. It seemed to me that the marvellous music on gospel records and the tremendous strength of the sermons needed recognition and research. Now, over thirty years later, I'm still of that opinion.

A few articles followed: on seeking Big Bill Broonzy and Blind John Davis in France, on 'Jazz in Negro Literature' and on the early Jubilee singers, among them. Then Tom Cundall got in touch with me about a new magazine he was going to edit, *Music Mirror*. It was to be about all music, and he wondered if I'd write on subjects of interest to me. I'm rather dismayed today to note that my taste was rather broader then; I wrote what was, I believe, the first article in English on the current developments in France on *musique concrète*, and reviewed concerts of modern American music. But with the first number, I started a series called 'Sources of Afro-American Folk Song' which brought together some of the material, and the records, I'd gathered in my fast-growing library.

All my life I've been a bibliophile and my principal exercise is using the step-ladder to reach the top shelf in secondhand bookshops. 'Jazz in Negro Literature' was a by-product of that book hunting, but the gleanings from books on the South, black culture, labour relations, railroad lore, census statistics, accounts of slavery, agricultural production and a hundred other themes went into the articles. They were hammered out on a forty-year-old Oliver typewriter (bought for the name, I suspect), standing on the tea-trolley which served as a desk. As what little we had to spare from a teacher's pay in those days was going on books and records, there wasn't much room for other indulging. But we used to take school parties to France each year and, having safely deposited the boys on their temporary foster-parents, were able to enjoy a paid-for (just) stay in Paris. Our friends ranged from out-of-luck painters to trans-Sahara truck drivers, but one day a fellow teacher, Dennis King, asked me if I knew of a black American named Richard Wright who 'said he wrote books' and would like to see me. Having devoured *Black Boy*, *Native Son* and *Twelve Million Black Voices*, I could hardly believe it. Like most writers in Paris he didn't spend much time at his home on Rue Monsieur la Prince, but used a café table as an office. His particular haunt was the Danton and there we met often, talked for hours over occasional cups of coffee bought when the proprietor eventually got a little fidgety for lack of custom, and met up with many of the black Americans who were then living in Paris. They included, I recall, Ollie Harrington, a black cartoonist, and Rudy Aggrey, the son of 'Aggrey of Africa' whose autobigraphy I had read.

Some years later those threads wove together again, when in Ghana I met up with Richard Wright's daughter, a student sociologist who was making a study of the 'Mammies' who controlled the market trade, and also went to Achimota where I discovered Aggrey had been a teacher. But that was a good while after the Paris days. There was a restaurant also patronised by expatriate Americans, especially musicians, run by Gabby Haynes. There I met the strange, battered 'White Negro', Mezz Mezzrow, whose *Really the Blues* was one of the seminal books for me. And always there was our friend Jacques Demetre to look up and to spin discs with, and a lot of music by Bill Coleman, Sidney Bechet, Lil

Armstrong, Sam Price or others who came to Paris, or were living there, and who played in the dank cellar clubs of the Rue de la Huchette – now alas, and inevitably, a tourist trap.

From them all I learned a great deal. They were curious about my questions, but always helpful; after all, it was a subculture of talking, writing and music. I had plans to publish 'Sources' in book form, but as I proceeded it became obvious that the subject would be too vast; I decided to narrow it to the music I enjoyed most, the blues. So often the meanings of terms remained elusive; I had a record by Leroy Carr titled 'Eleven Twenty-Nine Blues', and it was Richard who told me that it meant a sentence of one day less than a year. Obvious enough, afterwards. I put it in my book, which was shaping up as a study of what blues were *about*: I called it *Blues Fell This Morning*, and rather nervously asked Richard if he would read it. His enthusiasm and his offer to write an introduction to it astonished me. A young but quietly militant black church leader came to Paris that year, 1958, and Richard showed the book to him. His name was Martin Luther King. He laughed at the fact that a white Englishman had written the book, and then brooded on it for quite a while; as a churchman he was uncomfortable with the secular content of the book, and while he didn't criticize it he would have preferred to have seen religious song in it. Richard Wright had no such desire; he rejoiced in the 'lusty, lyrical realism' of the blues and saw in them 'an almost exultant affirmation of life, of love, of sex, of movement, of hope'. His support for the book I valued then, as I do now, more than I can say.

After the publication of *Blues Fell This Morning* Richard Wright wanted me to join him in a publishing venture concerned with the problems of minorities – not only racial ones. We discussed it at length but I was tied up with educational matters and time slipped by; suddenly he died, and I felt a deep loss. By then I had made my first trip to the States and, with a grant from the State Department, had travelled through the northern cities including Detroit and Chicago, south to Memphis, and on through Mississippi, Arkansas, Louisiana, Texas and the West Coast, before returning via St Louis and Washington. I was helped by numerous enthusiasts in various places: Bob Koester and John Steiner in Chicago; Charley O'Brien in St Louis; Mack McCormick in Texas; Dick Allen and Bill Russell in New Orleans, among many others.

The State Department offered help of its own, which was sometimes embarrasssing. In Detroit a wiry, lively sexagenarian named Mrs Florence Cassidy was determined to arrange my programme, and I was just as determined that she was not going to. We compromised, with my agreeing to attend a performance by a black dancer in the theatre of Wayne University, which she put on especially for me. The dancer was named LaRogue Wright and when the curtains parted he came prancing on stage in a leopard skin, and brandishing a spear. I found it excrutiating and asked if he could stop; Mrs Cassidy was not pleased, so I suggested an interview. 'Where,' I asked LaRogue Wright, 'does the dance come from?' 'Africa,' he said. 'Where in Africa?' He didn't know. Then where had he obtained it? 'From Katherine Dunham's dance troupe . . .'

I had to do something to save the situation. Did he know how to dance the Eagle Rock? He did, and went into a routine, leopard skin and all. The Camel Walk? That, too. It turned out that his mother had been a hoofer on the vaudeville stage and he'd learned from her the Turtle Twist, Elephant Squat, Falling-off-a-Log and much else. So

I had a personal command performance. It wasn't what Florence Cassidy had in mind, but I admired the old (to me) lady; she was busily scribbling down notes on the dances, doubtless to increase the range of her offerings when the next State Department visitor came to Detroit. For my part, I turned down all official invitations after that.

I'd corresponded with Chris Strachwitz (later, the producer of Arhoolie Records) and we decided to meet up in Memphis and travel together through the South. The only address that we knew mutually was the Peabody Hotel, where the Memphis Jug Band had been recorded, so we planned to meet in the hotel lobby. When we got there we found that it was the swellest hotel in town, with deep leather club chairs and a convention of chicken breeders going on. A large stuffed chicken was a centrepiece in the lobby and red-faced breeders came to shake hands and introduce themselves as 'Al, from Muscle Shoals'. Our rough clothes were conspicuous and we were eased out by the management, so we booked in at a cheaper hotel near Beale. It was the following morning when we discovered that the hotel we were in was being picketed for discriminatory practices – hardly a good start for blues research.

In Mississippi the going was a little tough and strange whites in a car with California plates – even a 1953 Plymouth – were not welcome. We decided to stay in a black motel on the grounds that no-one would expect to find us there. A crazy decision as I think back, but as Howling Smith says 'God looks after old folks and fools' and we had no trouble. We met up with Wade Walton, and I interviewed Aaron Henry, the 'leader of the Mississippi battlefront', as he was then called. Later he became an important black politician but then he was a strong and militant fighter who ran a pharmacy near Wade's Big Six barbershop. He disapproved

of Wade's humour, his habit of wearing his shoes backwards, and his tall tales. But he gave me a valuable insight into the problems that blacks were facing in Mississipi at the time. Some weeks after we left, his shop was bombed and I always feared that my visit may have led to the violence.

A kaleidoscope of memories plays across my mind's eye as I recall that trip, and did again when I was asked by David Evans to participate in a Blues Conference in Memphis in 1980 – made possible, incidentally, by the money generated by the Elvis Presley Memorial. We went down to Clarksdale again, to find it a far more prosperous looking town than it had been in 1960. Wade was still there, but had lost his teeth; he was one of a mixed audience, half black, half white, for a small symposium held at the Blues Museum in the Clarksdale Public Library. Such an event was inconceivable, unthinkable, twenty years before, though it was still slightly ironic that of the five speakers, two – Bruce Bastin and myself – were British.

While there we were able to hear one or two country singers, like Jessie Mae Hemphill, whose cabin in a clearing in the long grass near Senatobia was as impoverished as any we'd seen on our previous trip, though she was turned out smartly in a black cowgirl outfit. In South Memphis we heard at a local juke a band of mainly young blacks, the Fieldstones, who were playing for dancing and drinking much as the bands always used to do. Gradually in my writing I had come to play down the importance of blues for dancing, and blues as entertainment and background noise, in the course of examining the blues as expression.

This is an outcome, of course, of listening to blues on record. However much field recording or club visiting one might do if the opportunities were there, blues records provide the most familiar means of hearing the music. I still marvel at what actually did get on record and I still can recapture the excitement of finding unexpected items while junk-shopping. This activity, now more or less passed, was one way of spending a Saturday. Every town, and every old sector of London, had its junk shops. They may go by that name occasionally now, but today they prefer to be called antique shops, and most of the owners know their subjects pretty well. There used to be piles of old 78s in every junk shop, usually without covers and mostly dross. You had to turn over seemingly endless stacks of Foden's Motor Works Band, Denza Dance Orchestra or Frances Langford before you could find anything of even mild interest. (I did find a record by Paul Oliver once; I learned that this was a pseudonym for Frank Munn. Later, I did some book reviewing for a magazine in which I was already writing and was asked for a pseudonym: I chose 'Frank Munn' and felt that I'd got my own back, somehow.)

There were occasional rewards that made the heart leap, though. Like the day I found a shining Decca of 'The Black Diamond Express to Hell' by Reverend A. W. Nix, and the mint copy of 'K. C. Moan' by the Memphis Jug Band on Regal Zonophone. Then there was 'Skip Scat Doodle Do' by the Dixieland Jug Blowers backed by Bobbie Leecan's appropriately named Needmore Band playing 'Washboard Cut-Out'; all items that had been once issued in England, and like the washboard, cut out of the catalogue. There was Kokomo Arnold's 'Old Original Kokomo Blues' in a junk pile in Bournemouth and, eventually, many more. The point about collecting 78s and by this method, was that you got to know the records very well indeed, with an intimacy that has never seemed possible where LPs are concerned. I suspect that it was very like this for the black purchasers of the original 78s in the twenties and thirties. 75¢ was a lot to pay for a Columbia in the 1920s and they weren't bought to be discarded; the very fact that the collectors can canvass for them and still find rarities half a century later proves that. The range of blues forms, styles and individual singers that got on record was nonetheless, quite remarkable and I wrote an article 'Special Agents' (with a punning title that some took literally) on the 'agents', or influencing factors, which may have accounted for the appearance of some blues singers and non-appearance of others on disc. It was published in *The Jazz Review*, the excellent long-lamented jazz magazine edited by Nat Hentoff and Martin Williams, and it's reprinted in this book.

Included with it are some of those early articles on the settings of blues, on the dances, the country bands, home-made instruments, early instrumentalists and the juke joints where they played. They sketch in a few lines, some indications of the milieu in which blues developed and some of the ways in which it came to be heard.

That Old Time Religion
GOSPEL MUSIC AND THE CHURCH

For well over half a century jazz bands have been fleeing as birds to the mountain, and today the musicians are legion who want to be numbered with the Saints as they go marching in. Since the music was in its infancy, spirituals have formed an important part of the jazz band repertoire. But though the themes and words remain the same, though the record labels still bear the legend 'spiritual', they have long been divested of any spiritual significance. Like the Christmas Carols in the Community Song-book, they are good tunes to play and good tunes to listen to; they may be played with fervour but it is not of the religious kind. As the meaning of the spirituals has been forgotten, so too have we tended to forget that Negro sacred music is a living force.

One welcome aspect of the swelling tide of interest in Afro-American music in this country is the steadily increasing issue of authentic religious recordings, in which the record lists were for many years sadly deficient. It is the contention of many collectors that Negro religious music has very little relation to jazz and in this they have the ready support of a large majority of church-going Negroes. For in all strata of Negro society, jazz music is anathema to the main body of 'church-folks'. It is a fact, however, that the members of the Negro hierarchy do recognize, and incidentally deplore, the strong jazz elements which have entered the sacred music of the middle and lower-class churches. Improved education induces restraint, and the churches of the small upper-class incline to the pattern set by the corresponding white congregations. The desire to emulate the modes and manners of white society has eliminated to a consider-

able degree the essentially negroid elements of their services. Though the integrity of the upper-class Negro church is not to be questioned, it is nevertheless true that music that is likely to appeal to the jazz enthusiast is not to be found therein. In the middle and lower-class churches, however, where the congregation is not infrequently of a darker hue and where worship acts as a safety valve for the emotional turmoil which is a result of depressed living conditions, many of the qualities of traditional jazz are to be found in the music that accompanies the ritual.

Most collectors nurture a mental picture of a simple, virile, and uninhibited religion still practised at revival meetings deep in the brush, or in remote frame buildings amidst a sea of cotton. But it is generally a source of considerable surprise that it should flourish no less in the big cities of the urban North. In the Black Belt of Chicago alone there are approximately five hundred churches of more than thirty denominations, only a few of which are exclusive to the 'dicties', the Negro upper class.

During the great migration which introduced jazz to the North, the coloured people brought with them a religious fervour and an ability to improvise which extended far beyond music. As the white people were forced to vacate whole blocks of buildings before the oncoming black tide, their churches and synagogues were absorbed and the empty halls, theatres, stores and houses adapted to the requirements of the Negro and of his church. Buildings so converted became the 'store-fronts' which form more than three-quarters of Chicago's churches. With an assemblage seldom exceeding a couple of dozen persons, the store-front service takes on some of the attributes of a rent-party, the congregation being able to sing and dance freely. Theirs is not the 'sinful' dancing of the Savoy Ballroom, but 'Holy' dancing. To the lay observer the distinction might be a fine one.

Dancing, jazz music, gambling, card-playing, even knee-length skirts are to the 'church-folks' the Devil's temptations, as Chicago's seven hundred preachers stress with vehemence. There are far more preachers than churches; the surplus are the 'jack-legs' who, though seldom trained and often illiterate, have answered the 'call'. Their impassioned sermons, terrible in the power of their delivery, can be heard on the records of such preachers as Reverend W. M. Chambers or Reverend R. Burnett. Some enliven their sermons with their own instrumental performance, such as Elder Charles Beck, who plays good trumpet at his converted theatre in Pittsburgh. Pastors and preachers in the big cities have to make many concessions to the taste of their 'flock' in order to keep them within the fold of the church. Cinema shows, dramatic performances, bazaars, even horse shows are held in the church building; fashion displays with Negro beauties modelling the dresses are held in Clayton Powell's Abyssinian Baptist Church in Harlem. Many a man is kept 'free from sin' through the social life built around the church, for it provides him with his club and his amusement at a considerably cheaper rate than more worldly sources. And music no less than other forms of entertainment. Though jazz may have largely disappeared from the Negro world with the depression, the spirit was kept alive in the music of the Race churches. Not that their bands have followed the traditional structure of jazz, nor have they crystallized into a set instrumentation of their own. Money for instruments can seldom be spared; it is a fortunate church which has paid off its mortgage. The accompaniment may be just that of a pianist such as George Hornsby, or it may even be provided by a group of several pieces: horns, drums and strings. To its music the congregation sings, low and solemn or rocking with a steady beat. In the Baptist churches which represent nearly half the total number, and indeed, in any Black Belt service, the assembly like to sing, loudly and with gusto.

It is the insistence of the rhythms, and the urgency of the music, which stimulates the excitement and hysterical fervour of the Holiness service that culminates in the 'Holy Rolling' and 'speaking with tongues' of those who have got happy with the Power of the Holy Ghost. And, whatever the service, out in front – perhaps as 'angels' robed in muslin, but generally uniform only in the music and spirit that inspires it – is the gospel choir or rhythm quartet. Bearing names such as the 'Righteous Four' or the 'Heavenly Trumpets' they travel from store-front church to converted cinema, admired by a large following. Frequently they have an extensive itinerary, travelling between the states of the North and West, sure of an audience, their fame preceding them. Undeniably 'hot', their music has largely superseded the spirituals. Often the influence of jazz has been direct, as in the case of Thomas A. Dorsey, one-time pianist of Ma Rainey's Jazz Band and now a prolific writer of gospel tunes, some of which he has recorded. Similar music can be heard on the recordings of many such groups – the Evangelist Singers or the Harmony Four, for example. So widespread has their music become that they have organized the National Convention of Gospel Choruses and Choirs as a measure towards unity. It is the popularity of these groups and of the gospel singing soloists of Sister Rosetta Tharpe's genre, which has drawn and held many Negroes to the churches.

It would seem that musical creation is so

essentially a part of the coloured man's nature that if it does not find an outlet in his secular interests it still finds expression in his religious activity. When the Negro is unashamedly himself, his music thrives even if it takes extravagant forms which may alarm the collector. Only when his contact with white society has altered its character, or when for some other reason he consciously sublimates this creative desire, does his music become supressed. Thus the Moorish Science Temple of America, whose followers assert that they are Asiatics and Moslems, exclude music from their ritual. Wearing fezzes, facing Mecca when they pray, the Moorish-Americans admit neither the terms 'Negro' or 'coloured' nor what they imply. Their only hymns are slow chants and in all respects their behaviour is non-negroid. On the other hand, the members of a non-Christian cult, the Church of God, Philadelphia, while believing themselves to be the lost tribe of Israel nevertheless do not deny that they are Negroes, but in fact claim that Christ himself was black. Tambourines, drums, rattles and guitars form the orchestra; the preacher Prophet Cherry, himself beating the drum whilst gospel singers improvise their songs before the congregation.

In his far-famed Peace Mission Movement, Father Divine – who modestly admits himself to be God – has orchestras which closely follow the jazz pattern. Piano, drums, clarinet, cornet and strings join in extempore music to the shouting and hand-clapping of the assembly. Indeed the trumpeter of his New York mission plays in a style strongly reminiscent of Louis Armstrong. Stomping and dancing accompanies the music of the band in the United House of Prayer. Bishop Grace – who has 'given God a vacation' – unable to play an instrument himself, strums an imaginary banjo before the group!

Similar music can be heard in the Mount Sinai Church and a score of other denominations, sects and cults, whether or no their leaders are charlatans and 'fakes' as some assert. That some unscrupulous Negro 'preachers' play on the emotions of the congregations cannot be denied, nor can the fact that many live handsomely on the profits of churches run purely for commercial reasons and personal gain. One hears with horror of the five cent bottles of Holy Baptism Water sold in the streets; of the Holy Floor Wash and Sacred Powders. The music is in danger of suffering from similar exploitation. Violins, saxophones and electric guitars have streamlined the services of more than one church. Yet today the folk music of the Negro churches still thrives without the need of either injections or blood transfusions. But there is much need for more recordings, more critical appreciation, more understanding of the function of the music in the Negro church and of its value in its own right, as a folk art. We must not find out too late that a great urban folk music has passed virtually unrecognized, whilst we bewail the departing of another.

Jazz Journal, February 1952

Backwater Blues
ON THE RIVER LEVEES

I'm gwine down to the River, baby,
bye n' bye . . .

So runs the blues, 'The River' – the Bayou Teche perhaps, or the Magdalena, the Ouachita or even 'Ole Miss', – the Mississippi herself – provides a precarious livelihood for thousands of Negroes in the Deep South of the United States. In the crumbling shacks of the 'catfish rows' on a hundred river waterfronts live the stevedores, the long-shoremen and the loading crews; the shanties of the mule-skinner, the swamper, the raftsman and the logger line the bayous; and dotted over the bottomlands are the homes of the field hands and cotton workers. These are the people whose gift for self expression in the art of improvised song has produced a great body of music which the trials and vicissitudes of a life on and by the river has inspired.

Until the emancipation there were relatively few coloured people in the river towns. Planters kept their slaves on the plantations, and the flat-boat bullies and crews of the 'broadhorns' which plied the river until the early nineteenth century were white, and largely Irish. But a new era in river transportation began in 1811 when Fulton's steamboat, the 'New Orleans', successfully navigated the Mississippi – in spite of the New Madrid earthquake which reversed the current. A few years later, Henry Shreve's 'Washington', double-decked and shallow-hulled, set the pattern for the Mississippi riverboats. After the Civil War, many thousands of newly emancipated Negroes wandered to the river: free men, but uneducated, and a vast resource of potential cheap labour. As deckhands and roustabouts – loading crewsmen – they found employment and virtual slavery once more.

Work as a roustabout was strenuous and the hours interminable. Cruel and merciless, the white mates controlled their rough crews with their bull-whips – 'black snakes' as the roustabouts called them. But the roustabouts boasted of the lashings they had endured, were proud of the searing weals on their sweating backs and of the loads they could carry. Whilst they staggered up the gangplanks with their barrels of molasses and sacks of corn, or rolled the five-hundred pound bales of ginned cotton in their coarse jute wrappings aboard the sternwheelers, the raising crews – two men to raise what one man would carry – taunted the rousters:

Drop yo' sack, boy,
Drop yo' sack.
'Nother coat here
Gonna fit yo' back.

Git yo' bone, dog,
Git yo' bone,
You'se raisin' no mo'
Than you eats at home!

There was little rest for the crews for speed was all-important. Riverboats raced each other to the planters' wharves, and on to New Orleans to be first with the cotton cargoes. The trip from Natchez, which took the early steamboats five-and-a-half days, was reduced to ten-and-a-half *hours* by the 'Robert E. Lee' in 1870, racing at full pressure with a rouster sitting on the safety valve! For the Negroes the pay was better than in many occupations, but the danger of death from an exploding boiler was real; the fate of Shreve's 'Washington' was

17

freqently re-enacted. Whilst his companions 'monkeyshined' an improvised dance between the wharves a rouster would sing:

> *Gonna build myself a raft,*
> *Gonna float this river down.*
> *Gonna shack up with some*
> *Sweet Mississippi brown,*
> *Fo' the blues ain't nothin',*
> *Lawd, the blues ain't nothin'*
> *But a good man feelin' bad.*

until the honky-tonks of Rampart Street, New Orleans or the barrel-houses of Gayoso and Beale in Memphis, cured his blues, dissolved his aspirations and emptied his pockets.

With the opening of the railroads in the 1880s the long distance cargo trips of the riverboats came to an end. But numbers of the 'swimming volcanoes' and excursion steamers and later, oil-burning 'tow-boats' which *pushed* the barges to the Gulf, continued to ply between the river towns and provided work for many Negroes. Others became mule-skinners, driving their teams for a mere pittance with wagons loaded with cotton bales for the wharves, or with timber-laden skiffs splashing through the swampy bottomlands to the river where the lumber from the logging camps would be floated to the sea.

> *This man is a long way from home,*
> *An' he's got a brownskin woman . . .*

sings Huddie Leadbetter – 'Leadbelly' – improvising a typical mule-skinner's song to his own brilliant accompaniment on a twelve-string guitar:

> *. . . he knows pay day's coming*
> *pretty soon*
> *An' the ole woman's shoutin' for*
> *some mo' pay day.*
> *An' the ole mule is honin' an' the*
> *sun is goin' down,*

> *An' the man wishes that pay day*
> *would move off a little further,*
> *So he wouldn't have to pay the woman*
> *nothin'.*
> *I'm goin' t'tell ma woman like the*
> *Dago tol' the Jew . . .*
> *'You don' wan' me an' honey I don'*
> *wan' you . . .'*

his words giving a hint of the inter-racial jealousy amongst the underprivileged. The mule-skinner's is a hard life with the ever-present danger of sinking unheeded in the swamps, of being crushed by rolling timber or of mutilation from a roustabout's cotton-hook or a woman's cleaver.

> *. . . other men on the levee*
> *Holler 'Don' you murder me,*
> *Please baby, please baby . . .*
> *I'm down in the Bottom . . .*
> *. . . putting in my initials*
> *Honey, on the mule's behind,*
> *With ma line, babe, with ma line,*
> *babe . . .'*

In his thigh boots and rubber coat the mule-skinner fought mosquitoes and 'gally-nippers', snakes and the steaming, suffocating heat of the Delta timberlands, and struggled through to the flooded bottomlands. The bottomlands are the flat alluvial plains which stretch from the influx of the Ohio down the Mississippi for five hundred miles, and similarly on the Brazos and many another Southern river. Constantly changing its course, creating ox-bows and cut-offs, the Mississippi meanders through the rich and fertile lands which fall at a rate of only eight inches to the mile.

The work of constructing levees to reinforce the river banks as a safeguard against the annual inundation of the Delta lands during the spring floods was begun in the eighteenth century, and by 1828 these extended to the Red River. During the Civil War the levees were neglected and their repair after the conflict was executed to defective plans. Their inadequacy was proved when hundreds of persons lost their lives as the floodwaters of 1874 surged across the bottomlands. Some action was prompted by the catastrophe and many Negroes sang willow-cutting songs as they wove the mattresses and made the hurdles to repair the levees. A government grant was made of $5,000,000, but this was specifically for the repair of levees that would improve navigation, and not for the protection of the land. Disastrous floods during the Eighties did nothing however, to discourage the subsequent mass immigration of Negroes from the hill country to the river basin of the Yazoo–Mississippi Delta.

> *This is a song, was sung in eighteen
> and 'ninety-two,*

relates Big Bill Broonzy, who had himself worked in the levee grading camps at a later date.

> *There was a terrible flood that year,
> An' the people cried an' sung this
> song.
> To let everybody know how they felt
> About a whole year's work, an' no
> pay.*

With tragic frequency the disaster was repeated, and forced by economic circumstances to live in the Delta the Negro people were the chief sufferers from the effects of the floods. Control of the river was still the responsibility of individuals or the district levee boards, many of whom were very remiss in discharging their duties.

Then, on 21 April 1927, the greatest catastrophe occurred, when hundreds of square miles in the Yazoo–Mississipi Delta were inundated. Trees and debris were swept with the bodies of drowned people and animals past the disintegrating packing-case shacks, to the roofs of which terrified Negroes were still clinging. Countless persons lost their lives and emergency stations on the high ground at Vicksburg and Yazoo City attempted to house and clothe some of the 700,000 homeless and tried to check the spread of epidemics.

> *It thunders an' lightnin's an' the wind
> began to blow.
> When it thunders an' lightnin's an'
> the wind begin t'blow,
> There's thousands of people ain't got
> no place to go.*

Her strong voice full of pain and grief, Bessie Smith sings of the tragedy in the traditional folk idiom of her race, the blues:

> *Then I went an' stood upon some
> high old lonesome hill, (repeat)
> Then looked down on the house,
> where I used to live.*
>
> *Backwater blues done cause me to
> pack ma things and go (repeat)
> 'Cause ma house fell down an' I cain't
> live there no mo'.*
>
> *Mmm, Hmm, I cain't move no mo'
> (repeat)
> There ain't no place for a poor ol'
> girl to go.*

The blues is the common folk song of the Afro-American Negro, simple, yet almost unique in its twelve-bar structure, and based on the tonic, dominant, and sub-dominant chords in the major scale. Its form allows the singer the maximum freedom for improvisation and through the medium he finds a natural vehicle for the expression of his emotions.

Thus the blues is a safety-valve which helps the Negro to endure his trials. Inevitably, innumerable blues were born of the floods:

*I woke up this mawnin'. cain't even
    git out of ma door,
Woke this mawnin'. cain't git out ma
    door,
I was snowbound' in ma cabin an'
    water creepin' up through ma
    floor.*

*Snow began meltin', an' the rain
    begin t' fall,(repeat)
The backwater's done broke the
    levee, an' I cain't stay here no
    more.*

Stirred to action by the disaster, the
following year Congress passed the Flood
Control Act which authorized US Army
engineers to study and effect the control of
the river, nearly $600,000,000 being voted
for this purpose during the following
decade. When the Ohio floods of 1937 swel-
led the waters of the Mississippi the scheme
was put to a supreme test, and the new
levees held fast.

But still there is danger of severe flooding
in the bottomlands as the post-war catastro-
phes have proved too well. The steaming
swamps, the mosquitoes and the snakes,
and the long hours of heavy labour from
sunrise to sunset still remain. And still an
embittered Negro sings:

*Michigan water tastes like cherry
    wine,
Michigan water tastes of cherry wine,
But that Mississippi water done taste
    like turpentine.*

Music Mirror, May 1954
'Sources of Afro-American Folk Song: 1'

Down the Line
THE RAILROAD AS SYMBOL

It was not until the 1850s that the supremacy of river traffic as the principal means of freightage for the produce of Slave States was seriously opposed by the railroads. During the previous twenty years the railroads had been primarily constructed for the purpose of establishing links between the rivers and the townships in the interior. Laid in 1831, the second railroad in the Mississippi Valley, for example, connected the river with Woodville, the only township in South West Mississippi which lacked a means of floating cotton to the Gulf. But in 1858 the New Orleans, Jackson and Great Northern linked with the Mississippi and Tennessee railroads to provide a fast and important line from Memphis, and soon a number of other roads began to threaten the riverboats.

At this time it was impossible for a Negro slave to travel by train without a written bond from his owner. As the slave in the cotton rows watched the flame-spitting engine thunder towards the North and the Free States it inspired in him a fascination which his descendants still retain. It was natural that for him the escape route to the North was the 'Underground Railroad'. The hay-lofts, barns and cellars where he hid with trembling limbs were the 'stations'; the 'conductors' were the anti-slavery sympathizers who risked imprisonment and sometimes death to free the coloured people from bondage. Fine old spirituals such as 'Steal Away', 'Go Down, Moses', and 'Run To Jesus', now had another vital if secular meaning, being used as codes by escaping slaves. But to the God-fearing, spiritual-singing Negro the possibilities of imagery in the railroads were not lost. He sang of the 'Gospel Train':

I hear her bell an' whistle,
She's coming down the line.
O, sinner, you' forever lost,
If once you' left behind.

– and called to the 'children' to 'Get on board, there's room for many-a-more'. 'Oh be ready when the train comes in,' implores another spiritual. But this Holy Train to Heaven numbers no idolators, no pipe-smokers, no idlers nor even snuff-takers among its passengers. There is room enough for these on the 'Black Diamond Express to Hell' on which, as the Reverend A. W. Nix reminded his congregation:

. . . Sin is the engineer, Pleasure is the
*   headlight,*
And the Devil is.the conductor.
I see the Black Diamond as she starts off
*   for Hell,*

he continues:

The bell is ringing: 'Hell-bound! Hell-
*   bound!'*
The devil cries out: 'All aboard for
*   Hell!'. . .*

and the train stops at Drunkardsville to collect its first passengers, some drinking Jump Steady; some drinking Shinny, Moonshine, White Mule and Red Horse. Then on to Liar's Avenue to take on board more sinners, and so on through Deceiversville . . . Conjuration Station . . .

If the influence of the railroad on the religious music of the Negro lay in its metaphoric significance, it had a more direct impact on his secular music during the Reconstruction. Through the ravages of the

Civil War many of the railways had been destroyed. These had to be rebuilt and many new lines were scheduled for construction. Within seven years the total mileage of track in the United States was doubled, resulting in the virtual eclipse of the river trade, and a marked redistribution of the population. For numbers of the newly liberated slaves the boom in railroad building meant employment.

Then as now, however, convicts from the state prisons worked in the hardrock gangs, whose job it was to break up stone for the hard core of the road beds. Mechanical methods have not entirely supplanted the cheap convict and Negro labour even today, and the songs of the construction gangs have survived. A score of tools flash in the sun and as many parched throats sing together. 'This ole hammah . . .' a great gasp is heard as the heads smash the stone.

> . . .*killed John Henry – huh!*
> *Killed him daid   – Law'!*
> *Killed him daid   – huh!*
> *Won' kill me   – Law'!*
> *Won' kill me . . .*

Each operation in the never-ending work of track-laying and maintenance produced its own songs. One group of Negroes tamps the ties 'Solid, – so dey won't come down!' whilst another lays the one-and-a-half ton, thirty-three foot rails across the ties. With 'lining-bars' strained against the iron the gang 'track-lines" – straightens – the rail ready for spiking into position.

> *Sun gwine down, wu'k all day,*
> *Cap'n done t'rowed his watch away.*
> *Ease 'em over, ease 'em over,*
> *Hey, Hey, cain't yo' line it? . . .*

Now the steel layers faced each other in pairs and with swift strokes spiked the lines to the ties, their two-headed, ten-pound

hammers 'ringin' lak Jedgement' on the steel. Inevitably the prowess of strong and prodigious workers spreads from line to line and their exploits are celebrated in song. And of these none more than John Henry, who is to the Negro railroad worker as Mike Fink was to the flat-boatmen, Paul Bunyan to the loggers or Pecos Bill to the Western cowboys. John Henry, who could stop an express train with the flat of his palm; who drove a twenty-pound hammer in each hand . . .

John Henry was a 'steel-drivin' man', a railroad worker who tunnelled through the mountains by filling with nitroglycerine the holes that he bored with his steel drills and hammer, blasting away the rock. He died whilst competing against the steam drill which threatened to put his kind out of work. That John Henry lived seems certain, and though many places claim honour, his celebrated feat probably took place during the construction of the Big Bend Tunnel in 1872, on the Chesapeake and Ohio Line. Big Bill Broonzy sings 'John Henry' not as a work song but as a ballad that has stirred the hearts of countless track gangers. Against the guitar rhythm rolling like an express train in the Big Bend, he sings:

> *John Henry said to his Capt'in*
> *'Now-a man ain' nothin' but a man,*
> *Befo' Ah let those steam drills beat me*
>   *down*
> *Ah will die with that hammah in ma –*
> *Yes, I will die with that hammah in ma*
>   *han', ma Lawd,*
> *Ah'm gonna die with that hammah in*
>   *ma –*
> *Gonna die with that hammah in ma*
>   *han'.'*

> *John Henry sid to his shaker,*
> *'Now man, why don' you sing?*
> *I'm throwing twelve poun' from ma hip*
>   *on down,*

Why can't you hear that col' steel –
Why don't you hear that col' steel ring?'
(repeat)
John Henry wen' down that railroad track,
With a twelve poun' hammah by his side.
Yes, he wen' down the track but he never
came back,
Cause he lay down his hammah and he –
Yes, he laid down his hammah an' he died.
Gonna cry, he lay down his hammah an'
he –
Yes, he lay down his hammah an' he died.

There are no steel drivin' men today: John Henry's sacrifice did not stay the advance of machine methods. But the Negro crews maintained by the lumber companies perpetuate the old work songs whilst laying the 'spur' roads and 'dummy' lines which serve the lumber camps. As the timber is exhausted the branch railroads which bring the loggers to their sites and carry the logs back, are moved and the track laid to the new timber lands.

The Main Stem, the principal railroads, nevertheless offer a livelihood to many a coloured man. Labour troubles arising out of the employment of Negroes for certain railroad jobs make as distressing reading as do such disputes in other spheres. But Negroes have long worked in the sheds and 'roundhouses'; in the coveted posts as Pullman porters; as firemen on the foot-plates. Here the white and the Negro workers meet and their folk songs overlap. Joe Mica and Casey Jones were white, but the firemen and the folksingers who per-petuated their names were Negro. Both white and coloured 'boomers' – itinerant workers – wandered from line to line; the life of the white brakeman Jimmie Rodgers, whose early death from consumption was a major loss to industrial folk songs, reads like a directory of the American railroads.

. . . He was born in Mississippi away
down South,

And he flagged on the T. & N.O.
He yodelled to fame on the Boston Main
The Wabash and the T.P.
From the old Grand Trunk to the Cotton
Belt
He yodelled on the Santa Fe.
On the Lehigh Valley he yodelled a while
Then he went on to the Nickel Plate.
From the Old Lake Shore to the Eerie
Line . . .

. . . and later on the Lackawanna and the 'Katy' – the Missouri, Kansas and Texas Line. On the Illinois Central he rode the 'Cannonball', the famous New Orleans-Chicago run recalled in Jelly-Roll Morton's 'Cannonball Blues', on which the engineer or driver, Casey Jones, lost his life.

There are a great many railroads in the United States, but there are songs and blues about them all. They are characterized by their pace and rhythm, their short, clipped lines which are redolent of the clatter of wheels on the track. Such a song is 'The Rock Island Line', which is sung by cotton workers throughout the South.

Well, The Rock Island Line is a mighty
fine road,
Yes, the Rock Island Line is a line to ride.
The Rock Island Line is a mighty fine road,
An' if you wan' t'ride it,
Gotta take it as you fin'it,
Get yo' ticket at the station
On the Rock Island Line.

Many are the blues about the 'Yellow Dog', the Yazoo and Mississippi Valley road, which meets the Southern at Moor-head. Some contend that it got its name from the initials of the briefer phrase 'Yazoo-Delta'. But in Rome, Mississippi, they say that it was named after a mongrel hound who noisily greeted every train that came through. On the line itself they say it was the derisive term of a rival firm, for railroadmen know a small, dummy-line train as a 'short dog', but it is immaterial; another piece of railroad folklore has been created and has inspired innumerable songs.

Before the standardization of the railroad whistles, the coloured firemen would arrange the 'quills' until they could play a veritable blues on the engine whistle. Developing their personal styles they thrilled the hearts of the workers in the fields who told the time by the passing trains, knew them by special names and sang of their schedules. There are blues about that 'K.C. whistle', of the '2.19' and the '3.50'. The Negro sings of the 'Red-Ball', the 'Sunshine Special', and the 'Flying Crow':

> *Flying Crow leaves Port Arthur, calls on*
> *Shreveport to change her crew,*
> *Flying Crow leaves Port Arthur, stops at*
> *Shreveport to change her crew,*
> *She will take water at Texakarna, yes boys*
> *and keep on through.*

sings Washboard Sam of a well-known Texas flyer. The 'Shorty George' was a Texas train also, but its route was to the State prison. The prison trains, too, have been recorded in song. When there are five Sundays in the month, the fifth is reserved as a visitors' day for the prisoners at Parchman, Mississippi. Then the 'Midnight Special' brings their wives and lovers for a twelve-hour break in the hard monotony of prison life.

> *Well, you wake up in the mornin', hear*
> *the ding-dong ring,*
> *Go a-marchin' to the table, see the same*
> *damn thing.*
> *Well its on-a one table, knife a fork an'*
> *pan,*
> *An' if you say anythin' about it, you' in*
> *trouble with the man.*
>
> *Let the Midnight Special, shine its light*
> *on me,*
> *Let that Midnight Special, shine its ever-*
> *lovin' light on me.*

> *Well the biscuits on the table, just as hard*
> *as any tack,*
> *An ef you try to swallow them, break a*
> *convic's heart,*
> *My sister wrote a letter, my mother wrote*
> *a card,*
> *'Ef you wan' t' come an' see us, you'll*
> *have to ride the rods'.*

Riding the rods was a hazardous mode of travel, but the penniless Negro bum was prepared to risk death from frozen fingers losing their hold on the trusses, brake rods, and axle beams beneath the freight cars. But the tramp on the bumpers and the hobo 'on the hog' – riding the hog and cattle cars – were little better off.

'I'm leavin' here tonight if I have to ride the blinds,' sings Papa Charlie Jackson.

> *Leavin' here tonight, if I have to ride the*
> *blinds,*
> *Gonna take a freight train special, that's*
> *an engine won't lose no time.*

The baggage car next to the tender is 'blind', that is, it has no door, and thus the hobo sitting on the step is out of reach of the brakeman's club. Here he may ride with only the 'mean old fireman's' hose to fear . . . The 'snakes' and 'stingers' – the switchmen and brakemen whose Brotherhood lapel buttons 'S' and 'B' have given them their names, are the traditional enemies of the bums. So the hobo sings with pride of Railroad Bill, who 'was a very bad man, shot the lights from the brakeman's hands'. But in spite of the hazards the Negro with the wanderlust and no money to pay the fare, still 'nails a rattler an' bums his chuck'. But if railroad songs such as Trixie Smith's 'Freight Train Blues' are numerous, so too are the railroad blues played by the boogie-woogie pianists. Rolling with its eight-to-the-bar bass the 'Honky-Tonk Train Blues' recalls the Southbound Express as she leaves the rail centre of America, Chicago. A more subtle example of the piano music of those who live 'down the line' is Cripple Clarence Lofton's 'Streamline Train'. Red Nelson, who sings the blues, speaks for the naive coloured boy whose fascination for the railroad is mingled with fear, hate and humiliation.

> *Streamline Train, fastes' train that runs.*
> *Heartless thing, ain' gonna help you none.*
> *I'm gonna leave in the mawnin',*
> *Baby on that Streamline Train.*
> *Only thing I can say, mamma,*
> *'Take your mind off that cruel thing.'*

> *Went down to the Union Station, ac' jes'*
>   *like a chile,*
> *Had to ask the cardboard mamma,*
> *'What train do I ride?'*

The railroad holds few illusions for the Negro. Firing the engine, greasing the bearings, riding the gondolas, he is too close to the tallow and grime for romantic notions. But for some of the coloured race, the railroads are their lives; for others, a symbol of release. And whatever the significance of the railroads might be to them, the key is to be found in their music.

Music Mirror, June 1954
'Sources of Afro–American Folk Song: 2'

Strut Yo' Stuff, Boy!
DANCING AFTER HOURS

Everybody – fall in line!
Grab your partners – git back on time!
Big Fat Ma and Skinny Pa's
Gwine to do a dance you never saw!

Though the world was dancing-mad in the 1920s, it was still possible then for the older Negroes visiting the North for the first time, to show a step or two which were still new to the young Negroes and their girls who crowded the State Street halls. Some of the most venerable of them could even recall the plantation dances before the emancipation, and they looked askance at the frenzied cavortings of their grandchildren in the big cities. But though the elders may not approve the passing of the traditional dance figures, dancing of some form is a natural mode of expression for the Negro. His African heritage might have been lost in the assimilation of centuries of western culture but his sense of music and of rhythm, and his innate grace in the co-ordination of mind and body have ever remained with him and have enriched the culture of the world to which he now belongs. In the beauty of his running, jumping, swimming, athletics and sport the Negro has no peer, and his use of the body as a vehicle of self-expression reaches its ultimate in dancing.

Negro dances and dance-songs have suffered from a lack of adequate documentation of their early phases as have all other aspects of Afro-American folk song and music. For the most part there was little interest in such Negro arts during the slave era; such practices were treated with indifference or suspicion. Most forms of Negro dancing and music were suppressed at one time or another, only to be permitted at a later date when the plantation owners recognised them to be safety valves through which the coloured slaves were able to release pent-up emotions. Nevertheless, the fury and primitive nature of the 'ring-shouts' must have caused much anxiety amongst the occupants of the Big House as they listened to the endlessly repeated chants and the monotonous pounding of bare feet on the earthen floor of the 'gallion' – the slave quarters.

Elbows bent, wrists loose, bodies relaxed and feet stamping in rhythm, the dancers of the 'ring-shout' slowly revolved in a circle to the accompaniment of hand-claps and their own singing. They chanted meaningless, tangled phrases whose pattern and sounds appealed – and continued until they fell exhausted. The dance was essentially African, deeply rooted in the souls of the Negroes far from that continent; so fundamental in its appeal in fact that in the most backward of Southern Negro communities it may still be found. African memories shaped many early dances, all of which were performed to a background of singing and of rhythmic patterns. Most elementary was the 'pat', a rhythm created by slapping the knees and limbs at different points to produce a variety of sounds. There were innumerable pats: one of the earliest, yet one of the longest-lived, is the 'Juba Pat'. Juba was an African ghost:

Juba here, Juba dere,
Juba, Juba ev'rywhere!
Juba up an' Juba down,
Juba runnin' all aroun'!

Juba seldom flits through the canebrake today, but the spirit is still a familiar presence in the West Indies, where the pat survives.

The African drum appeared in the form of the Bamboula. Originally fashioned from a joint of bamboo from which its name is derived, it was also made from a hollow log with a goat-skin stretched across one end, and was eventually made from discarded casks. The name also applied to the vigorous dance which it accompanied, which became an attraction for early nineteenth-century tourists visiting New Orleans. There, in Congo Square, large gatherings of Negroes met to perform the dance to the delight of the French Creole population. The dances provided more of interest than the accompanying song which consisted of the endless repetition in Creole patois of such a phrase as 'When the 'taters are cooked, don't eat 'em up!'

Another popular Negro dance of the period was the Counjaille. Technically it was a version of the minuet which the coloured people copied from the French. Their adaptation was so free and the dance song so ribald that it shocked the inhabitants of licentious New Orleans and was banned. Many of the Negro dances were taken from those which were popular with the white people. The Pas-Ma-La and Falling-Off-A-Log were modifications of square dances, simple but gay. Others, which they invented themselves, were modelled on popular mid-nineteenth-century dances but had a distinct character of their own: the Carabine, for example, was a colourful dance in which the women, waving red handkerchiefs, revolved beneath the extended arms of the men. In the lay-off period after the harvests had been gathered in there were more opportunities for dancing. Many of these had some relation to the work of the plantation. When the corn had been shucked and a huge pile of husks remained in the yard the men would chase the girls round it to the steps of a dance, the women singing teasingly:

Five can't catch me, ten can't hold me,
Ho, round the corn, Sally!
Round the corn, round the corn,
Round the corn, Sally,
Hey, Hey, round the corn, Sally!

Many of the Negro communities were extremely isolated and local dialects developed which confused the meaning of many of the songs. One verse of the above-quoted dance song runs 'I cin bank, ginny bank, ginny bank the weaver!' Most extreme of the Negro dialect is that known as Gullah or Geechee, which is still in use in the remote communities near the South Carolina and Georgia Coast, and on the Georgia Sea Islands. There, far from the influence of the towns, the Negroes made their own amusements, composed their songs, invented their dances. The fondly-loved picture of the Negro family gathered at the door of the hut where an old Negro entertains on banjo or guitar became, here, something of a reality. Blind Blake plays a Southern rag of the type to which people danced: 'Way out there on that cotton field, where them people plant all their rice 'n big sugar cane and so forth grow.' As he plays he speaks a commentary and taunts an 'old Geechee' standing by:

Hey mamma, I wanna match an you cin light
*   my pipe, yeah!*
Go on, old Geechee, I ain't talkin' 'bout you!
I know, this sweet mess begin to roll . . .
I could help you pick this cotton . . .
You cain't dig potatoes – either one!
I can stook more rotten sugar cane
Than you cin stook in ten years!. . .
Now we gonna do that dance now,
We call it the Geechee dance.
I'm gonna give you some music we call the
*   Geechee music now,*
That's ma gal, git away from here! Play 'em!

and he 'hits his guitar every way but loose!' To the music of such guitar and banjo rags the coloured folk danced at their 'play-parties' and backwoods 'breakdowns'. Individual dancers competed with each other when cutting their capers, bringing even more complicated steps of their own invention to the dances. So new dances and dance songs are created, sometimes with the plantation as inspiration, as for example the Buck and Wing with its chicken-like flutters and quick-steps. Some dances are funny; others bizarre. In the early days of the Cake-walk the dancers actually balanced the cake upon their heads and attempted difficult steps without dropping it. The high kicks and struts of the Cakewalk remained, but the cake soon became the prize for the best dancer. The plantation dances frequently had a local fame and appeal only, but the Cakewalk, with its origins in the banjo rags largely precipitated the piano rag-time era, and its popularity was widespread. Talented couples 'strutted their stuff' before excited crowds:

> *Here they come, look at them demonstratin'*
> *Goin' some! Ain't they syncopatin'?*
> *Talk of the Town, teasin' brown,*
> *Liftin' 'em up and layin' 'em down!*

sings Eva Taylor.

> *They're in a class of their own!*
> *The only way to win is to see them,*
> *You may try but you will never beat them!*
> *Strut your stuff boy! You won't do nothin'*
> *   diff'rent –*
> *Cakewalkin' babies from home!*

The trend was to wilder, still less inhibited dancing, and the respectable members of the communities looked askance at the dizzy gyrations of the happy sinners. They had some justification: the dancing in the hole-in-the-wall dives of the Wicked Cities was always sensual and often sexual. No city had a more notorious reputation at the turn of the century than New Orleans with its vicious though superficially gay segregated area, Storyville, where the Negro marching bands were learning the new dance tunes. The dance halls, honky tonks and cabarets were legion: places like the Red Onion 'Tonk, Dago Tony's and the Pig Ankle where the women tried to kick the pig's foot hanging from the ceiling. Here the early jazz bands played hotter versions of old dances, and the halls were packed with pleasure-loving people of every colour. But it was primarily a Negro quarter and everywhere dark-skinned dancers were snaking their hips to the suggestive motions of the Shimmy. Originating in the swamplands of Florida the Shimmy was a truly Negro dance, but in New Orleans it became common property.

> *I wished Ah could shimmy lak ma Sister Kate,*
> *Well she shakes it lak jellies on a plate . . .*

New dances appeared in places throughout the South during the first two decades of the twentieth century. From the grim waterfront of Nashville, Tennessee, on the banks of the dirty, sluggish Mississippi river, an area known as the Black Bottoms, came a new dance, a 'twister' with hand claps and hops. It became known as the Black Bottom, and doubtless the punning significance of the name added to the popularity of the dance.

> *They say that when that river bottom covered*
> *   with ooze –*
> *Started to swirl –*
> *That's the rhythm they use – jump like a*
> *   whirl!*
> *Black Bottom, the new rhythm,*
> *When you spot 'em, you go with 'em,*
> *You do that Black, Black Bottom all day long!*

In its original form the Black Bottom made few concessions to respectability. Nor did the close-hugging Grizzly Bear or the many dances that employed the 'Bumps' and 'Grinds' forward and rotating movements of the hips and abdomen. But the dancers did not mind. With pride and delight Lil Hardin sang:

Papa, Papa, just look at Sis
Out in the backyard shakin' like this!
Doin' the Georgia Grind, that old Georgia
  Grind!
Now ev'rybody's talkin' 'bout that ole
  Georgia Grind!

I can shake it East, I can shake it West!
But way down South I can shake it best!
Doin' the Georgia Grind, that ole Georgia
  Grind!
Well everybody's ravin' 'bout that ole
  Georgia Grind!

. . . and her meaning was more anatomical than geographical.

Up the river from New Orleans came the jazz bands to take Chicago by storm. The effect of the hot music of the jazzmen from the South was electrifying. After the initial paralyzing shock the North was charged with energy which found expression in an unprecedented craze for hot music and wild dancing. 'The world's jazz crazy, Lawdy, so am I!' cried Trixie Smith.

Last night down in a cabaret
That's where we heard a jazz band play.
Just my daddy and me, we broke 'em down till
  three . . .
. . . Jazzin', everybody's jazzin' now,
My pretty papa, he don't know how –
All night long the band kept us awake
So we could jazz away until daybreak.
I like the motions that my daddy has
But everyone likes a real good jazz . . .

Best-loved dance of the Twenties was the Charleston with its back-kicks, crossed-leg steps and wagging fingers. But Negro in

origin though it was, it typified the white Jazz Age. More characteristic of the coloured people were such dances as the Soft-Shoe Shuffle and Suzie-Q. The pattern of the Fishtail often involved intricate locksteps whilst the close dancing of the Bunny-Hug presented its problems. Negro couples Walked the Dog and Balled the Jack in a score of dance halls, cabarets and cafés on State Street during the Roaring Twenties. The Dreamland Café, Buckner's Dance Hall, the Mecca Flat and the Elite Café were only a few of the centres of jazz and dancing, whilst on 35th Street which crossed State at the 'hottest' place on earth, were the Apex Club where Jimmy Noone played; The Plantation, which rocked to the music of King Oliver; and the Sunset Café where the dancers went wild to the inspired improvisations of Louis Armstrong. 'Sunset Stomp starts folk jumpin'' sang Mae Alix. 'Just go bumpin' up and down, all around – They yell "Band Man, Play some more!"' The dancing was reckless and the enthusiasm of the dancers infectious. Lord, it was going to drive people insane it seemed. 'Created in the Crazy House that's what folks'll say . . .' In the smaller resorts and cafés, in backroom parlours and obscure gin-mills people 'messed around' to the stomping of a three-piece band or the pianist's rolling boogie.

Swing down low, and come up slow
Shake to left and right,
Lean right back and double-track
And twist with all your might!
It's all over the town, wherever there's music
  to be found
You'll find them breaking 'em down,
Mess, mess, messin' around!

It is tempting to trace atavistic tendencies in Negro dancing: every Negro cabaret for white audiences has its 'jungle scene'. There even seems to be an echo of totemism in the persistence of animal imitations in such dances as the Eagle Rock and the Turtle Twist, the Grizzly Bear and the Bunny Hug, the Turkey Trot and the Buzzard Lope . . . Negro dances from the Bamboula and Counjaille of the 1830s and 40s to the Lindbord – or Lindy-Hop and the Jitterbug of the 1930s and 40s have been vigorous and uninhibited, sometimes to the point of licentiousness, but they have always had an inherent beauty which, if occasionally barbaric, is none the less real. The Negro has reintroduced extempore dancing to improvised music in western culture after a lapse of centuries, and though no thorough study of his unique contribution has yet been made, we cannot afford to ignore the Negro dance indefinitely.

Music Mirror, March 1955
'Sources of Afro-American Folk Song: 10'

Tub, Jug, Washboard Bands
MUSIC ON IMPROVISED INSTRUMENTS

Somewhere between the loose spontaneity of the blues singer and the formalized, semi-sophisticated music of the jazz band lies a little-documented territory of music for which no convenient name has been coined. To call the creations of Negro musicians who play on unorthodox or home-made instruments 'rural dance music' or to label their groups as 'country bands' narrows the field, for many seem to have sprung up in Southern urban communities as well as in the juke joints of Mississippi or Alabama. In jazz histories of course, the playing of 'the second line' of children imitating the marching parade bands has often been noted, and the 'spasm bands' of New Orleans which can be justifiably considered as part of this genre, by their very proximity to the traditionally accepted birthplace of jazz, have been given some attention. It is generally assumed that these groups of Negroes, who played on instruments as improvised as their music, were the antecedents of the jazz musicians and some reference to them precedes a discussion of emergent New Orleans jazz. It is a simplification which does not take into account their continued existence for many years after New Orleans music had flowered and withered; nor does it discuss their popularity in areas separated from New Orleans by many hundreds of miles and very different musical traditions.

In the blues the use of less conventional instruments than those of jazz is familiar enough. Jazz musicians depend largely on instruments originating from the military band whilst the blues singer uses the guitar or piano of the nineteenth-century parlour – and when none is available, makes his own. The biographies of blues singers are peppered with references to one-string fiddles, cigar-box guitars and wires on fence palings on which the instrumentalist-singers first tried to accompany themselves. So are the reminiscences of at least some jazz musicians though they soon forsook the home-made substitute for the real instrument when they had the chance. Mature musicians might use a folk instrument for novelty effect, like Baby Dodds' slide whistle (on a few of the recordings of King Oliver's Creole Jazz Band). Also, to increase the range of their instruments they might use derby hats and sink plungers to choke and mute their trumpets; such departures did not affect their dependence on a certain orthodoxy of instrumentation, even when it moved away from the conventional three-part-harmony against background rhythm of the classic New Orleans 'line-up'.

It is not difficult to see why this was so. Jazz in its early forms was largely an improvised music but it clearly depended on the mutual acceptance of a certain structure in the organization of the bands, the selection of keys and the sequence of collective and solo choruses on agreed themes or chord progressions. The agreement was basic to the development of jazz; any compromise here would have led to chaos. Only decades later, with the eventual emergence of highly sophisticated forms of modern jazz, were 'free form' experiments even possible. The folk musician, whether from the country or from the Southern town, making his instruments or exploring the possibilities of household articles, could scarcely enter the jazz band on equal terms. It is interesting to note how seldom, at least on record, such links occurred. The folk banjo player and singer, Papa Charlie Jackson, recorded with Freddy Keppard – but only to sing, not to play.

Clarinettist Johnny Dodds did play with the Dixieland Jug Blowers – but this was a jug band so close to jazz that many collectors do not accept it as part of the admittedly ill-defined tradition. When a blues singer was fully accepted into the jazz band structure he had to be of the calibre of Lonnie Johnson to play with Louis Armstrong's Hot Seven – and many blues enthusiasts do not consider Lonnie Johnson to be a blues singer of the folk idiom.

On the other hand, the blues artists who have expanded their number to something of a band are faced with problems which they do not encounter when working by themselves. The solo blues singer can vary his rhythm, extend his lines, cut the number of measures in a stanza according to his personal whim, and frequently does so. Inevitably he is obliged to give his songs some formal order when he is accompanied by a companion, and it is no accident that the blues became a much more rigid structure in Chicago in the Forties when the blues bands expanded to four or five members. Only by a common acceptance of the formal progression of the twelve-bar blues or the sixteen-bar blues songs of the day could the performances be cohesive as group creations. However, these bands *were* the logical extension of the earlier, more primitive folk bands, and the harmonicas and washboards which played with the piano and guitar in such groups were in a direct line of succession. Chicago blues of that period was tough, aggressive music and its emphatic form gave strength to the performances of the South Side blues bands. In this it was extremely exciting but it lacked the charm, the ingenuousness and the unexpected quality of the earlier and more primitive folk bands.

In the light of recent developments in the blues, with the pressure of modern commercialism threatening to crush all spontaneity from the music, it is instructive to look back at the simple groups who might be considered the forerunners of the rhythm and blues bands of the Sixties. The appeal of these bands sparked off the skiffle craze in Europe a decade ago. The imitative British groups unashamedly plagiarized the songs and tunes of forgotten folk artists from Memphis, Tennessee, and even travelled to the United States to play them. Now the wheel has turned another half circle and with few areas of Negro music left to be exploited, (traditional jazz, country blues and even rhythm and blues having been all copied, exploited and discarded in turn) groups of young white Americans are now imitating the music of the jug and washboard bands. But the present collection presents the authentic, unassuming music of these groups as it was played and recorded three, even four, decades ago.

The tradition extends further back in time than these recordings reach, but documentation is scattered and poor. It is customary to relate the rhythmic emphasis to the African inheritance; to suggest that the improvised nature of some of the instruments has its origins in the jawbones, marimba brett and cask drums described by George Cable in the 1880s. The desire to make music is itself the inspirer of instrumental invention and probably such seeming direct heritage is more the common need to invent instruments, when the economy prevents the purchase of them. Serious arguments have been advanced however to support the view that there are echoes of African culture in the music of the folk Negro bands. The ethnomusicologist Harold Courlander, for example, first suggested in the pages of the *Record Changer* that the tub bass found in some of these groups and heard in the recordings here of the Tub Jug Washboard Band is a direct descendant of the African earth-bow. It is important to bear in mind, however, that many primitive societies use adapted shooting-bows as monochords; a variant used by white folk communities in the United States survived until recently in Arkansas. Conclusions as to the provenance of these instruments must therefore be made with caution; as yet the subject has not been examined with sufficient attention. Whatever its origin, in the form as used by Negro folk bands – and copied by the skiffle groups – the tub was merely an inverted washtub from which the handles had been removed to ensure stability. A broomhandle was then held against the rim and a cord, or better, a bass fiddle string, was attached to the top of the broomhandle and to the opposite side of the tub's rim. As the handle was tilted back the string tautened and it was possible to pluck it with the fingers, 'fret' it against the handle and produce a deep, bass-like sound.

Courlander and others have also noted the basic similarity in principle of the washboard used as a rhythm instrument and the West African scraper. But again, the 'musical rasps', as they are known to the anthropologist, are common to many societies. They employ serrated edges or surfaces over which nails or other scrapers are passed in rhythm. The common washboard, a domestic companion of the washtub and a musical one too, is played by the folk Negro in imitation of the drums. Generally he favours a zinc washboard, for it produces a louder sound, and he plays it with forks or spoons or, in more recent times, very often with his fingers protected by thimbles. Some washboard players put two washboards back-to-back and even mount them on a 'horse' and sit astride them so as to play both surfaces at once. They are frequently decked out with cowbells or other metallophones to add to their musical and rhythmic potential.

A similar ancestry is claimed for the jug, which in many ways is the most colourful of the folk instruments. Primarily though, it is a novelty. Gus Cannon, leader of one of the best known jug bands, got the idea of playing a jug from watching another folk artist blowing down a metal pipe. Cannon's jug was a metal paraffin can – but he was quite able to play without it. When he demonstrated his jug technique to me in Memphis he pursed his lips in a 'bronx cheer' and produced the fruity sound which is featured on many of his recordings. The jug is in fact a fairly unspecific instrument and for Hammie Nixon a whiskey bottle will do. He blows not only into the bottle but on it, spinning it, blowing on the bottom as well as in the neck – variations which he claims affect the sound. Perhaps they do – they certainly add to the visual effect. The large stoneware seven-gallon jug can be considered as something of a true instrument though. Blown into at various angles it vibrates differently, the internal column of air being altered and producing a strong and resonant vibration in the jug. It is probably a jug of this type that is to be heard on the recordings of the Cincinnati Jug Band in which the rhythms of the washboard are also clearly audible.

The foregoing instruments are all, in one way or another, rhythmic and are thus suitable for accompanying a guitar or fiddle. Even the jug, with its reliance on the direct formation of the lips and some element of vocalizing presents many problems arising from keys and tuning. Melodically, the successor to the old Negro instrument of the alley fiddle is the harmonica. The fiddle scarcely survived into the recording era and it is significant that it is only featured on the earliest of these recordings – those by Whistler's Jug Band made in 1924. The harmonica seems to have taken over and makes an excellent companion to the guitar. Blues harmonica players favour the simplest of instruments – the ubiquitous Höhner Marine Band was especially popular – 'vamper' or sophisticated chromatic models were eschewed. Variety was achieved by techniques of overblowing, unconventional lip and tongue work and by muting with the cupped hands. With no orthodox tradition to hinder the development of blues harmonica technique the instrumentalists evolved original and expressive styles. These were largely the result of 'mocking', or imitation of sounds, particularly those of speech and song. 'Mocking the trains' was also common to every blues harmonica player and simulating the train whistles and rhythms as well as speech patterns led to blues harmonica styles that were both melodic and rhythmic. Eddie Mapp 'mocks the trains' in 'Riding The Blinds' and anticipates a technique of imitation which was brought to a remarkable virtuosity by Sonny Terry in later years. Haromonicas in most keys are obtainable but the commonest are C and G models, with occasional E 'harps'. These are easy keys for the guitarist and it is not uncommon to find guitar and 'mouth harp' duets in the blues. More ambitious keys can be carried on the kazoo which requires only that the instrumentalist can sing in tune. The kazoo is a submarine-shaped metal – or sometimes wooden – tube about six inches long with a thin membrane mounted in a dipper-like conning tower on top. The player vocalizes through one end of the tube and the vibrations of the membrane, which is often set in wire gauze, give a buzzing tone not unlike the quality achieved by the harsher trumpet players like Natty Dominique. With the kazoo the group can arrive at some hint of a jazz band without the problems involved in learning a wind instrument, and the use of an oil funnel to give a bell on the kazoo gives it considerable carrying power. It is the kazoo player who figures prominently at the commencement of Walter Taylor's 'Thirty Eight and Plus', a folk musician known only as Anderson.

Given a choice of string instruments – guitar, banjo, mandoline, fiddle perhaps – and drawing upon tub bass, washboard and jug to augment the rhythm, only a kazoo or harmonica is needed to create a folk band with a full sound, suitable for providing the music in a roadside juke joint as in a Beale Street cabaret. It seems unlikely therefore, that the folk groups of this type originated in any one place, or even that they were the sole prerogative of Negro musicians. Indeed, the first documented group of this character, the oft-noted Razzy Dazzy Spasm Band, which performed before Sarah Bernhardt in New Orleans in 1901, was made up of white musicians: it is unlikely that the great actress would have heard them if they were coloured. But the peculiar qualities of intonation and timing that characterize the blues give colour to the music of the Cincinnati Jug Band or the Piccaninny Jug Band and set it apart from the equally interesting but totally 'white' music of the Moatsville String Ticklers or Gid Tanner's Skillet Lickers.

Most of the players on these recordings are anonymous and even their places of origin are a matter of speculation. Some, like the Cincinnati Jug Band, proudly declare their home town and it seems likely that Bob Coleman is one of the guitarists on this item as he is on his own 'Cincinnati Underworld Woman' and the charmingly ingenuous 'Tear it Down'. Guy Lumpkin and Eddie Mapp only made the coupling included here; without this evidence there would be no testimony to the very real talent of these humble musicians who recorded in Long Island City one summer day in 1929. From the title 'Decatur Street Drag' one would be justified in guessing at an Atlanta, Georgia, origin for these two men. They are closer to the blues than is the enigmatic Whistler whose actual name, like that of the members of his accomplished little band, is unknown. They played in a jaunty, near-jazz style, with strong overtones of ragtime, tunes like 'Smoky Mokes' or 'Come Back Sweet Papa' and in their first recordings 'Chicago Flip' and 'Jerry O'Mine', with their leader whistling fluently the lead melody on the latter. A few years later Whistler recorded with his jug band again in St Louis, Missouri, and a single coupling in 1931 made in Louisville, Kentucky, ended his recording career and perhaps indicates his home town.

A 'hot' kazoo player who had listened to King Oliver – or at any rate his records – leads the Tub Jug Washboard Band. It has been suggested that this is Tampa Red (Hudson Whittaker) but it seems unlikely that the rest of the personnel will ever be ascertained. The group provided the great Gertrude 'Ma' Rainey with one of her earthiest supports on eight of her blues titles. Perhaps she didn't give them enough opportunity to show off their abilities: in any event 'Tub Jug Rag' is the celebrated showpiece of the Original Dixieland Jazz Band of a decade before, 'Tiger Rag' under a different guise. They also put in a creditable performance of the Lindsea McPhail – Walter Michels hit tune of 1920, 'San'. With George 'Chicken' Wilson and Jimmy 'Skeeter' Hinton we are very much in the blues idiom and their gentle 'House Snake Blues' with Hinton's interpolated cries in his harmonica line betokens a Southern origin. Nothing is known of these two artists, but 'Myrtle Avenue Stomp' suggests Memphis where the notorious Myrtle Avenue runs off the Eastern limit of Beale. Beale Street, Memphis, was the home of one of the most famous jug bands – Will Shade's Memphis Jug Band which masqueraded on this Champion recording of an old blues favourite 'Bottle It

Up and Go' as the Piccaninny Jug Band. Better known than most of the artists here, Shade, his rumbustious partner Charlie Burse, the blues singer 'Casey Bill' Weldon and their companions Jab Jones, Vol Stevens and Otto Gilmore made up one of the finest and most spirited of all the folk bands. At times they could be extremely moving but in these recordings they are exuberantly extrovert. The cowbells and washboard rhythms provided by Gilmore, Jab Jones' syncopated jug playing, and Shade's swinging harmonica playing on 'You Got To Have (Move) That Thing' are definitive of this form of music. Their mastery of their unassuming instruments, and extraordinary cohesion in playing, contrasts with the more primitive sound of Walter Taylor's group playing and singing of the frankly libidinous 'Diamond Ring Blues'. Yet this group, which on one coupling shared the same pseudonym of the Piccaninny Jug Band, is perhaps most typical of the folk band: gauche at times, but also delightfully primitive and uninhibited when in form. 'Thirty Eight and Plus' – presumably 'thirty-eight plug' and referring to the revolver bullet of this calibre – with its kazoo choruses, banjo accompaniment, washboard rhythm, succession of traditional verses and growled refrains, epitomizes as well as any item in this collection the spirit of these under-rated folk groups.

Of the artists represented in these old recordings only Tampa Red (if he is the kazoo player with the Tub Jug Washboard Band) and Will Shade are known to be living. Tampa Red lives obscurely in Chicago, the modern blues having passed him by, whilst Will Shade survives on public relief in a bare frame building at the back of Beale Street. As for the remainder, they are as unknown now as they were at the time of their brief appearances on record. Only their music remains to remind us of a

Negro tradition which has all but disappeared.

★ ★ ★ ★

Grey perhaps with the residue of soap suds and dirt, worn down by the rough brushing of hard bristle, the common scrubbing-board or rub-board was never a particularly attractive object even when it was fairly commonly seen. Today, even the idea of a rub-board is an anachronism when automatic laundries and washing machines have made machine laundering available to all but the poorest income groups. It was to these – by and large, the Negro population and Cajun French, though not Puerto Ricans or Indians – that the washboard offered possibilities, however unlikely, as a musical instrument. An instrument of a fairly primitive order it is true, though the drums, which the washboard sought to imitate, are themselves elementary in conception.

Just when the washboard came into use as an instrument remains uncertain, but a number of nineteenth-century observers noted the long improvised songs of the Negro washerwomen in the outhouses of the large plantation buildings where the laundry for the entire plantation-owning family would be done. These songs were termed 'rubbing songs' and though they were probably sung to the rhythm of rubbing the heavily soaped clothing against large timber sections, at some indeterminate date the manufactured washboard with its regular corrugations must have come into general use. There is room here for an obscure thesis by a researcher interested in the remoter corners of jazz. As commentators noted throughout the last century, Negroes then had a talent for the improvisation not only of their music but also of their instruments, and when the washboard was idle at the end of the day many a man must

have picked it up, to find by scraping it with a stick an excellent rhythmic accompaniment to his singing. Guitar pickers and banjo players would certainly have welcomed its superiority over the 'pat' accompaniments, those latter-day juba rhythms which were made by slapping the fingers, the ball of the thumb or the palm against knees, thighs and ribs to produce a variety of sounds. But the 'pats' were soft in tone; the washboard was crisper and louder in volume.

Among the first recordings of a washboard band were those of Lem Fowler's Washboard Wonders in 1923; ragged, rather crude music with some staggering rhythms from Fowler's unknown player. For a washboard band required only one washboard, as a jug band required only one jug – the rest of the instruments could be conventional though the washboard made good company with other improvised instruments like the jug, the washtub bass, the musical saws and jews' harps that were pressed into service. Such bands were by no means uncommon in Negro communities throughout the South, and Walter Taylor's Washboard Band, Ed Kelly's Washboard Band, Chasey Collins' Washboard Band are just a few of the washboard and jug bands featured on Blues Classics No. 2, which gives an idea of the distribution of these spirited groups.

In the jazz field the washboard made its appearance and added to the quality of many recordings by notable jazzmen – Baby Dodds, the New Orleans drummer playing the boards on his brother Johnny Dodds' Beale Street Washboard Band, Jasper Taylor playing on the recordings of the Blues Grass Footwarmers, or Jimmy Bertrand even doubling on drums and washboard in Erskine Tate's Vendome Theatre Orchestra. Clarence Williams, apart from using Taylor, also exploited the talents of Floyd Casey and Willie Williams on a number of his recordings with his washboard bands, and even a big band like McKinney's Cotton Pickers used the washboard on occasion. Of course the oddity of the washboard in such a context in itself appealed, and the comic potential was exploited by Spike Jones' City Slickers, the Hoosier Hot-shots and other strictly 'hokum' bands. Nonetheless, the boards did provide in their staccato quality of sound and suitability for clear, brisk rhythmic backgrounds, a setting for many major jazz performances.

The blues, no less than jazz, profited from the washboard, though the volume of the boards when played with nails or forks made singing against them something of a competition. Blind Boy Fuller's washboard player, George Washington, who rejoiced in the nickname of Oh Red was one such player who worked well with a blues singer, and though Brownie McGhee had a lighter voice, he employed Washboard Slim – Robert Young – to similar good effect. A rougher singer like Bukka White sounded best with the boards behind him, where the textural quality of his voice was in accord with that of the boards. Here lay the particular merit of Washboard Sam, who was almost unique in being both vocalist and washboard player.

Washboard Sam, as Robert Brown was known, is believed to have been born in Arkansas in 1910 and by the age of fifteen to have been playing his rub-board in small groups in Memphis, Tennessee. Big Bill Broonzy, not always the most reliable of informants, claimed that Robert Brown was his half-brother; at all events they worked closely for a great many years following Sam's move to Chicago in 1931. He was a large man, with broad features and a somewhat ingenuous expression which apparently belied his character. He played the washboard with thimbles on his fingers.

This was a technique often, but by no means exclusively, employed for many washboard players preferred to use spoons or metal bolts and even knuckle-dusters to produce their rhythms. Washboard Sam added two metal cowbells to the top of his board which had individual notes, and a personal invention – a phonograph turntable which he screwed through the centre and which he used as an effective cymbal. Though photographed holding the boards in his arms he generally played with it held between his knees. The sheer volume of sound would have been difficult to sing against but Robert Brown had a rich, strong voice with a peculiarly rough texture. He sang with a very marked vibrato and this pulsation in the notes, coupled with the hardness of his loud singing, produced a sound which was admirably suited to that of the washboard. It was an ideal, though rare, combination and undoubtedly contributed to the extraordinary popularity that Washboard Sam enjoyed.

Three or four years after his arrival in Chicago he was well enough known to record a couple of titles in April 1935 under his own name. His next few titles were under the name of Ham Gravy but he soon returned to Washboard Sam and for the next seven years almost every title he recorded was issued, with over one hundred and sixty items appearing on 78s. This placed him in the forefront of recording artists of his day and is due as much to the originality of his ideas as it was to the vigour of his performances and the high quality of his groups. The bands featured a succession of excellent pianists – Black Bob, Joshua Altheimer, Horace Malcomb, Simeon Henry, Roosevelt Sykes, Memphis Slim and Bob Call amongst them, and apart from Big Bill Broonzy who was on nearly all his records, he used in later years Willie Lacey on guitar. Washboard Sam favoured a sax or clarinet

player on a great many of his records –
Arnett Nelson, Buster Bennett, Frank
Owens, J. T. Brown, Oett Mallard and
Eddie Penigar amongst them whose gas-
pipe style was eminently suited to the
rough-and-ready atmosphere.

Like Big Bill and Sonny Boy Williamson,
Washboard Sam was one of the innovators
of the Chicago style with its tough, brisk
sound. He was also a highly prolific and
original composer of blues – he wrote
several for Broonzy and over twenty for Jazz
Gillum, and though he occasionally used
compositions by Little Son Joe or Memphis

Slim himself, most of his records were of his
own blues. 1949 saw the end of a long recording career and though he made a brief
attempt at a comeback in 1953 it is only
within the past couple of years that he has
occasionally played again. Washboard Sam
is as tough as his music and has led a rather
tempestuous life – the suggestion that he
was a policeman was Big Bill's ironic joke.
Now settled and virtually retired, his recordings, of which these are some of the best, are
testimony to the part he played in the
creation of the distinctive Chicago blues.

Notes to Riverside RM 8807, 1964
and Blues Classics 10, 1964

Will Shade died Memphis, September 1966,
aged 68
Tampa Red died Chicago, 19 March 1981
Robert Brown was born Walnut Ridge,
Arkansas, 15 July 1910 and died Chicago,
13 November 1966

Railroad Piece
HARMONICA PLAYERS

There are many neglected areas of blues research, but one of the most seriously overlooked is blues harmonica playing. Only one book has been written on the subject – *Blues Harp* by Tony 'Little Sun' Glover. Though written in a relentlessly mid-Sixties 'hip' style it is an informative guide to anyone who wants to play the instrument by studying a manual, and is instructive on modern blues harmonica techniques. But it says little about origins and nothing about the early players who are to be heard here, and who certainly did not learn to play from a manual. This selection gives many pointers to the formation of blues techniques on the 'mouth harp' – since the beginning of the century the American term for the harmonica.

Modern harmonicas were first commercially developed by M. Höhner of Trossingen in Germany in 1857 but it was the influx of German immigrants at the end of the nineteenth century that popularized the instrument in America. Even today the states, with concentrations of German immigrants – Texas, the Carolinas, Illinois – also appear to have higher concentrations of black harp players. Bluesmen still play harmonicas made in Germany by Höhner or Holz, with the Höhner Marine Band ten-hole, twenty-reed instrument the most popular.

In common with concertina players and fiddlers, harmonica players seem to have learned much of their technique through mimicry. In an idiom like the blues, which is so dominated by the voice, it is not surprising if vocal elements of wailing and moaning are to be heard played on the harp. But the techniques may have been learned by other imitations. Freeman Stowers, for instance, reveals on 'Sunrise on the Farm' a very close familiarity with animal noises which he convincingly imitates by purely vocal means. Dogs, chickens, cockerels, cats, cows, donkeys and hogs are all captured by impressions. So his 'Texas Wild Cat Chase', with its participants, Charlie and John, and dogs like Yellow-hammer, sound as if they are accurately portrayed as the wild cat is treed, spitting and snarling, before being killed by the dogs. In fact, the vocal imitation is more accurate than El Watson's 'Fox Chase', partly because Robert Cooksey's second harmonica overcrowds the sound, partly because the 'Fox Chase' here is still a tune. It is likely that the chase, which is still a standby for harp players, has its origins in fiddlers' showcase playing of the same theme.

Another subject for mimicry was the train. Stowers imitates a journey from a platform parting to arrival in St Louis, but he doesn't spend much time on starting off; his skill is in shrieking into the reeds to imitate the train whistle. A note in the Gennett Ledgers after his name says 'the Cotton Belt Porter' so perhaps this is a sound he had heard very often. Palmer McAbee's 'Railroad Piece' recorded in Atlanta is that of a player with a keen ear for nuances of sound, from the letting off steam at the start, to the flares of noise as the train is heard passing objects or trees and crossing bridges. He appears to use a form of cyclic breathing for the sustained fast-rolling passages and you can detect the sound of his intake of air. A ledger note 'hillbilly' raises a doubt as to whether he is black, but chase and train imitations were popular with white players too. 'Lost Boy Blues' is also a kind of train improvisation with a slight dance beat, while El Watson's 'Narrow Gauge Blues' imitates a 'dummy line' train, or spur to the work camps, and has more of a blues character.

Playing for dancing was expected of any player with a melody instrument. Watson's 'Bay Rum Blues' is a skipping dance of considerable age for it is modelled on 'Polly Wolly Doodle'. He also contributes a waltz, 'Sweet Bunch of Daisies', which gives food for thought, for it was composed by Anita Owen in 1894 and made popular by a white singer, Phyllis Allen; perhaps Watson played it for white dances. Ballads were generally as good for dancing as they were useful as work songs, the sixteen-bar form of so many ballads fitting the structure of many country reels. The totally obscure William Francis and Richard Sowell recorded just two titles, both of them ballads and common among both white and black communities. Sowell, who played harmonica, took 'John Henry' at a medium pace and with a mellow quality, only occasionally introducing a more howling note. 'Roubin Blues' is a ballad seldom recorded by black musicians and singers, but which was popular among white performers who also knew it as 'Nine Hundred Miles', which was a railroad song. And in fact, Richard Sowell does play a short and fast train imitation at one point.

Compared with these folk performances Blues Birdhead, as James Simon called himself, seems quite sophisticated. He obviously had been listening to records, especially those by Louis Armstrong. His 'Mean Low Blues' owes a lot to Armstrong's solos, while 'Harmonica Blues' is also jazzy in feeling, with a vaudeville tune of the type popularized by Butterbeans and Susie. Standard blues tunes also form a basis for Freeman Stowers' 'Medley', on which he plays 'All Out and Down', 'Old Time Blues' and a blues tune of possible white derivation, 'Hog in the Mountain'. 'All Out and Down' was a favourite theme in Texas, apparently confirming the evidence of the 'Wild Cat Chase' that this was his state of origin. These then, were some of the routes into blues harmonica playing which find their resolution in 'Pot Licker' and 'One Sack', played by Palmer McAbee, on which he both states and answers each phrase on the harp. They gain their purest expression in the virtually unbroken improvisation by Alfred Lewis, 'Mississippi Swamp Moan' and 'Friday Moan', in which he sings and even shrieks into the reeds fragments of lines '. . .Lord have mercy . . . I'm gonn' play these blues for my baby . . .' His falsetto words are blended into the harp phrases so that the instrument becomes an extension of his voice. From the various sources of chase and train imitations, ballad and dance tunes, even jazz influences, the techniques of cross harp playing and bending of notes through lip, tongue and breath control were evolved, enabling the players to exploit the potential of the mouth harp as a blues instrument.

Notes to Matchbox Bluesmaster
MSE 209, 1982

Dallas Rag
COUNTRY STRING BANDS

It is to be expected that we base our knowledge of blues and related black music on the records that are available to us, and tend to overlook the importance of the idioms that are thinly represented on disc. This is particularly unfortunate when string bands are considered, because they were extremely active in black communities throughout the South during the period when the blues was emerging and maturing. Important string bands like Sid Hemphill's in Mississippi, Willie Walker's in the Carolinas and the Wright Brothers' in Texas were not sought out by the talent scouts; their reputations survive but not their music. Luckily, two bands of note *were* recorded: the Mississippi Sheiks and the Dallas String Band, the former led by Bo Chatmon and the latter by Coley Jones, the subject of this significant collection.

In Texas, everyone it seems, heard Coley Jones and the Dallas String Band in the 1920s and 30s, and the older people remember the band that his father, Old Man Coley, ran early in the century. It was a big family band with a varying personnel that sometimes included one or two violins, two guitars, at least one mandolin and a string bass. In later years it was noted for the clarinet playing of Jesse Hooker, and sometimes a trumpet player would sit in. Most of the time it was a five or six piece string band which worked for dances, picnics and shows, or serenaded. 'Serenading' bands were a feature of the South: string bands which performed in the streets, outside theatres, or in the courthouse squares. They would play a tune for a small sum of money or serenade a lover, probably acquiring the technique from the Mexican bands and mariachi groups who played in South Texas. They were also known as 'shivaree' bands, their name being a corruption of *charivari* by which Italian groups that played on home-made instruments were once known.

Coley was about forty when he recorded, so Alex Moore recalled, and this would place his date of birth before 1890. He had a brother Little Coley, or Kid Coley, (who may or may not be the singer who recorded under that name) who played fiddle; Sam Harris played guitar and the bass player was Marco Washington who had himself run a string band which included his stepson, Aaron Walker (later T-Bone Walker) as a child guitarist. Coley Jones himself played guitar, somewhat indifferently, and mandolin, which he played brilliantly. His voice was strong and coarsened by years of street singing, and his sense of timing was that of an experienced entertainer.

A group like the Dallas String Band played where they were wanted, and where they could draw a crowd. They were professional musicians who performed on Central Tracks in Dallas by Ella B. Moore's Park Theatre for the 'sporting' people, appeared on stage at the Park from time to time, and entertained the crowds at ball games. They travelled from Tyler to Fort Worth, to Waco, to Austin, Houston and Beaumont – 'they had Texas covered,' T-Bone Walker said. They played for white dances and barbecues as well as black functions and all these facets of their performances are hinted at in their recordings.

'Dallas Rag' is one of the very few folk recordings of a rural rag, and if it were only for this beautifully integrated performance the name of the band would be assured. Each strain is made of a pair of sub-strains and the sequence of the fast piece is *abbaabcba*, led with great élan by Coley's mandolin. 'Say, Coley, can you sing?' asks one member of the group on 'Hokum Blues'. 'No,' says Coley, 'I lost my voice in jail; I was always behind a few bars and could never get a key.' The item was recorded just as the Hokum Boys were being recorded in Chicago and it is a moot point as to which group had the term on record first. The blues element is fairly conventional with familiar words, for a string band of this kind played blues as a song type rather than as a form for personal expression. This is evident too, on 'Sweet Mama Blues', which is equally well played.

Minstrel show songs were still popular; in fact Ella Moore had minstrel shows at the Park. It is probably through them and other stage productions that they picked up such a song as 'So Tired', by Jack Little, who was also the composer of 'A Shanty in Old Shanty Town'. Another show song is 'Shine' by the black writers Cecil Mack, Lew Brown and Ford Dabney which was published in 1924; the String Band plays it with accomplishment and there's a hint of parody in Coley's vocal. On 'Sugar Blues', composed in 1923 by Lucy Fletcher and Clarence Williams, he concludes with a scat vocal, but there is more than a touch of Jolson-styled singing and the 'coon' song on 'Chasin' Rainbows' and 'I Used to Call Her Baby', set against jaunty playing and with occasional harmonizing.

In the appropriate setting, at an entertainment or on stage, Coley was also a monologuist, aiming a few light barbs at the church deacons with 'The Elders He's My Man' (the label had a misprint) and his alleged affairs, and gently mocking on 'Army Mule in No Man's Land'. His other solo items draw from both white and black traditions; 'Drunkard's Special' is an eighteenth-century European song, known as 'Our Goodman' (Child 274) in Britain and the Eastern United States, while 'Travelin' Man' was a standby of the minstrel shows and a popular folk song from Texas to Virginia. With Bobbie Cadillac, a Dallas woman of some reputation, he made four titles, all of them variants of 'Tight Like That'. Regrettably it seems that Coley Jones and the Dallas String Band's kind of 'hokum' blues was not as appealing to the Chicago-based record companies as Georgia Tom and Tampa Red's urbane variety. In Texas the band continued to enjoy its state-wide fame, and throughout the 1930s provided music for both black and white functions. They did not record again though, and efforts to trace Coley Jones in the 1960s, or even to ascertain his subsequent career, were sadly unsuccessful.

Notes to Matchbox Bluesmaster
MSE 208, 1982

Ragtime Blues Guitar
BLUES BEGINNINGS

It seems that the blues appeared in the Old South several years later than it did in the states closer to, or beyond, the Mississippi. In the eighteenth century the settlement of the eastern seaboard states had extended beyond the big plantations of the tidewater regions into the rolling hills of the Piedmont, stretching from Virginia southwards, through the Carolinas to the northern half of Georgia. Perhaps the physical and cultural divide of the ranges of the Blue Ridge and the Appalachians, which had formed such a barrier to early settlers, also acted as a watershed between the black cultures of the Old South and the New. Whatever the reason, the older styles of song and dance persisted in the Piedmont and, as the researches of Bruce Bastin, Peter Lowry and Kip Lornell have shown, survive there to some degree even today.

So it is not surprising to find that country dances and jigs, ragtime rhythms played with great virtuosity, minstrel songs and other older traditions were predominant in the recordings of Piedmont musicians, even when they played blues. All these elements are evident in the playing of William Moore, who was born in Georgia in 1894 but who moved with his parents to Virginia eight years later. He lived for many years at Tappahannock, the county east of Essex county on the Rappahannock River, to which he refers on 'Old Country Rock', a slow drag dance with sliding notes for the drawn steps. He was a barber – 'the only barber in the world can shave ya and give ya music while he's doin' it,' as he claimed on 'Barbershop Rag'. His injunctions to the assistant to bring water and brush, strap the razor with a feather edge and 'shine that man's shoes', are complemented on the guitar.

It seems likely that Moore was a barber for white clients too, who could well have been entertained with his 'Ragtime Millionaire', an Edwardian fantasy of a poor man who drives a '28 automobile, takes his 'sweetie' to a ball, and brushes his teeth with diamond dust. Or they were amused at the description of 'Tillie Lee', 'my yellow honey-bee, she's bow-legged and lazy, cockeyed and crazy', and much else. Even when 'Raggin' the Blues' Moore was playing a ragtime dance with stop time steps. 'Jazz 'em boy, jazz 'em,' he drawled, but it was more ragtime than jazz or blues. He was mainly a dance musician playing sand-dance time on the 'flang-dang' piece 'Ragtime Crazy', on which he called on the children to 'go crazy . . . look foolish, cross-eyed and everything'. Such novelty steps lasted for many years in black rural dance.

When he played blues, as on 'One Way Gal' or 'Midnight Blues', William Moore displayed his remarkable skill, using the slid drag notes to blues effect. He used a four-line form on both, and two verses of Mamie Desdume's blues, as recalled by Jelly-Roll Morton, creep into 'One Way Gal'. Traditional blues verses also figure strongly in the two blues by Steve Tarter and Harry Gay, who lived at Gate City, Virginia, and who played for the miners in the coal mining camps of southwestern Virginia. The vocals were taken by Tarter, who also played lead guitar, excellently supported by Gay. They were primarily ragtime guitarists and typical of such musicians who assimilated the new blues, did not sound particularly involved in the content of their songs.

Nothing is known of Bayless Rose, and it has even been suggested that he was a white musician. Nevertheless he sang and played blues in a manner characteristic of musicians of the northern Piedmont, including 'Black Dog Blues', a variant of 'Honey Where You Been So Long', which admittedly, was popular among white singers. Capable of fast finger-picking, he displayed a hint of old-time banjo technique on his 'Frisco Blues'. His instrumental 'Jamestown Exposition' refers to the Tri-centennial celebrations held in Jamestown, Virginia, in 1907, which he may well have attended and played at as a young man.

One can only guess at the extent of the undiscovered talent that existed in this much neglected area from the few examples by these obscure, but in most cases, locally famous musicians. Willie Walker is an outstanding case in point, remembered by Josh White as 'the best guitarist I've ever heard . . . this man played so much guitar it wasn't even funny'. How much guitar is evident on the two takes of the beautiful 'South Carolina Rag' on which he was accompanied by carpenter and guitarist, Sam Brooks, who

also acted as his guide, for Willie Walker was born blind in 1896. He lived and played around Greenville, South Carolina, where he was widely recalled as an exceptional singer and musician with a repertoire which is only hinted at by his version of the old ballad 'Betty and Dupree' which he called 'Dupree Blues'.

Unfortunately, the Piedmont singers were not sought out so rigorously as those in, say, Memphis and Mississippi and none of these men recorded again. Blind Willie Walker died in 1933 and Stephen Tarter a few years later. But William Moore lived until 1955, Sam Brooks to the late Sixties and Harry Gay was reported as still living at that time. Because these were more laconic singers than those from further west they have been largely overlooked, but their relaxed vocals, casual air and breathtaking instrumental command created an alternative, distinctive model of a regional blues approach deeply rooted in older traditions.

Notes to Matchbox Bluesmaster
MSE 204, 1981

Juke Joint Blues
PLAYING IN THE BARRELHOUSES

We were taken out to the juke joint by Columbus Jones and Wade Walton. It lay a mile or so out of Clarksdale on Highway 49, a wooden-frame structure of two rooms. The front room had a high bar and a single, bright lamp bulb swinging from the ceiling. There were ten or fifteen people round the bar and they stepped back a little as we came in, rather as if we were players in a Western movie. Wade muttered words of explanation to the barman and, telepathically it seemed, everyone relaxed a little, or appeared to; we *could* have been police though; cautiously they invited us to a Coke, for Mississippi is technically 'dry'. Chris stayed and talked in the front room but Wade wanted me to go through to the room beyond. I was very reluctant and sensed the barrier of black figures and blue faded overalls in front of the doorless doorway. But we went in anyhow, Wade proudly and excitedly, myself excitedly too, but feeling qualms. The noise coming from the juke-box somewhere – it was hidden by bodies – and the shouting of drinkers trying to be heard above its din, was indescribable. But at least there wasn't the dramatic effect of my entry that I half expected, with everyone falling silent; perhaps because the room was so crowded that my presence was probably unknown to most of its occupants. In a babble of words Wade explained where I'd come from, who I was and why he'd brought me. There was incredulity, amusement, friendliness; I was half forced down into a chair, the ubiquitous tube steel chair with shaped metal seat, and given a drink. Then I felt and realized the open hostility of two young women in the crowd around the table, mistily seen through the dust rising off the bare wood floor, the tobacco smoke and the poor light. We had no communication; I knew and understood how they felt. Wade made some apologies for the coldness and I wished he hadn't. Another record - it was by Howling Wolf but I cannot recall which – blared out. There was no dancing, for there wasn't room, but gesticulating figures were magnified in the shadows cast against the ceiling, boarded like the floor. When we left I saw the wall for the first time and noticed it was papered yellow with sheets of old newpapers.

Most country jukes are not so very different, although some are long and narrow, and others ridiculously tall on their brick piers. Generally they are wood, patched and remade on their balloon frames, but covered sometimes with tarpaper and imitation tiles stamped on sheets of roofing felt. The fronts often have deep, projecting eaves in the shade of which the old men can sit, and ads for Dr Pepper, Nehi, Barg's, Budweiser and so on, are nailed to the front boards in a crazy assemblage. The only unifying factor, though, seems to be the name of the juke joint, stencilled in emasculated green sans serif letters and flanked by the bottle-cap trademark of one or other Cola firm. The sign may proclaim the name of the proprietor, or a colourful image – 'Lone Star' or 'White Rooster' – or merely say baldly, Colored Café. One thing it hardly ever says is 'Juke', for though the numbers of juke joints may be thousands and everyone calls them this, their owners seem loath to state the term. In the towns they assume a certain respectability – in St Louis the popular phrase is 'Recreation Parlor'. But inside they're not so very different from the rudest of country joints. A few more tables, a little more space, a bandstand perhaps, a plastic

Winchester '73 in a plastic case, courtesy of a beer firm, last year's Cola calendar, not much else. Juke joints are English pubs and Western saloons without the charm of the former or the romantic appeal of the latter; they're social clubrooms to which the church members don't go; they're dance halls that are too small for more than a few couples to hully-gully. They are, in fact, unappealing, decrepit, crumbling shacks, which never seem to have been built yesterday, but always thirty or forty years ago, and unpainted since. They are dusty and rather squalid, littered with flattened beer and soft drink cans in the yard in front, stained to shoulder height inside. They're the last retreat, the final bastion for black people who want to get away from whites, and the pressures of the day. It was in these juke joints that the blues found a home.

Dr Lorenzo Turner has disclosed the ancestry of the word 'juke' or 'jook', revealing its American origins in the Gullah 'joog', meaning 'disorderly' and, in turn, its African source in the Bambara 'dzugu', meaning 'wicked'.[1] To the law-abiding, the jukes are still suspect. They can be very rough places and more than one blues singer has been involved in shooting or knifing affrays in them, some even to die in them. Their origins probably lie in the social community rooms that were occasionally built on the plantations, even during the slavery period, and which kept the field hands within the confines of the plantation spread, in the early decades of this century. The 'barrel-houses' and 'chock-houses' of the forest regions of Mississippi, Louisiana, Arkansas and Texas were maintained by the sawmills and the big lumber companies to entertain the loggers, and these rough buildings, constructed in the same pattern as the commisary stores or dwelling units, may well have been the first instituted jukes. But juke joints sprang up all over the country at the highway crossings and the railroad intersections. Many were, and are, closed during the weekdays when the workers are employed in the fields, but open at weekends when there is spending change available, casual musicians to play, and time to fill. After a week of strenuous work the field hands in the country and the factory workers in the cities look for an opportunity to 'let off steam'. The dice rattle, the liquor flows in 'dry' state or 'wet', and the couples 'dance on a dime'. During Prohibition the juke joints proliferated, their front rooms presenting an innocent face to the police who came to collect their percentage, and their backrooms, where there *was* more than one – crowded and impenetrable. It wasn't easy to be heard and for this reason, if for no other, many blues singers developed powerful, strained voices, and played steel strung, sometimes steel-bodied guitars, for greater resonance.

Describing the music of Florida juke joints Zora Neale Hurston wrote: 'One guitar was enough for a dance. To have two was considered excellent. Where two were playing one man played the lead and the other seconded him. The first player "picking" and the second was "framming", that is, playing chords while the lead carried the melody by dexterous finger-work. Sometimes a third player was added, and he played a "tom-tom" effect on the low strings.'[2] Or drummed on a suitcase; or a pianist was added, or a guitarist or harp player supported the pianist. Sometimes a harmonica player held his own by himself, and sometimes a single instrumentalist played guitar, harmonica, even kazoo, drums and cymbals as well, using the combination to give the sound of a full blues band.

In 1930 out of some six million farms only one in ten had electricity and at the outbreak of the Second World War two-thirds of America's farms were still without power. A heavy electrification programme during and after the war narrowed this gap until, in 1950, four-fifths of the farms had electricity and there were enough spare lines to feed even the most rural of jukes. The effect on the music of the jukes was felt first in the amplification of instruments which commenced in the city joints and spread to those in the country. The increased volume created a stimulating new sound and with the growing popularity of amplified guitars and microphones, the juke joints of the early Fifties rocked on their shaky piers and even collapsed under stamping, dancing feet. These recordings come from this period and demonstrate not only the vigour of the music but the ubiquity of juke joint blues, with Eddie Burns and Harvey Hill playing in Detroit, Big Boy Spires and Mr Honey in Chicago, Sonny Terry and Square Walton in New York, Buddy Lewis and Sonny Boy Holmes in Los Angeles, Dr Hepcat and L. C. Williams in Houston and Lightning Leon in Memphis.

But if the live blues in the juke joints was to be heard throughout black America it was soon to be threatened by mechanical reproduction and canned music. The juke joints gave a new term to American vocabulary with the widespread installation of the jukebox. It didn't entirely destroy live blues but it did a lot to drive it from the jukes.

1. For the implications of this derivation see *Savannah Syncopators (African Retentions in the Blues)* by Paul Oliver, Stein and Day (USA), and Studio Vista (UK), 1970.
2. From *Mules and Men* by Zora Neale Hurston; French, Taubner, 1936.

Notes to Blues Classics BC23, 1970

Special Agents
HOW THE BLUES GOT ON RECORD

Now Special Agent, Special Agent, put me
  off close to some town,
Now Special Agent, Special Agent, put me
  off close to some town,
Now I got to do recordin'; ought to be recordin'
  right now
(Sleepy John Estes: Special Agent)

As anyone who has made the attempt will be well aware, the transcription of a blues or a Negro folk song into musical notation or of its words into dialect or phonetics singularly fails to convey the very qualities that are most essential to the music. Subtleties of inflection, nuances of tone and timbre and line elude the pen, and the peculiar characteristics of the blues are lost in the fruitless effort to convey them in the formal terms of musical or written language.

'I cannot begin to tell you of the difficulties that Mrs Buie met with in trying to translate the songs "from the African to the American" as she explained the process,' wrote Mrs Tom Bartlett to the folk collector Dorothy Scarborough early in the century. 'There are slurs and drops and "turns" and heaven knows what of notes not to be interpreted by any known musical sign. You are experienced enough with Negro music to know that it is entirely different as sung from the regular accompaniment.' Hers was the *cri de coeur* of the sincere collector who has encountered the insuperable problems involved in trying to preserve folk music material in the days before gramophone recording techniques. Through the medium of literature we may learn more about the singers, their lives and their environments – with all the considerations of the fallibility of the human memory in giving and receiving information, of inadequate reporting of

the untrained techniques of the amateur observer borne in mind. But it is to the recording (gramophone, tape, it makes little difference) that we must turn in order to study the work of the singers, though there is no substitute for the first-hand experience of listening to the singers at work.

With all the technical imperfections of the past and the present, the recording remains the only satisfactory way in which the blues of the past may be preserved and still experienced, and it is the means whereby students and enthusiasts of this form of folk music may turn to identical terms of reference. Through the careful observations of Odum and Johnson we know more of the life of 'Left-Wing' Gordon than we do of the lives of Robert Johnson or Blind Lemon Jefferson, but as a blues singer he means far less to us because some impression of their voices, of their instrumental abilities, have been preserved for us whereas Gordon was to remain unrecorded.

Understandably, the written material on the activities of blues singers has been primarily devoted to those whose work appears on record, though it is possible by comparison of styles to convey an impression of the singing and playing of an unrecorded folk artist as more examples on disc are made available. The numbers of recorded blues run into many thousands though many are far from easily obtainable. They are profuse enough, however, to encourage many a writer to try his opinion as to the identity of the 'greatest (living) blues singer' or to spur him to draw conclusions as to the 'Mississippi style' of singing, the 'purest form of blues' or the contender for the title of 'the Father of Blues Piano'. It is important therefore to bear in mind the many considerations, whether commercial, economic, physical, geographical or born of human temperament that have conditioned the recording of blues, for these have the greatest bearing on any conclusions that might be made from examples available on wax.

Mattie Hite was one of the most esteemed of the vaudeville-blues singers of the Twenties but she left only two records to prove that she was the peer of Alberta Hunter and Trixie Smith with whom she worked. Son House made a handful of superb blues recordings before the Depression: he is still alive and active in Clarksdale. Beside the monumental discographies of Amos Easton (Bumble Bee Slim), Big Bill Broonzy, Casey Bill Weldon or Tampa Red must be placed the single discs made by the Otis Harrises and Joe Linthecomes of the blues. What were the causative factors that made Pink Anderson a forgotten name for a score of years? What were the 'Special Agents' on which have depended the recording of the blues?

In the recording of Negro folk song, history has been curiously inverted, for the more sophisticated forms of vaudeville entertainment were to be heard on wax before the Southern blues, whilst examples of the most primitive forms of field cries and hollers, of children's songs and unaccompanied blues were not to be found on commercial labels until after the Second World War. That there was a market for the former before they ever appeared on wax was well demonstrated by the remarkable response to the issue of Mamie Smith's first sides, whilst conversely, the recent recordings made of folk songs in the field may have been possibly, though not necessarily, impressions of a music which had been subjected to change and even the influence of some three decades of commercial issues.

In the mid-Twenties Odum and Johnson noted the influence of gramophone recordings made in the Northern cities on the singing of folk Negroes; a quarter of a century later the 'field blues' of Rich Amerson recorded by Harold Courlander had strains that can be heard on early recordings of Blind Lemon Jefferson and it is an open argument as to whether folk repertoire, direct or indirect influence, or traditional form explains the coincidence.

Many of the vaudeville and tent show singers who included blues in their repertoire learned them as they travelled 'in the sticks' whilst others stemmed from a folk environment and broadened their repertoires for vaudeville audiences. On the other hand, folk singers such as Peg Leg Howell, Henry Thomas and even Stovepipe No. 1 (Sam Jones) include amongst their songs totally unsophisticated variants of vaudeville melodies. Thus the interchange between the folk and the professional stage is exceedingly complex, confusing still further the general impression that the picture of Negro song has been given a perspective seen through the wrong end of the telescope by its representation on wax. As an indication of the stages of blues history, therefore, recording dates can be vastly misleading.

Indicative of the initial prejudice against Negro singers held by the recording companies were the struggles of Perry Bradford with Okeh and elsewhere to secure recognition for his artists. Soon after Bradford's first promotion success, the Okeh Company was happy enough to boast in its *Blue Book of Blues*: 'Who first thought of getting out Race records for the Race? Okeh, that's right. Genuine Race artists make genuine Blues for Okeh . . . It's a cheerful day, folks for everybody . . . ' But a few years later Ralph Peer, who had been Okeh's recording manager, recalled that they had records by numerous foreign groups, German Swedish, Polish 'but we were afraid to advertise negro records, so I listed them as "Race" records and they are are still [1938] known as that.'

Once the sale of recordings by Negro artists had proved that a whole new market existed, other companies were not slow to follow suit. Within the space of a few months Mary Stafford (Annie Burns) recorded for Columbia, Lillyn Brown for Emerson, Gennett introduced Daisy Martin, Arto commenced with Lucille Hegamin, and soon Paramount started its celebrated Race series with Alberta Hunter, and Black Swan came forward with Katie Crippen.

Pressure salesmanship followed as competition became keen: fly-sheets, throwaways, illustrated supplements, full page advertisments in the *Chicago Defender* and other Negro newspapers were exploited and the importance of individual singers became submerged in verbiage; extravagant cajoling, sycophantic, according to the copy-writer's current assessment of his audiences' reaction. 'How we love that girl, Eva Taylor! Sugar cookies, if she ain't the berries we've jes' been samplin' the blues and know nuffin'. She jes kisses dem vocal tones good-bye and the very next thing you heah is somethin' sobbin' sweet and gruesome . . .'

Separate catalogues were issued for white and Negro records with suitable photographs or decorations embellishing the covers: a Negro roustabout sings to his guitar whilst a Mississippi Riverboat passes in the distance on a Victor catalogue that does not mention 'Race' but advertises 'Vocal Blues, Religious, Spiritual, Red Hot Dance Tunes, Sermons, Novelties' amongst its contents. Paper record sleeves bore drawings of singers inset in decorative stars; bore vignettes of tuxedoed entertainers or 'Plantation' scenes according to the intended market. And with the coming of Southern country blues on the record market, items such as Blind Lemon Jefferson's ''Lectric Chair Blues', 'See That My Grave is Kept Clean' and Blind Lemon's 'Penitentiary Blues' appeared somewhat surprisingly beneath the legend 'Favorite Hits You Will Enjoy'.

Undoubtedly such methods of salesmanship stimulated a chain reaction between purchasing public and recording companies as indeed they were intended to do, the fever to obtain the latest releases creating queues that were blocks in length outside the South Side music stores. Companies secured their 'Exclusive Artists' and tied them to contracts; measures that were a safeguard for some singers and prejudicial to the success of others. To promote further interest, blues singing contests were held, commencing in January 1922 at the Manhattan Casino, NYC, on the occasion of the 15th Infantry's 'First Band Concert and Dance' at which Trixie Smith won a loving cup after competition with Daisy Martin, Lucille Hegamin and Alice Carter. Three years later an eight-week marathon blues contest at the Booker T. Washington Theatre in St Louis was finally won by Lonnie Johnson from New Orleans, the event setting the seal on his career. In 1926 Richard M. Jones organized a 'Race Record Artists' Night' at the Coliseum Theatre, Chicago, at which Hociel Thomas, Sippie Wallace, Butterbeans and Susie, Bertha Hill, Davenport and Carr and other Okeh artists took part; and a few months later brought Sarah Martin, Lonnie Johnson, Nolan Welsh on the stage of a 'Cabaret and Style' show which featured the bands of King Oliver, Al Wynn, Louis Armstrong and Doc Cook.

So was established a pattern of commercial exploitation, salesmanship and star building within the gramophone industry which is still very much with us today. It may have changed in kind; the radio networks with their autocratic disc-jockeys have altered the vehicle, but the means and the end are fundamentally the same. Many great singers were thus given their due and many inferior ones were 'built up' beyond their merits, but the effect was beneficial not only to the record industry but to the vaudeville circuits and the nightclubs. Some singers – Melissa Rainey and Ada 'Bricktop' Smith for example, much admired in their day – floated on the resultant tide of popularity and, entertaining at their Harlem Clubs, did not need or seek a recording career; whilst others, many of whom must now be completely forgotten, were content enough to maintain their touring engagements without the interruptions of recording sessions in the North and the restrictions of exclusive contracts.

'We want live agents everywhere' demanded Black Swan in 1923, seeking representatives in drug stores and furniture shops, hairdressing salons and roadside cafés. Record salesmen touted the discs from their suitcases and barrows; hawked them from bar parlour to gin-mill; sold them by mail-order. In beer taverns and jukes, brothels and honky-tonks, the back rooms of tenements and the parlours of dog-trot cabins, the discs were worn grey on battered victrolas. In the process of disseminating their products through the Southern States the representatives soon became aware that there was a market also for the untutored singing of the folk blues men as well as for the more conscious artistry of the vaudeville entertainers.

In recording the latter, they were assisted by the numbers of coloured theatres that employed such singers in the Northern cities where the majority of the studios were established; but the great Northward migration of Negroes during and after the First World War brought many Southern folk artists off the streets of Chicago and Detroit to put on wax for a few moments their blues creations.

Nevertheless, the wisdom of employing talent scouts within the race or amongst men who circulated freely in Negro districts encouraged them to commission Mayo Williams, Dan Hornsby, Richard Jones, Aletha Robinson, J. B. Long, Lester Melrose, J. C. Johnson, Will Shade, Joe Lee Williams and many others with the task of seeking and recording folk musicians. Many of these showed considerable perspicacity in their choice of singers and their fingers were clearly on the pulse of Negro taste; nonetheless they were capable of favouritism and prejudice and were in a position to dictate the terms and to reject those who were not in accord with their ideas of contractual obligations.

Some companies maintained regular recording studios in certain Southern cities as, for example, those owned for a number of years during the later Thirties by the American Record Company in Dallas and San Antonio, Texas. Mobile recording units were also extensively used and they visited Southern townships for brief periods ranging from a few days to a couple of months. These would feel their way to Birmingham, Alabama, to Nashville or to Charlotte. Brief recording spells were made by mobile units in Hattiesburg, Mississippi, and Savannah, Georgia; Jacksonville, Florida, and Fort Worth, Texas, whilst Memphis and St Louis were frequent stopping places for many companies. Even Gennett made a trip to Birmingham, Alabama, for a short spell in 1927 when Jaybird Coleman, Whistling Pete and Daddy Stovepipe made their contribution in the temporary studio. Such recording tours were singularly beneficial from the point of view of the student of Negro folk song for they preserved much talent that may otherwise have remained totally unknown. For the companies themselves, they proved to be a lucrative move, especially during the lean post-Depression years, for the singers did not expect to be paid more than a fraction of the sum required by a professional entertainer. Five dollars for a coupling was a commonly paid fee which made the casual street singer happy enough and could scarcely be considered a risk on the part of the company's agent. In the Southern districts where they were marketed, the recordings of folk blues singers sold almost as well as did those of the bigger names, but in spite of this, there are many established instances of singers receiving no payment at all for their work; of non-payment or misappropriation of royalties, or the all too frequently employed device of causing a singer to 'pay off the debt' he owes through having 'wrecked' the recording machine by the loudness of his playing.

A close study of the movements of mobile recording units in relation to the talent discovered at specific periods is long overdue. As an indication, a glance might be made at the information revealed by the seemingly hard and unrelenting facts contained in the ledgers of one company. Outstanding amongst the 'Race' catalogues was the Columbia 14000 series which was commenced in 1924. The quality of the material recorded was exceptionally high and the standards of recording and surface in contrast with those of the justly celebrated and contemporaneous Paramount series compares favourably with those of thirty years later. Though Columbia recorded primarily in Chicago and New York, it did maintain a touring recording unit which had its own blocks of matrices and recorded soloists and groups, white and coloured, religious and secular.

As far as the blues collector is concerned, these tours commenced in earnest on 8 November 1926, when four sides of folk guitarist and singer Peg Leg Howell were recorded in Atlanta, Georgia. Four months

later, the unit returned to cut the first items made by Barbecue Bob – Robert Hicks – on 25 March 1927, together with items by Reverends Weems and Tomlin. Five days later Hicks was again recorded and so was Earl MacDonald's Original Louisville Jug Band. Apparently they were satisfied with Barbecue Bob for he was further recorded a week later on 5 April and so too was 'Talking Billy Anderson' who was, in fact, on one side at any rate, 'Cow Cow' Davenport. 7 April saw the deep-voiced Emery Glenn in front of the machine along with Reverend Thrasher and the next day, Peg Leg Howell returned with an unknown violinist to accompany him, and Dan Hornsby, the talent scout who had discovered these men recorded his own trio.

It was to be eight months before the group returned to Atlanta but when they did so it was to record the now familiar Peg Leg on 1 November. Barbecue Bob was in the studio on the fifth and tenth of the month, sharing it with Weems and Thrasher once more. This November block used tried and proved artists for the most part but a new discovery in the person of Charlie Lincoln was waxed on the fourth, with one title under the name of Laughing Charlie under which pseudonym he also recorded a two-part title with Barbecue Bob. Two more titles with Hicks on the tenth and the company hit the road for Dallas, Texas.

In Dallas, where they arrived three weeks later, a week of intensive recording activity brought Lillian Glinn before the machine on 2 December with the date shared by the wandering evangelist Blind Willie Johnson who recorded again the following day, sharing the date with Coley Jones, Billiken Johnson and Fred Adams. Coley Jones came back on the fourth and sixth of the month including, on the same date, sides with the Dallas string band and sharing it with Hattie

Hudson, Gertrude Perkins and the har-monica soloist, Willie McCoy. As far as the Negro artists were concerned, the coarse-voiced Lewis Black concluded the block with his four blues sides on 10 December.

Returning to Atlanta again in April 1928, the company recorded Charlie Lincoln on the eleventh and during the subsequent ten days, still more sides were cut by Howell and Hicks. The talent scout – presumably Hornsby – had also discovered the street entertainer Pink Anderson and his partner Simmie Dooley who made some charac-teristic minstrel-influenced sides; Henry Williams and Eddie Anthony who made a primitive guitar and fiddle blues duet, and Nellie Florence who was accompanied, it seems, by Charlie Lincoln who contributed a characteristic evil laugh in the back-ground. Including sides by Jim King and his 'Brown Mules', these were all recorded before 21 April. Three days later the unit was in New Orleans.

Between 24 and 28 April, Will Day, Will Harris and Alberta Brown were recorded, and so too was Lillian Glinn, still playing the Southern time. It was a short stay, but the unit returned to Atlanta for the end of Octo-ber to record Hicks, Howell and Eddie Anthony yet again, but finding new talent in Curley Weaver, Too Tight Henry, Billy Bird and the minstrel singer Alec Johnson who was accompanied by the brothers Joe and Charlie McCoy, destined to be cele-brated blues artists in later years. The restless unit was back in Dallas a month later for a few busy days when Coley Jones, Blind Willie Johnson, Billiken Johnson and Willie McCoy came to the machine again. But Bobby Cadillac, Laura Henton, Willie Reed, Otis Harris, and Jimmy Davis were recorded for the first time and Leroy's Dallas String Band was supplemented by Frenchy's String Band. Also recorded was Blind Texas Marlin but his sides were never

to be issued. Later in the month a brief stay in New Orleans brought Lillian Glinn to the studio once more and Dorothy Everetts and the unissued sides of Barrelhouse Pete were enregistered.

The pattern of the tours of the Columbia mobile unit now begins to emerge and it is no surprise to find it back in Atlanta in March and April the following year, record-ing Peg Leg Howell, Lillian Glinn – now in Georgia, and Barbecue Bob who commen-ted in one blues on 'Miss Lillian's' presence. Familiar names, but new talent was dis-covered in the banjo-playing Lonnie Coleman, Barefoot Bill and Blind Sammie (who was to record under his correct name of Blind Willie McTell for Victor) were added to the company's files in the next Atlanta session which occurs, as one is now inclined to expect, at the end of October and the beginning of November. Again accord-ing to the well-established rule, three days in Dallas in early December brought further sides by Willie Johnson, Coley Jones, Bobbie Cadillac – and Lillian Glinn. But fresh discoveries in the persons of Texas Bill Day, Perry Dixon (sounding remarkably like Atlanta's Emery Glenn), Whistling Alex Moore and one Oak-Cliff T-Bone, just sixteen years old and eventually famous as Aaron 'T-Bone' Walker, were made and recorded. To round off the year just four days later in New Orleans, Blind Willie Johnson cut a few more tracks for the company. With the approach of 1930 and the Depression years the activities of the mobile unit were curtailed, but the old favourite Barbecue Bob in Atlanta was still recording in April, together with Pillie Bolling and Jaybird Coleman, and in November of that year he made a final set of four sides. He died soon after.

From this outline sketch which tends to read at first as a list of names and dates almost devoid of meaning, several facts do emerge and certain conclusions may be drawn. In the first place, the tour of the Columbia Company's unit or units would seem to follow a set and almost invariable pattern with dates for specific centres corresponding in successive years. Certain artists were much favoured by the company: Robert Hicks, under his name of Barbecue Bob, heading the list with some fifty-six sides ultimately to his credit issued, and Peg Leg Howell with just half that number. These folk singers were among the first to be recorded in Columbia's ventures abroad and their early issue ensured that their popularity amongst the Negro purchasers could be ascertained. They were also among the last to be recorded before the Depression put an end to the trips, their value to the company assured. But at the same time many obscure blues singers were given an opportunity to record, and many of these had no little ability both as folk singers and as instrumentalists on the much favoured guitar.

Nellie Florence, Lonnie Coleman, and Otis Harris are represented by a single disc each; Billy Bird and Glenn by four sides apiece. Curley Weaver, however, though only recording two sides for Columbia was to appear on Champion, Decca and ARC labels in later years; Blind Willie McTell, continuing to beg on the streets of Atlanta for twenty years, recorded for Victor and eventually for the Archives of the Library of Congress; Too Tight Henry was to appear on Brunswick in Chicago some three years later; Laura Henton in Kansas City the following year; Pink Anderson in North Carolina some twenty-two years later; whilst Jaybird Coleman had been recorded by Gennett, as has been seen, some three years earlier in Birmingham, Alabama, where incidentally, he still lives. Whereas some of the singers may have been dropped by Columbia through lack of talent or

unsuitability in other directions, others may well have moved on or have been difficult to trace.

In the course of their movements, the Columbia unit was clearly following an established routine dictated by the size and importance of the towns in the states (Georgia, Louisiana, Texas) that they visited. Lillian Glinn was almost certainly on tour, possibly with the TOBA circuit and traced a similar course. She may well have travelled with the unit at one time and it is most likely that Blind Willie Johnson travelled from Dallas to New Orleans with the company in December 1929. It is conceivable that they were committed to the Columbia concern and neither they nor Hicks and Howell recorded for any other company. Rabbit Brown was available in New Orleans, but he recorded for Victor; Sloppy Henry and Macon Ed were in Atlanta recording for Okeh; Bo Jones and Jake Jones were in Dallas (Brunswick, Vocalion) but they were not employed. These artists were therefore apparently exclusive to the other companies working the districts at the same time, a factor which accounts in part for the bewildering use of pseudonyms by folk blues singers and vaudeville and city singers alike when they wished to work for another company.

Contracts clearly limited the availability of folk artists but there were many physical factors that must be borne in mind. A glance at the map will show how widely dispersed were the three centres used by Columbia, hundreds of miles separating them from each other and no casual stops were made. Many singers would have lived in areas untouched by the recording units, unvisited by the talent scouts. Others would not have heard of the visit of the unit or would have arrived too late to benefit from their arrival. The Columbia concern made use of the 'layoff' period in the South when chances to earn extra money would be welcome and Negroes would be less committed to employment that would prevent their attendance; many singers were garage hands, factory workers, levee graders, turpentine workers, sharecroppers, tenant farmers, section hands. Others worked with medicine shows and were themselves making use of the 'lay-off' period, so that they were barred by the nature of their work from attending recording sessions at the dictates of the engineers. Some recording firms paid travelling expenses for their artists (Will Ezell is said to have claimed expenses from Texas when he came from St Louis), but others did not do so. Expenses, the lack of transport and the difficulties of travel in rural areas must have precluded others from being heard. The short duration of many of the session visits would have limited the field still further, though Columbia may have attempted a 'session habit' by appearing at exactly regular dates.

Apart from these considerations of selection, trial, route, disposition of centres, contract limitations, notification, labour commitments, travel and date, there were innumerable human factors to be surmounted. Reluctance to perform before a recording machine may have affected many blues singers, especially when the medium was comparatively new. It may be recalled that Johnny Dodds, an able performer on the clarinet before the recording horn, was quite incapable of speaking a few words into it when a 'hokum' routine demanded it. Negroes in the early recording days may have displayed similar reactions to those experienced by John Lomax when recording in the Southern penitentiaries in the Thirties. One man, he reported, fell flat on his back in terror when he heard his own voice issuing from the machine, whilst another, Joe Lee, screeched at the top of his voice, burst into tears, beat his head against

the wall and threw himself violently about the room in fright at hearing himself.

More sophisticated singers still experienced nervous reactions when recording. Victoria Spivey had to make three takes of 'Black Snake Blues' because she was scared to death, and burst into tears on hearing her voice on record. Unsophisticated country Negroes encountering recording conditions for the first time must have been unsettled in many instances by the novelty of the experience, and the numerous listings of names and titles known to have been recorded but never released may well be accounted for by attacks of nerves which have impaired performances. Laziness, lack of ambition, disinterest or failure to realize the possibilities of recording may have deterred some folk artists, whilst the reluctance of Freddie Keppard to record in 1916 for fear that his work might be copied by others may have been echoed amongst folk singers.

Of equal significance in affecting the scope of recording would be human characteristics of quite opposite nature. If some singers are unnerved by the circumstances of recording, other are undoubtedly stimulated to superior efforts by the necessary concentration and a realization of the finality of the performance. Whilst some singers would be reluctant to record, others could well have been as eager as the Negro convict who approached John Lomax with a request to record: 'Boss, I can beat on a bucket just as sweet as you please.' Singers who rose to the occasion would have been encouraged by session supervisors to record again. Similarly, if idleness affected some men, others more ambitious might have seen in recording a chance to achieve more than local fame and an opportunity to go North. 'I would have gone for the trip!' said Brownie McGhee, recalling his excitement at obtaining his first recording date and the offer of payment. Some recording sessions are known, in fact, to have been financed by the singers themselves. For some Negroes, recording meant a supplementary income and in some instances even freedom from other forms of work. To the sharecropper tied to a system of debt serfdom, recording meant much. The Mississippi singer Tommy McClennan who worked a farm on Highway 61 out of Jackson, Mississippi, was recorded by the Victor-controlled Bluebird label as a result of the advances made on his behalf by Big Bill Broonzy, and his dependence on this source of income was amply demonstrated in his 'Bluebird Blues'.

> *Bluebird, Bluebird, please fly right down*
> *to me,*
> *Bluebird, Bluebird, please fly right down*
> *to me,*
> *You don't find me on the M & O, you'll*
> *find me on the Santa Fe.*

> *Now Bluebird, when you get to Jackson,*
> *please fly down Charles street,*
> *Now Bluebird, when you get to Jackson,*
> *please fly down Charles street,*
> *Tell 'em Tommy's too bad, oh well, cause*
> *you know every time I play the blues, I*
> *got the Bluebird beat.*

Through an ill-chosen verse, McClennan lost his contract with Bluebird. Only for some singers could recording be a dependable source of income; for others it was a lucky break in a piecemeal life, forgotten as soon as the fee had been paid. The nature of Negro employment, the loose family structures occasioned by insecurity of tenure, the migration of labour, has produced through the doors of the recording studios a stream of casual singers whose origins were vague and whose destinies were unknown. Though Southern blues singers walked the streets of Chicago and some came to stay, others made the Northern cities a very temporary home. Finding the severity of urban life, not to mention mid-Western climate, contrasting violently with the sedentary lives that they had led before they migrated, many soon followed the railroad tracks homewards. Uneasy when staying in one place for any length of time, others, 'nach'l born ramblers' drifted on. How many singers appeared before the recording machines by a matter of a chance meeting, a desultory conversation, a sudden impulse, can never be known. Who introduced them, cajoled them, tempted them? Where did they come from, where did they go? As the years pass, their records become rarer and their names assume a nostalgic mystery.

What percentage of the possible talent do the recorded blues singers represent at any one time; what creative abilities have been lost in the great gaps in the calendar of recording dates and the vast spaces between the recording venues; in what ways have our judgments been moulded by the limitations of recording, our opinions shaped by human, physical and commercial agents? There is no way in which the problems may be answered conclusively, but a conscious awareness of the material factors that have governed the availability of recorded blues may lead to more balanced assessments of those that it is our good fortune and privilege to hear, and a more charitable consideration for those unknown talents that 'ought to be recordin' right now'.

The Jazz Review, February 1959

2
Picking
the
Box

Illustration for "The Development of the Blues", *Radio Times*, January 29, 1967

'Do you play an instrument yourself?' I'm always being asked. To which the answer is usually something like 'I used to play several instruments – very badly'. This is taken as being an example of English self-deprecation, or modesty; rarely as the simple truth. My first stringed instrument was a metal-bodied banjo. It's a fine example, and I still have it, even though it hasn't been played for fifteen years or more, and then very rarely. Then, inevitably, a guitar. Val played guitar better than I did, and had bought an Austrian Herwiga, which no-one seems ever to have heard of, but which was a nice instrument. Brownie McGhee played it a number of times on his visits in the late Fifties, and in one reckless moment even suggested an exchange with his Gibson 'Dreadnought'. In all fairness we couldn't really take up the suggestion, and he wisely changed his mind and didn't change his guitar.

Then we had a Gibson Kalamazoo, with white edging and shaded toning on the wood. It was metal strung and the strings were so high off the fingerboard that it was more effective as a digit exerciser than as a musical instrument. Don Kincaid let us have it; he did the musical transcriptions for *Screening the Blues* and *The Story of the Blues*. We played together in a little group of teachers called The Crawdads and it was then I began to realize that this wasn't my scene. It was great fun, but Don was a vastly better player, as well as being a performer on several other instruments and a composer. I switched to mandolin, and was actually a lot better on that instrument, trying to play like Charlie McCoy backing Ishmon Bracey and Tommy Johnson. It's usually stated that he played a guitar capo'd high, but anyway, this was the sound I was striving to get and, up to a point, succeeded. By which time I was wondering why I was attempting to do so. Not very hard, it's

true; I didn't practise enough. But this was partly because I had a strong feeling that it wasn't for me to try and play guitarist (or mandolin player) – I had no association with the world of blues singers nationally, racially, environmentally, even by class. We used to go to the one or two London clubs – the Good Earth in what is now the West End's Chinese quarter, or Alexis Korner and Cyril Davies' Barrelhouse and Blues Club at the Roundhouse pub in Wardour Street, Soho. There Rory McEwan played astonishingly adept imitations of Blind Gary Davis and various aspiring blues singers including the later, successful Long John Baldry, tried their hand, or rather, their voices. I never met one who seemed to be remotely like a blues singer in background, approach or personality, apart from Cyril Davies. Cyril was a laconic, (or loquacious when drinking, which was heavy and often) burly, working-class panel-beater who made a living taking the dents out of wrecked automobiles; he had a devotion close to total identification with Leadbelly. It seemed to me that he had bridged the impossible gulf between the cultures in a way no other blues-singing Britisher did or could. He died suddenly and tragically, and that possibility went with him.

These were pre-Beatles, pre-Stones days. There was a way in which blues could generate a new music, or play a part in the process. But it hadn't happened then, and I certainly didn't expect it, and cannot claim to have welcomed it, particularly when 'beat' became a generation's music. Not for a few months anyway, and when I did, I found my views about popular music were beginning to change. Today, I'm much involved in the establishment of the International Association for the Study of Popular Music and have had no aspirations to become a performer (expect in private and a good while ago) for years. Perhaps my sense of the absurdity of comfortably-off middle-class white Englishmen (or Frenchmen, or American college students) declaring that they're 'goin' down to the river, baby, take me a rockin' chair', has been slightly tempered by an interest in the phenomenon itself. But only slightly.

In all this popularization of the blues in the Fifties and Sixties the guitar took on a symbolic importance among young people, even when it wasn't being played. Just to *carry* a guitar, especially in a canvas bag tied with string, or with a coloured webbing strap and a list of songs taped to the side of the box, was a sign of a role being played and a position in relation to the rest of society. Up to a point it applies still, though now the guitarists are expected to play well; at the time they were almost suspect if they *did* play well. This isn't the place, I regret, for the semiotics of the guitar-player but it cries out for analysis.

For me, what has been absorbing has been trying to find out what the blues guitarist really was like; how he worked within his community, where he got his influences from, how he was regarded by others, how he regarded himself, his instruments, his playing and his blues. In *Conversation with the Blues*, based on field recordings made synchronically in 1960 as a point in time in the history of blues, I quoted some of these observations about their music from blues singers I met: Mance Lipscomb, Lil Son Jackson, Muddy Waters, Blind James Brewer. Brewer talked about very little *but* guitars, his interest in them was obsessional. Other singers were extremely reticent, like Robert Lockwood or Percy Thomas. Percy Thomas was painfully out of practice, and suspicious when I endeavoured to interview him. His answers seemed almost deliberately designed to challenge anything I said: 'We knows nothin' much *about* the blues . . . we called it blues, we called it breakdowns, we called it blues and some people say it's square dances . . . We didn't know what it was; the achin'-hearted blues is slow, breakdowns is fast.'

I felt a bit frustrated, and his poor playing was all the more uncomfortable because he was claiming to have 'made a record with Muddy Waters'. I decided he was trying to fool me, and I left. It wasn't until the publication of Dixon and Godrich's *Blues and Gospel Records*, second edition, that it was confirmed that Percy Thomas *had* recorded with Muddy Waters as a member of the Son Simms Four, for the Library of Congress in 1942. His description of blues and breakdowns was, I now believe, very accurate; to some extent we have imposed upon blues a rigidity of definition which the singers and musicians themselves didn't share.

But if that was a failure, other encounters were successful and informative experiences as well as being musically exciting ones. There was nothing in Lightnin' Hopkins' stage performances that was like his appearance in neighbourhood bars, playing for dancing in noisy black clubs, burning his lips by singing with his mouth against a microphone with a short-circuit. Nothing quite so enthralling as seeing Black Ace lay his guitar across his lap and play his Thirties-styled blues by stroking the strings with a small medicine-bottle. Nor anything quite as infectious as the swing generated by Big Bill Broonzy when he was playing a rag dance or a fast ballad like 'John Henry'.

The hobo with his 'easy rider' slung across his back may be a romantic fiction (I've *never* heard a guitar called an 'easy rider') but the guitar as the instrumental voice of the blues singer – that's fact.

Guitar Blues

MARTIN, GIBSON AND NATIONAL

Early in 1964 C. F. Martin and Co from Nazareth, Pennsylvania, announced their new twelve-string guitar, the D 12-20, tuned to the cord of E. The D 12-20, costs $329.50 – a lot of money by any ordinary standards and far out of the pocket range of the country blues singers. Many aspiring young city folk blues singers will buy it, hoping that the rich tones of the twelve-string will make them sound a little more like Leadbelly. It takes more than the guitar to make a blues guitarist though. Perhaps this is why the makers of guitars are the unsung heroes of the blues and American folk music. For whilst the guitar may be no better than the man who plays it, some American guitar-makers have had a long experience of catering for the special needs of their players, and though their new 'box' may be directed to a particular market, their scores of others have been no less tailored for the folk instrumentalist. Not that Martin & Co were necessarily aware of the specific requirements of the blues singer – he probably didn't know in as many words himself – but they knew what sold and in what areas particular guitars were most popular. The college blues or folk guitarist who longs for a Gibson or a Martin is acknowledging, in fact, the not inconsiderable part played in traditional American music by the guitar manufacturers.

C. F. Martin came to the United States from Germany in 1833, and since that time his firm has made close on 200,000 guitars. Their simple form and classic proportions, their hand-inserted frets, their rosewood, mahogany and birch construction make them fine, desirable instruments. The position of Martin is rivalled by that of Orville Gibson's firm; the big Gibsons have been made in Michigan since 1894 and were important in the popularization of America's music. It was Gibson who is generally acknowledged as having introduced the violin-breasted, F-hole instrument and the rounded keyboard with its easy-action frets. These were tailor-made guitars with a folk musician in mind. Gibson also invented the cut-away box, designed to permit the instrumentalist to reach the additional couple of frets of his new 17-fret guitar. Gibson made cheap models, too, like the Kalamazoo with its familiar white outline, named after the city of its manufacture. Not a classic instrument by any means but one which has been handled by unnamed generations of blues singers.

Perhaps the most romantic of guitars is the National from North Carolina, the steel-bodied, loud-volumed guitar which seemed to be designed for street singing and juke joints. This was the guitar, in one or other of its forms, played by Blind Boy Fuller, Bo Carter and Bukka White. The diaphragms that act as resonators beneath the outer casing are fixed by rivets which give the basis to the characteristic patterns on the top of the guitar. To the blues enthusiast there is something magical in the National guitars, for being virtually indestructible they have been in the hands of their owners for twenty-five years or more, or have exchanged hands through successive singers in their long history. Unhappily, they are no longer made.

Most of these guitars are six-string models, but there are others – particularly the twelve-string with its massive body and double-stringing. This is the instrument to which attention was directed by Leadbelly, the self-proclaimed 'King of the

Twelve-string Guitar players of the World'. It was played by Barbecue Bob, Charlie Lincoln and Blind Willie McTell amongst others, even in a couple of instances by two of them together! Among the other firms who have made this contribution to the blues, Gretsch and Harmony are important too, but there are a host of other makers who have accounted for some of the less familiar models like the bizarre cut-away that Big Bill Broonzy played as a young man.

Give a guitar to a blues singer and he soon starts making adjustments to suit his own voice and his personal conception of the blues. He may replace the gut strings with metal ones (likely to warp a classic guitar); replace the flat-wound strings with metal non-compound strings. He may fit an end-piece on a conventional guitar; he may even add extra strings. Big Joe Williams, for instance, adapted his six-string guitar by adding three 'machines' across the top of the head to make a highly original nine-string guitar. With the bass strings double-strung, but single-stringing in the treble, he was able to combine resonant rhythms in the bass against which he could contrast the ringing notes of the treble strings. Later, he attached an amplifier to his guitar, his playing becoming a flurry of adjustments and finger-picking as he continually altered the amplification according to the passages he played.

Many blues guitarists have very unconventional techniques: Elizabeth Cotten plays the guitar 'left-handed' with the treble strings at the top so that the fingering is reversed. Yank Rachell on the other hand sometimes plays a left-handed guitar on which, however, the order of the strings is reversed and the fingering is thus normal. Josh White reports that when he first learned to play guitar he placed his left hand over the *front* of the finger board, fingering the frets in an odd and extremely awkward manner. Later he learned the more customary fingering but his ability to control a most difficult playing position made his execution that much easier subsequently, permitting the dexterity and ease which typifies his work.

Blues singers frequently learn from watching other bluesmen; sometimes they learn by experiment. No blues singer learns from a book, and from this variety of beginnings stems the individuality which soon becomes the hallmark of each guitarist.

Notes to Storyville SLP 166, 1965

First Generation
EARLY COUNTRY BLUES GUITARISTS

Blues as a distinct form of black folk song was already a quarter of a century old when the first country singers from the American South were placed before unfamiliar horn microphones to record their music. Quite how the blues began, and why it gained such rapid popularity that singers from the East Coast to West Texas could be found in such numbers and in such variety, may always remain a matter of speculation. But we can be sure that the first generation of singers who recorded blues were performers who knew the songs of other black secular traditions. Such was the case with three of them represented here: Papa Harvey Hull, Long Cleve Reed and Richard 'Rabbit' Brown.

Several decades have passed since those few days between March and May in 1927 when they made these titles and today we know the voices and the songs of the singers better than we are ever likely to know the men themselves. But Richard Brown, apparently called 'Rabbit' because of his small stature, is known to us at least in outline. He was a native of New Orleans where he grew up in the same James Alley between Gravier Street and Perdido Street where Louis Armstrong was born. A slum by a turpentine factory, it was near the tenderloin district of Storyville where he gained employment as a singer-guitarist, 'serenading', as the casual street entertainment was termed. He also worked out at the resorts on Lake Pontchartrain, where he was heard by the recording director Ralph Peer. Brown was probably well into his forties when he made these few titles in his home city.

Harvey Hull and Cleve Reed are far more shadowy figures, and nothing specific is known about them. 'Have you ever took a trip babe on the Mobile Line?' they sang on 'France Blues', leading some to speculate on an Alabama origin. But the M & O ran up the east side of Mississippi and there is much in the light fingerpicking and rolling guitar rhythms to suggest that they came from the hill country of northern Mississippi. Cleve Reed appears in copyright lists as the composer of the popular Thirties blues-song, 'Hey Lawdy Mama', but this may just have been a confusion arising from the refrain of 'France Blues'.

Most of the songs here relate to the period before the First World War, when blues was still competing with other song types. Rabbit Brown's 'Never Let the Same Bee Sting You Twice' was a comic 'battle of the sexes' song typical of the 1890s vaudeville stage, while his 'I'm Not Jealous – I just don't like it, that's all' – has evident minstrel and ragtime song characteristics in the verse and chorus structure of popular songs of the day, and in the deft and spirited guitar accompaniment. A reference to Rampart Street gave it a local touch but it was probably a song he had picked up from a travelling show.

More directly from the folk tradition were the ballads that Brown and Reed sang. Oldest of these was Cleve Reed's 'Original Stack O'Lee Blues', among the most complete versions on record of the famous levee ballad. By tradition, Billy Lyons is said to have been shot by the bully Stack Lee in a Memphis bar-room, probably in April 1906 – though police records do not confirm it. The couplet and one-line refrain structure of this and other contemporary ballads may have influenced the shaping of the blues. A few years later, the sinking of the liner Titanic on her maiden voyage pointed a

moral about pride and supposed infal-
libility which provided the theme for
several songs, including Rabbit Brown's
'Sinking of the Titanic'. This was probably
already in the tradition but the long and
local ballad of a kidnapping, 'The Mystery
of the Dunbar's Child', was almost certainly
his own composition.

Only one of Brown's songs was a conventional blues (another, 'Great Northern
Blues', was unissued), but 'James Alley
Blues' was a subtle song with its lines built
up of a series of oppositions, and its verse
sequence divided between statements about
himself and dissatisfied reproaches to his
woman. Most of Hull and Reed's songs on
the other hand, related to blues, though
'Don't You Leave Me Here' was a version of
a song widely collected at the beginning of
the century by this title, or as 'Alabama
Bound'. Early collections also included the
words of 'Gang of Brownskin Women', particularly the theme of the 'woman for every
day of the week'. On this they hummed,
haahed and scat vocalized together in the
manner popularized by black vocal quar-
tets, while the refrain of lines of 'France
Blues' also linked with the songs of these
groups which were popular in the 1890s.
'Two Little Tommies (or Tonys) Blues'
conformed more closely to the emerging
twelve-bar form, though one verse was of a
single line repeated three times; another
repeated twice. With 'Mama You Don't
Know How' though, we hear Cleve Reed's
awareness of the newly famous recording
blues singers: the first verse is modelled on
Blind Lemon Jefferson's 'Black Snake
Blues'.

For these singers the blues was one of
several song types from which they could
draw, but already it was on its way to
becoming the dominant black song form of
the century.

Notes to Matchbox Bluesmaster
MSE 201, 1981

Match Box Blues
BLIND LEMON JEFFERSON

A thickset, bullet-headed man weighing around 180-pounds, his head held alertly on his broad shoulders so that his ears could detect the gathering of a crowd that his sightless eyes could not see: Blind Lemon Jefferson. Bright of skin colour, short in build yet stocky and compact, in Sam Price's words 'a chunky little fellow', he was a familiar figure in the streets of Dallas, Texas, for more than a score of years, his tapping stick, his big guitar, his broad-brimmed black hat making him a memorable character. But he is remembered today less for his appearance than for his importance as one of the greatest of the folk blues singers.

Of his origins, little that is definite is known. Aaron T-Bow (later T-Bone) Walker believed that he came from the Texas port of Galveston, born there perhaps in 1883; Samuel B. Charters has elicited the information that he was born nearer Dallas, raised 'outside Coriscana' in the neighbouring country of Navarro. Wherever he was born, Blind Lemon made his name and his home in Dallas.

In 1900 Dallas had a Negro population of less than ten thousand; the figure doubled in a score of years, and it was during these years of considerable expansion that the blind blues singer was to be heard on the street corners and in the saloons, hollering his folk songs and rattling his begging cup. 'Blind Lemon an' me was runnin' together for 'bout eighteen years roun' Dallas, Texas . . .' said Huddie Ledbetter – Leadbelly – on one occasion. Leadbelly settled in Rockwall County, east of Dallas when he married his first wife, Lethe, at the age of eighteen. May 1918 saw Leadbelly charged with the murder of Will Stafford, and that December he was sent to jail with a thirty-year sentence. The ''bout eighteen years' was perhaps a slight exaggeration, but he must have shared his life with Lemon from early in the century. This he confirmed at his famous last session recorded by Frederic Ramsey Jr., when he discussed the provenance of 'Careless Love'. 'White people's version is "Love, Oh Love, Oh Careless Love", but down in Louisiana we sing it, "See What Careless Love Have Done". Now to my ideas, what I think is true, Blind Lemon was the first man to put out that record of "Careless Love" . . . since then . . . he was the first man that did it. Because him and me was singing it in 'round Dallas, Texas. That was in 1904, you know. Him and me was about the same age. Yeah, that was a' old field song – old when you was young.'

Blind Lemon's stay in Dallas must have been close to twenty-five years in duration, broken at intervals by his tours to other States. In age he was probably only a little older than Leadbelly: 'Him and me was buddies,' said Leadbelly on more than one occasion, implying a relationship of close friendship rather than that of blind singer and lead boy, though he guided the blind man '. . . he was a blind man 'an I used to lead him aroun'. When him an' me was gwine to the depot, we'd sit aroun' and used to talk to one another . . .'

While they waited for the incoming trains and fresh visitors to Dallas to whom they would sing, Leadbelly learned and profited from their association. Often Leadbelly would play a mandolin or 'windjammer' – accordian – while Lemon would play his Hawaiian guitar and sing. Much of their time was spent on the barrelhouse circuit – wandering from saloon to gin mill, singing for food and drink and for the coins of the patrons. But at other times they would beat their way southwards to the wide-open town of Groesbeck, or to the equally rough haunt of the tougher Negro elements, Silver City on the route to Fort Worth.

As the Texas and Pacific train came through, Leadbelly would help his blind companion onto the steps and into the coach. 'I'd get Blind Lemon right on', he said. 'We get out two guitars; we just ride . . . anything. We wouldn't have to pay no money in them times. We get on the train, the driver takes us anywhere we want to go. Well we jes' get on and the conductor say: "Boys, sit down. You goin' to play music?" We tell him "Yes." We jes' out collecting money; that's what we wanted – hitch some money. So we set down and turn the seats over you know. He sit in front of me, and I'd sit down there and we'd start.'

By their playing and singing they hitched free rides to the townships, not only on the trains but in the buses also. 'We go to Silver City out there too. We allus go to Silver City. When we got on the bus we Silver City bound first. There's a lot of pretty girls out there, and that's what we looking for. We like for women to be aroun' cause when women's aroun' that brings mens and that bring money. 'Cause when you get out there, the women get to drinking . . . that thing fall over them, and that make us feel good and we tear those guitars all to pieces.'

Blind Lemon lived a full life in spite of his handicap and he was as popular as the tough and handsome Leadbelly with the women of Silver City. 'That was me and Blind Lemon's hangout. We had twenty-five – thirty girls apiece out there . . . have a good time! They be around . . . it was a killer I'm telling you!'

In the familiar districts Blind Lemon's sense of direction was uncanny to those who watched him. He could find his way with-

out a lead boy to act as his eyes but when he was travelling he welcomed assistance. Sang Leadbelly:

Me and Blind Lemon, goin' to ride on down,
Catch me by the hand – oh baby,
Blind Lemon was a blind man.
He'd holler – 'Catch me by the hand' – oh baby,
'And lead me all through the land.'

When Leadbelly's fracas caused him to be sent to jail, Blind Lemon employed young boys to lead him around as was customary among the blind blues and gospel singers. Aaron Walker, not even in his 'teens – he was only sixteen when he made his first record for the Columbia 'Race' series – acted for some time as Lemon's eyes and learned much of his guitar playing from the blind man. So, too, did Josh White, whose childhood from the age of seven was spent in the bitter schooling of travelling with many of the blind beggars. Jefferson, he remembered, would get up late in the day, and around noon when the crowds in the streets were thickest, would take up his stand on a particularly busy intersection and commence to holler from the street corner. While he sang and played his guitar, Josh White would accompany him on his tambourine, tapping it in rhythm against his knee until a good and appreciative crowd had collected. Then he would turn the tambourine over, and crying, 'Help the blind, help the blind,' in his shrill boy's voice, would beg coins from the assembled gatherings. So popular was his playing that it was possible for him to make as much as $150 over a week-end. Where Lemon was to be heard, there was always a crowd. When Jimmy Rushing was an itinerant pianist and singer playing the townships of the Midwest and South, he listened to Jefferson whenever he could. Short in stature himself, he could not see the stocky, blind singer, but the clear, shrill voice that could be heard for a couple of blocks guided him to the spot, and the crowd that gathered around him was large enough to halt the traffic.

In spite of his blindness, Blind Lemon was an inveterate gambler, relying on the witnesses that stood about him to ensure that he was not swindled by a crooked dealer. He drank heavily and was a strong man, capable of defending himself better than most persons similarly afflicted. His blues were fierce and violent, and Josh White recalls that he would drink heavily for several hours and, returning to his Dallas home, would lie on the bed with his guitar and shout his blues into the night air. Blindness had given him acutely developed senses in other respects, and Sam Price avers that he was able to tell if any drinks had been taken from his whiskey bottle when he was absent, by shaking the bottle. If there was any missing, he said, Jefferson would thrash his wife. This appears to be the only reference to a wife, and it would be of considerable interest to know if, in fact, the singer was married, and what became of the woman.

Whether Jefferson had been blind all his life is a matter of conjecture. 'I ain't seen my sugar in three long weeks today . . .' he will sing; or 'Want to talk to my baby in South Carolina who looks like an Indian squaw' – his blues have many visual references. Sam Price, who knew him well, argued that he needed no leading. It was Price who was largely responsible for the blind singer's appearance on record. As a young man, the pianist from Honey Grove, Texas, was a record salesman in R. T. Ashford's Dallas store, and he recommended Blind Lemon to the Paramount company representative. It has been often rumoured that his first records were cut in the rug department of a Dallas store – perhaps Ashford's – but whether these were test recordings made for the consideration of the Paramount company, or whether they were his initial sides, it is difficult to say. The first coupling made, though not the first released, was 'Old Rounder's Blues' and 'Begging Back', which was cut in May 1925, some eight months and some 450-odd matrices away from the next title, 'Got the Blues', made in February 1926. It is possible, therefore, that these two tracks were cut in Dallas, and winning the approval of the Paramount directors, caused Blind Lemon to be brought to Chicago.

'Got the Blues' is exemplary of Blind Lemon's art, and the brilliant accompaniment, with its rapid arpeggios and rippling phrases produced by dexterous 'hammering on,' marks it as one of his finest recordings as well as among his first. Here are to be found, fresh and hitherto unrecorded, the folk verses that have been the stock-in-trade of many a lesser singer.

You can never tell what a woman's got on her
*   mind, (repeat)*
You think she's crazy about you and she's
*   leaving all the time.*

Ain't so good-lookin', teeth don't shine like
*   pearls, (repeat)*
But that lyin' disposition'll carry her through
*   this world.*

So commenced a remarkable series of recordings which preserve the blues in its folk form at the point of transition from the field holler to the street corner and the barroom floor. There are many echoes of the past tradition in these blues, as in the comparatively early 'Shucking Sugar', where the phrase is interpolated inconsequentially within the verses:

I've got your picture an' I'm goin' to put it in
*   a frame,*
I've got your picture, I'll put it in a frame –
*   shuckin' sugar,*
Then if you leave town I can find you just the
*   same.*

The voice crying 'shucking sugar' seems to die away as the memories of the plantation shucking parties were even then disappearing. Among his recordings are songs which have a long folk ancestry, such as 'See That My Grave Is Kept Clean', which is the old white folk song 'Two White Horses in a Line' sung to a tune closely related to 'Careless Love'. But the majority of his recordings are his own blues, relating his experiences without malice or bitterness; blues that tell of the life of a blind beggar in hard times:

I stood on the corner and almost bust my head,
(repeat)
I couldn't earn enough to buy me a loaf of
bread.

My girl's a housemaid and she earns a dollar a
week, (repeat)
I'm so hungry on payday, I cain't hardly speak.

Now gather round me, people, let me tell you
true facts, (repeat)
That tough luck has struck me and the rats is
sleepin' in my hat.

And there are blues that tell of the miseries of others of his race:

Water in Arakansas, people screamin' in
Tennesee,
Oh – people screamin' in Tennessee;
If I don't leave Memphis, backwater be all
over po' me.

Children standin', screamin' 'Mama, we
ain't got no home!
Oh – we ain't got no home!'
Papa says to the children, 'Backwater left us
all alone.'

Paramount surfaces obscure many of the qualities of Blind Lemon's work, and it is only the single coupling issued by Okeh: 'Black Snake Moan/Match Box Blues' that does justice to his singing and playing, as comparison with the Paramount recordings of the same titles bears eloquent witness.

Repeated performances of his blues are rare in his work, and the two sets of masters for 'Lock Step Blues' and 'Hangman's Blues' are therefore of considerable interest, both issued as Paramount 12679. The earlier version of 'Hangman's Blues' (20751-2) is the more dramatic, the guitar accompaniment with its rapid pulsations like the racing circulation of a frightened man, being intensely affecting. The later version (20816), though better recorded, does not quite measure up to the former, and the added spoken phrase adds relatively little, though this, and the slight differences in the words, give a valuable indication of the extent to which the singer improvised his blues for recording purposes. In either version it is a grim and stark blues:

The mean ole hangman is waitin' to tighten
up that noose, (repeat)
Lord, I'm so scared, I'm tremblin' in ma shoes.

Jurymen heard my case and said my hands was
red, (repeat)
Judge he sentenced me to be hanging till I'm
dead.

The crowd round the courthouse, an' the time
is goin' fast, (repeat)
Soon a good for nothin' killer is goin' to breathe
his last.

It would seem that Blind Lemon made casual trips to Chicago to make his recordings, and it is possible that he returned at intervals to Dallas. A significant gap appears in his recording career in 1927, which was followed by such recordings as 'Hangman's Blues' together with a considerable number of items, among them 'Lockstep Blues', ''Lectric Chair Blues', 'Blind Lemon's Penitentiary Blues', 'Prison Cell Blues' and others which are related to prison themes. Such morbid material would appear to have a somewhat limited market, but Blind Lemon sings with the conviction born of personal experience, and one cannot help but speculate whether the blind man had spent a period in jail prior to these recordings. During the years of his recordings, Blind Lemon's fame spread. He was soon a well-known figure in Chicago as well as in his native Texas, and the proceeds from his records made him, for a brief period, relatively wealthy. According to Aletha Robinson, however, he remained a rough and untamed character, who, she maintains, tore his food apart with his bare hands and never used a knife and fork. But it would seem unlikely that the fingers that played the Spanish and Hawaiian guitar with such dexterity would be incapable of such manipulation; unlikelier still if the signature on his photograph was genuine. On the label of 'Lemon's Cannon Ball Moan' appeared a scroll with the words 'Blind Lemon Jeffersons' *(sic)* Birthday Record' and a portrait taken from the previously mentioned photograph, which in the original was three-quarter length. The sightless eyes still look proud, the dull features are strong but not arrogant, and the bearing of the thickset man is erect – far removed from the emaciated figure that appeared on the sleeve of a Riverside long-playing record – the blues-singing beggar of popular fancy.

Lemon Jefferson's fame spread throughout the coloured world, and a visit by the singer was long remembered: remembered by Horace Sprott a quarter of a century after the singer, with Richard Shaw to guide him, had travelled through Alabama; remembered with pride by Red Willie Smith when he told Harold Courlander how he had played in Blind Lemon's travelling folk band in Alabama; remembered by Adam Booker in Texas in conversation with Sam Charters: 'He was about the best we had.'

Frequently Blind Lemon Jefferson's blues are termed 'primitive' and in the anthropological sense of being unlettered and untutored, they are. Aesthetically, too, they may be considered the 'primitive germ', in Parry's phrase, that fertilizes the seed of music. But though there is not a trace of sophistication in Blind Lemon's singing or playing, there are subtle qualities of rich individuality that fortify the development of jazz music, as a young sherry is fortified by the blends that precede it. Blind Lemon's blues have a primitiveness that is in no way synonymous with crudity, but his blues were undoubtedly strong meat; full-flavoured and rare without garnishings or fussy trimmings; the savour of the barbecue rather than of the chef's cuisine, making the gorge rise in sensitive stomachs, but relished by those who delight in chitterlings and hog's maws and pigfeet.

On his best recordings, and those best recorded, Blind Lemon's voice is clear, and the notes of his guitar have a pristine quality. Deceptively simple though some of his discs may appear on first hearing, he had a remarkable gift of phrasing and the technical accomplishment to give the fullest expression to his ideas. Though he was a street singer, he did not have to shout: he had a way of pitching his voice high, of calling out his words so that they could be heard at a considerable distance. At times he would declaim his blues with an emphasis that brooked no denial, but at other times his voice had sad, tragic tones that nonetheless never descended to self-pity. Even when the words of his blues told of trivial things, of irresponsible parties and reckless drinking, there was always an underlying pathos that indicated not only the plight of one blind man, but that of all members of his people. For his hearers his records had a deeper significance than that indicated by their literal meaning alone. Jefferson had the unassumed ability of the natural artist to be able to give the greatest range of expression to his chosen media: his voice had considerable light and shade which he used to advantage, at time striking the note that he required with unerring accuracy and at other times soaring up to it through the course of his syllables. He would permit his natural vibrato to swell and fade, cause his words to gain in effect through every nuance of inflection, introducing the subtlest rhythms by fractional suspensions in the timing of his phrases.

Throughout, his guitar amplified his mood without a note of inessential decoration. Behind his voice he generally played a simple rhythm, occasionally in a different time to that in which he was singing but miraculously meeting at the close of the sung phrase which would be carried on instrumentally without a break. He picked his strings in rapid arpeggios of beguiling facility, the wordless utterances of his guitar eloquently amplifying the lines that he sang. In his work there is no rancour, but there is no diminuition of brutal facts, no sentimentality, either. Starkly dramatic, stripped of all superfluities, cruelly beautiful as the Texas landscape, Blind Lemon's recordings burn their way to the heart of his hearers. They sprang from the oil wells, they were rooted with the cane, grew with the cotton – and they lie with the dust of the Dallas sidewalks.

Blind Lemon Jefferson died on the streets of Chicago in 1930 from a heart attack, leaving behind him a legacy of personal blues that peeled the onion of his soul as Peer Gynt was incapable of doing. His uncompromising blues were the irrepressible outpourings of a true folk artist, and he was sadly mourned.

'I take my text from First Book of Corinthians, fifteenth chapter, forty-fourth and forty-fifth verse, which reads as follows: 'It is sown a natural body; it is raised a spiritual body; and so it is written that the first man, Adam was made a living soul and the last man Adam was made a quickening spirit.'

It was the Reverend Emmett Dickenson who was preaching. His voice was not that of the 'straining' preacher, hoarse and gasping; he spoke simply and warmly, in softly enunciated words that carried the conviction of utterance that was sincere. He continued:

'My friends, Blind Lemon Jefferson is dead, and the world today is in mourning over this loss. So we feel that our loss is Heaven's gain. Big men, educated men and great men, when they pass on to their eternal home in the sky – they command our respects. But when a man that we truly love for the kindness and inspiration they *(sic)* have given us in our uppermost hearts pass on to their rewards, we feel that there is a vacancy in our hearts that will never be replaced.'

Blind Lemon Jefferson, a blues singer and a singer of 'devil songs' was dead. As the devil's advocate singing the blues, he would seem to be a strange subject for a sermon, except for the purpose of pointing a moral. But the Reverend Dickenson knew his congregation and he spoke in terms that they could understand. 'The world . . . is in mourning over this loss,' he said, but the world as a whole had never heard of Blind Lemon Jefferson, nor heard his voice. It was the Negro world, compact and largely separate in those years when the clouds of the depression were breaking over the United States, to which the preacher referred, though as a sincere member of the Church he knew that the loss extended far beyond the boundaries of race. To the world, Blind Lemon was not a big man, an educated man or a great man, but within the Negro world, as Reverend Dickenson knew, the blues singer was valued and loved, for he spoke to them who were members of his race.

'Is there harm in singing the blues?' asked Reverend Dickenson in one sermon; and he made the earthy standard of the blues singer, 'Tight Like That', the subject of another address to his congregation. He once recorded what he called 'The Preacher's Blues' but now he was speaking of one who had 'preached the blues'.

'Let us pause for a moment and think of the life of our beloved Blind Lemon Jefferson who was born blind. It is in many respects like that of our Lord, Jesus Christ. Like Him, unto the age of thirty he was unknown, and also like Him in the space of a little over three years this man and his works were known in every home.' In making a comparison that might seem even somewhat blasphemous on first hearing, the preacher was in fact dwelling on coincidental details. He was in no way suggesting that the blind blues singer was of similar stature to Christ, nor that he was in any way a spiritual being. But at the same time, while recognizing Blind Lemon's vices as well as his virtues he could pass no word of censure, for:

'Again I refer to our text: I believe that the Lord in Blind Lemon Jefferson has sown a natural body and will raise it a spiritual body. When I was informed of Lemon's death, I thought of our Lord Jesus Christ as He walked down the Jericho road and saw a man who was born blind. And His disciples said: "Master, who did sin? Did this man sin or his parents, that he is a man born blind?"

And Jesus Christ answered, "Neither did this man sin nor his parents sin but that I may be manifested in him."

'Lemon Jefferson was born blind and was cut off from the good things of this life that you and I enjoy; he truly had a cross to bear. How many of us today are crying about the crosses we are to bear; "Oh Lord, this is too hard for me; Oh Lord, I have a pain here and an ache there, and Oh Lord, my life is miserable to lead." Blind Lemon is dead. As Lemon died with the Lord, so did he live.'

The whole man still eludes us, but the Reverend Dickenson's sermon gives more than a little indication of the importance of Blind Lemon Jefferson to the Negro world of the Twenties, whose members bought his records and listened to his blues; revealing a character, proud, devoid of self-pity in spite of considerable handicaps; loved and esteemed in spite of his personal foibles and defects of behaviour – a man in whom was 'sown a natural body' with human weaknesses and appetites, but a man whose sins did not put him past redemption and whose example in his honesty, his self-examination, his forthrightness of purpose, blues singer or no, could be raised in death 'a spiritual body'.

The Jazz Review, July 1959

Blind Lemon Jefferson was born Couchman, Texas, July 1897 and died Chicago, *c.* January 1930

Cool Drink of Water

TOMMY JOHNSON AND ISHMON BRACEY

It's difficult to assess what the Mississippi blues would have been like without Tommy Johnson. Of course, there would have been the unquestionable supremacy of Charley Patton or the agonized sounds of Robert Johnson to indicate the quality of its traditions. There would have been the sweeter, more lilting melodies of Bo Carter and the Mississippi Sheiks, and the gentle, rhythmic, introverted playing and singing of Mississippi John Hurt, and much more to underline the richness of the musical forms of blues, ballads, breakdowns that could be heard in the State at almost any time in this century. Yet Tommy Johnson added something so special, so uniquely his own in its conception and yet so influential among his contemporaries, that without his singing and playing an essential ingredient in the musical mixture would have been lacking, and Mississippi blues much the poorer for it.

If it had not been for the perspicacity of the Jackson music-store owner, H. C. Speir, we might never have heard him on record and could have judged his importance only from the recollections of other bluesmen and the many imitations of his blues, above all 'Big Road Blues' which have been recorded. As it is, these historic titles which virtually epitomize blues feeling and expression were made over a short span of time; he continued to make effective music for at least another decade, sadly unrepresented on disc.

Fortunately, if he was not fully served by recording he has at least been well served biographically. Credit for this must go to the ethnomusicologist David Evans, whose two books *Tommy Johnson* (Studio Vista, 1971) and *Big Road Blues* (University of California Press, 1982) provide an extensive narrative of his life and a close examination of his songs and influence. The sixth child of Idell and Mary Ella Johnson, Tommy was born on the George Miller plantation about 1896. This was in the south of Hinds County, close to the Pearl River and the township of Terry on the Illinois Central line, a score or so miles south of Jackson. Idell Johnson was related to Alonzo 'Lonnie' Johnson, though Tommy did not get his music from him but from his mother's many brothers who played a variety of instruments. An elder brother among the thirteen Johnson children, LeDell, began to play guitar and to teach Tommy when he was fifteen or so. The following year he ran away from home with a woman several years older than himself; the liaison did not last but the move seems to have shaped his music.

It seems very likely that he had made contact with the cluster of blues singers gathered around Charley Patton at Drew in the Delta and to have learned a lot from them. Back in Terry in 1914 he played for a while with his brother, down in Crystal Springs in Copiah County, or up in Jackson. He married Maggie Bidwell around this time and together they went to the Delta, meeting up with Patton, Willie Brown, Dick Bankston and other celebrated musicians on the plantations around Drew and learning from them. Mott Willis from Crystal Springs was also one who shared the 'Drew tradition', as Evans has termed it, and when Tommy returned to the region south of Jackson it was to bring some of that tradition with him. Yet it is tempting to overstate this: the influence of Patton and his circle is undoubtedly present in Tommy Johnson's work, but he seems to have built upon it in an individual way which impressed his hearers then and lingers still in the blues of Mississippians.

Part of this special quality lay in his voice; it was quite unlike the much admired 'heavy' voice of Patton or the rasping tones of Willie Brown. It was pitched much higher, which enabled him to introduce calling falsettos of quite remarkable accuracy, as on his beautiful 'Cool Drink of Water Blues'. He had a powerful voice, with full chest tones and a natural vibrato, which he used to slide up to notes or to hum a syllable without loss of projection. This is particularly evident in 'Maggie Campbell Blues' or in the range of 'Bye Bye Blues'. Unlike the Drew singers who often conveyed an intense, rather urgent and aggressive quality in their vocals, Tommy Johnson was relaxed as if he were singing a field holler.

No less remarkable was Johnson's guitar playing, which was superbly complemented by his friend Charlie McCoy on three titles, of which 'Big Road Blues' was quite outstanding. The interweaving of their instrumental lines was impeccable, but on 'Big Road' the climbing bass pattern that Johnson played imparted a compelling movement that is irresistible and impressed itself on his hearers. Many of his accompaniments have extremely difficult guitar figures in them but Johnson plays them effortlessly. He was remembered as being something of a clown with the guitar suggesting that he was different in person from the serious singer on record; no doubt he was, but the clowning was made possible by his mastery of instrument and voice.

Though most of Johnson's blues stanzas appear to be traditional and shared by other singers in the area, 'Canned Heat Blues' with its references to the 'Sterno' cooking fuel, which was used to obtain its alcohol, was certainly his own; as he predicted, alcohol eventually killed him, though he seems to have had a prodigious capacity to indulge in it. He died on 1 November 1956, his memory living on in these masterpieces and the memories of his friends.

★ ★ ★ ★

There is something hard and uncompromising about the personality of Ishmon Bracey, something challenging and direct. It is evident in the known photographs of him when he was in his late twenties, staring fixedly at the photographer. In one shot his expression is steady, even sullen; in the more familiar cut from an old Victor catalogue he struggled a mirthless and unfriendly smile. Dressed in a suit, with collar and tie, in each case he was carefully up-to-date. In 1925 he had a natty hat with turned brim, and three years later he was in a different suit with the wide-notched revers that had lately come into fashion. Insignificant details perhaps, but they are glimpses of a proud and confident man who may have been up from the country but who was a sharp dresser, aware of the times in which he lived.

'A rare combination of braggart, entertainer, musician, showman and eventually an ordained minister' is how Gayle Dean Wardlow, who interviewed him many times, chose to describe him in *Blues Unlimited* (No. 142). By Ishmon Bracey's own account to Dave Evans, he was a fighter too, 'mixing it' with Saturday night drunks and the jealous lovers who came after his friend Tommy Johnson. It seems that he had always held strong religious sentiments, and had been a member of the Baptist church as a child in Byram, Mississippi. So his eventual ordination as a preacher, which was a personal relief after his 'wicked ways' and life 'in the world', was not so surprising.

One might expect a singer with his self-esteem and interest in current modes to effect a more sophisticated approach to his music which might mask his rural background. But it seems a part of Ishmon Bracey's character that his blues are as uncompromising to the listener as his attitude. His singing is natural and unelaborated, with a markedly nasal tone. This rasping, buzzing quality is not as seductive to the listener as the vocal range and falsettos of his friend Tommy Johnson. Compared with Johnson's use of calling notes and glissandi, Bracey's singing is stark and we might be tempted to think that it is entirely the result of innate ability rather than deliberate performance. That this is not the case is evident when we compare the two takes of 'Trouble Hearted Blues' and listen to the way in which he shapes the first stanza. So what determined Bracey's approach to his blues?

Ishmon Bracey was born on 9 January 1901 (or 1900. He died in 1970, aged 70) at Byram in Hinds County, Mississippi. This is a mere ten miles south of Jackson, halfway between the city and the township of Terry, the home of Tommy Johnson, though today, Terry is in danger of being engulfed by expanding Jackson. He learned to play guitar from two obscure local musicians, Louis Cooper and Lee Jones, though Rube Lacey also claimed to have taught him to play. A keen young musician, he doubtless picked up all he could from any good guitarist that he heard. He worked on neighbouring farms and, like any young black man, picked cotton on the larger plantations. Later, when he moved to Jackson he worked for an oil seed company, did casual labouring and played music for a living whenever he could. The group that centred around Rube Lacey included Ishmon, but he travelled around a good deal on his own, playing for picnics, dances, and for the Saturday night spenders in the street. Down in Crystal Springs he met up with Tommy Johnson and the two played a good deal together in 1927. When H. C. Speir, the Jackson record store owner and talent scout, made a successful test of Ishmon he asked the singer for the names of other artists in the area. He, Tommy Johnson, a minstrel show singer named Rosie Mae Moore, and the younger musician – mandolin player, Charlie McCoy, took the Greyhound bus on Thursday, 2 February 1928, and arriving in Memphis, were soon to make blues recording history.

Bracey's blues are an extension of the man but they come it seems, from two basic sources. 'Rock, church rock . . .' comments Charlie McCoy at one point, and the moaning of the elders on the mourner's bench at the Baptist church of his childhood can be heard coming through his blues stanzas. His delivery is powerful, the singing of a field hand; the holler is never far away. Ishmon synthesized these two contemporary currents in his youthful experience as a singer in a convincing and personal style. With him on the 1928 sessions was Charlie McCoy: 'Charlie couldn't lead. He just seconded,' as Bracey explained. But he was a remarkably sensitive seconder and the matching of the two guitars is impeccable. On 'Leavin' Town Blues' the manner in which one guitar echoes the phrase of the other, and then moves into integrated phrasing, is a joy to hear.

It must be admitted that the Paramount session of 1930 was less successful because of the presence of Kid Ernest Michall, a clarinet player from New Orleans who played a gaspipe style not overly suited to jazz in that city, and highly unsuited to Bracey's style. Ishmon didn't think so, for Michall and '44 Charley' Taylor, a pianist on the session, worked with him in Mississippi. At this last session we hear Bracey unaccompanied and on 'Woman Woman Blues' introducing a hint of Tommy Johnson's falsetto. They worked together intermittently for another ten years or so and must have made a formidable team. Eventually Tommy died and Bracey joined the church; uncompromising as ever, never to play blues again.

Notes to Wolf Records WSE 104
and 105, 1983

Though his first name was Ishmon, on all Bracey's records it is spelled Ishman.

It's Just Too Bad
BARBECUE BOB

Harlem has its Lennox Avenue; Chicago its State Street. Through the heart of every Negro sector courses the life-blood of the Negro world and every coloured quarter has its main artery: Rampart Street in New Orleans, Beale Avenue in Memphis, Baltimore has its Pennsylvania Avenue – and Atlanta its Decatur Street. Atlanta is the principal town in the South between the Mason-Dixon Line and New Orleans, and Decatur Street is the main thoroughfare in the Negro quarter, which in the late Twenties had some sixty thousand inhabitants. It was a teeming, bustling, blowsy area to which came some of the most famous names in the Negro entertainment world to play before its colourful, rowdy audiences. Ma Rainey, Bessie Smith, Butterbeans and Susie, Stringbeans Butler May, Eddie Heywood and scores of others playing the circuit appeared at Charles P. Bailey's TOBA theatre at 91, Decatur or at the Jewish-owned playhouse next door at 81. Their wildly enthusiastic audiences were drawn from the rib joints and pads, the saloons and speakeasies, the brothels and dives which fronted the road.

> They got plenty good liquor
> And everything for sale,
> If you get into trouble
> You won't have to go to Jail.
> If your man won't give you lovin',
> An' he won't treat you right,
> Step out in Atlanta
> Any time of the night,
> You'll get your lovin' down on Decatur Street,
> In Atlanta, down on Decatur Street.

sang Lillian Glinn, who played Atlanta often and recorded her 'Atlanta Blues' (Columbia 14421) on 9 April 1929. She recorded a couple more sides the following day before leaving shortly to continue her tour which was to take her on to Texas. Before she left, though, she may have met Barbecue Bob, for he recorded himself only a day later on 11 April. True, Lillian Glinn was a vaudeville entertainer and tent-show blues singer but on Decatur Street all types and conditions of artistes met and though a folk singer, Bob's reputation was not small.

Barbecue Bob – Robert Hicks – lived with his brother Charlie in the little village of Lithonia about a score of miles out of Atlanta. Together they worked at a small pull-in and gas station which was situated near Buckhead, one of the suburbs of Atlanta which lay some four miles from the city. They swept the yard, filled the cans which every driver carried on the running board of his Model T, wiped the screens and serviced the puttering engines. Whilst one brother toted a grease can the other would fix a hamburger or jerk a soda drink for a customer. One day the drive-in was visited by a customer who was to play quite an important part in the life of Robert Hicks. The newcomer listened to the two Negroes as they sang to themselves whilst going about their work. Eventually he heard Bob Hicks accompany himself on his guitar and was very impressed with what he heard. The visitor was Dan Hornsby, who was employed as a talent scout for the Columbia record company and was now on the look out for original singers and musicians to record for the Columbia Race series. Satisfied with what he heard he arranged a recording date at the company's Atlanta studio for 25 March 1927.

When he presented himself at the studio Robert Hicks, who liked to call himself by the name by which he was popularly known – Barbecue Bob – recorded appropriately enough 'Barbecue Blues' and 'Cloudy Sky Blues'. Apparently his two titles that day met with the approval of the company, for Bob Hicks embarked upon a series of recordings during the next three years which included more than fifty titles. Barbecue Bob was one of the most talented of a great many folk singers and instrumentalists who included such characters as Eddie Anthony, Pillie Bolling, Blind Sammie, Laughing Charlie, Peg Leg Howell, Barefoot Bill and Henry Williams. The favourite instruments of these folk blues singers were guitars, fiddles and banjos, which they played with a crude virtuosity. For the most part the guitar was favoured and it was this instrument that Robert Hicks played, wire strung and tuned with a subtle but perceptible flatness. To the instrumental purist this is a contradiction in terms and a horrifying practice. But Bob was not an instrumental purist, nor even an orthodox guitarist, and he knew how best to achieve the strange flatness of his strong, masculine singing. These modifications in tuning were no accident: in the three years of his recording activity Bob always strung his guitar consistently. The result is hard to describe but thrilling to hear, for the fractional 'edge' to the tone gives a bite to his playing that rings in the mind's ear long after listening.

As a master of his instrument, Barbecue Bob had achieved a rare standard of accomplishment long before he commenced to record and his first sides demonstrate how original an artist he was. He continued to develop and his accompaniments to his own singing have few of the repetition of ideas which occur in the work of the greatest musicians in the blues and jazz fields, Armstrong not included. His finger work was rapid and he never resorted to the monotonous strumming of a single chord that plagues so many contemporary recordings. Instead he would alternate strong, driving rhythms with light runs of great delicacy and ingenious pattern behind the rare phrasing of his vocal line. Resounding notes on the bass string would follow a treble run; phrases of unequal length – of a bar, a bar-and-a-half, a single emphasized beat, a suspension in the rhythm, succeed each other with swift ease; syncopations with stresses on second and third beats would be further marked by hand-slaps on the fingerboard or across the strings and a piece might end in a beguiling, broken rhythm ceasing with one whining, ringing note. Nor is there any disparity between his singing and playing, for the characteristics of one are the characteristics of both, and Hicks' vocal line has the same variety with verses rapidly sung in a torrent of words followed by a drawled, half-time refrain. Lines repeated, half-lines dropped, verses running into each other, choruses echoed or omitted; all this with the ease and assurance of a man to whom improvisation is a natural act of creation. And interwoven, freely but surely knit together, his instrumental and vocal threads produce a fabric rich in textural variety, warm in colour, stimulating in pattern.

On 15 and 16 June, Barbecue Bob had his next two sessions at which he recorded eight more sides – including, rather surprisingly two spirituals, 'Jesus' Blood can make me Whole' and one of the earliest solo recordings of the 'Saints'. These were issued under Robert Hicks' own name, the only issue apart from a duet with his brother made in 1930 on which his actual name appears. Bob's excursion into the religious field was hardly characteristic, but his other recordings at the time certainly were. As one expects from a folk musician, his records have the coloration of one whose experience is intense but limited, and aspects of Negro life both humorous and grim are reflected in his work. The caste system determined by skin hue which sadly exists in the Negro world is demonstrated in 'Brownskin Gal' (Columbia 14257D).

Now if a Brownskin woman got a dollar in 'er
hand.
She takes two bits for 'self, six bits for her man.
– A Brownskin woman, best Brownie after all.
She will stick by you, winter, summer, spring
and fall
A Brownskin woman, best Brownie after all.

High Yeller woman she may have a cent
But she'll tell all you men, she ain't gotta thing
– A Brownskin woman, best Brownie after all.

Anybody tell you Brownskin gal's all right –
When they get Twenty-five they drive a black
stripe.
Brownskin woman, best Brownie after all.....

Ashes to ashes an' Dust to Dust
If You cain't ride the train catch the Ginger bus
A Brownskin woman's best brownie after all
She will stick by you, winter, summer, spring
and fall.
Brownskin woman, best Brownie after all.

Bob's use of folk idiom and metaphor is well demonstrated in the third and fourth stanzas quoted, the one referring to the tendency for coloured girls to darken in hue as they get older, a point which only a dark-skinned Negro such as Barbecue Bob would consider to be in their favour. The second reference is a customarily fatalistic one which underlines that a Negro of a particular social group must not despair if he cannot mate outside it. (Similar contentions account for 'Chocolate to the Bone'.)

In his autobiography Big Bill Broonzy says that he met Barbecue Bob in 1924 in Chicago, together with Blind Blake and many other 'Race' artists and that they had already recorded, persuading him to do the same. It seems that the passage of thirty years impaired Bill's nonetheless remark-

ably good memory for there are certainly no records by Hicks known to date from that time, nor is there any corroborative evidence that he visited Chicago. Such recordings as 'Mississippi Heavy Water Blues', 'Way Across Georgia Blues', 'Goin' Up the Country' and 'Mississippi Levee Low Blues' suggest that he had nevertheless ventured beyond Atlanta before April 1928, whilst 'Mama You Don't Suit Me', 'My Mistakes Blues', 'Crooked Woman Blues', 'She's Gone Blues' and 'Beggin' For Love' suggest that this was not a very successful period in Bob's amorous affairs! Matters appear to have come to a head with 'It's Just Too Bad' (Columbia 14424) which Bob recorded when Lillian Glinn was in town. The words are more brutal than is customary with him, though his usual sense of humour creeps in the final verse quoted:

Have a story to tell you honey an' it's just too
bad,
Get a l'il closer, tell 'bout a dream I had.
Saw a Big-Time rounder hanging round my
high-brown's bed
If I shoot that rounder honey it will be too bad.

Won't you tell me pretty mama, who you fool
aroun' with him?
I can't tell you papa, It will be too bad.

I want to take my razor cut you from end to
end,
When that rounder call you, honey then you
cain't send.
I'm goin down to the river, jump off so brave
and bold,
I don't mind the drownin' honey, but the
water's so cold.

Fortunately the April waters successfully dissuaded him from this disastrous step, and Bob had half-a-dozen recording sessions during 1929 when he made many sides of commendable variety and experimented with different verse forms which defy written description or musical notation to give anything of their true worth. Typical, though only because of its originality and not because it repeats a pattern, is 'Freeze to Me, Mama' (Columbia 14507D). The verses are sung rapidly in double time with scarcely a break between words or lines and the refrain follows instantly as part of the verse. The words 'Freeze to me' are sung on the beat; a beat is played before and after the word 'mama' of which the first syllable is stressed, and the words 'with both skin and bone' are stressed in syncopation on 'both' and 'bone' so that 'both skin' sounds more like 'buckskin'. In the third line of the refrain the stress is on the first syllable of the second half, i.e. on the syllable 'be' and the line runs out with slight variations of emphasis. This clumsy and pedantic description may perhaps give some indication of Barbecue Bob's unique use of rhythm and verse form.

> *Come along mama give me a hug*
> *You got the world I got the stopper in the jug,*
> > *so*
> *Freeze to me, mama, please don't let me roam,*
> *Freeze to me, mama, with both skin and bone.*
> *Freeze to me, mama, before I go home.*

> *Girls they call me Big Bad Pete*
> *But they's crazy 'bout this little pigmeat so*
> *Freeze to me etc.*

> *Skinny gal in the summer may be all right*
> *But a fat gal in the winter is just too tight, so,*
> *Freeze to me . . .*

During the following year Bob made a few more sides including versions of the ancient Negro folk themes of 'The Monkey and the Baboon' and 'The Spider and the Fly' and a couple of sides with his brother Charlie called 'Darktown Gamblin' in which they gave some indication of the sing-song methods of playing Craps and the Georgia Skin game, the latter incidentally being also recorded for the Library of Congress by Jelly-Roll Morton. One more session on 5 November 1930 and Barbecue Bob's recording career, like that of so many other folk artists who felt the repercussions of the Depression on the recording industry, came to an end. Robert Hicks, Barbecue Bob, is dead now, though his brother is reputedly still around somewhere in the environs of Atlanta. Only the records, all more than a quarter of a century old, remain to testify to the genius of a rough, rare, Negro who sprang from the Georgia soil, and comparatively few persons know them.

Music Mirror, September 1958
Barbecue Bob was born Walnut Grove, Georgia, 11 September 1902 and died of pneumonia, Lithonia, 21 October 1931.

Lazy River
BILL WILLIAMS

Throughout the Sixties, it seemed there was one 'discovery' or 'rediscovery' of a blues singer after another; a succession of methodical searches, happy accidents and dramatic events which brought not only a number of legendary figures to life, but also revealed that the wealth of talent in the black traditions had been even greater than might have been supposed. Already though, the circumstances which brought about these discoveries seem to have passed and the events themselves slipped into history. Not many collectors would be sanguine enough to expect any major discoveries to occur now. And so, just to challenge any incipient pessimism, along comes Bill Williams.

Bill Williams is not just the shadow of a tradition, a lone survivor whose longevity has preserved a relatively minor talent after his greater contemporaries have passed on, as is sadly the case in New Orleans today. On the contrary, he is a find of outstanding importance who makes a few more pieces fit into the complex jig-saw puzzle of blues history, and who is, in his own right, a musician of outstanding ability. Kentucky is a State which, on the evidence of records, has contributed relatively little to the blues, though in the groups of Clifford Hayes, Earl McDonald and the anonymous Whistler there was apparently a fairly strong jug band tradition, centred perhaps, in Louisville. A solitary field trip made by Victor in June 1931 resulted in quite a few unissued titles, some recordings of a contingent from St Louis including Roosevelt Sykes, Walter Davis, and probably Clifford Gibson and Henry Townsend, a couple of items by Kid Coley, and very little else. With not much to go on the blues enthusiast might be forgiven for assuming that 'My Old Kentucky Home'

had killed off any tradition that might have been in the State.

It's inappropriate to consider Bill Williams as essentially a Kentucky musican anyway, although he has lived in that State for almost fifty years. He was born in Richmond, Virginia, on 28 February 1897 and lived out in the country some sixty miles from the city in his youth. His brother, James Williams, appears to have been his first inspiration. A ragtime guitarist, he was an unwilling tutor; Bill nevertheless picking up the rudiments of a ragtime technique which has remained in his music to the present day. At the age of fourteen he began a life of manual work, first as a waterboy at Wilmington, Delaware, for the railroad company, and subsequently far out west in Colorado where he worked in the mines at Lester and lived with relatives. Eventually, after a spell in Bristol, Tennessee, he dropped off a freight train at Greenup, Kentucky, and took a job with the C & O Railroad in Russell. Greenup, and that region has been his home stomping ground for half a century, a sector in the extreme west of the State in the loop of the Ohio River where Kentucky, Ohio and West Virginia all meet. It's a region which has had quite a part to play in the story of country music in the white traditions – Merle Travis, Ike Everly – the father of the Everly Brothers, Don and Phil – and lesser known musicians came from that area. It also produced Arnold Schultz, a Negro guitarist of considerable local repute who would probably have remained unknown to us if it hadn't been for the fact that he played for country dances around Rosine, and was the first important influence on Bill Monroe. And it produced Jim Mason from Webster County, a guitarist just two years Bill Williams' junior, though it's doubtful if we would have known about him if it didn't just happen that he was the man who shaped the guitar styles of both Merle Travis and Ike Everly in Muhlenberg County and neighbouring parts. Bill Williams didn't have the luck to be an influence on a famous white country or hillbilly guitarist, at least by name. He was one of the several black guitarists and fiddle players who played their boxes in the region where, across the river from Greenup, Kentucky, the towns of Coal Grove, Ironton, Franklin Furnace and Scioto Furnace betray their mining, industrial character.

It's coal mining country right through that region, at the knuckle of a great finger of bituminous coalfield which stretches from western Pennsylvania through the intersecting corners of Ohio, West Virginia and Kentucky, down through Tennessee to probe the northern part of Alabama. Maybe the pay wasn't high but there was work in the coal mines and Bill Williams went after it. Shift work too, which meant that, as in the lumber industry of the piney woods further south and west, there was always a shift looking for recreation: to a musician, a naturally attractive situation where he could earn a little money on the side from his fellow workers, or if he was exceptionally good, so inclined or handicapped, could make a living from his music. As a fit man in his mid-twenties – he's still vigorous and looking ten years younger than he is – Bill worked in the mines of Pike County. But after the day's work he'd sit and jam on the porch of his house with one of the guitar-pickers who came into the region, attracted by the opportunities for entertaining, a smiling oval-faced man who wore a suit with broad revers but whose extensive travelling was hinted at by the high, laced-boots he wore. He was sightless and one of

the best guitar-pickers to hit that area, or indeed any other. They called him Blind Blake.

Blind Blake came from Georgia. According to his friend Blind Willie McTell he was named Arthur Phelps, but it seems his name was Arthur Blake. He travelled a lot – to Jacksonville, Florida, where he had a home and may have died, and as far west as Dallas, Texas. He was well-known in Chicago where, fortunately, he was extensively recorded for Paramount in the later Twenties. Five years before his first session in September 1926, he was in Kentucky and he proved to be the strongest influence on Bill Williams. He had met him earlier in Bristol and had worked with him there as his regular second, accompanying him and learning from him. Listening to Bill today he seems at times to be Blind Blake reincarnate; he has the same ease and facility, the same dexterous thumb-roll, the same rapid picking. But he's not a carbon copy of Blind Blake, though he readily admits that the famous guitarist was, and still remains, his favourite musician. At times Bill Williams recalls Mance Lipscomb – whom he may never have heard, even today – and at other times he reveals hints of Big Bill or Mississippi John Hurt, both guitarists whom he admires and whose early records could conceivably have had some influence on his style. Like many of the 'eastern' guitarists (to the blues enthusiasts all musicians from east of Mississippi tend to be called 'East Coast'), he clearly admires technical skill and places more importance on a sweet-flowing instrumental line than on any deep emotional involvement in the words of his songs and blues.

Back in 1921, when he was playing with Blake, Bill Williams would have earned the name of a 'songster'. It has been suggested by Eddie Lambert in an article a while ago in this magazine's predecessor that the songsters did not precede the blues singers, but that recording has tended to give an undue importance to blues. There is a lot of truth in this, I think, but nevertheless blues singers tend to talk of their guitar-playing fathers as old-time songsters, and not as blues singers, suggesting that the songsters of the past fifty years have been the tail end of a much older tradition. Generally I think it is still fair to assume that the songsters preceded, as well as overlapped, with the blues singers. They have been poorly documented and the chances of doing so adequately get less and less virtually with every passing month. One clear characteristic is that they had a very wide range of repertoire with dance tunes, instrumental rags, minstrel and medicine songs, all included in a spectrum of song and music which took in the blues as that music began to appear.

Bill Williams, then, is a songster rather than blues singer and his music contains examples of all the types mentioned above. Recently he was recorded by Nicholas Perls, the proprietor of the important reissue label Yazoo, for his subsidiary Blue Goose. A collection has now been released on Blue Goose 2004 which gives a remarkable indication of this hitherto 'unknown' talent. Included are three ragtime pieces called simply 'Banjo Rag', 'Bill's Rag' and 'Total Rag'. Guitar rags have been recorded by the eastern songsters to a far greater extent than by Mississippi and Texas men, although the latter were geographically as near to Missouri. His rags may refer back to his brother's repertoire. Nevertheless, Williams has long been a Kentucky man and the two States meet at Cairo and share a short stretch on the Mississippi River. Perhaps this is a misleading trail to follow, but the relationship of piano rags to guitar rags has been so little explored that the point might be worth making. The first two of Williams' rags have stop-time elements which relate them

to country dances of this title in which the action is momentarily suspended or the foot is slid to its partner as an unexpected pause in a faster movement. 'Bill's Rag' is a buck and wing dance quite close to Mance Lipscomb's 'Buck Dance' and appears to be of the kind that might well have been performed on the Ohio waterfront in his younger days.

Typical of the songster is his version of a minstrel song which he calls 'The Chicken'. It is the same song as that recorded by the Negro Frank Stokes and the white Clayton McMichen under the title of 'Chicken, You can Roost Behind the Moon'. This fact serves to emphasize the manner in which these early songs crossed the colour line. It makes an excellent vehicle for Williams's scintillating technique. He slightly rushes the playing and fractionally slows up to sing, not as did Little Hat Jones as a stylistic characteristic, but presumably because the concentration required slightly inhibits singing. I find it instructive because it is quite obviously the speed at which he must have played it in his younger days, and doubtless sung it too, and one can imagine the startling effect of this tremendous finger-work when he was a young man.

Catholicity of taste is common among songsters. It's the quality they admire and one which separates them from blues singers. Bluesmen have a dislike of published standards; try for instance, to count the number of versions of 'St Louis Blues' recorded by bluesmen, compared with those recorded, endlessly, by jazz groups. Can you count Bessie Smith's as a blues? Well, yes of course, but not one from the folk tradition. Or Jim Jackson's? For Jim Jackson was himself a songster. You'd be hard pressed to think of others. Bill Williams plays it in a straight version which he appears to have learned at an early age. Unashamedly he settles for 'Up a Lazy River', as engagingly as Big Bill Broonzy playing and singing 'Shanty in Old Shanty Town' (and annoying the purists in so doing). I was slightly surprised to hear Bill Williams singing 'Frankie and Johnny' by this name and with the verses he chose, for to most songsters this semi-pop song is known by its earlier ballad title of 'Frankie and Albert'. It suggests that he may have learned it rather later in his career than some of his songs.

'Frankie' is played with a confidence and freshness which makes the over-familiar song very acceptable. Williams' dazzling playing makes every track of great interest and is specially evident on 'I Know What it Means to be Lonesome', a theme which has the descending phrases and structure that relate it to 'Ella Speed' as played by Lipscomb, and to a certain extent to other favourites like 'Salty Dog'. Several of Williams' tunes are original re-workings of some older blues melodies. His 'Lucky Blues' is on an eight-bar framework which is closely related to the 'Trouble in Mind' – 'Key to the Highway' complex. Apparently he learned this in Virginia which suggests, in view of the popularity of the theme with eastern musicians, a local traditional 'tune family'. Such tune families ask for more thorough examination than they have so far received. After writing the chapter on 'The Forty-Fours' in *Screening the Blues*, I received many letters pointing out that I had missed this or that recording of the theme. But instead of labouring this it would have been valuable if other writers pursued other complexes in greater detail. One of them must surely be the 'Highway' – 'Trouble in Mind' family and someone interviewing Bill Williams might ascertain whether his 'Lucky Blues' is, in his view, a separate song or one derived from the others mentioned. Similar thoughts come to mind in listening to his recording of 'Pocohantas' which is reminiscent of a very fast, virtuoso guitar

performance of 'St James Infirmary Blues'. Perhaps specialists in New Orleans jazz might comment on whether this is the same theme as the tune of 'Pocohantas' which was, I believe, a fairly popular parade and Mardi Gras tune. According to Stephen Calt, Williams learned it from an Italian railroad man.

It is clear that if Bill Williams was influenced by Blind Blake he was certainly not dependent on him. One is impressed by his individuality, though of course, it is not the kind of single-mindedness that encourages a blues singer to compose his own blues. On present evidence Williams is not an innovator of blues as such, which presumably Blind Blake was. Bill's voice is quite different from Blake's. Where Blake could be smooth and wistful he is inclined to rasp; where Blake sang from the front of the mouth, Williams sings from the back of the throat in a somewhat constricted manner which links him aurally with that Virginia songster thirty years his junior, John Jackson. But there are echoes of Blake's musicianship in a number of items, the instumental rags recalling 'Blind Arthur's Breakdown', and being by no means eclipsed by that classic. More evidently influenced by Blake is 'Too Tight' which was twice recorded by the blind singer himself and which also had a rough-and-ready treatment from Peg Leg Howell and His Gang. And there are the blues items, with 'My Girlfriend Left Me' being very obviously based on Blind Blake's 'Georgia Bound'.

Apart from a demo tape made by a local guitar teacher, Charlie Parsons, these are the first recordings that Bill Williams has ever made, but hopefully, they won't be the last. In the summer of 1970 he played at the Mountain Heritage Festival at the County Fairgrounds in his home town of Greenup and received a standing ovation from the crowd. True songster, he played the National Anthem in response. Soon after, he performed at the Community College in Ashland some fifteen miles up river, appeared on John Skagg's Coffee House show on WIRO and even on the Kentucky Educational TV network. All pretty local, but he had his biggest adventure when, in the winter of 1970, he played at the University of Chicago Folklore Society Festival. There'll be many demands for Bill Williams in the future, and one of them will be this summer when he plays at the Festival of American Folklife which Mack McCormick is directing in the Buckminster Fuller Dome on St Helen Island, Montreal, Quebec. It will be Bill Williams' first international performance. Wherever he goes he'll doubtless be following the pattern established by his fellow West Kentuckians, Jim Mason and Arnold Schultz – showing the young white guitar-pickers how to tease the frets.

Jazz and Blues, August/Sept. 1971

Bill Williams died Greenup, Kentucky, 6 October 1973.

Ramblin' and Wanderin'
BIG JOE WILLIAMS

The 'D' shaped stretch of country that lies between the Mississippi and the Yazoo Rivers which has been known since the latter part of the nineteenth century as the 'Delta' – though it lies a couple of hundred miles from the mouth of the larger river – has been associated with a whole blues tradition. It is a markedly rural area with many small and liberally scattered communities and only a very few large towns.

Outside the Delta there are also innumerable 'li'l ole country towns', often of little more than fifty small shacks which provide the homes for the workers on the neighbouring plantations and large farms. In slightly more outlying areas small cabins stand in the fields surrounded by cotton and cottonwoods. It is from these country towns, cottonfield cabins and occasional larger towns that the many blues singers of Mississippi have come. Big Joe Williams is one of them.

In many ways Big Joe Williams fits the collectors' ideal of the country blues singer. In his music, his character, his way of life and his blues verses which relate to it, he completes the image of the Mississippi bluesman. His parents were tenant farmers – one stage up from the sharecropper and scarcely better off – and they had some fourteen children. Large families in Negro communities are usual, for though there are more mouths to feed there are more hands to work. Though his father was a farmer, and sometime sawmill worker, Big Joe was disinclined to labour in fields or mill as he had done. He seems to have inherited from his mother's side an innate musical talent which found primitive expression when he began to accompany himself at only four years by beating on a bucket of water and altering its tone by the pressure of his fingers on the

side. He wasn't much older when he made himself a crude instrument by stapling a length of baling wire to a length of fence-wood and using a cotton reel as a bridge. With a bottle held against the 'string' he had made what was in effect a one-string guitar. It seems that he had a succession of instruments of a like nature and made the 'cigar-box' guitar of the type which many singers – Big Bill Broonzy for example – first learned to play. By the time he was in his early teens he was getting around on his own and playing at country suppers, levee camps, turpentine camps.

For some time Joe worked at a tough levee camp near Greenville, Mississippi, where the work was hard, the conditions brutal and the food poor. But if the life was grim it was relieved by Joe's music and he made himself 'spending change' from his blues playing. Soon he was making more from his music than the sweat of his brow and he cut across the State line to Alabama. It was there on the coast of Mobile that he got his first guitar. It was a big twelve-string; only later did he get the more usual six-stringed instrument. His ability to master the double-strung box served him in good stead in later years when he made his own, famous nine-string model. He played in Mobile, Biloxi and way over in Florida, making his way to the M & O Bottoms of Tuscaloosa, Alabama, at some indeterminate time in these years of rambling. Bossed by a local gangster named Totsy King, this wide-open area provided work for Joe, who played for local functions, country suppers and at the neighbourhood jukes. His years of 'ramblin' and wanderin'', took him from State to State – as far as Pensacola, Florida, New Orleans, or Dallas, Texas.

A rambling life has more than one

meaning in Negro idiom: Joe Williams had several clashes with the law and was jailed on a number of occasions. He spent a time in Parchman Farm, Mississippi, but managed to avoid working too hard by entertaining the convicts and warders alike with his blues. It was there that he composed his 'Baby, Please Don't Go' – 'Don't You Leave Me Here' is a version of it – and sang his way out of jail with it. A hard life made him at times an irascible and difficult man and his independence of action hardly endeared him to every person that he met. He is a more mellow man now, but in his cups can still be a little 'evil', as he would say himself. If he was in and out of jail, hoboing on trains, thumbing rides, playing in jukes and brothels – somehow he held on to his guitar. It was a guitar that was changing; the rough treatment that the instrument suffered necessitated much patching up and at times he added a peg when another broke. Somewhere along the line he found himself playing what was in effect a nine-string instrument and liked the sound.

'Poor Joe', as the blues world knew him, played a style of guitar which owed much to Mississippi with its ringing treble notes, pronounced rhythm and marked swing, so different from the contemplative arpeggio style of the Texas blues guitarists. Originally Joe played the normal, standard guitar tuning, but eventually he adopted the Spanish tuning favoured by many blues singers in which the guitar is tuned to a chord. Especially when played with a bottle neck against the strings, this is a most effective tuning for the blues, and though it has certain limitations Joe was able to introduce great melodic variety against the bass rhythm that he maintained. His vocals were strong and declaimed, but he liked to tail off his voice or soar to a note before hitting it hard. At times there is evidence of the influence of his partner Peetie Wheatstraw too. Peetie and Joe ran a club in St Louis for a considerable time in the company of Charlie Jordan. Peetie was killed in a car crash and Big Joe inherited his guitar, though for the most part he continued to play his own battered instrument. Innumerable blues singers from St Louis and blues centres in Missouri and Indiana gravitated to the St Louis Club and it was not until 1954, when Charlie Jordan was murdered, that the venture ended.

By this time 'Big Joe' – as he was now called – had a score of years of recording behind him. It seems that his voice became heavier as he matured. Later recordings have the familiar Joe Williams sound with the urgent guitar work and the strong, dramatic blues singing. His words were always interesting, being frequently derived from his experience or his own peculiar imagery. In this present collection 'Old Saw Mill Blues' has obvious personal significance; so too has 'El Paso Blues' with their reference to stages in his long and colourful career. Other songs come from the great Mississippi tradition of which he is an active part; 'Shake Em' On Down', for example, is a tune frequently associated with Tommy McClennan and Bukka White.

Though he had been recorded by Bob Koester in 1958, Big Joe continued to ramble and in 1960 he and his wife were beating their way across Texas and the West on his way to California. That year, however, his wife died and he, in a disturbed state of mind, found himself in jail in Oakland. Blues enthusiast Chris Strachwitz bailed him out and he too recorded Big Joe. Soon after, he was back in Chicago with Bob Koester and Pete Welding of Down Beat giving him a helping hand. He played at Koester's club, The Blind Pig, and at a coffeehouse which featured blues singers, the Fickle Pickle. Both places are described in 'Pick a Pickle' in which he pays a tribute to those who have helped him to overdue recognition.

In 1963 Big Joe came to Europe with a blues package show, when these items were recorded. To European blues enthusiasts his visit was particularly exciting for he was quite the most primitive blues singer to have played here. He returned to Chicago with a wider audience, but this has meant little change for Big Joe in his way of life or his blues. He cannot change either his habits of living or of playing. Less than any other blues singer whose audience now embraces white college students and folk enthusiasts has he found it necessary or possible to change his repertoire. So he remains and will continue as one of the last of the truly untutored folk blues singers, his country style of blues becoming less and less in keeping with the slick modern trends.

Notes to Storyville SLP 163, 1965

Big Joe Williams was born Crawford, Mississipi, *c.* 1903 and died Macon, Georgia, 17 December 1982.

Catfish Blues

ROBERT PETWAY

As you descend from the hilly, wooded land-scape of De Soto, Tate and Panola Counties in Mississippi to the flat bottomlands of the Mississippi River flood-plain, the landscape changes. Not dramatically, because the hills aren't high enough to be a dramatic contrast, but very noticeably so, all the same. Between the Mississippi River and the meandering Yazoo River which meets it north of Vicksburg is the so-called Mississippi Delta. It is well watered and the soil is rich, the weather is mild in winter, hot and steamily humid in summer, combining to make the ideal conditions for growing cotton which was for so long the basic crop of the region. It isn't pretty country; it's too flat and the trees too scattered. The towns aren't particularly attractive either, though in recent years since the mechanization that has made the farms and plantations more efficient – and thinned out the black population that worked them by hand – some of the townships look more prosperous than they did even a score of years ago. Even so, going through this rather featureless land-scape with its settlements and poor cabins dotted all over it, it is hard to picture even now how so vital and powerful a music as the blues came out of it.

In the southern part of the Delta is Yazoo City, a small town served by the Illinois Central railroad and situated on the Yazoo River itself; not much to distinguish it from several others of similar size in the region though it is the largest in the county. It's on the edge of the Delta; the land begins to rise to the east. It is blues country; to the south about twenty miles away is Bentonia where Skip James and his circle lived; to the west about thirty miles away is Rolling Fork where Muddy Water grew up. Jackson,

Crystal Springs and the focus of the Tommy Johnson nexus of bluesmen lies about sixty miles to the south. We know these names and places because of the blues singers who became famous through their recordings. If they came from, or worked in them they fit into our mental map; if we haven't heard of them this way they seem not to exist. But for the diligent researcher there's still a great deal to be found out about the blues-making culture in these settlements in between, and doubtless much to learn of the men who never did get on record.

Robert Petway is one of the Delta singers who *did* make it on disc – just. Like several other bluesmen he recorded at two sessions only, far away in Chicago. It's tempting to think of his style of blues as anachronistic, an approach more suited to the generation of Charley Patton or Willie Brown than to the period when Sonny Boy Williamson, Jazz Gillum or Mississippi-born Big Boy Crudup were recording. But in the compressed history of blues the span of a decade is made to seem significant. Only the record companies and their marketing, and the tastes of the record-buying public that to a great extent they moulded as well as reflected, really changed. Blues singers whom we mentally associate with one point in time by the date of their recordings, tended always to play in much the same way, both before and after cutting their few tracks.

Big Bill Broonzy told me that 'Robert, he played along with Tommy. They were in there together – kids together, grew up together. But Tommy got better known.' Tommy was Tommy McClennan, who was born and raised on the J. F. Sligh farm about ten miles north of Yazoo City in 1908. It seems likely from Broonzy's recollection that Robert Petway was about the same age and raised on the same farm. Later, when McClennan moved on up the Yazoo River to Leflore County he was an influence on David Edwards, as 'Honeyboy' told Peter Welding: 'He lived from Greenwood over to Itta Bena, Indianola. He was playing house parties like I was, so I was learning under Tommy, practically . . . he was playing the same things he made, "Catfish" and "Bullfrog" . . . he had a different style; him and Robert Petway had the same style 'cause they played together all the time. They didn't always play together, I mean. It'd be in and out; sometimes Tommy would be by himself and then when he got something pretty large he'd go get Robert . . . so they'd play together.' (*Blues Unlimited* No. 54, p. 7)

They were certainly close to each other in approach. Both had deep, gravelly voices, both could hit the guitar hard. They tended to talk between lines to themselves, to their listeners or to the women who were generally the subject of their songs. But

Robert Petway could be the more delicate of the two, using a light arpeggio which became something of a personal trademark both behind the vocal line and in the breaks. Neither singer was as subtle as Patton but they had the same 'heavy' delivery. One can't help wondering if the subject of 'Bertha Lee Blues' – 'you sure been good to me' – was in fact, Bertha Lee Patton.

In 1939 McClennan moved to Chicago and he'd had three successful recording sessions by the time Petway had his first. It seems likely that Tommy sent for him. 'Catfish Blues' was a big hit for him and he came up again to record a year later at a session which he shared with McClennan. A photo taken at one of these sessions shows a small, shy-looking man with a steel guitar, still wearing his blue duckins. Neither of them recorded again and McClennan, at any rate, died later in Chicago. But Robert may have returned to Mississippi; he *could* be there still.

Notes to Wolf Records 108, 1981

Jerry's Saloon
OSCAR BUDDY WOODS

Shreveport, Louisiana, lies in the Tri-State region where Louisiana, Texas and Arkansas meet. It's the capital of Caddo Parish, the most north-westerly parish in the State and one which has along its western border the mounds that marked the boundary between the United States and the Republic of Texas. Like the Parish, Shreveport has a large non-white population, a third of its people being black or Indian in origin, and the booming, hustling city has always attracted blacks from the Tri-State region who have sought to get some spin-off from its continually expanding economy.

Growth is a characteristic of Shreveport. It was the clearing of the Red River by Captain Henry Shreve in the mid-1830s that made the town possible and it was incorporated in 1839 with a name that honoured his Shreve Town Company who laid out the site. It flourished with the trade that its situation on the Texas-bound route encouraged and by the cotton produced on the big plantations along the Red River. They depended on slave labour before the war between the States. Not only was the city on the Confederate side; it was the last bastion of the Confederacy even though it was never devastated by the war.

All this has a bearing on its culture and, incidentally on the music of its black population. For there was money in Shreveport and when the railroad link with Dallas was established, soon after the war, it continued to thrive even as the river traffic died. Relatively speaking, blacks in Shreveport were well-off, sharing a little in the general prosperity and circulating their cash in the bars, saloons and red-light districts of the city. In 1880 there were still only 8,000 people in Shreveport; nevertheless, this number had

doubled by the time Huddie Ledbetter, the celebrated Leadbelly, made his first visit to the brothels of Fannin Street at the turn of the century. Still a small town, even if, to the young rebel in knee-pants from Mooringsport and the Caddo Lake region, it had the temptations of a big city.

It was the oil-strike at Caddo Lake in 1906 which made a boom city of Shreveport. Oil, like cotton, required cheap labour, at least in pre-mechanized years. Blacks were seldom employed at the rig, but there was still plenty of heavy work and, with the discovery of oil, the expanding economy of the city brought many opportunities for domestic, menial and semi-skilled work. When the strike seemed to have burned itself out by the end of the Twenties, the opening of the East Texas field in 1930 and the Rodessa Field five years later gave the city the boost it needed.

The Depression years had been tough for Shreveport as for every other urban district but it recovered quickly and avoided the malaise that affected many Southern cities. But then it had none of the aspects of a Southern city; it was pragmatic, hard-nosed, commercial, unromantic, go-getting. When John Avery Lomax came there in 1940, the population had hit the 75,000 mark and blacks had tipped 35 per cent. If they'd stayed longer they would doubtless have found many more musicians among the black community that centred on the West Allendale and Cedar Grove sections. But they stayed only two days, the Tuesday and Wednesday, 8 and 9 October, before going on to Oil City, the site of the 1906 strike. Writing a few days later Ruby Lomax reported: 'After jiggling around considerably in East Texas with Sacred Harp

Conventions and a Negro Baptist Association and guitar-pickers and an ex-slave, we struck out for Shreveport. Except for some pretty newsboys' cries, all our recordings there were made by Negroes – blues singers from Texas Avenue, French Creole singers, guitar and mandolin pickers.'

Though John Lomax's autobiography was published a few years later and therefore could have thrown light on how he found the Shreveport singers, the event was obviously insufficiently memorable for him to include. But it is likely that he merely encountered them on the street and later followed them to a bar. His field notes report that 'Oscar (Buddy) Woods, Joe Harris and Kid West are all professional Negro guitarists and singers of Texas Avenue, Shreveport, Louisiana. The songs I have recorded are among those they use to cajole nickels from the pockets of listeners. One night I sat an hour where the group was playing in a restaurant where drinks were served. I was the only person who dropped a contribution in the can. I doubt if the proprietor paid them anything.' This brief note suggests that all three musicians were working together as a group. But if so, it seems not to have occurred to Lomax to record them as a three-piece band. Instead, Oscar Woods was recorded on the Tuesday; Joe Harris and Kid West on the following day.

In a brief interview at the conclusion of the session, when Oscar Woods had sung and played 'Look Here Baby, One Thing I Got To Say', John Lomax elicited a little further information.

Lomax: Buddy, when do you – when do you play this song?
Woods: Oh, well, down 'n' around these little hop joints and things like that – when they having a good time.
Lomax: That's a – that's a stimulator?
Woods: Well, they kinda get a li'l stimulated.

Lomax: How do you make your living regularly, Buddy?
Woods: Oh, just different – hanging around the corners, lyin' around the joints 'n' takin' up where I can. Once in a while-n-y' know, that way.
Lomax: You pass the hat around? Don't you . . .
Woods: Oh yes, sir, passing the hat around, don't forget it.
Lomax: How long have you been a street singer?
Woods: Ohh – I guess around fifteen years.
Lomax: Done nothing but pick since then?
Woods: That's all – practically all.
Lomax: That so? Where did you grow up did you tell me?
Woods: Always in the State of Louisiana.
Lomax: Whereabouts?
Woods: Oh, down near Nachitoches.
Lomax: Worked on a farm?
Woods: Yes sir.
Lomax: Where did you get your music?
Woods: I guess I just settled on it. Just picked it up somewhere, something. I didn't read up on it.

'Thank you' said Lomax in a rather bored voice; he'd heard it all before, the same vagueness, the same lack of detail. As an interview with a blues singer it was perfunctory but in 1940 there was little to relate it to and no picture emerging that would make a more probing interview necessary. Woods was easy, but respectful, and didn't advance any information of his own accord.

The record session itself was slightly more revealing, though it may have given John Lomax a surprise. He had collected a number of versions of the 'Ballad Of The Boll Weevil', and probably requested one from Oscar Woods. At any rate Woods obliged with a song of this title, 'Boll Weevil Blues'. It was however a version of Ma Rainey's 'Bo-Weavil Blues', recorded in

1923 and her first issued record. Oscar Woods had transposed the tune skilfully to his individual technique of guitar playing, subtly changing the phrasing to suit the steady rhythm of his own accompaniment. By his own account to Lomax, Woods had been working on the streets since 1925 and may therefore have heard the record at his farm home a year or so before.

Buddy Woods, as he was generally called, was no stranger to recording when the Lomaxes found him. His earliest titles were with a second guitarist, who sang blues vocals and played kazoo, Eddie Schaffer; their 'Fence Breakin' Blues' and 'Home Wreckin' Blues' were recorded a decade before in Memphis, Tennessee. This was only four days after James 'Kokomo' Arnold made his first recordings, at the same location and with the same recording crew. The fact is a tantalizing one, for as far as can be ascertained, these may have been the first four recordings made of a comparatively rare style of blues guitar playing. It seems unlikely that Woods and Arnold could have learned this technique with such virtuosity in so short a time and direct influence is therefore unlikely. Arnold claimed to have come from Georgia, while Woods came from Louisiana. Only a few days later, Booker Washington White (and companion, Napoleon Hairiston) also made his first recordings of slide guitar, again to the same recording team in Memphis.

Unlike Tampa Red, who used a slide on the treble strings only, Arnold, Woods and White all played in open tuning with the slide laid across the strings. On occasion, Booker White would play with his guitar laid across his lap, but more frequently he played with a slide made from a length of brass tubing, slipped over his finger, with the guitar in the customary position. Arnold usually, and Woods invariably, played the guitar flat across the lap. Black Ace (B. K. Turner), who learned much of his technique

from Buddy Woods, employed the same method. This was also the manner of slide guitar playing used by Leadbelly, who may well have learned it in Shreveport. It appears that the flat guitar technique was particularly favoured by Shreveport musicians but it seems likely that it was derived directly from the Hawaiian style, which had been made popular by Hawaiian musicians appearing at the Chicago World's Fair and the subsequent annexation of the islands.

Arnold, Woods and White, who were to make their names in later years, had already formulated their personal styles. Arnold's complex picking on 'Rainy Night Blues' and almost frantic playing on 'Paddlin' (Madeline) Blues' was indisputably his own; White's train imitations were in a percussive form that he repeated often later. By comparison Woods' playing was more relaxed, seeming to be less interested in impressing the recording executives. Not that any of them was to owe a career to Victor – though Oscar Woods with Eddie Chafer (*sic*) made a coupling for Victor under the name 'Eddie and Oscar' on 8 February 1932. This record (Victor 23324) which backed 'Nok-'Em-All-Blues' with 'Flying Crow Blues' was the first recording of the latter title, a popular Texas-Louisiana theme. The session was in Dallas and was probably held at the instigation of Jimmie Davis, a white country singer with political ambitions, whose songs were clearly influenced by black records. On the same day Davis made four titles with Woods accompanying, on one of which they shared the vocals, 'Saturday Night Stroll' (Victor 23688). Indeed, Buddy Woods may have accompanied Davis recordings as early as 1930, in Memphis. Jimmie Davis was later to become Governor of Louisiana in 1944 and was to serve a second term in 1960. Woods seems not to have exploited the connection by seeking more recordings on his own initiative. Within the next couple commenced his four-year long contract with Decca during which he recorded prolifically.

Buddy Woods, however, stayed in Louisiana, unambitious, disinterested in making a career. 'Calls himself "Troubadour", "Street Rustler",' Lomax noted. When Woods had an opportunity to record for a unit of the Decca company it was in New Orleans in 1936 where he cut 'Don't Sell It – Don't Give It Away'; one of the tunes he chose to play for John Lomax four years later. He'd recorded it, too, in San Antonio with the band fronted by a Shreveport singer, Kitty Gray. It's not surprising, therefore, to hear the ease with which he plays the tune and the almost casual, swinging manner of his singing. 'Words and music by Buddy Woods' Lomax added to his hastily penned transcript, adding 'Buddy Woods claims to have composed the words and music.'

Though Buddy Woods had recorded several blues at his few sessions, he made only one for John Lomax, 'Sometimes I Get To Thinking'. The verses were slight modifications of traditional lyrics and the whole blues had only three stanzas. But Woods seems to have considered them as a composition; asked to make a second take, he introduced only slight variations, opening with different instrumental phrasing and changing a word here and there while the sense remained the same. Buddy's final item 'Look Here Baby, One Thing I Got To Say' was a remodelling of 'Hey Lawdy Mama' (a theme made popular by Bumble Bee Slim a few years before) played with his customary fluency.

John Lomax could have obtained more music from Buddy Woods if he had been familiar with his records. Lomax was motivated to record songsters rather than blues singers and was far more interested in those singers who reflected in their repetoires the vestiges of an older tradition. Buddy Woods,

of years Kokomo Arnold had moved to Chicago where, in September 1934, he recording with his 'Wampus Cats' and playing, at times, with small jazz-inclined groups, must have seemed too urbane to Lomax. Kid West and Joe Harris were more to his taste; at any rate he recorded more items by them. However, they had even less to say about themselves, and Lomax left no further notes to fill in the biographical details of the two street singers.

Their first title was probably rather unexpected. Though it was called 'Railroad Rag' (AFS 3990 A3) it was a novelty ragtime number of the kind that years before they had played to white audiences; decades before, even. After a second take of the song, with its pathetic closing line 'Here comes that Choo-choo, choo-choo-choo-(poop-poop)-- that's the Railroad Rag', Lomax avowed that it was a 'pretty thing' and asked Kid West when he first played it. 'Thirty-five years ago.' Lomax asked him had he heard 'anybody else play it?' 'Nobody' Kid West assured him. John Lomax turned to Joe Harris: 'What do you do Joe?' 'Play music', came the brief reply. 'In a drinking place?' Lomax asked. 'Yes sir,' said Joe. 'Play and sing?' enquired Lomax. The interview wasn't going well so Joe played the 'Baton Rouge Rag' to a banjo-like theme with a heel-and-toe dance timing. Lomax asked Joe where he had learned it. 'I jus' studied it up myself.' 'Didn't you tell me that somebody else started you on it?' Lomax asked in a reproving tone. 'Yes sir, the boy – he was was a trumpet player and he learned it to me.' 'How long ago?' Lomax asked. 'Been around thirty-three years ago,' Harris replied, explaining in answer to a further question, that this was in Bunkie, Louisiana. Harris revealed a little more of himself when he recorded a song in Creole patois, 'Creole Song' (AFS 3990 B4). This he learned in New Iberia, he explained, thirty-six years before, when he was sixteen.

> Lomax: Did you speak any French Creole
> down there?
> Harris: Yes sir.
> Lomax: What do the words mean?
> Harris: I got no razor, and I got no gun,
> I got no money, and I don't
> want you.

They moved hastily on to the next tune. It was 'Nobody's Business', a version of a traditional theme first popularized by Bessie Smith in 1923 by its full title of "Tain't Nobody's Business If I Do'. On this Joe Harris took the vocal, his voice being stronger than Kid West's, who, on the evidence of the recordings, appears to have been the older of the two men. It was one of three older themes which the duo recorded, the other two were 'Bully Of The Town' and 'Old Hen Cackled And Rooster Laid An Egg'. Although 'I'm Looking For The Bully Of The Town' had been recorded by, for example, the Memphis Jug Band in 1927 it seems unlikely that the Harris-West version was derived from such a source. Part of every songster's repertoire early in the century, this song seems to have survived in the duo's memory in a fragmentary form. Kid West's mandolin playing is sufficiently adept to suggest that he may have been a dab hand at playing the tune in earlier years. 'Old Hen Cackle' was more popular with white communities, a dance theme which was recorded by a number of old-time white musicians. There is some relation to 'Cacklin' Hen And Rooster Too', by The Skillet Lickers, the Atlanta based white string band which featured Kid West's contemporary, Gid Tanner, on fiddle. It was in fact a fiddle showpiece permitting instrumental imitations of the fowl. One might conclude that Kid West had been a member of a string band playing for white dances at

some time in his life, when a fiddle player performed the mimicry.

Though older 'musicianers' than Buddy Woods, both Kid West and Joe Harris played and sang blues. 'Kid West Blues' has an engaging touch of irony which declares his intention to stay single and not be bothered by 'no worryin' kids'. Though Joe Harris's 'East Texas Blues' is fairly conventional with its verses derived from Blind Lemon Jefferson, his reference to getting to Texas 'across the line' emphazises the persistence in the folk memory of the boundary between the States and the Texas Republic. His 'Out East Blues' (AFS 3991 A2), a wistful blues with echoes of earlier recording, includes the line stating that he had 'a woman in Franklin, one in Donaldsonville'. These towns in St Mary's and Ascension Counties respectively have, even today, populations below ten thousand. Bunkie, incidentally, lies south-west of Natchez-on-the-Hill in Avoyellas Parish. The final blues, well played by Kid West, 'A-Natural Blues', is otherwise notable for the inclusion of a verse usually associated with Huddie Ledbetter's 'Good Morning Blues'.

The Shreveport sessions were over, and none of the participating singers ever recorded again. What happened to them?

Almost exactly twenty years later, in the summer of 1960, with my wife Val and Chris Strachwitz, I tried to trace Oscar Woods. It wasn't easy to make any kind of research in Shreveport at that time. The city facilities were still segregated and whites weren't welcome in the tougher black districts. Only a few blocks away the white proprietor of a gas station pretended that he'd never heard of Fannin Street. When we got there, finally, it looked oddly pleasant and shaded, the smaller timber framed cabins that clung to the side of the steep hill appearing very domestic with linen on the washing lines. But a couple of black women soon let us know we weren't wanted.

In 1940 Oscar Woods had given his address as 1403 Patzman Street, with a mailing address at 1529 Alston, and Harris and West were living at 816 Lawrence. This information was not available to us at the time of our own searches, but in the event it would have been of limited use. From one poor lead to another we eventually met up with Alex 'Snooks' Jones, a piano player and one-time musician in a little band which included Woods, Kid West and Joe Harris. Sadly we learned that Alex Jones had been one of the pall-bearers at Buddy Woods' funeral when he died at the age of fifty-three in 1956. Ironically, Kid West, a much older man, survived him by a year, while Joe Harris 'just faded' and nothing more was heard of him. We went out to Club 66 on a deserted, chalky hill-site on the edge of town where the band used to play. A clapboarded, white painted dance-hall, it had lurid murals on the walls and a juke-box in one corner. We tried to imagine it when the Shreveport string musicians provided the music, but in its silent, stuffy, unused space the images were slow in coming.

Notes to Flyright LP 260, 1975

Piccolo Rag
BLIND BOY FULLER

Though popular conceptions of the cultures that have produced the blues tend to concentrate on the Deep South, on the blues of Mississippi, East Texas, Louisiana, Georgia, and Alabama, those States that border them have been no less productive of the music. Arkansas, Missouri, Tennessee, the Carolinas have been the working territories of innumerable blues singers who have travelled east and west as their more southerly brethren have moved northwards. Some remain virtually unknown to all except those who heard them in person in roadside 'jukes' and on street corners – men like Peg Leg from Ashville, North Carolina, who could play two harmonicas simultaneously, one with his nose and one with his lips, or could accompany his own singing; or De Ford Bailey who is known to blues enthusiasts by a couple of obscure titles, but who was famous in Tennessee amongst the wandering singers and blues musicians. Curley Weaver and Fred McMullen, Georgia-born but more frequently to be found in Kentucky or Tennessee, Pink Anderson or Floyd Council – these were a few amongst the many blues singers that were to be heard in the rolling hills of the Piedmont, or meandering with the streams through the wooded valleys. Of this considerable body of folk talent, anonymous and legendary alike, none was more famous than Blind Boy Fuller.

Blind Boy Fuller was the name by which a small, compact Negro guitarist, Fulton Allen, was known to farmers and millhands, tobacco-cultivators and hog-keepers – and to countless thousands of Negroes who bought his records in the Thirties. He was born in North Carolina in 1908, but when he was a boy he moved to Rockingham and there learned to play the guitar. From older country folk he learned field hollers and country rags, traditional songs and traditional blues; played them at suppers and outings much as scores of other Negroes would do, with few forms of ready-made entertainment available. He may have lacked stature but his ability to sing and play earned him many admirers, and jealous ones too. An ugly story is told of an unnamed woman who put acid in the water in which he washed his face; in his early twenties he was cruelly and tragically blinded.

A blind Negro has few opportunities for work – still fewer in times of depression – and the young Fulton Allen had to turn to begging in the streets and obtaining what employment he could as a singer and entertainer. What had been an agreeable leisure activity as well as a means of self-expression now became a way of life. Allen moved to the tobacco-producing centres where there was employment for Negroes and a chance for him to win money given over to tobacco production and he gravitated there. His small frame, his big guitar, his sensitive but sightless features, and his gritty voice were soon known in the 11th Street Bottom and at the corners of Fourth and Vine or Seventh and Patterson. The returning shift-workers who gave him coins soon got to know his name; they called him 'Blind Boy' Fulton – but Blind Boy Fuller ran more easily off the tongue and so his name became. There were so many street beggars in Winston Salem that a city ordinance against begging was introduced. Blind Boy Fuller moved on to Durham. There again he worked in the streets and occasional dances provided him with extra pay. He married Cora Allen and settled down as best he could, making forays to townships along Highway 70 and the Southern railroad: Greensboro, Graham, Burlington, Hillsboro.

He was aided by a local boy named, with parental pride, George Washington, who acted as his eyes – his lead boy. George was pink-complexioned and somewhat freckled, had sandy-coloured hair, and was known, like many Negroes of this skin pigment, as 'Red'. There was a popular league baseball pitcher of the time named 'Bull' Durham and the town of Durham was sometimes called 'Bull City' by way of association. When George Washington recorded by himself he recorded as 'Bull City Red', playing guitar with the obvious and marked influence of Blind Boy Fuller. His guitar playing was competent and his singing good, but they paled somewhat beside his teacher's. He was, however, a superb player of the washboard-and-bells, and with this as his instrument he accompanied Allen, giving constantly varied rhythmic patterns behind the blind man's vocals.

They worked together well and sometimes teamed up with another blues singer working in the same area, Gary Davis. Eventually Gary Davis was to become a preacher and gospel singer but at this time he generally sang blues. Sometimes he showed a leaning towards gospel songs and even encouraged Blind Boy Fuller to sing outside the churches with him, but usually they sang and played in accordance with Fuller's tastes, Davis playing second guitar.

Then, in 1935, Blind Boy Fuller and his companions came to the notice of the mayor of a nearby township and manager of a department store in Durham, J. B. Long, whose esteem in the neighbourhood was such that he could show interest in Negroes with less vulnerability than others slightly less well placed. J. B. Long arranged for Blind Boy Fuller to record, and so com-

menced some five years of steady recording, during which the blind singer made more than 120 sides, had his records appear on more than half-a-dozen labels, and became widely celebrated as a blues singer.

'Evil-hearted Woman' is a typical blues as sung by Blind Boy Fuller at this time. The blues is slow and the voice tough yet sad, whilst the excellent guitar accompaniment is a perfect complement to the words. At this session, in July 1935, Blind Gary Davis was present and he joined Blind Boy Fuller on 'My Brownskin Sugarplum' and 'Keep Away From My Woman' both slow blues with powerful guitars played more or less in unison in Fuller's phrasing but with interesting and telling variations.

It has been said that Blind Boy Fuller was a dirty, a vulgar, a leering singer, but such was in no way the case. He was a rough singer at times and, as with so many singers, there was often a fierce directness in the content of his blues which could offend the prudish. Like that of many another blues singer his sexual imagery was rich and uninhibited; his expression was a natural one and he did not couch his ideas in vague or delicate phraseology. Were this the sum total of his blues there might indeed be some grounds for criticism, but in fact he drew from every aspect of underprivileged life with which he was familiar: from the pawnshop to the jail-house; from the bed to the graveyard; from love to disenchantment; from entertainment to sickness and death. To all his themes he devoted the same attention, the same sincerity, the same lack of sophistication or affectation. He had no need to be salacious on the one hand or sentimental on the other; the greatness of his folk artistry largely lay in the integrity of his self-expression. In 'Evil-hearted Woman', 'My Brownskin Sugarplum' and 'Keep Away From My Woman' there is love, there is desire, there is menace, there is jealousy, there is disappointment, and there is humour. Above all there is honesty and the artistry of a folk singer of rare calibre.

Far from being a singer of narrow resources, Blind Boy Fuller drew from all that was a part of his immediate experience both in content and in music 'Cat Man Blues' begins:

> *Went home last night heard a noise, I asked*
> *my wife 'What was that?' (repeat)*
> *Says 'Man don't be so 'spicious, that ain't*
> *nothin' but a cat.'*
>
> *Lord I travelled this world all over, taken all*
> *kinds of chance, (repeat)*
> *But I never come home before, seen a cat*
> *wearin' a pair of pants.*

Another song concludes:

> *'Oh wifey, please tell me, explain this thing*
> *to me,*
> *'Stupid, oh foolish, cain't you never see?*
> *That's nothing but a cabbage-head where*
> *you head ought to be.'*
> *I've travelled this world over, ten thousand*
> *miles or more,*
> *But a moustache on a cabbage-head I never did*
> *see it before.*

The latter is from 'Our Goodman' or 'The Drunken Cuckold's Song', a traditional song which has been known in England since the mid-eighteenth century and was widely current in the Appalachians a century later: 'Cat Man Blues' is the Negro blues-singer's variant of it. But if 'Cat Man' draws from the common heritage of Negro and white song, 'Hungry Calf Blues' or 'Mojo Hidin' Woman' come essentially from Negro life. 'Hungry Calf Blues' employs the rural metaphorical imagery frequently employed in the blues and immediately communicated to its original hearers, whilst 'Mojo Hidin' Woman' is drawn from the folklore and popular super-

stition of the country Negro, whose regard and respect for the occult is especially concentrated on the power of the 'mojo hand' charms made in Louisiana and still sold in shops from Houston to Detroit.

Blind Boy Fuller played for all kinds of functions, particularly country suppers where lively guitar and washboard groups provided the music, which had its roots in the early banjo and guitar rags. He could 'pick a low rag' himself and the punning 'Piccolo Rag' is proof of his instrumental virtuosity and the crisp, exciting washboard rhythms of 'Red' Washington – 'Oh Red', as they called him after the title of a popular Race song. The origins of 'Piccolo Rag' are to be found in the words, the traditional guiding cries to the mules and horses appearing in the lines:

> *Can't stop doin' what you doin' to me, mama,*
> *just go run me wild,*
> *Can't stop doin' what you doin' to me, baby,*
> *mean just what I say,*
> *Say when I'm on the farm hollerin' 'Whoa,*
> *Haw, Gee!'*
> *My gal's in town hollerin' 'Who wants me?'*
> *Can't stop doin' what you doin' to me, you*
> *just goin' run me wild.*

A number of variations of country dance tunes and rags appeared in Blind Boy Fuller's recordings, spirited performances which proved him to be far beyond the technical limitations of the majority of blues singers, very inventive in his improvisations and fluent in his ideas. 'Oh Red' accompanied him on a number of these, sometimes playing the washboard with a pair of forks instead of the usual thimbles, as on 'She's a Truckin' Little Baby'. A number of such rags were in sixteen-bar form; others were more complicated, in particular the unusual 'Big Leg Woman Gets My Pay' with its verses that vary from twenty to twenty-two bars.

In the mid-Thirties a tall and gangling young Negro who had been blinded, on different occasions, in both eyes, frequently played harmonica for Blind Boy Fuller. His name was Sanders Terrell, though in the customary manner in which names were changed and adapted he was known as Sonny Terry. Later he was to be a celebrated harmonicist, playing in the company of Walter 'Brownie' McGhee, who even at this time was playing in the streets of townships between Tennessee and their own territory. Later, too, Sonny Terry liked it so much that he recorded it as 'Custard Pie' a number of times himself in later years. On this his voice and harmonica are so much a continuous melodic line that the 'harp' appears to sing the falsetto '. .'fore you give it all away . . .' in his solo.

As a result of his extensive recording Blind Boy Fuller was in demand in the country districts between Durham and Memphis, Tennessee, and wherever he travelled he was exceedingly popular as a singer. The hundred recordings that he had made had in no way impaired his style and he made no concessions to commercialism, if indeed he could have done. In fact his last recordings included some of the finest in his whole career. That he remained close to the roots of the blues is clearly evident in the echoes of the field holler that are to be heard in his recording of 'Little Woman You're So Sweet'. This is an eight-bar blues so close to the field cries that more than ten years later it was recorded as one of Frederic Ramsey Jr, who heard the Alabama sharecropper, Horace Sprott, singing it as he worked his land, in a version clearly derived from the recording. And in the ringing chords played in unison to his hollered words there is something chillingly primitive in Fuller's record.

19 June 1940, was the date of Blind Boy Fuller's last appearances on record. Such a recording as his 'Lost Lover Blues' is pure folk poetry, moving and sad, the blues of a great artist:

And I went down to that freight depot
And that freight train came rollin' by
Lord and I sure ain't got no lovin' baby now
And I sure ain't got no lovin' baby now.
(refrain)
And I went off in that far distant land,
I wasn't there long before I got a telegram –
what did it say? –
Sayin' 'man won't you please come home.
Now man won't you please come home.'
Then I went back home and looked upon
the bed
And that best old friend I had was dead.
(refrain)

Now I'm sorry, sorry, sorry to my heart,
But that best old friends some day must part.
(refrain)

There was a tragic presentiment in Fuller's last titles: 'My left side jumps, baby, and my flesh begin to crawl', he sang in his last recording 'Night Rambling Woman', and there seemed to be a double meaning. Soon after, he developed kidney trouble and had to enter hospital for an operation that winter. Unhappily the operation was unsuccessful and he died under the anaesthetic.

Blind Boy Fuller had many disciples, many followers. Buddy Moss and Ralph Willis were two of the best known, but closer to him was 'Little Boy Fuller' – Richard Welley Trice – and Floyd 'Dipper Boy' Council, the 'Devil's Daddy-in-law'. Their recordings and those of 'Bull City Red' Washington, were unashamedly based on Fulton Allen's though none achieved his greatness nor his singular qualities.

Notes to Philips BBL 7512, 1962

Fulton Allen (Blind Boy Fuller) was born Wadesborough, North Carolina, in 1908, and died Durham, North Carolina, 13 February 1941.

Fox Chase
SONNY TERRY, FULLER'S ACCOMPANIST

It is one of the curious paradoxes of the improving status of the Negro in American society that the increasing interest in his art form, and particularly those of jazz and blues, is resented by a great many Negro intellectuals. To refer to the Negro as a born entertainer is to rub salt into a gaping wound, which though beginning to heal, still festers easily. Negro leaders – 'Race Men or Race Heroes' as their people call them – far from being proud of the great musical, terpsichorean and histrionic gifts of a multitude of coloured persons, frequently ignore them. Blackface and 'nigger minstrel' shows, plantation dances and banjo playing Uncle Toms, Brer Rabbits and golliwog sambos rankle in the mind. Such are the associations that the concepts of the Negro entertainer and Negro folk lore still induce and with them jazz and Negro folk song are often linked. Shadows of slavery still flit in the darker recesses of the racial memory and for many the cap-touching, lick-spittle servility of the plantation worker and the crude, gauche, superstition-ridden speech of the uneducated Southern 'boy' is inextricably linked with the arts which arose as a form of escape from them.

Reflections of the attitude to the folk heritage largely adopted by the intellectuals are mirrored in the approach of the Northern, generally more educated Negro to the unsophisticated arts of his Southern brethren. The shame that he feels when confronted with aspects of their behaviour, trends of thought and modes of speech, which to him let down the race and are a barrier to its progress, is filtering to the Southern communities and the coloured people of the backward states are themselves striving to cast off the mantle of their own provincial-ism. This rapidly spreading attitude has had its effect on the creative music of the Negro populace. In the Northern cities the new jazz forms have a more intellectual basis; the music is significantly cool, and emotional feeling, whilst present, is well controlled. In Southern towns the brash, noisy, superficially extrovert music of rhythm and blues copied via the radio networks – there are many Negro disc jockeys specialising in this music, whose easy flow of jive patter makes them popular with both coloured and white – and the phonograph records, is assumed by local groups: blues in the country idiom is fast disappearing. But it has not gone yet, and the issue of the LP entitled 'Folk Blues' and featuring Sonny Terry (Vogue LDE 137) is of great importance because it shows that this music is for some still a small but vital living force. Changing economic circumstances, improved educational facilities, the exodus from the country to the towns, may eventually bring about the complete disappearance of folk blues of this nature, but it is earnestly to be hoped that whilst the opportunities still present themselves this great music will continue to be engraved in the wax. When the battle is at last won and parity of esteem for racial and religious denominations in the United States is finally secured, the Negro people will be able to look back with pride on the art of their predecessors and will be free to embrace such folk music into their own artistic heritage.

Sonny Terry has been more generally known as an accompanist than as a solo player and his magnificent harmonica playing can be heard on many fine sides recorded by Huddie Ledbetter, Brownie McGhee and Blind Boy Fuller. In recent years he has, however, recorded a number of fierce performances with his own washboard group, and these have given collectors a better opportunity to study his technique and brilliant style. The most outstanding feature of this is Terry's ability to alternate vocal passages with phrases played on the harmonica with such skill as to avoid any break in the beat. In itself this could be developed as a trick, but quite apart from it he is a technical virtuoso. By slurring, overblowing, tongue vibrato, half sealing apertures with tongue and finger, Sonny manipulates the instrument as if it were his own voice – which in fact is just what it becomes. With his outstanding ability he makes the harmonica a perfect vehicle for his deeply expressive blues improvisations which are played with great intensity of feeling and emotional power.

Born in the tobacco producing state of North Carolina, Sonny Terry was taught to play the harmonica – the mouth-harp – by his father. It was from his father that he learned to play the 'Fox Chase'. In common with many Negroes in the coastal States, Terry *père* kept hounds for hunting. He had six, and on his harmonica would imitate the thrills of the chase.

'Down South, my father get on a horse y'know,' explains Sonny in his recording, 'Ride the horse an' the fox chase'd be goin'.' 'He used to play a li'l harp y'know, I say "Pa, how do you do that?" He say, "Some day I'll be dead an' gone. You grow up and you can do the 'Fox Chase'." I say, "I play it a li'il bit, I play it like dis."' – demonstrating his immature style. His father told him: 'That ain't no way to play the 'Fox Chase'. Why don't you play it like I play?' 'Hear my father play the 'Fox Chase'.'

The baying of the dogs, the cries of 'Catch Him!' the fury of the chase, are captured in the wailing of the notes and the underlying pulse of the rhythm. To his father Terry

says, 'You tellin' d'truth. You tell me to play like you play, now I play like I play the "Fox Chase",' and into his playing he introduces the excited squeals of the pup hounds and the growls of the older dogs until the piece closes with the plaintive cries of the dying fox. 'The Fox Chase' is a virtuoso piece of a type which is common in many lands. But it was in playing such tunes which strained his technique to the utmost that Terry learned the possibilities of his instrument.

'I played the harp, I play the harmonica ever since I was fourteen years old, an' I play when I was nine years old, but I went, got profession playin' the blues. An' now I can still play the blues,' he explains in 'Talking about the Blues'. He became an itinerant folk singer, playing his blues in the streets and earning a precarious living by casual labour or by begging 'on 28th Street', by 'the brick wa'house', in Barrack Street Market or on the 'Big Four'. His repertoire increased:

'Way down in North Carolina y'know, I used to sing the blues. People used to throw me nickels and dimes and they say "Sonny, what you doin'?" I say I play the "Fox Chase" an' I play the blues.' With his own improvised cries he was playing and singing traditional folk tunes, including the celebrated railroad construction song, 'John Henry'. With the fine guitar playing of Alec Stewart providing a rhythmic foundation, Sonny sings this in a wild, rough manner, scrambling the verses and interpolating a spoken commentary the while. His harp is the perfect complement to his voice and with tremendous swing he plays his version of the wind-sucking hammer of Polly Ann, John Henry's woman who 'drove steel like a man'.

He may never have worked with the section gang, but Sonny almost certainly worked as a field hand. The inclusion of

'Moaning and Mourning Blues' on this LP is of great importance for it is the nearest to the field 'Moan' which has yet appeared in Britain. The moan is the precursor of the blues, the outpouring of a man's heart hummed between closed lips with scarce a word uttered except a despairing 'Lord, Lord!' Sometimes the words do break to the surface . . . 'Lord, boy, I get to moanin' sometimes . . . I moan in the mornin', Lord an' I moan at night . . . ' But the anguished cries punctuating the hummed phrases that follow the melodic pattern of the blues are more eloquent than any words.

Most of the Negroes who lived primarily by singing and playing the blues wandered slowly from State to State. 'Red River' is a song of the levee grading camps on this great tributary of the Mississippi. To the tune which has been recorded elsewhere as 'Crow Jane' Sonny sings a ballad which recalls the untamed life of the camps. Terry's own unsettled career, and the difficulties of waging a ceaseless battle against the flooding and silting of the river.

Which way, which way, does that blood-red
    river run?
Honey turn my back door to the risin' sun.

I just stopped here honey, to catch ma lovin'
    wind.
Soon as the weather break, honey, I'm up an'
    gone again.

Go down to the camp, an' tell ma Brother
    Bill,
That woman he love is sho' gonna get him
    killed.

Well the dumper, tol' the loader, 'Oh send me
    six feet of clay,'
Well the Blood River rises six feet ev'ry day.

In the levee camps it is the loader who fills the skiff with clay and rubble, the muleskinner who brings the cart to the levee and the dumper who unloads the material for the grader to build the artificial river bank.

In 1933 Sonny was playing with Blind Boy Fuller in South Carolina. A year later they were to be found in Memphis. Inevitably they gravitated North as all blues men do. Blind Boy died in 1940 and Sonny Terry was himself now stricken with almost total blindness. When Leadbelly found him in 1943 he was ill and destitute. With Martha his wife, Leadbelly took Sonny to live with them in New York and supported them all whilst he worked at the Village Vanguard. Sonny recorded a number of sides with Leadbelly (issued on Melodisc) and learned much from their association. They recorded together in 1944 Leroy Carr's beautiful blues 'In the Evenin'', a favourite also with Big Bill Broonzy, but it was unissued. Here Terry sings and plays the tune again and if his singing has neither the range nor the feeling of those consummate artists there is great poignancy in his blues phrasing on the harp, and Alec Stewart's subtle guitar is not unworthy of Blind Blake himself.

'Mr Leadbelly, me an' him we had no fallin' out,' says Sonny, and he felt the death of his companion keenly. Leadbelly was an enigmatic character, unpredictable to those who knew him slightly, but a generous and constant friend to Sonny Terry.

Well me an' Leadbelly, I done tol' you people
    he was my lovin' frien'.
I done tol' you people, Oh Lord, he was my
    lovin' frien'.
When I hadn't got the price of a bottle of
    whiskey,
He say, 'Here Sonny, Get me a bottle o' gin.'

Bye-bye Lead. this is all I got to say,
Bye-bye Leadbelly, this is all I got to say.
I gonna tell you people he was the same thing
    ev'ry day.

Today Sonny Terry records under his own name. He is a good singer; a harmonica player without peer. He has come a long way since the day when his mother spoke to him as a child: 'Well,' she says, 'Sonny Terry, you too big a devil to be so foolish and wild.' A devil he is, a wild singer, a playing fool – and a great folk artist; one of whom both his mother, and his Mother Race, have good reason to be proud.

Music Mirror, July 1958

Milk Cow Blues

JAMES KOKOMO ARNOLD

In the blues, as in other arts, it is not by any means the finest artist that gets the greatest recognition, nor are the most successful singers necessarily the greatest ones. There are many reasons that account for the popularity of certain singers, and it is fortunate that in some instances the best are also the best known even if this is no rule and cannot be the basis of critical assessment. In some instances the reputations of the best-known and best-loved blues artists have been founded upon the early success of a single, outstanding item that has brought an extension of the idiom, a new interpretation, or in some other way has filled a gap in the recorded music. One can think of many obvious examples: Jim Jackson and his 'Kansas City Blues'; Leroy Carr and 'How Long How Long'; Tampa Red and 'Tight Like That'. The outstanding success of his composition 'Milk Cow Blues', and its backing of 'Old Original Kokomo Blues' established Kokomo Arnold as one of the most popular of blues singers of the Thirties and a major singer in the Decca company stable.

Few but a handful of blues singers rate any attention in the jazz histories and these are drawn from the same limited list of names. Even Marshall Stearns and Rudi Blesh, writers who give more attention than many to musical forms related to jazz which are not strictly within the music itself, make no mention of Kokomo Arnold and not surprisingly he does not appear in Leonard Feather's *Encyclopedia*. Hugues Panassié in his *Dictionary of Jazz* is singular in according recognition to the singer, considering him to be 'one of the greatest blues singers who has been recorded. His singing has the roughness, the strength and the purity of the Mississippi countryside; his playing is no less impressive – it is so rich that it gives the impression of two guitars instead of one', and Panassié continues to write of his 'sounds of great beauty, with frequent glissandi and inflexions of extraordinary subtlety'. In his book *The Country Blues,* Samuel B. Charters makes brief reference to Arnold, comparing him with Blind Boy Fuller as having the 'same kind of self-confidence' and acknowledging his ability: 'Kokomo was a fine guitar player, using a bottleneck on his little finger in a frenzied rhythmic style. The basic rhythm was almost lost in a blur of rhythmic elaborations. For two or three years their records sold with about the same success, but Arnold had less variety than Fuller and Decca was forced to drop him.'

Both writers have given fair, if short, assessments of Arnold although it is by no means easy to make a direct comparison with Fuller, for whilst they certainly shared the same confidence, their styles were very different. Fuller, of course, made a dozen sides for Decca and had an energetic agent finding new companies for him. Arnold's ninety-seven issued titles recorded exlusively for Decca make for formidable competition one would have thought. Most blues enthusiasts have considered that Arnold came from Mississippi, the bottleneck style of guitar having been considered a Northern Mississippi tradition exemplified by Eddie 'Son' House, Robert Johnson, Muddy Waters – and Kokomo Arnold; Black Ace, too, a deduction I made myself which was equally unfounded as I was to learn to my surprise when finally meeting him in Fort Worth, Texas. It was not until Jacques Demetre, the inexhaustible blues authority who writes for *Jazz Hot*, finally discovered Kokomo Arnold in Chicago in 1959 that some of his story came to light.

James Arnold came to record with reluctance, and as reluctantly he agreed to talk of his life. Few blues singers could be more retiring in their retirement; few more enigmatic than Arnold. But Demetre's enthusiasm and energetic interviewing melted his resistance temporarily and he talked freely of his life. James Arnold was born in the small township of Lovejoy which lies south of Atlanta, Georgia, 15 February 1901. His family were farmers and as a small child he was introduced to the work, but at the age of ten began to play the guitar in his spare time. His cousin, John Wiggs, was an accomplished guitarist and it was from him that he learned the rudiments of his playing. Wiggs used the 'knife' style, sliding the blade across the strings, and Arnold copied him. Later he met another guitar player who showed him how to play with a bottleneck on his little finger. But Arnold's style was unusual in that he wore the bottleneck on his *right hand*. He is left handed and learned to play the guitar picking with his left hand and holding the neck of the fingerboard in his right.

At the age of eighteen James Arnold left Georgia and moved to New York State, obtaining work in a steel mill in Buffalo. He became an accomplished steel worker and except for a brief period in the Thirties has worked all his life in steel mills since moving North in 1919. After ten years in Buffalo he moved to Chicago and settled there. He had continued to play the guitar throughout his stay in Buffalo, working in the evening in clubs and at small joints. He followed a similar mode of life in Chicago and was eventually discovered by Joe McCoy, who drew the attention of Mayo Williams to the very able blues singer. They invited him to record, but Arnold had no mind to do so.

He preferred to remain fairly anonymous, and had his reasons. During the prohibition period he had developed a profitable sideline in putting a country tradition to urban use by making moonshine liquor in a bathtub still. The demands of his customers continued after repeal and James Arnold was not anxious to relinquish this source of income.

Joe McCoy and Mayo Williams were persistent in urging him to record and finally, in the summer of 1934, they induced him to come to the studio. The comedy situation that resulted was explained to Jacques Demetre:

'I was doing well with my moonshine business, making it in the basement. I always had customers coming to buy it when I returned from the steel mill, and I didn't wish to leave it. You see I couldn't leave my basement, otherwise I would lose my customers. When they took me to the studio first – that was Joe McCoy and Mayo Williams – they let me wait about for hours because the studio wasn't free. So I said to myself "What the hell's the use of this; I better go home to see to my customers and give them that moonshine." So I went out of the studio without recording and came straight back home; I asked the landlady to tell everybody I'm not at home. Yes, they came to look for me, but I was in the basement making my moonshine and I was hearing the landlady answering them and telling them I was outside. You know I was never interested in making records and I always preferred to live a quiet life; just unknown in my basement . . . Well, I met Joe a few days later in the street and he took me to the studio again. You know, there were several people there that time, and they didn't let me go until I cut my record!'

The result of this *force majeure* was 'Milk Cow Blues', and as Arnold opened up with his urgent guitar playing and began to sing

'Hollerin' Good Mornin', I said blues how do you do . . . ?' Decca had a winning record on their hands. The opening verses were in the twelve-bar three-line structure but played with a dexterity of bottleneck guitar playing that had never been equalled on record before. Then the pattern changed to a four-line structure on the twelve-bar base:

> . . . *Now you can read out your hymn-*
>   *book, preach out your Bible,*
> *Fall down on your knees and pray the*
>   *Good Lord will help you –*
> *'cause you gonna be, you gonna be – my*
>   *help some day;*
> *Mammo, if you cain't quit your sinnin';*
>   *please quit your low-down ways.*
>
> *Says I woke up this mawnin' and I looked*
>   *out doors –*
> *Says I know my mammy's missin' pretty*
>   *milk cow, Lord by the way she lows,*
> *Lord if you see my milk cow buddy,*
>   *please drive her home,*
> *Says I ain't had no milkin' butter*
>   *mammo,*
> *Lord since-a my cow been gone . . .*

With the appearance of 'Milk Cow Blues' a number of other versions soon appeared and before long every blues singer was introducing the blues or singing a variant; on a bovine theme – wild cows, bull cows, lowing heifers succeeded each other and Nappy Lamare even sang a pathetic version on a Bob Crosby Bobcats record. Arnold, however, was at this time using other singers' material as well as his own and apart from the various bovine themes used by Texas singers such as Alex Moore and Bert Mays at an earlier date, it is quite likely that he derived inspiration from the items featured then by Big Bill Broonzy. Be that as it may, it was his own 'Milk Cow Blues' which had such a resounding success, a success equalled by the backing of 'Old Original Kokomo Blues'. This was a blues

with a counting theme which has the natural resolution of verses that enumerated from one to twelve, recalling the 'dozens' and any number of children's recitatives. The verse was chanted, the refrain declaimed against fine guitar work:

> . . . *Now six and one is seven mama, seven*
>   *and one is eight*
> *You mess around here pretty mama, you*
>   *gonna make me late –*
> *Cryin' oooh, baby don't you wanna go?*
> *Back to Eleven Light City, to Sweet old*
>   *Kokomo?*
>
> *Says I told you mammo when you first fell*
>   *across my bed*
> *You been drinkin' that ole bad whiskey and*
>   *talkin' out your head . . .*   (refrain)
>
> *N' I don't drink because I'm dry mama, don't*
>   *drink because I'm blue,*
> *The reason I drink pretty mama, I can't get*
>   *along with you . . .*
>
> *Now eight and one is nine mama, nine and one*
>   *is ten*
> *You mess around here pretty mama, I'm*
>   *gonna take you in . . .*
>
> *Now ten and one is eleven mama, eleven and*
>   *one is twelve*
> *You mess around here pretty mama, you*
>   *catch a lot of hell*
> *Cryin' oooh, baby don't you wanna go*
> *Back to Eleven Light City, to Sweet old*
>   *Kokomo?*

Many versions of 'Kokomo Blues' were made by other singers – some like Frank Busby's, similar to Arnold's – others, like Willie 'Boodle-It' Wright's, quite different. Generally they were recorded as 'Eleven Light City Blues' and in all instances the strange phrase of 'Eleven Light City', apparently unrelated to any of the listed nicknames for towns, remained. Arnold explained the significance of the words in part to Jacques Demetre, telling him that Eleven Light City was the name of a drug store near 35th and State where a girl with whom he was consorting was working. The store sold a brand of coffee labelled 'Koko' and it was from this, with an alliteration of his own, that he devised the phrase of 'sweet Kokomo'. Mayo Williams however saw the commercial possibilities in exploiting the association of the brand name with Arnold and dubbed him 'Kokomo Arnold' for this and his subsequent records. He thought that Big Bill Broonzy's belief that he had owned a grocery store stemmed from this, for in fact he had never owned or worked in one. There still remain certain problems not wholly explained by this – not least of which is the significance of Eleven Light City as a name itself, or whether in fact a brand of coffee called 'Koko' was so marketed.

This first session was in some ways Arnold's best. His playing is furious and quite outstanding; superb on 'Back to the Woods'. This item, though credited to himself, was identical in the lyrics to Charlie Spand's Paramount recording with its excellent and poetic words:

> *Going down to the river, set flat on the*
> *   ground   (repeat)*
> *My heart strikes sorrow, the tears come rollin'*
> *down.*

On this Arnold encourages himself with cries of 'Play·it Mister Kokomo . . . I'm goin' in to fiddlin' now . . . now get ready to pick it up there, and holler a while . . .', later referring to himself as 'Mister Koko' showing that the name was at least agreed upon at the session. This rhetoric adds vitality to the recording and it is a pity that he seldom did this on record again. Most of the elements of his later recordings were to be heard in these first items, and 'Milk Cow Blues' used a tune which became uniquely his own and to which he returned time after time in such recordings as 'Black Mattie',

'Head Cuttin' Blues', 'Broke Man Blues', 'Back on the Job', and very many others. Not infrequently they used the same guitar phrases too, or simple variants on them, and yet the fascination of his records remains. Undoubtedly there is justification in the suggestion that he was repetitive – yet he was not monotonous. The blues audience that bought nearly a hundred of his recordings were clearly in no way dissatisfied, but whilst recognizing the high quality of his guitar playing, its very personal sound, as distinctive and instantly identifiable as Tampa Red's or Tommy McClennan's, one is led to enquire where else his attraction lay.

As a singer of the blues Kokomo Arnold was seldom disturbingly sad; more often he was fiercely declamatory and he tended to shout but not strain his words. This caused him to pitch his voice an octave higher than his normal speaking voice and very frequently he would raise this still further with a falsetto cry – often of 'please!' – which imparted a shrill intensity to his phrases. As his voice fell, his words resolved into a glottal hum which he would sing in tune to the guitar. Barely audible at times, this curious throat humming is nearly always present and gives a link between the whining of the guitar and the singing of the words that makes voice and instrument one. Musically he was interesting, but his tendency to repeat himself might have been self-destructive were he not an unusual and original composer of blues verses. Undoubtedly his appeal lay very largely in the consistently apposite content of his verses to popular feeling and common experience.

The personification of the blues occurred frequently in his songs and indicated in its unusual forms that this was both known by him and shared with his listeners, as in his 'My blues fell this morning and my love come falling down' in his initial 'Milk Cow Blues'. Or take the lines of 'Sundown Blues' which give new shape to an old theme:

*Now let me tell you mama why you treat me
    so mean   (repeat)*
*Ask you for a cup of coffee and you brought me
    gasoline.*

Now you pack your suitcase and hit the door,
*Wind done change and I don't want you no
    more,*
*I said Good-bye blues, blues why don't you
    leave me alone?*
*Says you been my best friend, ever since my
    gal bin gone.*

or again, in 'Coffin Blues', taking the familiar 'going to the River' theme:

Now I'm goin' out on Lake Michigan,
I'm gonna kneel down and say my prayer,
*Now if the blues overtake me, you goin' to
    find me in this lake somewhere.*

It was Arnold's particular technique to remould blues verses that had become comparatively standard and, by changing their inferences, to invest them with new life and meaning both for himself and his listeners. 'Backfence Picket Blues' for example, uses verse patterns from widely different sources and concludes with a verse very charactistically his own:

*Now I'm goin' get me a picket, right off-a my
    back fence,   (repeat)*
*And I'm go'n whup my woman, clean until
    she learn some sense*

*Now you know I'm your manager and you
    sure got to obey my rules,   (repeat)*
*Says you ain't no schoolgirl, you sure God
    ain't nobody's fool.*

*Now you sing just like Moses; walk just like
    the Good Lord above,   (repeat)*
*I bin had a gang o' women, but you the only
    one I really love.*

He would often use the same verse in different blues or, rather, the same base for a new verse, so on 'Black Mattie' the second

and third verses of 'Backfence Picket Blues' become:

*Now I know I'm my mamma's schoolboy an'
    I sho' got to obey her rule,   (repeat)*
Said I had a gang o' women – that is something I ain't learned at school.

whilst in 'Back on the Job' the theme recurs in different form:

*Now you acted bad, and you didn't obey the
    rules,   (repeat)*
*'Cause I'm back home again, I'm goin'
    t'take you to a brand new school.*

Certain ideas persist in Kokomo Arnold's recordings, the notion of the 'Fool man' being frequent enough to commend itself to the attention of Cecil Collins. 'My Well is Dry', already quoted, has the interesting lines:

*Says I ain't gonna be no fool man, I'm gonna
    hold up my head and walk,*
*Says ma mama get a chance to see me, but
    she won't hear me when I talk.*

Women in fact are the cause of 'the fool man' as he reiterates in 'Lonesome Road Blues':

*Says now I'm not crazy, sure God ain't
    nobody's fool,*
*Before I let you women mistreat me, I'll eat
    just like a Georgia mule.*

and he emphasizes his point in a blues entitled 'Fool Man Blues':

*Don't you be no fool man, think you the only
    one your woman loves,   (repeat)*
*There's other men wearin' britches will make
    her moan like a turtle dove*

*Now don't you be no fool man, now well it's
    time that you should wake up,   (repeat)*
*Cause you cain't satisfy no woman when you
    filled her in her cup.*

As with many of his blues this is bitterly sung and Arnold was clearly disillusioned with his women. The last line brings in another far from inconsiderable element, however, for his pronunciation of the words is such as to give a very much more pungent meaning to the lyric. In spite of the quantity of so-called 'obscenity' in the lyrics of records in the Decca listing, such a line sung straight would almost certainly have been forbidden. Even so, 'Sissy Man Blues' was uncompromising:

> *I woke up this morning with my pa-grinder*
> *in ma hand,   (repeat)*
> *If you can't send me no woman, please send*
> *me a sissy man.*

The Texas pianist Edwin Pickens recalled the item twenty-five years later : 'God I thought they'd put him inside for that!' although Pickens recorded for me 'The Ma Grinder', first cousin to the 'dozens', which is amongst the rougher of unrecorded barrel-house songs. 'The Dirty Dozens' was recorded by Arnold soon after his 'Sissy Man' but as the violence and bitterness of many of his blues suggests, he was singing in terms that he knew rather than for any 'special' market. The sexual element of many blues is essentially a part of its form; not sung specifically for the 'parties' of college freshmen.

In Texas, Kokomo Arnold's blues are particularly well known and Mack McCormick has listed a large number that are in Lightnin' Hopkins's repertoire in some form or another. Either by sympathy or by design Arnold made frequent reference to specific places in his blues and these locations must have added to their popularity in the areas. In 'Long and Tall' he sings of a woman 'shaped like a cannonball, says I found that woman where the Southern cross the Yellow Dog' – a reference to Moorhead Mississippi, and follows this with the line 'Then I heard the church bells callin'

way out on Dago Hill . . .' which is a reference to St Louis. 'I got a woman from Texas, got one from New Orleans' he sings in another blues, and in still another:

> *Says I did love my woman, better than a cow*
> *loves to chew her cud,   (repeat)*
> *But that fool got mad, and moved back to the*
> *Piney Woods.*

On 'Shine on Moon' he sings the familiar 'Red River Blues' with an erratic geography:

> *Now tell me pretty mama, which-a-way do*
> *that Red River run?   (repeat)*
> *She reaches from the Atlantic ocean, clean*
> *down to the Risin' sun.*

> *Now the big boat, she's up the river, sittin'*
> *way out on a bank of sand,   (repeat)*
> *If she don't soon strike the water, I do swear*
> *that boat will never land.*

> *Now the river, she's gone to risin' and spread*
> *it all over the land,   (repeat)*
> *And she reaches from Memphis, clean down*
> *into the darkened land.*

This recording, one of his most poetic, is sung in an unusually restrained voice, very similar to the young Brownie McGhee and scarcely recognizable as that of Kokomo Arnold. His guitar, too is played 'straight' – comparatively rare for the master of the bottleneck style, and Peetie Wheatstraw, his companion on the record, dominates with his piano playing. Such records, which gave immediacy to the content of his blues for people throughout the Negro world, must have greatly added to his popularity, whilst the appeal of 'Chain Gang Blues', 'Bo Weevil Blues', 'Hobo Blues', 'Policy Wheel Blues' or 'Mean Old Twister' for their content, is too obvious to require further particularization. It is of considerable interest however to learn that Kokomo Arnold remained in the North throughout the Thirties. If this statement to Jacques Demetre is true, and there seems little reason to doubt it, his sense of association was uncanny. Perhaps less easy to accept is his angry assertion that he sang and recorded entirely for the money that it brought him, for his records reveal an undoubted delight in his own playing and singing. The significance of his statement probably lies more in his agreeing to record instead of remaining in the obscurity that he preferred.

How influential was Kokomo Arnold? Stylistically one finds that he had his parallels rather than his immediate influences and the personal influence on any Mississippi style would appear to be non-existent. But he *did* have such an influence – to a degree at any rate – on Robert Johnson, for example, a rather more eclectic singer than is generally believed, his 'Sweet Home Chicago' and his famous 'I Believe I'll Dust My Broom' amongst others deriving from Arnold: the latter being adapted from 'Sagefield Woman Blues' and, in turn, taken from Johnson by Elmore James. Few singers came very close to his style, however, and he worked with very few. Most of the Arnold accompaniments that have been suggested are now disproved, but he did work closely with Peetie Wheatstraw. The partnership was excellent in some instances; 'Broke Man Blues', for example, shows clearly how the introductory phrase that each man had chosen for his trademark blended in perfectly. But 'Mister Charlie' is unfortunate, out of tune and ending on a strident discord. At their best they made an excellent partnership although Arnold told Jacques Demetre that he preferred to play with Roosevelt Sykes or Joshua Altheimer.

For the most part Kokomo Arnold was to be heard at his best when by himself, and if there was a certain tendency to repeat himself in some items he would come round magnificently with such an item as 'Sister Jane, 'Cross the Hall'.

Old Sister Jane right across the hall,
She got good stuff but no mule in her stall
Old Sister Jane right across the hall
She drinks her liquor and she sure God,
has a ball.
She got a kitchenette and an apartment too,
She don't do nothin but ballyhoo.
Now when I sleep, I lay flat on my back,
You come in drunk with one of those wise
old cracks
From Sister Jane, right across the hall,
When she gets full of her liquor you know
she gotta have a ball.

Although virtually all his recordings were twelve-bar blues he often favoured the four-line form which employed a couplet sung in the first four bars and a two-line refrain sung in the remaining eight bars. These appear to have given him more scope instrumentally and the swing generated by his remarkable guitar work on 'Sister Jane' would be the envy of any jazz musician. The rhythmic impetus and the polyrhythmic complexities with which he embellished such performances made them outstanding examples in the blues idiom. 'Down and Out Blues' was another example of this high order:

Says I ain't got no airplane, ain't got no
automobile,
I ain't got no money, guess I'll have to rob and
steal,
'Cause when I wake up in the mornin' I
cain't eat a decent meal,
I had bad luck in my family, I guess you
know just how I feel.

whilst one of his most wholly satisfying recordings with Peetie Wheatstraw, 'Running Drunk Again', is a powerfully swinging piece with guitar and piano stomping in a barrelhouse music entirely devoid of pretensions yet in its way without parallel. 'eeh . . . let's play it now . . . play it there now Peetie . . .' Kokomo cries during an instrumental chorus before hollering his last verses:

*Says now mammo don't need-a you keep
    raisin hell,
I know you been boogie-woogie'n by the
    way you smell,
Now here I come, running drunk again,
Don't you hear me knock mammo, please
    open up and let me in.*

*Now I'm gonna tell all you men you
    better work fast,
These Chicago women really shake a
    wicked yas-yas-yas,
Now here I come, running drunk again,
Don't you hear me knockin' mammo,
    please open up and let me in.*

Kokomo Arnold was a blues guitarist of
remarkable facility, and one with a very personal style and means of expression. He had
the capacity to compose unusual blues and
to give entirely new value to old ones. When
his musical invention flagged his blues ideas
were often still of a high order, and he had
the ability to project himself into other
people's physical and mental situations so
that his resultant blues had real meaning for
them. And at certain times he combined all
these qualities to make some of the most outstanding blues on record. He was not however a musician totally and completely; only
for a very short period did he give up his
work in the steel mills and in 1941 he was
happy to return to this mode of life. Sick of
the music world in the sense of business he
gave up music altogether; when, years later,
he was found by Jacques Demetre he was at
first an unwilling subject for interview.
'What is past is dead, I think only of the
future,' he said, and did not wish to be
reminded of his life as a blues singer, either
by records or by keeping a guitar. He was
making a good living at the mills and was
happy to tell stories to the local children and
to smoke his pipe in obscurity. Efforts to
record him are unlikely to succeed and are
unlikely to be met with appreciation. In
'Broke Man Blues' he had signed off
appropriately:

*Now I'm gonna close my conversation,
    an' I have no more to say . . .*

Jazz Monthly May, 1962
Kokomo Arnold died Chicago,
8 November 1968.

Just a Dream
BIG BILL BROONZY

On the back of the programme the London Jazz Club at Britain's Premier Jazz Rendezvous announced Saturday and Monday Night Jazz with Europe's Greatest Jazz Band Attraction, the Christie Bros Stompers. The programme was dated Saturday 22 September 1951 when, at the Kingsway Hall in Holborn, London, a recital was proudly presented of blues folk songs and ballads, by the famous American singer Big Bill Broonzy. An old photograph showed a youthful Broonzy with a stub of cigarette in his mouth, an open-necked shirt loosely worn and a cello-style guitar held away from him, machine-gun fashion. When he arrived in Max Jones's diminutive red sports car he looked very little different – remarkably young in appearance, immensely tall in the cramped circumstances, clad in an ill-fitting suit. As he eased himself out of the car with some difficulty and much laughter we wondered – could this really be Big Bill Broonzy whose voice we'd heard and whose guitar we'd marvelled at on those treasured Okehs and Meltones and Vocalions which we valued so highly, and incidentally paid the earth (or at least the price of this LP) for each of them?

It was Big Bill, and he proved it triumphantly to the small crowd that clustered round him at the bottom of the steeply ramped seats of the unlikely Kingsway Hall setting. The hall was only a third full, its enraptured audience the hard-core of blues devotees in a predominately 'Trad' world of American-orientated jazz music. Looking back, fourteen years later, it still stands out as a thrilling and singular experience. Jazz history is short and blues history is ill-documented, and even the recent history of the music has a curious way of getting distorted. Far from urging Big Bill Broonzy to sing folk songs, the cluster of blues enthusiasts were somewhat astonished by the catholicism of his music, expecting twelve-bar blues almost exclusively. It is interesting to note the songs that he sang without any prompting or adjusting to his audience at that time: 'In the Evening', 'John Henry', 'Keep Your Hands Off Her', 'Key to the Highway', 'Trouble in Mind', 'Back Water Blues', 'Just a Dream', 'When I Been Drinkin''. He included a number of blues, guitar rags, a boogie or two, ballads, spirituals and even popular songs like 'When Did You Leave Heaven?'. They were songs and blues that he liked to sing. 'I want to sing just as I feel,' he would often say and was always happiest when the audience let him make his own way through his songs and stories. For Big Bill was a great raconteur for whom fact and fantasy were sometimes a little confused but in whose stories there was always a nub of truth.

His life had been a remarkably interesting and varied one and he had outstanding aural recall, so that he was able to draw on his experiences and the song traditions that were a part of them freely and imaginatively. Arguments that Big Bill was a country singer or a city singer or a folk singer or a blues singer are fundamentally futile because he was all of these things, and a great artist. He did not claim to have come straight from an Arkansas cotton patch and responsible writers didn't suggest it either; Max Jones's notes to that initial programme were accurate in detail as to his career, his work and his recordings. This is not to suggest that Big Bill was never the darling of the folk-song circles; indeed he was. He was a man with great human dignity and feeling;

he responded easily to all people who were sympathetic to him and was happy to sing whenever there was an audience that wanted to hear him. He had no need for rigid classifications in blues and folk song and was not a lesser artist because he drew from the recollected songs of his youth as well as the blues of Chicago which he had been so prominent in shaping. One of sixteen children and a twin himself, William Lee Conley Broonzy was born on 26 June 1893 in Scott, Mississippi, in the heart of the Delta Pine Lands country. He moved with some of his family as a child to Arkansas and retained his connection with the two States until the late Forties, frequently visiting his family, although he settled in Chicago after the First World War. By that time he had worked on plantations, been married, owned and lost a farm, worked in the coal mines and had been drafted into the Army. For the next twenty years he did a variety of jobs, mainly labouring, and not until the 1950s did he earn his living entirely by his singing. When he was brought to Europe in 1951 he was a caretaker, a 'mopper', at the Iowa State College, and on his return resumed his menial work as janitor.

As a child Big Bill heard many itinerant blues and ballad singers but he recalled most vividly a 'rouster on the water' by the name of C. C. Rider, who sang the song which apparently gave him this name: 'See See Rider'. Normally this song is associated with a railroad tradition but Big Bill over several years never wavered from his story of the wandering minstrel with the one-string fiddle whose 'home was on the water, he didn't like land at all' and who gave him the idea to make himself a one-string fiddle in imitation. This was, as he recalled, in 1908 and for the next eight years he worked on the same Arkansas farm, learning to handle the big plough and the stubborn mules. In the long days and years on the farm he developed the spine-chilling hollering that remained a part of his vocal range for half a century, crying the blues in the open fields with the resolve to leave the country if he could 'feel tomorrow, like I feel today'.

*Bye-Bye Arkansas, hello Missouri, I'm
    on my way up North now baby,
I declare it ain't no foolin' gal if I can just
Feel tomorrow, like I feel today.
Yes, I'm gonna pack up, pack up now
    baby,
An' I declare I'm gonna make my
    getaway.*

It was the war that made the wish a reality and when Big Bill settled in Chicago in 1920 he came in contact with many blues singers and musicians including the banjo and guitar player Papa Charlie Jackson who taught him to play guitar. To his increased instrumental range Big Bill brought his magnificent hollering voice and in the ensuing years helped to model the development of the Chicago blues. He heard singers like Bertha 'Chippie' Hill whose singing of the New Orleans pianist Richard M. Jones's blues 'Trouble In Mind' impressed him greatly. Too much of an individual merely to copy, he made the celebrated blues on its traditional theme a vehicle for his own inimitable form of self-expression, and used the melody for another blues of his own, 'I Wonder'. Bessie Smith was another of the old blues singers back in the 1920s whom he liked to recall in later years. 'They was my friends – and your friends too,' he said, knowing of the widespread admiration of Bessie Smith and Leroy Carr.

★ ★ ★ ★

Big Bill was a leading figure in the development of the blues trends which evolved during the Thirties and Forties in

Chicago and, to a lesser extent, Detroit. He came of a generation of Southern-born men who found the brash, fast life of the city a stimulating experience after the conservative, slow-moving world of their youth and reflected this in the music they created there. Their music was given new form by the fusion of different elements – the rural blues with their origins in the field hollers; the songs of minstrel shows and the vaudeville stage; the guitar playing of the jukes and the medicine show entertainers and the rolling piano of the barrelhouse pianists. Meeting on the South Side of Chicago, blues singers and country field hands, sawmill piano players and steel mill smelters created a new style of blues which had its origins in the Southern traditions but was uncompromisingly of its time and place. Guitarists and pianists worked together: amongst the earliest were Blind Blake with barrelhouse piano man Charlie Spand. 'The Guitar Wizard' Tampa Red joined forces with Georgia Tom Dorsey who had played the piano for Ma Rainey. Scrapper Blackwell played the guitar to accompany one of the greatest of all the blues singers in the more urban forms, Leroy Carr. William Lee Conley Broonzy, 'Big Bill' to all his friends, belonged to this group.

After an uncertain start to his recording career, Big Bill emerged in the Thirties as one of the major artists of his day and remaining in Chicago, he was a prime mover in the blues music of the city. He came into his own as the pattern took shape. Bob Alexander – Black Bob as he was universally known – became Big Bill's pianist in 1933 and from then until his death in 1937 he was his constant companion both on record and in the Chicago clubs. This was the peak period of Big Bill's career, when his music was most significantly his own and bore the stamp of his own individuality. Through the Thirties he worked at a variety of jobs, com-

mencing as a railroad porter, then serving in a grocery store, acting as a janitor and all the time improving his guitar playing. Though he had played the fiddle since childhood he had not seriously played the guitar until he moved to Chicago but in the fertile period of the Twenties he became an adept guitarist and brought to his playing a swinging impetus that was entirely his own. His recording of 'Good Jelly', lightly ribald, is an interpretation of a traditional tune sung by Peg Leg Howell, amongst others, but invested with a new rhythmic quality. It was a quality of rhythm which derived from the guitar rags which Big Bill brought to the blues; the ragged syncopation of his playing in this idiom is perfectly demonstrated on the old song of the barnstorming vaudeville shows 'Keep Your Hands Off Her'. And behind his remarkable playing and the easy delivery of the amusing words his pianist Black Bob stomps out a raggy piano accompaniment.

These are recordings of Big Bill Broonzy in the mid-Thirties. A vast body of the records that he made late in life is available but little is currently accessible of his early recordings from the period when he was a leading figure on the blues scene. Coming from this period these recordings enable the listener to assess the degree of truth, if any, in the assertion that he was at this time 'trying to sound like Lonnie Johnson and Leroy Carr', or the merit of the observation from the same source, that his style on 'The Sun Gonna Shine in My Door Someday' was 'as close to being ingratiating as the blues can be'.

When Big Bill was cutting these numbers the effects of the Depression were still sorely felt throughout American society, but most bitterly by the Negro, whose very skin colour was a further barrier to his employment. In many different verses Big Bill illuminated different facets of the problems of the day. In 'I'm Just A Bum', for example, he sang:

Eeh, when my mother died, my dad give po'
*   me away,(repeat)*
Lord, I'm just a bum babay, that's why I got
*   no place to stay.*

Sometimes I wonder why my dad give po' me
*   away,(repeat)*
Lord because I was dark-complexioned, Lord
*   they throwed me away.*

A nostalgia for the South still lingered in many of his songs, 'Southern Blues' most obviously, but as the Thirties rolled on and the nation's economy picked up, his blues took on more city associations and reflected something of the growing optimism that was discernible in the Negro's music. In Chicago, always a rough, tough and exhilarating city, the blues hardened into a more brassy and extrovert music, and Big Bill, essentially a part of it, continued to be a dominant personality, whilst his guitar style lost some of the echoes of Scrapper Black-well that are still to be heard in some of his earlier records. Now in his forties, he was something of a father-figure to a younger generation of blues singers who arrived in Chicago after the Depression.

★   ★   ★   ★

Big Bill was a huge man whose physique belied his years. He was a tough man too, hard-living and hard-drinking. In later years when he was in greater pain than he would ever admit and much more distressed than we ever knew, he kept a bottle of hard 'medicine' always by him and drained it steadily. But he was fond of the bottle as he declares in 'I Love My Whiskey' and always joked about it as he said whilst introducing 'When I've Been Drinkin'' 'anyone who don't like this is crazy – oh brother . . .'

I don't need no money, I've got Lucky Oil on
*   my hands,*
Don't want no woman boys that's always
*   raisin' sand,*
When I been drinkin', yes when I been
*   drinkin',*
If I make it home to you baby, will you please
*   let me lay down and rest.*

He always had the capacity to laugh at life and to laugh at himself; his good spirits were infectious and his rocking semi-comic songs were as much a part of him as his hollered blues. He drew from old traditions and brilliantly adapted them so that an old medicine show song 'Keep Your Fingers Off It' became a witty number of his own 'Keep Your Hands Off Her'. It is a song which incidentally illustrates Big Bill's creative interpretations excellently, for the early recording of 1934 is much closer to the original than the later, very personal working which he sang as:

She's got a million-dollar figure and long
*   black curly hair,*
Big Bill's gonna foller her everywhere,
So keep your hands off her, keep your big
*   mitts down,*
Keep your hands off her boy, don't you hear
*   what I say*
She don't belong to you . . .

It was a form of song which he greatly liked, with rhyming couplets and witty refrain, occuring again on the brilliantly played and mercilessly sung 'Five Feet Seven':

Gal, you'se neat in the waist as a wasp
And you walks around like a hoss,
You know you cain't see straight baby,
You know your eyes is crossed.
Now tell me who baby, who'se been foolin'
*   you?*
Tellin' you you'se five feet seven, baby and
*   you'se pretty too.*

Maybe these songs are not as profoundly affecting as some of his blues but they are a part of the man, endearing, good-humoured, engagingly sung and played with impeccable swing. It was his unerring rhythmic sense that caused him to be a leader in the emergence of the Chicago style of modern blues, giving the drive that swung a whole band and the keen guitar sound that gave an edge to groups that might otherwise have been dulled by the weight of piano and rhythm accompaniment. 'You've Been Mistreating Me Baby' is a typical number in this form with its boogie piano, stop choruses, saxophone solo and Big Bill's voice roaring out from its background. Big Bill Broonzy died of cancer on 14 August 1958. After his death the iconoclasts moved in swiftly, attempting, in the words of the old blues, 'to tear his reputation down'. But his reputation remains secure and the recordings that he made are support for it – if any were needed – to be valued as highly as any of those worn 78s in their card wrappers that were prized by those who were privileged to hear him at the commencement of his 'comeback'.

Notes to Fontana 688 206, 1968
and RCA Victor RD-7685, 1964

Tupelo Blues

JOHN LEE HOOKER

For the greater part of his working life John Lee Hooker has lived in cities and for the past fifteen years his home base has been Detroit, Michigan. It would seem hard to reconcile his recent background with the picture of the country singer that has been drawn of him. But of all city singers who have attained prominence John Lee Hooker has retained the qualities of his rural origins longest. He was born on 22 August 1917 in Clarksdale, Mississippi. Although it is the principal town in the Northern Mississippi Delta country it is still a small place with two main streets in the Negro sector with brick-built shops, loan offices and surplus clothing stores and an ill-defined maze of wood-frame houses and dirt roads stretching out to the cotton fields. For all the Negro migrations this is still cotton country and, in the years when John Lee was growing up, had an intensely rural character.

Clarksdale and the Delta country around has produced a remarkable number of blues singers as all blues enthusiasts know. The list need hardly be repeated but the fact of the strong local blues culture that developed in the area is valid and relevant to John Lee Hooker's maturing as a singer. He was born into a family of eleven children. Negro families in the Delta were, and still are, large, for the children work in the cotton fields from an early age and larger families increase their earning capacity. For all that, living is barely above subsistence level and the iniquities of the sharecropping system tended until very recently to perpetuate a life of serfdom. John's father died when he was a small child and he was raised by his mother and his step-father, William Moore. William Moore was himself a blues guitarist and it was from him that John first learned

to play the instrument. Like most other Negro boys of his age he made his own instrument and learned the rudiments of music-making on the crude 'box'. His fingering was untutored and unorthodox – no doubt his step-father's was too. Today John Lee Hooker still plays in an unconventional guitar style which dates back to his childhood.

The singers that he heard as a boy are almost lost to his memory for it was the number of them that remains most clearly in his mind. Home music-making was the most popular of recreations; 'store-porchin'' with the guitar or indoors on the piano. The music of the juke joints and edge-of-town barrelhouses was an extension of the same and with their doors open in the hot summer nights a boy could still hear the music even if he was not permitted to go in. In the fields workers hollered as they toiled; over their tubs the women sang blues or gospel songs – there was a common tradition of song which formed the natural background to a child's life. By the time John Lee was ten, blues records were to be heard on phonographs in most homes, and always in the town. The blues of a Blind Lemon Jefferson or Leroy Carr became common property and local singers like Charley Patton or Son House were featured on discs which were aimed specifically at the regional market and which are consequently great rarities now. When he was about thirteen, John started to play the guitar with earnestness and was soon playing for country suppers and fish-fries. He was unsettled in the large family though, and, feeling capable of supporting himself, he ran away from home.

The centre to which all Delta people gravitated was Memphis, Tennessee. It was only just out of Mississippi but it marked the first stage north. It was to Memphis, along Highway 51, that he directed his steps. On Beale Street he got himself small jobs and eventually sold peanuts and candy in a movie house. Inevitably he was fetched home, but not for long. From that time on he made frequent breaks from home, finally being permitted to stay in Memphis. When he was there he sang with a gospel group in a Baptist Church. His mother had been a religious woman and had encouraged him to sing with gospel groups back in Clarksdale – the Big Six and the Delta Big Four were two of them. In Memphis he continued to do so and did not attempt to play guitar for a living. Instead he worked in a factory until he felt the need to move on again. John Lee Hooker's subsequent movements are fairly confused. Through the years of the Second World War he worked in factories both in Memphis and Cincinnati and hoboed to other industrial centres as the fancy took him and the work beckoned. 1948 found him in Detroit with a job at the foundry at Ford's. He decided to settle there.

Though he had continued to play guitar John had not thought of making his living from his music. The encouragement of other singers in Detroit and of his new friends in the city led him to concentrate on his playing. Detroit has a long tradition of piano players – there are fewer guitarists and John was welcome. He was offered evening spots in clubs on Hastings Street and other centres in the Negro sector. The Apex Club and the New Olympia Bar, the Forest Inn and the Muddy Colour Bar, the Vogue and the Club Basin – each offered him employment, first for after-hours sessions and later on a regular basis. He started to record for local labels and was a nation-wide success with his recording of 'Boogie Chillen'.

When John first made a pitch on Bernard Besman's doorstep on Woodward Avenue, Detroit, and begged him to record him he was playing a crude instrument that appeared virtually home-made. But his rapid popularity in Detroit clubs demanded a louder vehicle for his playing. He bought an electric guitar which amplified his heady rhythms and ringing high notes. He had behind him good blues men like Boogie Woogie Red, the pianist, or Little Eddie Kirkland who played organ, harmonica or guitar with equal ability. Sometimes Johnny Hooks or Ellis Johnson would play tenor sax and the music was jumping, exciting rhythm and blues. Mississippi seemed far away.

As John Lee Hooker's recordings mainly featured him playing in the rhythm and blues idiom, Bill Grauer of Riverside records had the idea of recording him in different vein. He envisaged a session on which John would play and sing the songs of Leadbelly. Leadbelly's recordings, though great in number, had been issued primarily on specialist labels and the records for the Negro market had been relatively few. Not altogether surprisingly therefore, John Lee Hooker did not know either Leadbelly or his songs. Perhaps it is as well, if only because the present album might not have been made if he had been familiar with them. Instead of singing the blues and songs of another man, which would have been second-hand experience at best, he was encouraged to recall the blues he had heard or sung in his youth. Instead of the electric guitar which he normally played but which would have been anachronistic in this context he played an acoustic instrument and the present anthology of John Lee Hooker's 'Country Blues' was the result.

It is an amalgam of blues from many sources and corners of his experience which have been personalized until they are essentially his own. There is no denying the autobiographical content of 'Behind the Plow' which puts the clock back over thirty years.

> *I was born in Mississippi out a little country*
> * town, (repeat)*
> *Livin' on a l'il cotton farm, not very far from*
> * town.*
>
> *I plow all day long, I plow from sun to sun,*
> *I plowed the ole grey mule, I plowed all day*
> * long.*
> *I be in the field at sun rise, I stay 'til the sun go*
> * down*
>
> *Me, me an' my ole grey mule get so tired, so*
> * tired he wanna lay down, (repeat)*
> *I say no, no no, you cain't carry me down . . .*

and he continues to talk to the mule. It is an irregular blues, half a recitative, sometimes sung, sometimes spoken to a strummed guitar with interpolated flourishes, far removed from his rhythm and blues idiom. In a similar vein is the moody 'Tupelo Blues' which tells of a tragic flood that occurred in his youth and which deeply impressed him. Tupelo is a long way from the Mississippi and the unexpected extent of the flooding caused much loss of life and livestock. 'Rowed a Little Boat', with its echoes of Bessie Smith's 'Back Water Blues', has a similar theme – one that is common enough to those who come from the river bottomlands.

'Water Boy' is a recollection of a gang work song – a form which is rarely to be heard now but which was common enough when John Lee Hooker was living in the South. There are echoes of Blind Lemon Jefferson's records in 'Church Bell Tone' and 'Black Snake', two sober and magnificent items, whilst 'I'm Prison Bound' shows some indebtedness to Leroy Carr.

Though their origins in the recordings of these singers can be detected they all probably refer back to common heritage of the blues. At all events Hooker's treatment is uniquely his own: his voice rich, full and vibrant and the guitar throbbing as he hammers on the strings. His guitar technique is unusual, relying to a large extent on the hypnotic power of repetition. Though he can use arpeggios with great effect, as 'Behind the Plow' amply demonstrates, he is a rare master of odd rhythms. Many of his rhythmic phrases heard in isolation have a curious abruptness and yet there is over the total performance a sense of easy continuity. The breaks and pauses play a tacit part in the performance as a whole and the syncopated foot tapping is not an intrusion but an important rhythmic device. The many and varied tracks, including the brighter numbers like 'Wobblin' Baby' or 'Bundle Up and Go', demand and bear up to comparison and analysis.

Today John Lee Hooker is a city singer and it is artificial and unwise to make a country singer out of him. Nevertheless this is an important record for it shows uniquely the roots of the music that he has shaped into a modern idiom all his own.

Notes to Riverside 673 020, 1962

Highway 99
LOWELL FULSON

A tall, heavily built man on whom voluminous suits hang rather uncomfortably, Lowell Fulson cuts a striking figure. He bears a certain similarity to Jimmy Witherspoon in his medium colouring, his carefully greased hair, his broad smile and his long, trim pencil moustache on his upper lip. Born on an Indian reservation, Lowell Fulson is proud of his part Indian ancestry and shows it both in his features and his stance. His inclination to run to fat and his other physical attributes puts one in mind of the Plains Indians whose bulky frames looked graceless when they were on foot but who came into their own when astride a mustang. Lowell's heritage may be Indian but he rides to the rhythm of a guitar rather than a horse and he comes into his own when he sings the blues.

For, if he is part Indian he is also part Negro and the mixed background, shared by a number of other blues singers and musicians from Oklahoma and Arkansas has found expression in his taut, sad, often high-pitched blues which carry in them both the tragedy and the pride of each race. Lowell Fulson was born in Oklahoma in 1921 in the vicinity of Tulsa. His father was a musician who played guitar and followed in the footsteps of Lowell's grandfather who had been a fiddle player. Such a musical background inevitably brought the young Fulson in contact with instruments when he could scarcely walk and by the time he was out of childhood he was a proficient performer. He played with his brother Martin, another guitarist, and when he was seventeen years old joined a string band. This group, one of the several under the banner of the Wright family was known as Dan Wright's String Band and comprised two guitars, two mandolins, three violins and two banjos — a considerable complement which could provide exciting music for almost any function. For the most part they were in demand for country suppers and dances, especially in the slack lay-off season. Lowell Fulson was employed as a farm hand for much of his youth, but when the work on the farm dropped off he would travel with Dan Wright to outlying parts for various engagements.

With the Dan Wright String Band, Lowell Fulson, playing second guitar, toured as far South as Texas and Louisiana and all over the Oklahoma country which was still known as 'The Territory' even though it had long ceased to be a totally Indian territory for four decades. Working down in Texas in 1939 he heard at a house party the great blues singer Texas Alexander. According to Chris Strachwitz, who interviewed Lowell Fulson some years ago and who has supplied much of the available data on the singer, Texas Alexander had been working with Howling Wolf Smith as his accompanist. Smith had just left when Fulson met up with Alexander in 1939 and was invited by the older man to play guitar for him. At this time Lowell was still only eighteen years old but the opportunity was too exciting to pass by. Texas Alexander was one of the most respected of Texas blues singers and countless guitarists from Lonnie Johnson to Lightnin' Hopkins worked with him at one time or another. Travelling with the veteran gave Lowell a breadth of experience which was to stand him in good stead in his maturity. He learned from Texas Alexander the art of improvising blues on situations and events from his own experience.

For close on two years Lowell Fulson worked with Texas Alexander until he was drafted into the US Navy. He saw active service overseas from 1943 until the end of the Second World War and though he was not playing continuously he had the opportunity to work with small groups and to entertain the seamen at Guam. He was engaged by Special Services to entertain on shows and became accustomed to working before large audiences and with accompanying bands. The experience undoubtedly changed the nature of his music, if not immediately, at least to prepare him for his future career. Discharged in 1945 on the West Coast he found himself with no job and few prospects back in his home State. Deciding to remain in California, he started to play for clubs in the Oakland area and became extremely popular with the many Oklahomans and Texans who had migrated to the coast during the war, attracted by the high wages in the defence factories.

It was in Oakland that he made his first recordings in 1946. Cut for Bob Geddins they were made with Lowell's pianist Eldridge McCarthy. Others with R. J. Russell, another piano player, and a small rhythm group followed and then he sent back home for his brother Martin Fulson. Martin was not an especially inventive guitarist but he could provide a sturdy rhythmic basis for Lowell's more imaginative melodic flights. The two men worked extremely well together and Martin managed his brother until his death in 1959. By this time, however, Lowell Fulson had long been depending on small groups; the 'down-home' quality of the two-guitar team which seemed to refer back to Lowell's country background had been appropriately replaced by a more urban sound, suited to the Oakland and Los Angeles settings. He had shown a preference for small rhythm groups even in the late Forties and often used Lloyd Glenn from Texas or the band leader Jay McShann as pianist on records, accompanied by a bass player and drummer. Sometimes the group would be augmented by an alto player, and later, in the mid-Fifties, he was being backed by an orchestra comprising a full rhythm section, saxes and sometimes an organ.

For the blues enthusiast, the recordings made with these later groups are sometimes disappointing because Lowell Fulson's excellent guitar work is drowned, or even virtually replaced, by the volume of the orchestra. But the earlier small group accompaniments suited him well, providing a full enough sound to give a solid backing but allowing him the room for inventive playing and the freedom to command by his singing. Centred in California he still looked with longing to Oklahoma.

> *Goin' to Oklahoma City baby, where the*
> *   black gold flows like wine.   (repeat)*
> *Keep plenty money in your pocket, live happy*
> *   all the time.*

The words of the 1953 recording echoed those of some years earlier when he sang:

> *The war is over, I'm broke and ain't got a*
> *   dime.   (repeat)*
> *My time is up in California, gonna hit*
> *   Highway 99.*

Eventually he made good the promise and moved back to Oklahoma and Texas, settling finally in Fort Worth where he lives today. His recent work shows that Lowell has been overtaken by younger men and is now finding it increasingly hard to keep apace with changes of style and technique. It is a pleasure to be reminded of the music of his best period when, pushing thirty, he was the best known blues singer on the West Coast. In those less self-conscious days when the histrionics of 'Soul' had not affected the blues, Lowell Fulson was singing and playing the music with authority and feeling.

Notes to Polydor 423 250, 1963

Can't Hardly Keep from Cryin'
JUKE BOY BONNER

Louisiana is hot and humid; in the summer the temperature never drops below 80 degrees Fahrenheit and the steamy swamp heat hides the sun. The country itself is flat and featureless – a large proportion of the State is less than a hundred feet above sea level – but the vistas are broken by the lines of trees along the bayous which give way to thick timberlands and swampy groves. The coastal strip is eerie and forbidding to the visitor and strangely compelling too, with the twisted cypress trees hanging festooned with Spanish moss imparting a haunted, magical quality to the landscape. This area is populated by the descendants of the exiles from Novia Scotia, the Acadians, or 'Cajuns' as they became known, French speaking settlers who came to the region two centuries ago after they had been expelled from their homeland by the British. They are still an insular people in character, voluble but at times taciturn, unambitious and living off the meagre profits from the shrimping and muskrat hunting. They share their strange country with the Negro descendants of slaves of the French colony with whom they have sometimes intermarried. To a large extent the pressures and strains of modern American life pass them by.

Between thirty and fifty miles back from the waterlogged coast runs interstate Highway 90 linking Houston and New Orleans in a four-hundred-mile ribbon by way of Beaumont, Lake Charles, Crowley and Lafayette, dipping South round Grand Lake to Houma and Thibodaux. This, the traditional route between the Gulf Coast centres – unless one takes the intracoastal waterway canal which cuts its way improbably through the swamplands a dozen miles to

the South – takes one through the principal towns in cajun country. It seems that the talent scouts of the Twenties did not care to take it to any marked extent when looking for vernacular music in America but, even so, a certain amount of white cajun music by Clemo Breaux and Joseph Falcon, Columbus Fruge and Mayeuse la Fleur did get on record. Their nasal singing to the music of fiddle, accordion and guitar represented a fascinating backwater of American folk music and one that has remained little known until recent years, outside this area. Even less known, however, was the Negro music of the country which shared the character of both cajun music and the blues.

Back of the coastal swamps lie the so-called prairie lands, still well watered and the heart of the rice-producing area. The landscape is animated too by the nodding heads of the oil pumps, and the derricks of the oil rigs rising above the trees. Timber and its derivatives, oil drilling and refining and the cultivation of rice provide the main sources of employment for whites and Negroes alike. Their local communities are generally separate and their entertainments likewise, but over long years their traditions have developed on similar lines and often overlapped. Small instrumental groups featuring guitars, fiddles, base fiddles and accordions were characteristic of the district and in the Thirties some of them, like the Hackberry Ramblers which included Ed Duhon and Lennis Sonnier and was led by Luderin Darbonne, became extremely well-known. Their members came from Hackberry, West Lake and Sulphur in the region of Lake Charles, and their French names are a confirmation of their cajun origin. Sometimes they were joined by

Eddie Shuler from Lake Charles but Shuler later started his own band which played many tunes in the 'Western swing' style as well as cajun numbers.

In the early Fifties Eddie Shuler and his brother-in-law Steve Fruge (with a respected name in cajun music) started a record label to promote the music of their own band. They called it Goldband and all·but one of the first fifteen records was by Eddie Shuler's group. The exception was a recording by the ill-fated Iry le June and its successful sale led Schuler to interest himself in recording other artists. Mostly they were cajun and western swing musicians from around Lake Charles but the occasional blues musician from the district began to appear on the label and the names of Big Chenier and Hop Wilson were to be seen in the catalogues along with those of Linus Touchet or Lionel Cormier. Some of these were working locally, like Chenier, whilst others were, like Wilson, from Houston where a large French-speaking Negro population can be found. Goldband records began to be played in Shreveport and Dallas and points further afield, and the names of musicians local to Lake Charles were becoming known in districts far removed.

It was a record on a juke-box in Sacramento, California, that brought Juke Boy Bonner to record for Goldband. Bonner had been playing at clubs in the Sacramento area and one day, happened to notice the Goldband record on the turntable of a juke-box in one of them. Liking the record he decided that he would record for the label some time. Weldon H. Bonner comes from Oakland. California, but he is an artist who is continually on the move, rarely playing more than a couple of nights at one place before packing up his instruments and moving on. In the course of time, by a circuitous route, he eventually presented himself at Eddie Shuler's recording studio in Lake Charles

and made good his determination to record for Goldband. He was one of the small body of blues artists who played several instruments – at the same time.

Carrying his instruments, packing them in the trunk of the Greyhound bus, Juke Boy Bonner travelled across the South-west seeking out jobs, playing one-nighters, packing up and moving on – enjoying the life of a rambling musician. His perambulations took him to New Orleans where he struck up a friendship with a pianist. Together they worked their way back through Louisiana and when Juke Boy recorded for Eddie Shuler he was backed by the pianist – unfortunately the man did not give his name. Only one coupling of Juke Boy Bonner was issued by Goldband, 'Can't Hardly Keep from Crying' being the other issued side. Eventually a copy crossed the Atlantic and was heard by Mike Leadbitter who wrote enthusiastically about the disc and endeavoured to learn more about the session from Eddie Shuler. As a result the remaining six titles from the session are now being issued on this album for the very first time. Any eventual history of the blues will have to take into account the unlikely chain of events that may lead to the issue of records and the discovery of virtually unknown items by blues artists, but probably few are as unpredictable as that of a blues singer from California who resolves on hearing a recording made in Louisiana to visit the studios and to record for himself; who achieves his aim but whose recordings for the most part are issued for the first time at the instigation of a blues enthusiast from England, to appear on a label based in Denmark!

Note to Storyville SLP177, 1965

Weldon Bonner was born Bellville, Texas, 22 March 1932 and died Houston, 29 June 1978.

3
Moaners and Shouters

Illustration to "In the Sticks" *Music Mirror*, Vol 2, No 4, April 1955

As every book on blues seems to point out, it was Mamie Smith's recording of Perry Bradford's 'Crazy Blues' on Okeh 4169, that opened the way for the blues on record. It was really her second disc, and it was so successful that she made half-a-dozen other titles in 1920 and almost had the field to herself in the following year. Bob Dixon and John Godrich have told the story in their book *Recording the Blues*, of how the recording of black singers, both sacred and secular, grew. It was one of a series which I edited in 1969–72, called 'Blues Paperbacks' – though I must admit that the real editing, the close reading and correcting was mainly done by Tony Russell. Tony's own book, *Blacks, Whites and Blues*, like most of the others in the series, is still the only work on its subject.

I wanted to have a book on the women singers of the so-called 'Classic Blues' vein in the series and the obvious person to ask was Derrick Stewart-Baxter. He alone had gone to the trouble to interview singers like Rosa Henderson and Lucille Hegamin, helped by 'the Queen', Victoria Spivey. It wasn't easy to persuade him for Derrick had his own way of going about writing on blues. For years his was the only column on the subject, written for *Jazz Journal*, and his enthusiasm was projected to a lot of young readers in the late Forties. He used to hold court in an upstairs room of a Hove record shop, a gathering place for blues enthusiasts who were prepared to brave the smoke of his pipe to share in the sounds and discussion on jazz and blues. Since *Ma Rainey and the Classic Blues Singers* there have been a few articles, a biography of Bessie Smith and a full-length study of Ma Rainey's work. But the entertainers who sang blues on the vaudeville stage, or toured on the TOBA and other circuits, have generally been very poorly served by blues writers.

My own introduction to the records of the women singers was, like most jazz collectors, through the work of Bessie Smith. Though 'Gimme a Pigfoot' was made at her last session it had been supervised by John Hammond especially for release in England in 1933, and ten years later it was still in the catalogue. So were many others, including an eight-record Bessie Smith Memorial Album; I knew every shading and inflection on every track. There were others, but it took me a lot of junk-shopping to find them, like Bessie's 'In the House Blues' on an old black label Parlophone, with its roaring vocal and splendidly incongruous vocal: 'Cain't eat, cain't sleep, so weak I cain't walk my floor.' Apart from one title by Mamie Smith, 'Jenny's Ball', and a couple by Ida Cox, there wasn't much else, but in the enjoyable pastime of junk-shopping I turned up Elizabeth Johnson's 'E-Flat Blues' and a record which gave a new dimension to this form of singing: 'You're Always Messin' 'Round with my Man' by Lizzie Miles.

I'm not quite sure why this record, on a plum-coloured HMV and with a Sissle and Blake coupling which I hardly played on the back, was quite so important to me. Her voice (then) was rather piping but with a catty sort of edge to it which I found very engaging. And the words were wryly amusing:

> . . . *If you don't keep your big nose in its*
> *proper place*
> *They're goin' to lose a member of the col-ored*
> *race,*
> *I'm warning you 'cause I understand*
> *You're always messin' 'round with my man.*

Perhaps it was because I was almost eavesdropping on a private dispute: Lizzie's song was directed at her opponent; Bessie Smith's seemed to be to the audience.

A close friend, Roy Ansell, who first played trombone with the Crane River Jazz

Band (he couldn't actually *play*, but he had a very fruity glissando which sounded extremely authentic), had found a way of getting blues records from American airmen and, after the War, from the United States. We struggled with transcriptions of the words of every item, and started compiling a lexicon of blues terms. In the process we gathered many recordings by Clara Smith, Ma Rainey, Edith Johnson, Victoria Spivey, Butterbeans and Susie, and many other less well-known names. Some we didn't like much: Eva Taylor Viola McCoy, and traded for others to collectors who (fortunately) wanted everything on which Clarence Williams or Fletcher Henderson appeared. There were no guide-lines; it was a hit-and-miss process. But the hits were exhilarating.

I didn't get to meet many of the women singers, but through the editor of *Record Research*, Len Kunstadt, I met Victoria Spivey in 1960. She was astonishingly youthful-looking then, very animated in conversation, flirtatious and confiding in turn. Over a decade later, at the Ann Arbor Blues Festival at which I had the great pleasure of being MC, I was happy to introduce her on stage; when I had seen her first she was contemplating making a come-back and I was glad to have played some part in getting her to do so which, generously, she always remembered. Val, my wife, noticed that Victoria used the stage performer's trick of always raising her chin and letting the light from the sky fall on her face so that the wrinkles wouldn't show. She was a professional, very aware of her stage presence, arch and ogling at times, but perhaps because she was a little younger than the other stage veterans I met – Sippie Wallace and Edith Johnson among them – she seemed closer to that old vaudeville tradition, almost as if she'd never left it. Edith Johnson was a warm and animated person,

who had been a proprietor of a music shop and manager of a restaurant as well as having been involved in public service in later years. Sippie, on the other hand, had long been a stalwart of the church and a singular gospel singer. She came back to her blues singing with marvellous expressiveness and composure.

It was always my regret that I didn't meet Ida Cox, and obtained her address too late. She was highly regarded by many singers and performers and was probably the last of her kind to run her own road show. In San Francisco I met up with her one-time pianist Jesse Crump, who was playing with Marty Marsala's band at the Kewpie Doll; dreary Dixieland jazz for which poor Jesse was playing mechanical piano with scarcely a solo for his talents. Standing among the tubs of unconsumed food scraped off the plates of a choosy but bored audience, we talked about the days when he was a young man playing for Ida at Ella B. Moore's Park Theatre on Central Tracks, Dallas.

I was able to talk about Ella B. Moore's partly because of the kind of odd coincidence that occurs to anyone conducting research in just about any field. At the Metropole, New York, I'd been listening to Sammy Price playing with Henry 'Red' Allen, seated, it seemed to me, on a kind of shelf above the bar. Next to me was an oldish man who'd remembered Sam Price when he was a youth in Dallas; his name was Isom Hisam and he'd been the janitor at Ella B. Moore's thirty years before. Her place, long ago destroyed in a major replanning of Dallas which totally obliterated Central Tracks, was just one of the theatres on the 'Toby Time' – the circuit of black theatres run by the Theatre Owners' Booking Agency.

Male shouters tend to get left out of studies in blues, as they are usually linked more with jazz than with the blues idiom.

Jimmy Rushing was a shouter who's work I liked; he had impeccable timing and the extraordinary capacity to generate enough swing to take a band along with him. He was no great innovator of blues lyrics, in fact he made much use of repetition of phrases to build up excitement and the content wasn't important. But he had a good appreciation of blues singers from Blind Lemon Jefferson at one pole to Eddie Vinson at the other. Jimmy was alert and interested in the world around him; he had a surprisingly shy smile and gentle behaviour off-stage and we kept up a correspondence – his letters on pink paper in capital letters – until his death. After a little typed joke he would put SMILE in brackets; perhaps it should have been (SHOUT), but (SMILE) was as appropriate to his friendly personality.

But then, blues singers don't always conform to the stereotypes we've drawn for them. I remember being rather intimidated by Big Joe Turner's sheer size: a vast girth which seemed to taper back to his head, and which somehow appeared to be a defence against any difficulty: who would mess with Big Joe? Strangely enough for a man who'd been raised in the Prendergast years of Kansas City, a wide-open town if ever there was one then, he was very nervous in London. He asked me if I would take him to buy a hat as he was feeling the cold on his head. We went to Dunn's and a grey-suited, grey-moustached gentleman with a tape round his neck came up to me. Then he seemed to dissolve in blushing confusion totally unlike the impression conveyed by his suave dress and reception manner. 'N-not Joe . . . *Turner*?' he asked me, incredulously. I told him 'yes', and endeavoured to introduce him. Here was an old jazz/blues fan in this smart gents' hatters' reduced to embarrassed, excited nerves, proud to have found a hat to fit his idol. As for Big Joe, his confidence was restored.

In the Sticks

BLUES ON THE STAGE

Of the many aspects of jazz and Negro music and song, one of the most neglected has been the influence of Negro vaudeville. But its importance is great for it was largely in the tent shows and dime theatres of the lower-class Negro world that the gap between folk music and sophisticated song was bridged. It is to be regretted that a singer's work in the burlesque shows and the vaudeville theatres is frequently dismissed by students and historians of Afro-American music who prefer to place emphasis on the singing of blues. Sitting in the 'nigger heaven' as even the Negroes themselves termed the highest balcony seats in a theatre, the peanut chewing truck-driver with his eyes and ears concentrated on the sequinned figure standing at the footlights made no such distinction. Whether she sang the 'Gulf Coast Blues' or chastised her stage partner with 'You're Always Messin' 'Round With My Man!' mattered little to him: it was his kind of music. In point of fact, all the great 'classic' blues singers of the first quarter of the century – Sippie Wallace, Ida Cox, Bertha Hill to mention but a few – made their reputations and their livelihoods with the little 'minstrel' companies which toured the small towns of the South and mid-West, until finally they were able to secure engagements in the principal Northern cities. And the material they used was not inhibited by any preconceived notions of what was artistic, acceptable or classifiable as blues. They sang the music of their people – folk blues, sixteen-bar stomps, the songs of Handy and Pace, Spencer Williams and Kid Sox Wilson – and when inspired to do so, they wrote their own.

Gertrude Rainey – 'Ma' Rainey – was known as the 'Mother of the Blues'. She was no more the mother of the idiom than W. C. Handy was its father. But she was one of the first and one of the most important women to sing in the classic style. Hers was not the spontaneous, improvised blues singing of the section hand or the field worker. Her singing was as heartfelt and sincere, but she was an entertainer with a public. Diamonds glittered at her fingers, gold pieces hung at her neck and combs were thrust in her wild, frizzy hair. She was given to flashes of temper and moments of jealousy but there was kindness in her eyes and warmth in her generous smile. The audiences loved her.

I went down the alley the other night
That piano man had just had a fight.
He beat Miss Nancy 'cross the head,
When she rose to her feet she said:
'You low-down alligator
Just watch me, soon or later
Gonna catch you with your britches down!'

Ma Rainey came from Columbus, Georgia, where she was born in 1886. Like the majority of the classic blues singers she was raised in the South and throughout her career she retained echoes of her folk heritage in her singing. Recognition did not come instantly and she reached Chicago only after a long apprenticeship touring 'in the sticks' – in the backwoods districts, where she performed in make-shift tent theatres and second-line halls in a vaudeville troupe called 'The Rabbit Foot Minstrels'. During one of her tours she played at Chattanooga in Tennessee and it was there that she discovered a twelve-year-old girl, just eight years her junior, whose talent she instantly recognized and encouraged. The girl was Bessie Smith.

To the coloured audiences in Decatur Street, Atlanta, and State Street, Chicago alike, Bessie Smith was the 'Empress of the Blues'. She too, toured the 'tank towns' – the isolated communities built around the fuelling stations of the railroads – and her varied repertoire of jazz songs, burlesque numbers and blues endeared her to her audiences and won her the attention of Frank Walker who brought her to New York, and launched her on a wave of great, if temporary, popularity, in 1923. When moved to do so, Bessie could sing with great poignancy and feeling but for her vaudeville audiences her main theme lay in the battle of the sexes. A strong, handsome woman, she sang or spoke her lines with equal intensity.

> *To the world I'll scream, no man can treat me*
> *   mean,*
> *And expect my love all that time.*
> *When he rolls away, he'd better stay,*
> *'Cause if he comes back he'll find:*
> *'You've had your chance and proved*
> *   unfaithful,*
> *So now I'm gonna be real mean and hateful –*
> *I used to be your sweet momma, sweet poppa,*
> *But now I'm just as sour as can be!'*

Many of the earlier Negro vaudeville theatres were of extremely poor quality, offering little or no changing room facilities, the barest stage equipment and inadequate lighting. Few of the 'white' theatres would permit Negroes except perhaps in the highest balconies, and they were forced to build their own theatres from such resources as they had. Some were in converted cellars, others in adapted warehouses. Many were but rude tents or open air theatres exposed to the weather. With the steadily increasing popularity of Negro burlesque, a number of persons, white and coloured, opened theatrical circuits – X. F. Keith's 'Orpheum' circuit with theatres in St Louis, Los Angeles and elsewhere, was a typical venture catering for Negroes. Negro vaudeville flourished in Macon, Georgia, and Lexington, Kentucky; in Charleston, Savannah, Atlantic City and New Orleans.

Almost as popular as Bessie Smith in these first decades of the century was Clara Smith, a great and much underrated singer who was no relation to the 'Empress'. Clara Smith's performances were in the true vaudeville tradition and her songs often consisted of advice to her audience. 'Don't advertise your man!' she would warn her sex. But her philosophy, which was always so evident in her songs, was to accept circumstances as she found them and optimistically to make the best of them.

> *Every day, somebody tells me 'bout my man,*
> *But I know he's not the worst in the land.*
> *They say he did this, he did that, he got*
> *   another girl in the next door flat,*
> *But I don't care, it is a fact*
> *I know his home is everywhere he hangs his*
> *   hat.*
> *If nobody wanted him neither would I*
> *That's why you hear me cry:*
> *A Two-Timing Poppa is better than no poppa*
> *   at all . . .*

Artists of the quality of Clara Smith soon reached the more important of the Negro theatres, the Big Grand near 31st and State in Chicago for example, or the famous Pekin, a few blocks north. Some adopted an extremist policy, such as the Howard Theatre in Washington which preferred to reserve its seats for light-skinned Negroes only. Amongst the most important Negro houses was Philadephia's Standard Theatre where such artistes as Alice Ramsey and Mamie Smith could be seen. Mamie would sing:

> *'You can't keep a good man down . . .'*
> *. . . no matter how hard you try.*

Any time he gets his own –
He'll find a way bye and bye.
No use trying to treat him rough
Cause he ain't used to that cave-man stuff!
Kissin' for breakfast, huggin' for lunch,
Give him plenty lovin' cause he's your honey-
  bunch,
'Cause you can't keep a good man down!

Listening hard to Mamie Smith as she sang at the Standard Theatre was a tall thin girl who was to be known as Sweet Mama Stringbeans. Posterity remembers her best by her real name of Ethel Waters, but at that time she was aspiring to become a blues singer. Never did she have the vocal intensity of Bessie Smith or the warmth and feeling of Ma Rainey, but as a blues-singing vaudeville artist she was far from negligible. With the excellent schoolteacher turned blues pianist Pearl Wright to accompany her, she would sing for her final number 'Shake That Thing', her satin dress shimmering in the low lights.

Why there's old Uncle Jack, the Jelly-Roll
  King
He's got a hump on his back from shaking that
  thing!
Yet he still shakes that thing.
And oh, man! how he can shake that thing!
And he never gets tired of telling young folks
How to shake that thing!
Now it ain't no Charleston, ain't no pigeon
  wing,
Nobody has to give you no lessons how to
  shake that thing.
I'm getting tired of telling you how to shake
  that thing!

Whilst Bessie Smith rocked the Lincoln Theatre, Baltimore, there were a great many other vaudeville performers in the Negro theatre world of almost equal popularity and ability. Some, such as Florence Mills, Eddie Heywood and Bill 'Bojangles' Robinson were not in any sense jazz or blues

singers but they were consummate artists in their own right as dancers and entertainers. Whilst some like Beady Smith and Stringbeans (Butler May) preferred to work as solo acts, others like Eubie Blake and Noble Sissle or Bilow and Ashes, preferred a partnership. The boom attracted the attention of two theatre owners: Milton Starr of Nashville, Tennessee, and Charlie Turpin of St Louis. Together they formed the Theatre Owners' Booking Agency – the TOBA. Amongst many Negroes the agency had a poor reputation and the initials were understood to mean 'Tough On Black Artists'. Nevertheless it was a source of work for many performers who might otherwise have been without employment. It was whilst working at Charles Turpin's St Louis Theatre that Ethel Waters had to follow one of the most celebrated of coloured teams, the vaudeville act of Butterbeans and Susie. They were a perfectly balanced couple with a faultless sense of timing. Butt's voice was full and round. Sue's was sharp and piercing. Their material whilst never being salacious was full of innuendo and metaphor, and was punctuated by constant interjections as they alternated their lines. 'There's a lot of chocolates on the stall,' Butterbeans would remark. 'But where can you get good chocs free?' 'In my market I never put no stocks out,' Sue retorts.

S. *Well nowadays Butter if you want*
    something that's nice,
   Well you can't get it, if you don't pay
    the price.
B. *Now each night you keep me out,*
    you sho' ain't gonna have my key.
S. *Well pay me for my goods and you can*
    have your fill.
B. *Let me know what I'm buying and I*
    cert'nly will; cause Pappa ain't no
    Santa Claus –
S. *And your mamma sho' ain't no*
    Christmas Tree!

After years of obscurity these veterans of the Negro entertainment world have recently been rediscovered and are playing to packed houses in Miami, Florida. Such, unfortunately, is not the case for Coot Grant and Kid 'Sox' Wilson. One of the most celebrated and gifted coloured vaudeville teams, they have written more than four hundred songs and blues. They too have been rediscovered but in desperate straits and poor in health. In the Twenties they were greatly esteemed – Kid Sox, dark-skinned and plump, his wife Coot Grant, fairer of skin and very beautiful. Whilst Wilson played the piano his wife would sing in words that belied their devotion to each other over many years of trial.

You are my heart's desire
I like your love supply,
I see you in my dreams.
And every night you go,
I call you on the 'phone,
And this is what you'll hear me scream:
If you miss me here you'll find me at the
    Greasy Spoon.

Replied Kid Sox:

Mama, that ain't no cabaret,
That's only a barrelhouse saloon.

to which Coot responded:

You can read my letters,
You can't read my mind.
You think I love you Daddy,
When I'm quittin' you all the time.
If you miss me here you'll find me at the
    Greasy Spoon.

Arguments, domestic quarrels, rival and faithless lovers are the stuff of many a vaudeville act, including those where a partnership is of persons of the same sex. Masters in this field were Liza Brown and Ann Johnson, who, with the excellent Race artist Jim Jackson providing a guitar accompaniment, enlivened many a programme by cameos which were gems of timing and craftsmanship. Ann Johnson, large, and with a piping voice would incur the displeasure of the slight, deep-voiced and aggressive Liza Brown. Liza tells her opponent to go – to 'take it on outa here'.

L. *You been bumming for six months*
    Nothin' but liquor and beer,
    Now you can tell hot momma, the reason I
        don't want you here!

A. *Yes, you sell that no-good whiskey*
    and that old rotten beer,

L. *I made it all myself!*

A. *But when I get to snitchin'*
    The police gonna have you right out of
    here.

L. *You went round next door to talk 'bout me*
    to Elizabeth.
    Well I'm gonna skeet some snuff through
        your keyhole
    And make you sneeze yourself to death!

One of the personalities of the day was Lonnie Johnson, to be heard with Sarah Martin or Victoria Spivey or any one of a dozen other performers. Miller and Lyles, Buck and Bubbles, Davenport and Carr – they were only a few of the singers and dancers to whom the coloured population of New York, Baltimore, Philadelphia and Chicago flocked. Once their names were on everyone's lips on Chicago's South Side – now few are scarcely remembered. The Depression closed the theatres, and a later generation had no time for vaudeville entertainment or even for blues. So a fascinating and important aspect of Afro-American music came to a close; one which has been little documented and which becomes more distant with every passing year.

Music Mirror, April 1955
'Sources of Afro-American Folk Song – 11'

Paramount Wildcat

GERTRUDE MA RAINEY

They called her 'The Songbird of the South', the 'Black Nightingale', 'The Gold Necklace Woman of the Blues', and the 'Paramount Wildcat'. But throughout the South, throughout the coloured areas of the Eastern and Northern cities – from Pittsburg to Dallas, from Rome, Georgia, to Cleveland, Ohio, she was known to her race above all as 'The Mother of the Blues'. Gertrude Rainey was the first and in many ways the greatest of the women 'classic blues singers' who bridged folk music, vaudeville entertainment and jazz. To hear her and to see her, coloured people and many whites too who were prepared to defy conventions and prejudice to share in her art, would travel many miles and would camp overnight near her travelling shows. And Ma Rainey was something to hear. Her voice was warm with the love of her audiences and of her blues; sometimes wry, sometimes sad, sometimes laughing and sometimes nostalgic but always moving, exciting, heart-warming. She was something to see, too. Her face was impish. Puck-like, her nose short and broad, her thick lips upturned, her eyes twinkling and narrowed with her generous smile. Above her round, full black face her hair was wild and uncontrolled, a thick head-dress, like a band of wampum, only just succeeding in keeping it somewhat in place.

Barbaric? Yes, in a splendid, brilliant, uninhibited but majestic way. Ma Rainey loved the glitter of the diamonds in her head-dress and in her long swinging earrings. Sometimes she wore a tiara of diamonds when times were good; sometimes a diamond necklace. Once she bought a tiara and necklet of diamonds only to lose the good money she had paid when the police confiscated the jewellery which, unknown to her, were stolen goods. In her hey-day, though, she wore about her neck a long chain of twenty-dollar gold pieces which flashed as she swung in rhythm to her singing and matched the sudden stabs of light that caught her gold teeth. When she sang, she sang not only with her voice but with her whole body, emphasizing her lines with sweeping gestures of her thick but shapely arms, stressing the beat with flourishes of her huge fan of coloured ostrich plumes. Then, when the number was a 'hot' one she would lift the skirts of her long purple dress and showing her pointed, shiny black shoes, dance with surprising agility on the hardwood stage, her feather boa flying and the rows of loosely stitched beads on her costume shimmering. This is what they came to see and to hear; if her audiences had not heard her humming the choruses of 'Deep Moaning Blues' or listened to her voice soaring through 'Jelly Bean Blues', if they had not seen her famous backdrop of a soaring eagle, and the colourful splendour of her costumes, they would have been bitterly disappointed. But Gertrude Rainey never disappointed her audiences.

Gertrude Rainey was born into Negro show business. Her parents performed in travelling Minstrel shows, singing and dancing to the thumping of pit pianos and the strumming of banjos, the clacking of the bone castanets and the rhythms of the tambourine which were essential to the traditional set-up of such troupes. They lived, when not on the road, at Colombus, Georgia, and it was here on 26 April 1886 that their daughter was born. Naturally enough they trained her to sing and dance and her first opportunity to perform in public came when the Springer Opera House in Columbus was entertained by a local talent show called 'The Bunch of Blackberries'. Her professional beginnings were humble enough, but she began to make a local reputation. When a touring show came to the town only a year later she met Will Rainey, and shortly afterwards married him. Will Rainey's show was known as 'The Rabbit Foot Minstrels' and Gertrude Rainey became a member of the troupe. She was soon to prove to be more lucky for Will than any rabbit foot and rapidly became a major attraction in spite of her age. She was fifteen when she married.

During the first score of years of her professional career Gertrude Rainey played in every conceivable type of location – on the waterfront at Mobile, in oil-camps in Texas and in backwoods villages in the South and mid-West. Sometimes she played in big theatres, sometimes in converted barns. More often than not she played in the big marquee tent which she packed in her 'house-trailer'. The caravan – if it can be so called – that she used was a crudely constructed wooden affair built by willing and voluntary if unprofessional hands on the chassis of a large automobile. Rough though her travelling home was, it served her purpose and took her to remote parts where the coloured folk had few opportunities to hear any professional entertainment, let alone the music and blues that she had to offer. Though still not very old, Gertrude was now being known as 'Ma' Rainey and so she remained the rest of her life. She had left the Rabbit Foot Minstrels but the show itself continued – and under the management of F. S. Wolcott was still playing the South a few years ago, and may be doing so yet. Now, as Ma Rainey, the great blues singer led her own show. Who dubbed her as 'The Mother of the Blues' or who in fact first

called her 'Ma' is not established. Sidney Bechet, Big Bill Broonzy and Lonnie Johnson are among the persons who recall another Ma Rainey who had been famous as a singer early in the century and a Melissa Nixon Rainey played a Harlem cellar in the early Twenties. It has been suggested that Gertrude Rainey had adopted the name of 'Ma' when her predecessor with that title died. To what extent this is true is a matter of pure conjecture but by the early 1920s it was Madame Rainey, or Ma Rainey, who topped the bills.

So the years passed by and Ma Rainey's fame continued to spread and her energies never flagged. It is hard to appreciate the full import of the fact that she travelled up and down the country from Chicago in the extreme north to Mobile on the the Gulf Coast, playing continually to audiences often rough and remote, bearing the hardships of her chosen mode of travel and the tedium of being constantly uprooted from one situation to move on to the next, for thirty-five years. She was a trouper of more than a score of years' experience when she waxed her first recordings for the Paramount company, and during the next decade, whilst she continued to record, her artistry did not pale but continued to gain in richness and power. Throughout this time she continued to travel with her companies or with such Carnival shows as that led by 'Wee' Donald MacGregor, the Scottish Giant. Ma liked to have young men with her and she performed with the youthful Pinetop Smith as her accompanist; with the equally young, almond-faced, bright-eyed Tampa Red (Hudson Whittaker); with Georgia Tom, now Thomas A. Dorsey the gospel song composer. Her different bands included amongst their personnel: Tommy Ladnier and King Oliver's trumpet-playing nephew Dave Nelson; Gabriel Washington the drummer, and saxophone player Ed Pollack.

But she liked to perform with older troupers too, and the late Cow Cow Davenport, pioneer boogie player from Alabama, and one of the true Negro minstrel folk artists, banjo-playing Papa Charlie Jackson, were among her professional companions at one time or another. Ma's close links with the folk origins of the blues manifested themselves in her choice of accompaniments which included tub and jug bands, kazoo players and Swanee whistlers. Fortunately some of these primitive groups were on hand when she recorded a number of her sides for Paramount.

In the mid-Twenties, a Nashville theatre owner Milton Starr became president of an organization designed to give greater opportunities to coloured entertainers. This was the TOBA – the Theatre Owners' Booking Agency which linked the principal coloured theatres into one chain, allowing artists to follow in succession on a planned circuit. Needless to say, Ma Rainey played the circuit and rapidly became one of its principal attractions. Whilst playing the route she met Oran 'Hot Lips' Page, a young trumpeter from Dallas, Texas, who had been touring in carnivals and minstrel shows from the age of fifteen. Ma was impressed by his playing and booked him in on a tent-show tour in which he acquitted himself so well with her that she brought him to New York City for a season at the Lincoln Theatre. It was in New York that Ma Rainey made some of her greatest recordings, accompanied by members of Fletcher Henderson's band – Joe Smith and Louis Armstrong, Buster Bailey, Coleman Hawkins, Charlie Dixon, and of course Henderson himself. The proceeds from her tours and from her highly popular recordings – she made nearly a hundred sides – Ma spent fairly lavishly, but not too freely. Wisely she invested some and became the owner of two theatres in Rome, Georgia – the Airdrome

and Lyric. She did not forget her family either and bought a splendid house for them in Columbus, Georgia. It was her devotion to her family which resulted in her sudden retirement from the world of Negro entertainment, for in 1933 both her mother and her sister died with tragic suddenness. In spite of her life-long attachment to her art she severed all her connections, withdrew from her engagements and hurried back to Columbus. There, in the big house that she had bought for her family, she lived with her brother Thomas Pridgett Jr until her death on 22 December 1939.

Fifty-three years of age when she died, Ma Rainey was mourned in the homes of coloured families throughout the States. Though her retirement was spent in almost complete seclusion she was remembered during that half-dozen years with affection and is remembered still. By listening to reissues one may get a very good idea of the range of Ma Rainey's art and the tremendous hold that she had over her audiences. Her voice was unusually well recorded, bearing in mind the deficiencies of Paramount equipment. At least half-a-dozen tracks and the accompaniments, though largely unknown, are typical of what is known to be her particular preference in supporting groups. Furthermore, the material she uses ranges from twelve-bar blues to vaudeville songs.

On some of her tracks, which were recorded in January 1926, in New York, the singer is accompanied by a Henderson group which includes Joe Smith (cornet), Charlie Green (trombone), Buster Bailey (clarinet), Fletcher Henderson (piano), Charlie Dixon (banjo), and Kaiser Marshall on drums. 'Wringing and Twisting Blues' is one such tune, a simple enough blues which tells how Ma is warned by the fortune-teller that she will be left alone by her man. After reflection in bed on the gipsy's words she plans to poison her man if he comes back, and then to despatch herself. The references to voo-doo practices obliquely implied here would have been well appreciated by Negro audiences. Appropriately enough, 'Chain Gang Blues' follows, a blues which had all too much significance in the South:

> *The judge found me guilty, the clerk he wrote*
> *   it down.   (repeat)*
> *Just a poor gal in trouble, I know I'm county*
> *   road bound.*
>
> *Many days of sorrow, many nights of woe*
> *   (repeat)*
> *And a ball and chain everywhere I go.*
>
> *Chains on my feet, padlocks on my hands*
> *   (repeat)*
> *It's all on account of stealin' another gal's man.*
>
> *It was early this mornin' that I had my trial*
> *   (repeat)*
> *Ninety days on the county road and the judge*
> *   didn't even smile.*

The truth of this blues which might appear far-fetched to those unacquainted with practices in the past in the backward Southern areas is well supported by Adam Clayton Powell who in 'Marching Blacks' (Dial Press, NYC 1945) recalls seeing aged women digging holes on the campus of Georgia State College under watchful eyes, and teenage girls working the road in Wetumpka County, Alabama. Ma's voice with its anguish and feeling suggests that she knew something about the subject she had chosen for her blues.

'Misery Blues' was recorded in 1927 and though the trumpet, banjo and tuba players are unknown, the trombone is played by Kid Ory and Claude Hopkins plays the piano. This is a vaudeville blues song and a fine example sung with great swing and played with gusto. The final track on this side has Hopkins alone and Ma sings of being dead drunk in Houston. 'When I was in Houston, drunk most everyday . . .' Like the trouper that she was she aimed many of her recordings at specific places and here she sings 'Give me Houston, that's the place I crave,' but other blues will extol the virtues of Kansas City or elsewhere. It was all the same to Ma Rainey. She was welcome everywhere and happy when she was welcome. On her 'Sissy Blues' the words and their meaning are likely to escape all but the practised student of blues. The subject is a phone call – 'Hello Central, it's bound to drive me wild; can I get that number or will I have to wait a while?' – and the singer is trying to contact her lover who has run off with a 'sissy': 'My man's got a sissy, his (*sic*) name is Miss Kate.' The accompaniment was by an interesting but unknown band which included a Swanee whistle and a really gut-bucket trombone which blasts a rough and ready chorus on 'Broken Soul Blues'. Some of her tracks may not immediately commend themselves to the listener because of the strange band accompaniment 'directed by Professor C. M. Russell'. Its organ-like tones make unusual blues but ultimately they have immense appeal. The recording of these two tracks, 'Moonshine Blues' and 'New Boweavil Blues' is quite extraordinarily good while the quality of Ma Rainey's voice can be heard with almost unprecedented fullness. No need to transcribe these words in order to assist those unfamiliar with blues to comprehend the verses – the cries to the engineer of the Southbound train in 'Moonshine Blues' and even the triple meaning of 'Boweavil', where the term refers at once to lover, insect and the state of being blue, are all fully audible and the greatness of Ma Rainey's voice is powerfully present.

Music Mirror, November 1956

Empress of the Blues
BESSIE SMITH

With her first week's pay as a singer on the professional stage, Bessie Smith obtained a pair of roller-skates and a 'whopping' from her mother. She was just nine years old – the year was 1907 – and already the excellence of her singing had earned her this brief engagement at the Ivory Theatre in her home town of Chattanooga, Tennessee. One of five children in a desperately poor family, she had little schooling but made use of such facilities as were available to appear in school plays and to sing in a local girls' choir. With the latter she made a trip to Memphis and in later years claimed to have received some encouragement there from W. C. Handy, though it was a Chattanooga singer, Cora Fisher, who was the first major influence on Bessie Smith's singing style. Cora Fisher did not record and remains in memory only as a name.

The extent to which Gertrude Ma Rainey played a part in developing Bessie Smith's talents is still a matter of some debate. Bessie herself made little if any acknowledgement to Ma Rainey, while the latter claimed to have taught her. The professional jealousies which both singers shared with more 'legitimate' stage artists may well have accounted for these claims and omissions, for Bessie might well have made use of the older woman's fame until she was established and able to ignore it, while Ma Rainey can be forgiven some envy of the 'Empress of the Blues', as Bessie became. But it seems reasonably certain that about 1910 the small contingent of the Rabbit Foot Minstrels, that Will Rainey and his more celebrated wife managed, gathered Bessie into their number while on a visit to Chattanooga, and that the girl learned both the music and the hard knocks of the profession during her

indeterminate stay with the travelling company. Whether or not Gertrude Rainey 'taught her all she knew', as the story used to run, seems unlikely, and certainly out of character, but there is little doubt that Bessie would have learned all that she could. Possessing a strong will and an obdurate disposition, she apparently 'cut out' on her own within a year or two, but her debt to Ma Rainey remained as evident as the unique qualities, so specifically her own, that she invested in her singing. These were still to be heard a decade later when both singers were recording.

Gertrude Rainey's first record, and her third, featured the two songs by which, more than by any other, she was remembered in her travelling show days. 'Bo-Weavil Blues' (on Paramount 12080) and 'Moonshine Blues' (Paramount 12083) were made in December 1923 and proved to be such continued successes that four years later she recorded them again (on Paramount 12063), a gesture without precedent in her career.

Bessie Smith must have heard her sing these great blues many times in person as well as on the original records. It was Bessie's frequent practice – or that of her manager – to record, and in doing so to 'carve', the recordings of other noted singers of her day. Few singers attempted to follow a recording of Bessie's with a recording of their own, but there is a certain grim determination in her consistent remodelling and invariable improvement of the blues that other singers had only recently issued. Much of Bessie's fame as a recording artist undoubtedly revolved round this fact, for a proportion of the buying public must have held back until her version of a song was issued, and it was surely no accident that the first of her blues actually to be issued, 'Down-Hearted Blues', was daringly one that had been recorded to a point where its possibilities must have appeared exhausted until her own inimitable version appeared.

Significantly, Bessie's closest rival, but also a Columbia recording artist, Clara Smith, was the only one of her contemporaries who did not receive this treatment, and with Clara alone she shared a couple of records. But with Ma Rainey? In April 1924 Bessie Smith made the two recordings here reissued for the first time which deliberately linked on Columbia 140180D Ma Rainey's two most famous items, 'Bo-Weavil Blues' and 'Moonshine Blues'. Were they a challenge to the older singer? Were they a declaration of her achievement with fifteen records already issued? Were they a gracious acknowledgement to her teacher? The reason must remain conjectural, but the recordings serve to indicate both the similarities and the differences between the two greatest professional blues singers.

Ma Rainey opened her 'Moonshine Blues' in her slow, majestic way, making her lines statements, virtually without embellishment:

I was drinkin' all night, babe, and the night
  before,
When I get sober ain't gonna drink no more,
'Cause my friend's standing in my door.

My head's been goin' round and around, babe,
I don't know if the river's running up or down,
But one thing's certain, mama's gonna leave
  town.

The blues is rough and knockabout, autobiographical; sung as if it were the events of the moment – as indeed, in spite of its repetition, it generally was.

Bessie sings the lines:

Drunk all night babe, drunk the night before,
But when I get sober, I ain't gonna drink no
  more,
Because my friend has left me, standing in my
  door.

– slightly remodelling the words, elaborating the ends of the lines and making the vowels musically expressive in themselves. Where Ma Rainey was inclined to break up phrases and introduce aspirates, singing 'My head's goin' roun' . . . anha . . . roun', babe . . . ,' Bessie sings 'My head's goin' rounanaroun', babe . . . her elision helping to give the impression of her condition. Ma Rainey, intent on her powerful declarations, frequently gives force to the opening of a line and is negligent in its conclusion, but Bessie Smith tended to dwell on the last words, giving musical value to the vowels as she does in the end words in the lines quoted. When they sing the lines:

You'll find me reeling and a-rocking, howling
  like a hound.
I'll catch the first train that's going
  southbound,
Stop, you hear me say, Stop. Right
  through my brain, O stop that train
So I can ride back home again . . .

Ma Rainey sings with tremendous authority and her commands of 'Stop!' are imperious, sung to a 'stop chorus' which leaves no doubt in the mind as to her demands. She sings the irregular verse with ease, using the last line to lead in to the next chorus. There is more musical flow in Bessie's use of the first line (which Ma Rainey wilfully divides by singing 'wriggle and rockin'), and her evaluation of 'Oh stop, you hear me say, stop, right through my brain' is not as an injunction as was Ma Rainey's but as an extension of a reeling sensation in musical terms. And she completes these words as a verse by repeating 'Oh stop that train' so that the last line is formally united. Bessie's treatment of the difficult and structurally illogical conclusion of 'Boweavil Blues' is very similar. Ma Rainey sings:

Lord, I went downtown; bought me a hat.
I brought it back home and laid it on the shelf,
Looked at my babe, I'm getting tired sleeping
by myself.

but Bessie, more conscious of the awkward structure which Ma Rainey sings to an uncompromisingly marked punctuation, fills out the words and repeats the second half of the last line till its shape is fully determined.

In this comparison is revealed the essential difference between Bessie Smith and Ma Rainey. The older singer was closer to the folk blues and the blues of the travelling tent and medicine shows. Her songs were her own or had long since become so and she sang, even bellowed, to her audience, as a country blues singer might, blues that were her personal experience. Any vocal elaborations were a part of her mode of expression and seem not to have been studied or used in their own right in a musical sense. For Bessie Smith, introducing to blues singing a high level of professionalism, the musical structure of her blues was extremely important. This is revealed on the few issued alternative masters of her recordings, which show them to have an intentional employment of expression, cadence, embellishment which would be far less marked and less deliberate in Ma Rainey. This is not to say that Bessie's blues were not deeply felt, for the converse is true. She took a song, a blues, frequently one that was featured or sung by another singer, and immersed herself in it. The resultant song was one which was a direct and personal expression of herself, enriched and made immeasurably greater by the strength of her artistry and the expressiveness of her phrasing. It is these qualities of improvisation, of extension, and sometimes of deliberate musical interpretation that endear Bessie Smith to the jazz enthusiast. For those to whom the blues rather than jazz appeals, the directness of personal expression of Ma Rainey attracts more strongly. That Bessie's artistry is very largely the outcome of the approach of Ma Rainey is evident in their many similarities of emotional depth, dynamic delivery, and choice of material.

By the time she started to record in 1923 Bessie Smith's style was largely defined. She had more years of experience behind her in rough country joints, travelling tent shows, and barnstorming tours of run-down theatres than her mere twenty-five years would seem to permit. For the paltry weekly wage of $2.50 she toured in Mississippi, Alabama, and Florida with Pete Werley's Florida Cotton Pickers' Minstrel Show. 1917 found her in Selma on the Alabama River moaning the blues in a gin-mill on the outskirts of the town, but the following year she was on the road in a travelling show, appearing in vaudeville in Indianapolis. Her performance gave her what was probably her first press notice – a brief mention in the *Chicago Defender* of 25 May 1918. Then she became a headliner in the TOBA leading her own show 'Liberty Belles', which exploited the wartime hit-song 'Liberty Bell'. She appeared at the 91 Theatre on Decatur Street, Atlanta, and a little later at the grander 81 Theatre close by. 1920 came and she was out of the South, and featured as a singer in the brassy resort of Atlantic City, New Jersey.

Each move gave her greater confidence and a greater appreciation of the needs of her audiences and the techniques required for singing in dance hall or theatre. Vaudeville songs broadened her repertoire, whilst her ability in her pre-recording days to 'hoof –

to introduce song-and-dance routines in her show – opened up new opportunities for her. She had teamed with Clarence Williams, and after an unsuccessful start she succeeded Gloria Harven in the show 'How Come', in which Sidney Bechet played the part of a Chinese laundryman. It was all experience, and when the show folded she moved to Philadelphia, where she got engagements at The Madhouse on 11th and Poplar and eventually at the celebrated Standard Theatre. Her reputation was made. Frank Walker, who had heard her long ago in Selma, Alabama, sent Clarence Williams, now a Race Record 'Judge', to get her for Columbia.

'Tall and fat and scared to death' is how Frank Walker later described Bessie Smith's appearance on her arrival in New York. Once she had settled down there he brought her to the recording studio and into the horn she sang the first item to herald her long association with Columbia, "T'aint Nobody's Business if I Do'. It was historic, but none of the nine 'takes' were issued from that session on 15 February 1923. Less than a couple of months later she recorded this first number again, and this is the song which opens the present LP.

Both Bessie Smith and Gertrude Rainey were blues singers and vaudeville singers, but Bessie was a jazz singer too, in a sense that was inapplicable to Ma Rainey. Though the latter had her Georgia Jazz Band she made a blues band of it, and gathered around her jazz musicians like Tommy Ladnier who were most at home with the blues, or blues instrumentalists like Tampa Red and Georgia Tom. If the distinction remains a fine one, it is a fact that bands or small groups that comprised musicians much in the jazz tradition and of the New York variety rather than of New Orleans frequently accompanied Bessie Smith in person and on record in her later years. In view of the wide interest in the instrumental forms, it is not surprising that reissues of Bessie's recordings have been drawn mainly from these later sessions, and the jazz enthusiast has been well served in the four records of the Bessie Smith story, Philips B 07002-5L. Before the first of the remarkable recording sessions with musicians from Fletcher Henderson's Orchestra and, in particular, Joe Smith, when 'Weeping Willow Blues' (B 07003 L) was made on 26 September 1924, Bessie Smith had recorded over fifty titles, of which some forty-six had been issued. Of these, however, only three have been reissued in LP form and only five in any form, with the result that a large and important body of her recordings has been unavailable to all but the most fortunate and passionate collectors.

On the present record are to be found sixteen of the best recordings made by Bessie Smith in the first year-and-a-half of her contract with Columbia. They range from the intensely moving 'Mamma's got the Blues', with Clarence Williams' sombre piano and emphatic crushed notes, to the gusto of 'Aggravatin' Papa'; from the magnificent version of 'See See Rider' entitled 'Beale Street Mama', with its splendidly timed final vocal chorus, to the ingenuous hokum of 'Haunted House Blues'; from the remarkable interpretation of 'Bleeding Hearted Blues' which invests the banal words with dignity and meaning to the equally remarkable version of 'Nobody in Town Can Bake a Sweet Jelly Like Mine', which ignores the obvious handling one is bound to admit Bessie might well have given it six years later, and instead gives it a depth of feeling that makes it linger in the mind. In many ways this is the most interesting period in Bessie's recording career, the period that moulded the course of her life as a major figure in the history of jazz music; the period that brought her name to the lips

As M.C. of the Ann Arbor Blues Festival Paul Oliver attempts to solve a problem: the audience didn't want Hound Dog Taylor to finish his set, 1970. *Valerie Oliver*

Bernice Reagon, gospel singer; Taj Mahal, blues singer; Daphne D. Harrison, historian and Paul Oliver at the Smithsonian Institution's Black History month symposium "Black American Blues Song: A Study in Poetic Literature", Washington D.C. 1982. *Smithsonian Institution*

Tractor driver Robert Curtis Smith, guitar, and barber/blues singer Wade Walton at
the Big Six barbershop, Clarksdale, Mississippi, 1960. *Paul Oliver*

Big Bill Broonzy and Brother John Sellers with Paul Oliver at his home, 1957.
Beryl Bryden

Brownie McGhee demonstrates a lick to Valerie Oliver while Sonny Terry accompanies, 1958. *Paul Oliver*

Little Walter, Paul Oliver, John Steiner and St. Louis Jimmy at Smitty's Corner, Chicago 1960. *Sherrod*

Lightnin' Hopkins and Arhoolie Records director Chris Strachwitz with Paul Oliver at his Story of the Blues exhibition, American Embassy London, 1964. *U.S.I.S.*

ppie Wallace singing at the Albert Hall, London, 1965.
Paul Oliver

Lillian Glinn in retirement, at her California home, 1970.
Paul Oliver

Victoria Spivey relaxes, 1970. *Paul Oliver*

Blues singer Robert Pete Williams and songster Bill Williams at the Smithsonian Institution's Festival of American Folklife, Montreal, Canada, 1971. *Paul Oliver*

Lowell Fulson in his London hotel room, 1969.
Paul Oliver

Pianist Henry Brown with his friend, the guitar-player Henry Townsend, St. Louis, 1960. *Paul Oliver*

Georgia Talbert (14) playing piano for her vocal group, while Jasper Love, blues

Whistling Alex Moore, piano, while on tour
in Europe, 1967. *Paul Oliver*

Mance Lipscomb at Ann Arbor, 1970.
Paul Oliver

John Henry Barbee in London, waiting backstage, 1964. *Paul Oliver*

and her voice to the homes of Negroes throughout the United States, paving the way to a wider audience; the period when her spirit was fresh, when she was a young woman who had much to sing and sang it in a way that moulded and epitomized the jazz vocal, when she was as yet untouched by bitterness, by the ravages of gin addiction, and by the shadow of her eventual fate.

Notes to Philips BBL 13651, 1960

Suitcase Blues
THE THOMAS FAMILY

Blues writing places great importance on the work of individuals but a fruitful area of research might be the study of mutual influences within blues families. In any such study the Thomas clan of Houston, Texas, would emerge as the 'first family' of the blues. George W. Thomas, a Southern Pacific railroad worker and his wife Fanny had a dozen children, all of whom being gifted as singers or musicians. Some played or sang locally or in church, but a few became widely known; they are the subject of this album.

Eldest of the family was George Washington Thomas Jr, who was born about 1885 and was a professional theatre pit pianist in his twenties. Clarence Williams met him in Houston in 1911. 'Although I was in my teens and Thomas was old enough to be my father we became staunch friends,' he wrote in 1940. 'Thomas composed "New Orleans Hop Scop Blues" which was the first tune with the Boogie Woogie bass movement. I first heard him play it in the theatre in 1911' ('The Boogie Woogie Blues Folio', NY 1940). Three years later George Thomas joined Williams in New Orleans and they were publishing partners for a while. Later he sold Clarence his 'Hop Scop Blues', and doubtless regretted it: Bessie Smith, Sarah Martin and Williams himself made several records of the theme.

Unfortunately George Thomas made few records – a solo, as by Clay Custer, of his celebrated theme 'The Rocks' in 1922; a few jazz titles with his own Muscle Shoals Devils, and some accompaniments to Houston singer Tiny Franklin made in 1923. 'The Rocks' has the earliest walking bass figures on record and these appear occasionally on the Tiny Franklin sides. For George Thomas as pianist and singer we have only the coupling included here; barrelhouse in character with rolling bass and a sardonic humour: 'Please Mister, please don't kill 'im in here, 'cause I'm the landlord I got to stand the beer.' There's a good knockabout rapport with the guitarist who might be Papa Charlie Hill, or even Blind Blake.

By this date, George Thomas had been in Chicago several years. When he had got his music house established he sent for his sister Beulah to join him. Born in 1898 she had a childhood lisp which earned her the nickname 'Sippie'. She married young, got divorced, and then 'took Matt Wallace to be my regular man', as she declared on 'Murder's Gonna Be My Crime'. The pianist on this recording was her youngest brother, Hersal, whom she regarded as her own child. She brought him with her to Chicago, and subsequently Detroit, where she settled with her gambler husband. Sippie's warm, generous, pretty features and fine voice for the blues were complemented by the wide-eyed appeal of her brother.

Born in 1910, Hersal gained a reputation as a child prodigy in Houston, exceeding his eldest brother as a blues pianist. He modelled his style on George's but elaborated it and developed new bass figures. In Chicago his fame was formidable, as William Russell ascertained from the boogie pianist Albert Ammons. 'Whenever Hersal Thomas, who made a deep impression on young Ammons, came to a party, the other pianists were afraid to play; so he became unusually popular and got all the girls.' (W. Russell in 'Jazzmen' NY 1939). That was in 1924. Early the next year he cut his first record, his celebrated solo 'Suitcase Blues'. A masterly composition, superbly constructed, it places tremolos against an ominous, majestic bass pattern, with occasional climbing breaks.

With George as entrepreneur, the Thomases were doing well. Hersal accompanied Sippie before his fifteenth birthday with no less a giant than King Joe Oliver as horn player; a few months later he was working with Louis Armstrong, then at his peak. By mid-1925 he had a new singer to accompany – none other than his own niece, George Thomas's daughter Hociel, who was a couple of years older than himself. Her first title with him, 'Worried Down with the Blues', revealed her powerful voice for the blues and her use of portamento and blues shading. 'Give it to me good Mister Hersal' she commanded on 'Fish Tail Dance' and he obliged, catching the swing of the 'wicked dance and shimmy right on to the floor'. The splendid tune was composed by George Thomas who didn't miss the opportunity to refer to the band playing his own 'Muscle Shoals Blues'.

Hersal was everywhere in 1925–26 making a dozen titles with Hociel, fifteen with Sippie, accompanying Lillian Miller and Sodarisa Miller and making his own beautiful 'Hersal Blues'. Sippie invited him back to Detroit and he was immediately employed at Penny's Pleasure Inn. It was a tragic engagement; after a meal there one night he developed food poisoning and within a week, despite all ministrations, he died. He was still only sixteen years of age. For Hociel the loss of Hersal was unbearable and she gave up her professional career; Sippie tried another session or two but her heart wasn't in it. A year later, in March 1930, she got the news that her brother George had died as a result of a street accident in Chicago. It was not until after the War that either recorded again.

Back home in Houston, Texas, Bernice Edwards alone maintained the Thomas tra-

dition. She wasn't a blood relative but she was, in Sippie's words, 'one of the family'. The same age as Hersal, she had grown up with the youngest Thomas children including Hociel, and it was from them that she learned to sing and play the blues. Mostly from Hociel, who was a very good blues pianist in her own right. When the Thomas family moved north she stayed on in Houston, running around with other piano players like Harold Holiday (Black Boy Shine). Her turn to record came in February 1928 when she went up to Chicago with Blind Lemon Jefferson to cut six titles for Paramount. Her voice and approach was more lowdown than that of the Thomas girls, but her blues were simpler in structure and less varied melodically. She reflected Hociel's influence in her use of blues shading and that of Texas Alexander in her penchant for slow tempo and heavy moaning. Although only in her late teens, her singing suggests both a physical and an emotional maturity far beyond her years. Both Hersal and Black Boy Shine can be heard echoed in her playing – 'Long Tall Mama' being reminiscent of Thomas, while its session-mate 'Mean Man Blues' has strong links with Holiday's style, light and easy. Later the same year, in the company of Ramblin' Thomas (no relation), she had one more session which produced several memorable blues though her piano playing was more subdued.

By 1930 the family of Texas blues had broken up: George and Hersal were dead, Hociel had left for the West Coast where she died in 1952, a few years after her rediscovery by Rudi Blesh. Bernice recorded just once more, in 1935, but soon after, she married, joined the church and drifted into obscurity. Sippie joined the church too, though she made a brief return to blues recording with Hersal's erstwhile friend Albert Ammons, in 1946. A score of years later she made a short comeback to give the audiences of the Sixties a last glimpse of the blues from the days when the Thomas family were unrivalled, forty years before.

Notes to Magpie PY4404, 1977

Mighty Tight Woman
SIPPIE WALLACE

A splendid anachronism, Sippie Wallace; a singular survivor of a long past blues tradition. There was a time, in the Forties, when almost the only form of blues which had any recognition was that called 'classic blues'. The term itself is vague enough and does not carry in it any specific form, or style, or means of expression. But though it lacks a real definition the classic blues has meant for collectors and jazz enthusiasts the singing of the blues artists who worked with the jazz bands of the 1920s. There were few enthusiasts of the blues in the early years of the traditional jazz 'revival' and, in consequence, the blues singers who had associations with jazz were those whose names appeared in the articles and the occasional books which mileposted the developing interest in this form of music. When the 'trad' boom was over and the Dixieland bands and the New Orleans bands had fought out their battles of authenticity and purity to meet at last over glasses of warm beer to rue the passing of a fad, attention to the classic blues went too.

In the past few years a rise in interest in the blues has echoed in some respects the traditional jazz phase, sustaining a large number of imitative musicians, developing a market for the issue and reissue of the music of the past, and promoting the rediscovery of veteran musicians. In all this activity in the blues field there has been little attention to the work of the classic singers. Sadly their link with jazz which had inspired interest in the past is now contributory to the present disregard. Once again, the arguments over authenticity have produced artificial barriers, have classified, often meaninglessly, the categories into which musicians and singers conveniently fall and have imposed a highly artificial form of arbitrary evaluation. And the arguments have weighed heavily against the classic blues singers when indeed, they enter the discussion at all.

The appearance of Sippie Wallace at the Folk Blues Festival concerts in 1966 must be counted from any point of view, a conspicuous success. Her single appearance has caused critics to reconsider their opinions, some writers to admit grudgingly that there may after all, be some value in the work of singers of her type and generation. As the reviews and the spontaneous acclamation of the audiences revealed, Sippie Wallace's majestic singing was both a personal triumph and a smashing blow against those who found the classic singer inadmissable to the blues pantheon.

To the extent that the term has any meaning, Sippie Wallace is a classic blues singer. But the term is elastic enough to include at one pole the work of artists of the stature of Bessie Smith and Gertrude Ma Rainey, and at the other the entertainment of Rosa Henderson and Viola McCoy. While the former showed in their every phrase the influence of the blues, the latter singers were vaudeville entertainers whose links were as much with white show business as they were with the Negro tradition of song. No derogatory implications are intended; only some indication of the looseness of the terminology. Nearly all these singers were women and it is probably a reflection of the recording patterns of the day that while there were few rural women singers recorded in the Twenties the classic singers were almost exclusively female. Those who showed the greatest association with the blues tradition inevitably appeal today to a greater extent than do those whose singing was a part of the vaudeville entertainment of the early years of the century, and for this reason Lillian Glinn, Cleo Gibson or Clara Smith are among the few that are remembered. Standing pre-eminently in their company is Sippie Wallace.

Born early in the century in Houston, Texas, Beulah Thomas came from a musical family which included her talented composer brother George Thomas and the ill-fated child prodigy Hersal Thomas who was one of the finest of early recording blues pianists. A childhood lisp gave Beulah the nickname of 'Sippie' and she was known as this when she began as a child to sing before the congregations in Houston churches. This background in singing gave her a valuable training before large audiences which stood her in good stead in later years. Her brother George left Houston to become partner to the New Orleans pianist Clarence Williams. Beulah stayed at home, but when eventually George arrived in Chicago he sent for his young sister to join him. In the North she married a gambler by the name of Matt Wallace and it was as Sippie Wallace that her name first appeared on an Okeh record a matter of months after Bessie Smith's earliest recordings. The song was her own composition 'Up the Country' and it contained a recitative about her family which fired the imagination of other singers. Sippie's distinctive phrasing and use of imagery was copied by many other singers and following the remarkable success of 'Up the Country' and its backing, 'Shorty George Blues', she had a succession of nearly a score of hit records. People lined up in dozens outside the record shops to get her latest disc and her beautiful features, dimpled cheeks and soft, winning smile was to be seen in Okeh advertisements and throw-away sheets in the Negro newspapers and the music stores across America.

On her earliest records Sippie was accom-panied by Clarence Williams or Eddie Heywood. Heywood played for her on 'Up the Country', but, forty-three years later she played the piano herself, a little timidly perhaps but revealing unmistakably the characteristics of the Texas piano tradition. The Texas tradition coloured the content of her songs too: 'Shorty George' was adapted from a folk blues current in the State when she was a girl. On this recent version she is accompanied by Roosevelt Sykes, himself a veteran from the recording era of the Twenties. His sensitive support on 'Bedroom Blues' or 'Trouble Everywhere I Go' is entirely in keeping with the character of the men who supported the classic singers four decades ago. Those accustomed to Roosevelt Sykes' ebullient, stomping piano playing may well be surprised by these gentle and contemplative piano accompaniments.

Hersal Thomas was Sippie Wallace's favourite accompanist in her great years. His premature death from poisoning profoundly affected her, for she regarded him as her own son. It was an irreparable loss to the piano blues as the memories and testimony of such singers as Jimmy Yancey and Albert Ammons have been witness. Every pianist tried to play his 'Rocks' and 'Fives', and learned his figures from his records. One was Little Brother Montgomery from Louisiana whose support to Sippie on 'Special Delivery Blues', 'I'm a Mighty Tight Woman', or 'Murder's Gonna Be My Crime', evoke the shade of the great Hersal. But it takes an artist of stature to inspire his accompanists and credit for this session of recreations of the Twenties must go, above all, to Sippie herself. Her moaned phrases, her long extended notes, her subtle inflexions and shadings which charge her words with meaning are the hallmark of consummate artistry.

Those who were privileged to hear her in person will never forget Sippie Wallace's utter disdain of such contrivances as the microphone as she stood yards back from the instrument and soared into her blues. Without mannerism, scarcely without gesture, without histrionics or mugging or any aid other than her own great talent she dominated her audiences and held them enrapt in her presence. Such an ability revealed the measure of a true professional but one whose involvement was totally within the blues. Or so it has become again, for Sippie Wallace is still a devoted member of the church in which she has been working for the past quarter of a century. The Depression brought the virtual end to her recording career and though, many years later, she had a brief comeback in the company of Albert Ammons she was increasingly drawn to the church in Detroit where she had made her home. The death of her closest relatives and of her husband convinced her that she should give up blues singing. She became not only a devout church member but an active leader of the choir and teacher of church singers. She accompanied them herself on the piano and played in church, so that her contact with singing and playing was never broken. A chain of circumstances including the encouragement of her fellow-Texan, Victoria Spivey, has brought her back briefly to the blues but she has wisely decided against an attempted autumnal comeback. These recordings are perhaps her last blues performances, but they are a uniquely valuable document of a great age made by one of its most outstanding exponents. They range from the entertaining, archly amusing stage songs of the vaudeville theatre, 'You Got to Know How' or 'Women Be Wise' to the moving and timeless 'Lonesome Hours Blues'.

Listening to them they will evoke for some the memory of a plump, bespectacled, regal and still beautiful woman whose great voice filled the Albert Hall and thrilled an audience whose grandmothers were of her generation; for all who hear them they must signify a last link with the classic blues, without compare at this time. Almost alone they give us a glimpse of a blues tradition that we missed.

Notes to Storyville SLP 198, 1967

We're Gonna Rock the Joint
JIMMY RUSHING'S EARLY YEARS

As one thumbs through the pages of the discographies of blues singers one is constantly aware that the amount of biographical information on them is lamentably small. Therein perhaps lies some of their peculiar fascination: the strange names, the colourful pseudonyms, the titles of blues that are couched in idiomatic phrases that have real meaning only for the members of a remote minority group, have an aura of romanticism that might fade away if the hard and often dismal facts that shaped them were commonly known. But as the blues collector stares at the record label or listens whilst the needle summons again three lost minutes of a man's life some thirty years ago, he cannot help but speculate at times on the possible chain of circumstances that finally brought him from the city sidewalk and before the crude recording apparatus to enregister for those brief moments his rough, untutored voice, his picked notes on his guitar and the fragment of human experience that constitutes his blues. Where did he come from; who were his parents; when did he leave home? – one wonders and falters, as the limitations of one's own personal experience make it almost impossible to imagine the succession of occupations, the wanderings from State to State, the contacts with a multitude of unknown characters that eventually led to the recording session, which for the singer himself was probably as speedily forgotten as it was effected. There are exceptions of course – and these give some stimulus to the imagination. A Ma Rainey, a Leadbelly, Josh White, Brownie McGhee, appears as a real person in the mind's eye, and the mental groping in order to humanize the voice that issues from the speaker is more easily accomplished. But even among the great or more popular blues singers who have recorded extensively and about whom many thousands of words have been written, there are still many whose personalities remain virtually unknown beyond those which they project on stage. In many cases we have little knowledge of the influences and incidents that shaped their styles.

In spite of his considerable popularity, his pre-eminence as a band blues singer and his close association with the remarkably influential Count Basie, Jimmy Rushing has been singularly neglected in this respect. Though much has been written on his work as a singer, particularly on record, accounts of his early years have been sketchy and often conflicting and little attention has been paid to his relationships with other singers and the degree to which they influenced him. Yet Jimmy Rushing is a man who is no less generous with his time, his enthusiasm and his conversation than he is in his celebrated proportions. Delighted with the opportunity to talk about singers he had known, and of the years spent before and during his periods of working with the bands whose reputations he helped establish, he relishes the recollections that he summons from as far back as two score years and more. At times he rolls over with laughter with the memory of humorous incidents that happened long ago; warm but not loud laughter; at other times he is thoughtful and grave, his lips pursed, his eyebrows raised, his eyes focussed on the past.

Jimmy Rushing was born on 26 August 1903, in Oklahoma City. His parents were musical and his mother, a very religious woman, sang in church choirs and was at one time a professional religious singer. His father played trumpet, more as a hobby than as a means of obtaining employment; he was, in Jimmy's words 'a professional man'. At one time he owned a taxi-cab stand operating a number of cabs and later he opened Rushing's Cafe a medium-sized restaurant for coloureds. It was his parents' desire that he should follow a career in music and Jimmy was persuaded at an early age to learn the violin. 'I didn't want to play no violin,' he exclaimed indignantly nearly half a century later. 'I never could get a note out of that damn thing anyway!' Following his parents' inclinations on his behalf, Jimmy went on to study musical theory at the City's Douglas High School and from the course of his education and the ambitions of his family it would seem surprising that he ever became a blues singer.

It was Jimmy Rushing's uncle, Wesley Manning, who decided the eventual career that he pursued. Wesley Manning was a pianist who lived in close contact with the Rushing family but in their perpetual disapproval. For he was the 'Professor' of a sporting-house. 'They were afraid he would influence me . . . And he did!' said Jimmy, laughing in delight at the thought. When he was still only a small boy his uncle would creep in by the back door and climb the stairs to Jimmy's room. The dark figure would lean over and thrust a hat beside him, saying in a hoarse whisper: 'Dip your hand in Jimmy, take what you can hold.' The hat would be full of golden dollars, the takings of a night playing to the 'sporting men' and Jimmy would smuggle a handful into his bed. From an early age he had taught himself to play the family piano and his uncle took whatever opportunities arose to teach him to play and sing the blues. It was all that he wanted to do, and though he paid attention assiduously to his studies in musical theory which were to stand him in good

stead in later years, he had no doubts as to his ultimate intention to be a blues entertainer. Among the other Negro blues singers and pianists that were playing in Oklahoma City during his youth none influenced him as much as Gerry Stoner, a barrelhouse pianist, unknown today, but whose reputation in the State was formidable at that time. 'Stoney' as he was known, 'played a mess of blues' and his powerful playing and rich voice left a considerable impression on the style of the young Jimmy Rushing.

His first employment as an entertainer came, not unnaturally, from his father, for whom he played piano in Rushing's Cafe. Jimmy's repertoire was strictly circumscribed, for he received the inevitable 'whopping' if he began to play the blues. In no way was the work a waste of his time for it helped him towards the liberal attitude to popular music that has been a characteristic of his singing in more recent years, whilst the technical knowledge and experience of playing before a company of people was invaluable. 'I'm just naturally a rambler; cain't stay in any one place for long. I've got to be on the move,' he says today, and perhaps it was as much because of this restlessness as it was from the resultant soreness from attempting to play blues in his father's establishment that led him to travel from home. In 1921 he first heard a New Orleans Jazz Band. It was Singleton's Jazz Band (emphatically *not* Zutty Singleton) which was touring through Texas and the Oklahoma Territory. Forgotten though it may be today, it fascinated Jimmy who still recalls the drummer playing the afterbeat on a suitcase as the band roared into 'Hold That Tiger'. The drummer in fact, was something of a trick entertainer who used to sing the band's vocals. It was a speciality of his to take a snare drum and, loosening the snares, sing with the drum held close to his face so that his voice vibrated the snares, producing a bizarre but obviously memorable effect. It was to be seven years before Rushing reached New Orleans, when he played a one-night stand with Walter Page's Blue Devils and spent the rest of his time listening to Sara Martin, but the band whetted his appetite for travel and made him realize that there was much music to be heard elsewhere.

During the next few years Jimmy Rushing made many excursions through the mid-West, though Oklahoma City remained his base. He liked to tour 'in the sticks' during corn-husking time and after the wheat harvest. The farmers were rich then, and happy. When the crops were gathered and stored there were lively barn-dances and hoe-downs through the middle States and Jimmy toured through Oklahoma, Kansas – even as far as Iowa – playing and singing at the dances, gathering money and experience. Sometimes he sat in with small groups – maybe two violins, or bass and drums with the piano carried from the farmhouse to the barn. Other times he would entertain alone. In the hectic days of the early Twenties the young people often called for more exciting dances than those their elders enjoyed and he would frequently find himself playing for a Turkey-Trotting group of youngsters at one end of the barn, whilst a square dance was in progress at the other end to the music of a country fiddle band. He was plump, bawdy and immensely popular.

Jimmy's excursions took him South too, to Texas, and he stopped off to play in Dallas. It was there that he heard many blues singers and most notably, Blind Lemon Jefferson. 'You could not see Lemon for the thick crowd around him, but you could hear him blocks away,' he recalled. The thickset, yellow-skinned street singer was immensely popular amongst the Dallas Negroes and earned good money doing the barrelhouse

circuit. He spoke and acted as if he could see, for his sense of direction, and of people and places near him, was uncanny. But Jimmy, who learned a lot from Lemon Jefferson and listened to him whenever he could, was convinced that he was blind.

In 1924 Jimmy decided to go to California. He arrived in the Western State and worked his way along the coast, playing at cabarets and clubs and in various establishments that gave him an opportunity to work under all manner of conditions. His voice had matured and he was making a name as a singer. All the time he listened to blues singers, many of whom were of considerable quality though they did not record and are forgotten now. He particularly remembers a fine blues singer named Jessie Derricks who had many admirers in San Francisco and Los Angeles and who had no desire to go East. But it was Caroline Snowden who most impressed him amongst the West Coast singers. She had a beautiful, rich voice with a full sound and sang to a packed house at the Quality Club on the corner of 12th and Paloma in Los Angeles, when Jimmy used to listen to her moving blues in the Fall of 1925. Later he was to hear her singing at the Cotton Club.

Still restless, he decided to return to the mid-West and 1926 found him in Dallas once more. There he met Sam Price from Honey Grove, Texas, who as a record salesman at Ashford's store had recommended that Paramount record Blind Lemon Jefferson. Sam Price was now working 'on the Track' – playing piano at Ella B. Moore's Theatre, and the two men struck up a friendship that has lasted over thirty years. Bill King's Show was in town out of Chicago, and playing in the show was Walter Page's band, The Blue Devils. It was the first time that Jimmy had heard them, though he had once played in a trio with Page in earlier years, for the bass player also came from

Oklahoma City. Back in Oklahoma City, Jimmy ran into the Blue Devils again; Count Basie had joined them and was playing piano and Page offered Jimmy employment as singer with the band. He jumped at the chance. The Blue Devils were famous in Kansas City and had many fine musicians including Walter Page's half-brother, Oran 'Hot Lips' Page in the line-up. They toured extensively through the South and mid-West playing one-night stands, going as far south as Louisiana and north to Chicago. Whenever he was in Chicago, Jimmy used to take every opportunity to listen to the singers there, but the first person he would seek out was Bertha 'Chippie' Hill. 'Me and Chippie used to run around, and when I was in Chicago we really used to do Town – the "Golden Dollar", places like that. We had a ball! She was singing at the "Elite" – 'course you know there were two "Elites", the Class one, and the Second one. Hers was the *Second* one. Man, it was rough. That was in 1929.'

Among the other singers whom he greatly admired at this time were Ida Cox and Leroy Carr. Ida Cox he knew well – 'Ida and her piano-player Jesse Crump' – and he profited much from the association, but Carr's influence was greater. Not that Leroy Carr's style of singing influenced his own driving band style, but Carr's intense feeling for the blues earned Jimmy's respect.

When the 'Big One', Walter Page, finally went bankrupt and the majority of band members joined Bennie Moten, Jimmy joined him too. In October 1929 he made his recording debut with Moten whilst in Chicago and a fortnight later, on 10 November, as a final gesture the Blue Devils made their only record – 'Blue Devil Blues / Squabblin'' on Vocalion 1463 – and Jimmy still recalls how they spent two days hanging blankets around the walls of an empty hall before the recording was made. This recording, which he considers to have been his first, he had never heard until this year when a San Francisco girl produced a clean copy for him to hear. With Moten he was a prominently featured vocalist and he gave up all ideas of playing the piano to any extent again. He concentrated now on singing forthright, driving, punching blues that would accord with the powerhouse band, but as they went on tour through Alabama, Georgia and the Deep South, he listened hard to the folk singers that he heard. In Atlanta the blues singers jostled amongst the crowds on Decatur street and Auburn Avenue where the band was playing. Before he joined the band for the evening show Jimmy would wander down the street listening to them as they walked unselfconsciously with guitars slung from their shoulders, quietly picking and singing. In the gutters the blind blues singers played and begged: he would give them his spare coins and ask them to sing the blues, any blues . . .

1930 saw Jimmy Rushing firmly entrenched in the Moten Band; the rest is a part of jazz history well recorded on disc and in print. It is a permanent part of jazz history, for Jimmy Rushing's fame is assured, his importance as a jazz and band blues singer is undeniable. But he is the same man; fame has not altered him and he is as ready now as ever to listen to other blues singers, to listen, to learn, to enthuse, to praise. His admiration for B. B. King is great and he speaks with lively interest and in generous terms of Smoky Hogg and Lightnin' Hopkins. And if today his tours take him to Galveston or Houston or to a score of other towns in the South he will be found amongst the teeming crowds in the Negro sectors, listening for the blues singers in the cabarets and on the sidewalks.

Jazz Monthly, December 1957
Jimmy Rushing died New York, 8 June 1972.

Ain't Nobody's Business
JIMMY WITHERSPOON

'Blues shouter' is a term that is often applied quite indiscriminately to blues singers. As a rule the singers of the Twenties and Thirties did not shout, and to take the term literally to shout and sing a blues is by no means easy. In rural Negro usage the term 'shout' meant 'making a joyful noise unto the Lord' and had mainly religious associations. In time, however, joyful musical and vocal expression was termed 'shouting' and in turn the word was taken over by jazz musicians and similarly applied. It was the spirit rather than the act that was implied in shouting and the use of overloud speech – literal shouting – was not necessary though by no means ruled out. Undoubtedly 'shouting the blues' had at one time a similar meaning: blues sung with conviction and feeling. Country blues singers might have felt the need to sing loudly to be heard above the noise of the juke joints but they did not have to be heard above a musical background any louder than their own guitars and pianos, which before the Second World War were unamplified. In the regions lying west of the Mississippi, in Missouri, Arkansas, Oklahoma and part of Texas, there was a strong musical tradition of bands which played the blues and, naturally enough, they had blues singers working with them. These singers had the task of singing in crowded halls, on band stands and in front of powerful swinging mid-West bands. They had to be heard and they developed a full-voiced style of singing which can properly be termed 'blues shouting' in any sense of the phrase. Jimmy Witherspoon is one of them.

Jimmy Witherspoon was born in Gurdon, Arkansas on 18 August 1923. His mother was a strong member of the local First Baptist Church and at the age of six Jimmy was already singing in a gospel choir. No doubt the experience did him good though any interest in the blues that he showed was met with disapproval. In fact it was not until the Monterrey Festival in 1961 that his mother heard him singing the blues when he invited her to the concerts. In his teens Jimmy did hear the records of the Kansas City blues shouters, and particularly Jimmy Rushing and Joe Turner whose names were then coming into prominence for the first time. If he envisaged singing for his own career at that time he had little opportunity to start, for at the age of eighteen, in 1941, he was drafted. From 1941 until 1943 Jimmy Witherspoon served in the Merchant Marine on regular runs in the Pacific Ocean; his opportunity to sing with a band arose unexpectedly from this when his ship put in to Calcutta. Ashore he made his way to the Grand Hotel Winter Garden where the music of Teddy Weatherford's Band greeted him. Teddy Weatherford was one of the rare and colourful figures of jazz who brought the music to the Far East long before the War. Though he was born in West Virginia in 1903 he was taken to New Orleans when he was twelve and there learned to play piano. By 1923 he had moved to Chicago where he played as pianist in the fine pit band of the Vendome Theatre led by Erskine Tate. Considered ahead of his time as a musician, he left Chicago for California three years later and, joining Jack Carter's band, went to China. Most of the rest of his career was spent in the East. He gathered bands of little known but very good expatriate Negro musicians about him and for nearly twenty years played in Hong Kong, Japan, Malaya, the East Indies and finally, India, where Jimmy

Witherspoon found him. It was a swinging band that he led, and Jimmy jumped at the opportunity to sing with him when the occasion permitted. Teddy Weatherford died in 1945 and by that time Jimmy was back in the States.

Returning to the West Coast fresh out of the Merchant Marine he heard Jay McShann's band from Kansas City which was briefly playing in Vallejo, California. The mid-West sounds were right from his own country and the meeting turned out to be a singularly opportune one for him. The KC blues shouter, Walter Brown, who had been a stalwart of the band that McShann had led with the young Charlie Parker in the line-up a few years before, had abruptly quit the band. McShann was on the look-out for a singer and Jimmy Witherspoon filled the bill. The next four years he spent singing with the McShann band, touring with them and getting to know the business. Joe Turner was his idol and if his style reflects any one singer it is Big Joe. The ex-bartender from Kansas City had a tremendous voice, rich and deep. Jimmy Witherspoon has similar characteristics but is capable of singing softly and with restraint when the occasion requires such expression. He came to the notice of musicians and other singers but it was some time before he made a name. The break came with 'Ain't Nobody's Business'.

Though he led a fine, swinging band, Jay McShann did not achieve the fame that Bill Basie did. Perhaps he played in the wrong places. His was largely a touring band, following the circuit of mid-West and Western locations which the Territory bands had played since the Twenties. He was born in Muskogee, Oklahoma, in 1909 and in 1929 formed his first important band in Kansas City. A pianist who played in the western blues piano tradition, with strong left hand and boogie flavour, he led a band which prominently featured blues. Such bands were the nurseries of many of the avant-garde musicians – the most famous alumnus of McShann's was undoubtedly Charlie Parker, but such musicians as Paul Quinichette or Gene Ramey got valuable experience with him. In the first couple of years of 'Spoon's association with the band there were numerous changes of personnel, but McShann's blues-based music gave it unity and Jimmy's strong, personable singing the continuity necessary. For while in 1945 he was joined by Crown Prince Waterford and Numa Lee Davis to make a particularly strong vocal team to front the band, when Waterford left, Jimmy stayed on to enter the period of his best work, from which these recordings come. All but two of the tracks were recorded at two sessions on 15 and 20 November 1947 in Los Angeles for Jack Lauderdale's Down Beat – Swing Time label. The full McShann band at this time had Forrest Powell on trumpet, Frank Sleet and Charles Thomas on alto and tenor sax respectively, Louis Speiginer played guitar, Benny Booker bass and Jay's brother, Pete McShann, was on drums. An accomplished band, it is to be heard to advantage on, for example, 'Frog-I-More', an old Jelly-Roll Morton tune which features the characteristic qualities of a McShann group – the hard-blowing saxes, the excellent trumpet obligato against the vocal played by Forrest Powell, the riffs in the closing choruses and the final ride-out. Comparison with "Spoon Calls Hootie' or 'Destruction Blues', two items made on 10 June the following year is instructive of the leader's influence. Though there is no trumpet and Frank Sleet remains in the band, Milburn Newman plays baritone, Tiny Webb takes over on guitar, and Ralph Hamilton and Jesse Sailes play bass and drums; it is essentially McShann's band and the accompaniment is as sensitive to the singer's requirements. Jay McShann himself is showcased on a typical boogie-blues,

'McShann Bounce' while his excellent and under-rated guitarist, Louis Speiginer is given a deserved feature spot on 'Jumpin' with Louis'.

But above all it is Witherspoon's record. Confident and extrovert, the twenty-four-year-old singer belts out 'Skidrow Blues' on 'Money's Getting Cheaper', original, modern blues with topical relevance in the late Forties. They are credited to one 'Boyd' but bear the stamp of Witherspoon's own blues compositions of the time. His respect for the blues singers of older generations is demonstrated in his more contemplative recordings, the versions of Leroy Carr's classic 'In the Evenin'' and 'How Long Blues', and the timeless Bessie Smith-James P. Johnson 'Backwater Blues'.

'Spoon, as he came to be known, left Jay McShann to work with other groups. He sang with a small four-piece band led by Gene Gilbaux on piano and including Don Hill on alto. It was this group that backed him at the Civic Auditorium, Pasadena, California, in May 1949 when he made a sensational appearance at one of Gene Norman's 'Just Jazz' concerts. Soon after he made 'Ain't Nobody's Business' as a two-part blues for the small Supreme label of Los Angeles and registered a hit. Accompanying him was a band led by his old mentor Jay McShann and featuring Forrest Powell on trumpet and the guitar of Louis Speiginer. It was an interesting group but it was Jimmy's voice that sent the disc to the top of the charts. Really a traditional blues as old as 'Spoon himself (Bessie Smith recorded it in the year he was born) 'Ain't Nobody's Business' is an eight-bar theme that is always today associated with him. He favours it as his own special number and has good reason to sing on 'When I've been Drinkin':

I'm looking for a woman who ain't never been kissed . . .

Who digs 'Ain't Nobody's Business' and I won't have to break my fist
When I been drinkin' . . . yeees, when I been drinkin' . . .

'When I Been Drinkin'' is a remodelling of a blues that used to be popular with Big Bill Broonzy, a singer of a very different genre but united with 'Spoon in the type of music which is common to both. There are acknowledgements to other singers too: 'Wee Baby Blues' is a fine Joe Turner number which gets appropriate treatment from Jimmy, whilst 'SK Blues' is a composition of the West Coast rhythm and blues singer Saunders King. It has some pungent lines:

You're a mean mistreater baby, don't mean no man no good,   (repeat)
'Cause all you do woman is to disturb peace in my neighbourhood.

I did more for my baby than the Good Lord ever done   (repeat)
I went down town and brought her some hair 'cause the Good Lord never gave her none.

Give me back that wig I bought you baby, let your head go bald,   (repeat)
'Cause if you keep on mistreatin' me baby you won't happen to have no head at all . . .

Listen to Harry Edison's tasteful muted trumpet work behind the singer on this number. The accompanying musicians on the two sessions which produced the present album were men whose experience and musicianship were of the type best suited to 'Spoon's singing. Harry 'Sweets' Edison came from Ohio where he was born in 1915 but his professional career was with the mid-West bands from the start; first with Alphonso Trent and later, in 1937, with Lucky Millinder and Count Basie. He played with Basie for more than a dozen years and afterwards worked with Buddy Rich, Benny Carter and Jazz at the Philharmonic. He is heard to particular advantage on 'Sweet's Blues'. Gerald Wilson held down the trumpet chair for one session. He came from Mississippi but most of his experience was with the big bands including the Plantation Club Orchestra in Detroit. He also worked with Basie and in the past has played with Jimmy Lunceford, Les Hite and Willie Smith. He takes a typical solo on 'Good Rockin'' which also featured the two tenor players Teddy Edwards and Jimmy Allen. Edwards is the same age as 'Spoon and has played with modern-inclined musicians at Bop City and Hermosa Beach's famous 'Lighthouse' where he worked with Gerald Wilson.

On one session Hampton Hawes played. A well-known West Coast pianist, he was born in Los Angeles in 1928 and worked with Dexter Gordon, Wardell Gray and the Lighthouse groups. His piano work is heard well on an extended solo on 'All That's Good', a number which, like 'Spoon's Blues', is a variation on 'Tain't Nobody's Business'. Henry McDode played piano for the other session and Herman Mitchell on guitar, Jimmy Hamilton on bass and drummer Jimmy Miller made up the group which gives the right backing to the full-blooded singing of blues shouter Jimmy Witherspoon.

Notes to Fontana 688 005, 1962

4
Let's go to Town

Illustration to "Another Man Done Gone", *Music Mirror*, Vol 1, No 4, August 1954

CHAPTER FOUR
Let's Go To Town

One of the most frequent questions I'm asked, and which I didn't mention to Tom Mazzolini, is 'how do you make the connection between blues and architecture?' Or 'how do you reconcile . . . ' or some such phrase. It always seems to me that the questioner is anxious about anyone having such divergent interests and wants, somehow, to make them link up. As a matter of fact they do have a relationship to me at a certain plane, because I am particularly involved in, and also write about, 'vernacular architecture'. That's the term for the buildings of tribal, folk, peasant or unsophisticated societies. It isn't very precise and some use the term even to apply to the architecture of the suburbs, though for others in the field there are overtones of community or self-building in the concept of the 'vernacular' that suburban housing does not have.

In the sense that Marshall Stearns described his study of *Jazz Dance* as a 'story of American vernacular dance' the blues is a vernacular music. There are specialists in vernacular architecture who consider that it can only be rural, and others who concede that there are such buildings in the town or the city, but that they are not 'pure' examples. Blues of course, is subject to such discrimination too. Many collectors and writers on the subject seem to imply that the rural forms are more 'authentic' than the urban ones. Which is not the same thing as liking the country blues better, though many people I've noticed equate what they like with their view of authenticity.

To me there isn't a fundamental difference in the value of rural versus urban blues as such, though there may be better artists in one context or the other. There are poor country blues singers – some *very* poor per- formers – and there are very fine urban ones; it's a spurious distinction. But it is made more so by the fact that most blues singers worked for part of their lives in the city, or at least, most of the recorded bluesmen did. There was a flow from country to city which often meant that blues singers eased off to town when work was light or money was short, and there was a move back to the country when times got hard, or cold, in town.

If you consider some of the major 'country' blues singers, like Blind Willie McTell, Barbecue Bob, Blind Lemon Jefferson or Tommy Johnson, they were at least as much urban singers as they were country ones, with Atlanta, Dallas and Jackson among the cities where they lived and played. They weren't born in the city, admittedly, but they were in touch with the city and probably considered themselves quite urban – remember those smart, sharp suits that all of these singers wore? In fact, I've often wondered if the blues wasn't a lot more urban in its origins than we've been inclined to think, with the influence spreading to the country from the cities. Well, maybe that would be a hard argument to develop or prove, but I do feel that the city played a big part in all stages of the blues.

For me, as one who is professionally involved in architectural education and writing, it came as something of a jolt when I realized after quite a few trips to the United States that I had really not seen much of the architecture of modern America. Instead, I had seen a lot of the ghettos and a good many rural communities. I had visited Indian reservations and studied mobile home parks in various parts of the States; I had spent time in urban areas with strong ethnic emphasis reflecting central European immigrant settlement. Very important to me – but it meant that for a long time I had a one-sided view of urban America.

I remember the first night I spent in Chicago; John Steiner, who had bought the old Paramount Record Company and was a storehouse of information on Chicago jazz and blues history, took me to a number of clubs. It seemed to me that he was trying me out, testing my nerve, for we visited some particularly rough areas. After we came out of one club we had difficulty getting through a crowd by the door. They weren't trying to get in; they were looking the other way, eyes focussed warily on a couple of young black men circling slowly in a semi-crouching side-step in the street. The light from a neon sign flashed on the open switch-blade that one was holding and the cut-throat razor that the other held out in front of him. We didn't stay.

Once on my own in the early hours of the morning on a Chicago street corner I was aware that small knots of young blacks were gathering opposite and behind me. It was the only time I felt really nervous and deep in the South Side, very alone and white. The situation seemed very menacing and I wondered what action I should take. Then the traffic lights changed and the small groups dutifully walked across the street and I realized that the ominous clusters were nothing more than citizens obedient to the traffic laws even at that time of night. My relief was mingled with shame, and I realized how easy it is to project one's own anxieties on to an innocent situation, perhaps to bring about the very incident that one might fear by a thoughtless action or word.

Many black urban communities are almost unbelievably miserable and deprived. A few years ago I was in East St Louis. It was like a vast war-devastated city with occasional houses standing in acres of debris, rubble and weeds. I felt the tragedy of disappointed lives and of families barely held together by threads of pride in the forlorn yards and tended flowers here and there. But mostly it was a scene beyond hope. What benefits there are in slum clearance and urban renewal aren't easily perceived. Old Hastings Street in Detroit was dark, low and unlovely, but it was still bustling with life at one end when I saw it twenty-odd years ago. The expressway that was already carving out the urban landscape and resulting in massive displacement soon demolished all that remained. Twelfth Street became 'the new Hastings' – until that was largely burned down in the Detroit riots of the Sixties.

And the magic names of jazz and blues: Basin Street and Beale Street? Basin was made into a housing project long ago, a dreary, colourless substitute for the old, notorious thoroughfare. I did see Beale Street – actually, Beale Avenue – in its declining years, still thronged with people, still with its winos on the corner of Fourth, still with its intersection where Highway 51 met it at the end of the long haul from the Mississippi Delta. Behind Beale were the long wooden shotgun houses with rooms off an endless dusty hall, where Will Shade, Gus Cannon and other veterans of Beale's palmier, bluesier days still lived. Just a few pieces of bentwood furniture on the bare boards; nothing else.

Some blues singers fared better in the city. Muddy Waters for instance, who lived in a high brownstone building, with an ornamental door depicting a wading heron or crane, and photographs and ornaments on the television set. Down below in his basement, among the pipes that passed from one house to another lived St Louis Jimmy Oden, poor, optimistic, very grateful to

Muddy for giving him a place to live, paying for it in occasional compositions. 'I'm going to write one called "Blues Fell This Morning"' he said. I don't know that he ever did, but I greatly appreciated his kindness in saying so.

There were surprises: the pleasant, well-kept home that Speckled Red had in St Louis. He could scarcely see, but it was comfortable, orderly and relaxed. There was Eddie Boyd's Chicago apartment, so close to the elevated railroad that all conversation had to stop at twenty-second intervals while the trains rattled by the side of the house and the walls shook. Seen from the window they looked as if they were going to crash right *into* the house. There was Walter 'Furry' Lewis, famed survivor of the Memphis blues, featured in concerts and on films and TV shows, who in 1980 was still living in a tiny, two-roomed frame house. A huge, lumpy feather bed took up almost all of the front room; what space remained was taken up by bentwood chairs and the narrow route to the back room which, beyond a dingy, hanging drape, served as kitchen and gathering place for one or two ageing women. In another part of Memphis, Robert

Wilkins, on the other hand, was living very comfortably: cars in the car-port, trees in the well-tailored front yard, a glass-screened side porch for sitting, talking and receiving prospective purchasers of his home-manufactured herbal remedies.

Making it, scuffling, losing out – the city holds an uncertain future for black migrants from the country districts, but the possibility of a regular job, playing at nights in neighbourhood clubs and maybe making a living from it, jostling with the crowds, striving to get a piece of the action too, are all reasons for 'going to town'. Most of the streets that got into the blues: Decatur Street, State Street, Biddle Street, Deep Morgan, Auburn Avenue, and many more, have been demolished or altered out of recognition. Today Beale Street stands like a decaying Hollywood stage set, its shored-up buildings closed and fenced with wire, projecting into a wasteland from which all traces of the surrounding streets and houses have been cleared away. But if the old blues locales have virtually disappeared, black migrants still come to the cities, shaping new environments while the memories of the old haunts linger in blues titles and stanzas.

Another Man Done Gone
MIGRATION TO THE CITY

Another man has wiped the sweat from his forehead with the back of his hand, has shrugged his shoulders, laid down his hoe and has stumbled away dispirited, his feet dragging through the infertile dust.

Another man has got the Leavin' Blues.

Of the many themes on which Negroes sing, that of parting and departing is one of leaving home, leaving work, of leaving families, lovers, friends. And this is to be expected, for folk song closely reflects the lives and environment of those who create it, and the story of the American Negro during the past half century has been largely one of migration.

It starts with the blues. 'Negroes,' said Leadbelly, 'was born with the blues.'

Sometimes they don't know what it is,
But when you lay down at night
Turnin' from one side of bed all night to the
other
An' cain't sleep, what's the matter?
Blues gotcha.
An' when you get up in the mawnin' an' sit on
the side of yo' bed
An' you have father an' mother, sister or
brother,
Boy frien' or girl frien', husban' or wife
aroun',
You don't want no talk out o' them.
You ain't done nothin' to them
An' they ain't done you nothin'
What's the matter? Blues gotcha!

For the Negro the blues is the personification of misery, of depression, of adversity, the ever-present companion to the under-privileged.

'Yo' gotta talk to the blues. They wanna talk to you. You gotta tell 'em something,' Leadbelly explained. But it takes courage to talk to the blues for that means remaining, and enduring, on the slender hope that one day perhaps, one will have saved enough for a little land and a home and a mule . . . It is more inviting to attempt to escape the blues, to move to another town, another county, another State and try again. The Negro sings:

When a woman gets the blues, she hangs her
li'l head an' cries,
When a woman gets blue she hangs her head
an' cries,
But when a man gets the blues, he flags a mail
train and rides.

Yet escape is not easy. The sharecropper and tenant farmer systems keep a cotton labourer almost permanently in debt so that he is forced to remain if he is not to break the law. And in some States it has been illegal for a coloured worker to leave a plantation once he has received from the owner the loan of the tools with which he is to work. So, dissatisfied and helpless against the perniciousness of the system under which he works, he assures himself that he will leave 'in the mawnin'! Sang Bill Bill Broonzy:

Bye-bye Arkansas. Tell Missouri,
I'm on my way up North now baby,
I declare I ain't foolin' gal, if I can just
Feel in the mawnin'
Like I feel today,
I declare I'm gonna pack up, pack up now
baby,
An' make my getaway.

and again:

Yes, I'm leavin', leavin' momma,
But I don't know which-a-way to go,

159

*'Cause that woman I been livin' with for
    twenty years
Says she don't want me no mo'.*

*I got holes in my pockets momma,
I got patches on my pants.
I'm behind in the house rent momma,
Lord, Lord, he want it all in advance.*

Misery, disease and broken homes inevitably result from poverty, and despair drives
many a man from his home. That he might
just as well die in trying to snatch a ride on a
passing train that may take him to a more
promising district, as stay in the South and
die slowly, is the theme underlying the
'Walking Blues' of McKinley Morganfield.
Betraying his Mississippi origins as much in
the timbre of his voice, his manner of
singing and his style of guitar-playing as in
his folk-name of Muddy Waters he sings:

*Well, I'm leavin' this mornin' babe if I
    have to –
Go ride the blind.
You know I had been mistreated babe,
    know I –
Don't mind dyin' . . .*

Watching the plantations fail, the saw-
mills close, the stump lands grow, Negroes
in Alabama, Georgia, Mississippi, throughout the South, were becoming restless by the
close of the nineteenth century. Thousands
felt the urge to leave irresistible and though
it meant parting from their families and
tearing their roots from the soil where their
slave forefathers had toiled through many
generations, great numbers gathered together a few belongings and made their
erratic and uncertain way north. Fraught
with difficulties though such an undertaking
proved to be, they reached the northern cities
where they were as yet not unwelcome.
Those that settled sent back stories of better

housing, or more rewarding employment
and increased civil rights. During the
quarter-century preceding the World War,
more than a million-and-a-half Negroes
migrated.

Then came the War. Industry demanded
more workers. European-born Americans
volunteered to fight long before America
entered the War, and the factories of the big
northern areas were starved of workmen.
Largely feeding and arming the European
nations, United States factories had to work
at maximum production. Representatives
poured into the South urging coloured
workers to migrate to the industrial areas.
Floods in the Mississippi Delta, boll-weevil
in the cotton, encouraged them if they had
needed any further inducement. The introduction of jazz music from New Orleans
and the Mississippi towns to Chicago and
the North was only symptomatic of the
general trend and not, as many jazz enthusiasts believe and contend, an important
migration in itself. Though their influence
was to be great, the jazz musicians were
only a wave in the mighty coloured tide
which swept northward during the war
years.

So great had the exodus from the South
become that soon the slave States were passing legislation to prevent the 'enticement' of
Negro workers. Labour agents and recruit-
ment officers from the industrial plants had
to buy expensive licences or risk jail before
they could operate; the fee in Macon, Georgia, being $25,000 and the agent required to
obtain the recommendation of nearly fifty
local dignitaries. But they could not stop the
flood. With promises of sure employment
they rode the trains, travelling in them on
free tickets, not on the rods beneath the cars.
For the simple, ingenuous and uneducated
coloured man who perhaps had never seen a
town, the move was an unnerving
adventure.

I left my babe in Mississippi,
Pickin' cotton down near New Orleans,
(repeat)
She says 'If you get to Chicago all right
Please send me a letter if you please.'

I said 'Baby, that's all right,
Baby, that's all right for you, (repeat)
You'll be pickin' cotton down there –
Oh Baby, shall I get through?

'Baby when I get to Chicago,
I swear I'm going to take a chance.
(repeat)
'I know when I get back to Mississippi
I swear I'm going to change your name.'

Tommy McClennan did reach Chicago as did tens of thousands of other coloured people. By 1920 the population had exceeded a hundred thousand in the Black Belt, having trebled in ten years. A similar story was enacted in Detroit, Cleveland, Pittsburg. Now the Southern Negro found he was no longer welcome. He was resented by Northern whites and coloured alike. The former were alarmed by the expanding Negro housing sectors and the continued coloured infiltration into hitherto white residential areas, whilst the Negroes already in the North rightly feared the damage to the established society and its relations with the whites caused by the rapidly increasing Negro population. Bitter race riots broke out, Negro homes were bombed, and coloured people were victimized. Returning servicemen added to the labour problem and the Depression added to the misery. Yet the coloured workers from the South continued to come. Between the wars two million Negroes came North. In the ten years following the First World War the Negro population in Chicago increased by a

further 125,000. To leave again seemed futile, yet many a Negro shared the sentiments of Leroy Carr when wives in domestic service were earning when their menfolk stood idle.

. . . Yes, I'm gonna leave you momma.
Yes, I'm going down South.
I'm gonna ride that 'Fifty-five.'
It's too bad momma, I'm gonna leave you babe,
An' you will say good-bye.

You mistreated me momma,
You didn't treat me nice and sweet,
So I'm goin' down South
Shake the dust of this town off my feet . . .

Then in the years of the Second World War the story was repeated. Again industry demanded more labour and again the industrial cities experienced an influx of Negroes. Race riots broke out afresh in Detroit and Chicago, riots more terrible than ever before. But the migration was not only to the North this time. The Negro areas of the West Coast cities rapidly inflated. In San Francisco the pre-war population of 4,000 Negroes multiplied eight times whilst that of Los Angeles increased by more than 80,000. And at a rate of a 1,000 a week the coloured people were still streaming into California at the close of the war. Sang Josh White:

I've wandered, early and late,
From New York City to the Golden Gate.
I've been working in freighters,
I've been working on a farm,
An' all I've got to show for it
Is the muscles on my arm.
An' it looks like I'm never going to cease
My wanderings . . .

Music Mirror, August 1954
'Sources of Afro-American Folk Song: 4'

Central Tracks

DALLAS, TEXAS

In 1899 there were 9,000 blacks in Dallas, a quarter of the population. By 1930 they totalled just short of 50,000 and made up a significant part of the whole population. The hub of the black community was an area known as Central Tracks, where honky-tonks, saloons, beer-parlours and brothels were wedged between warehouses, furniture stores and places of entertainment like Ella B. Moore's Park Theatre, or Hattie Burleson's dance hall.

Urban expansion in Dallas was due largely to its importance as a railhead, and many railroads whose names are familiar to blues collectors had termini there. Among them were the 'Katy', the Missouri, Kansas and Texas line; the Fort Worth and Denver; the Gulf, Colorado and Santa Fe; the Rock Island; and the Texas & Pacific, along whose line Central Tracks was situated. Dallas was tough and proud of it; and one would expect that its raw and brash character would be reflected in a noisy brand of barrelhouse blues. So it may have been, though little survives on record to confirm that this was so. Instead, the blues piano style of Dallas is slow or medium-paced and contemplative in its nature as if in reaction against the clamorous, sometimes brutal, world of the streets. But it's not quite as simple as that, for these pianists/singers have their eyes very much open. Blues in the Dallas school is about *Dallas*; in fact no other blues school, with the exception, perhaps, of Chicago, gives us quite such a picture of the urban life which inspired it. It could, of course, be coldly descriptive, sensational, or even sentimental, but the special quality of the Dallas tradition is its poetry. These are blues that are intended to be listened to, with words that have a strange folk lyricism about them. Here the piano is used as a complementary poetic instrument, setting off the words and the mood of the blues instead of challenging it with pyrotechnic displays.

As might be expected of a railroad centre, trains play an important part in these blues. One might also expect flamboyant pianistic train imitations – but such is not the case. Gently rolling bass figures evoke the distant train rhythms without resorting to mimicry, as on Neal Roberts' 'Frisco Blues' which refers to the St Louis–San Francisco line. The 'Sunbeam', or 'Sunshine Special' that ran on the Missouri–Pacific line to St Louis is another train that gets attention: 'don't need no aeroplane, steamboat or submarine,' sang the unknown Fred Adams. On this, as on other train blues, Billiken Johnson vocalizes the imitations of the whistle, turning that most evocative of all Southern sounds into blues melody. He does so too on 'Inter-urban Blues' which refers to the short haul trains which brought country people into the city.

Billiken Johnson is a pivotal figure though he did not play piano. His forte was vocal effects, and he was considered rather a clown by his blues musician friends. A roly-poly figure who died long ago, he was a natural entertainer and provides the braying noises on 'Wild Jack Blues' which, I suspect, is slyly sung at his expense. He vocalizes, probably through cupped hands rather than kazoo or comb-and-paper, Texas Bill Day's forth-right 'Elm Street Blues', on which the pianist sings:

*Ellum Street's paved in brass, Main Street's
   paved in gold. (repeat)
I've got a good girl lives on East Commerce, I
   wouldn't mistreat her to save nobody's soul.*

*These Ellum Street Women, Billiken, do not
     mean you no good.   (repeat)
If you want to make a good woman, have to
     get on Haskell Avenue.*

His references were to the respective success of the black sector of 'Deep Ellum', or Elm Street, which ran by Central Tracks, and the downtown business sector of Main.

The harsher aspects of the area emerge from a blues like Bobby Cadillac's 'Carbolic Acid'. Though Alex Moore knew Bobby Cadillac he had little to say about her, beyond that she was tough. And she sounds it as she sings:

*I told her I loved her man, grave will be her
     restin' place   (repeat)
She looked at me with burnin' eyes, threw
     carbolic acid in my face.
Layin' in my bed, my face burned to the bone,
     (repeat)
If carbolic acid don't kill me, penitentia' gonna
     be my home.*

Alex Moore's 'Ice Pick Blues' (like Day's 'Elm Street', transcribed in 'Blues Fell this Morning', item 231) tells a story of a violent woman, with the strain of humour and shrewd observation that is typical of his work. The folk blues poet *par excellence*, Alex Moore, shows in 'Heart Wrecked Blues' (BFTM item 96) the potential of the idiom for the expression of ideas and experience, given special significance by the sympathetic piano accompaniment. All his eighty years a resident of Dallas, Moore has spent most of his working life as a cart driver, and later, hotel porter. When I found him in 1960, he wasn't much better off than when he . . .

*Met a woman in West Texas, she had been
     left out there all alone,   (repeat)
Out by the 'Hooking Cow' crossing, where I
     wasn't even known.*

*She fell for me, a raggedy stranger, standing in
     the drizzling rain.   (repeat)
She said, 'Daddy I'll follow you, tho' I don't
     know your name.'*

*We snuggled closely together, muddy water
     round our feet,   (repeat)
No place to call home, wet, hungry and no
     place to eat.*

*The wolves howl till midnight, wild ox moan
     till day,   (repeat)
The Man in the Moon looked down on us –
     but had nothing to say.*

When one thinks of the colour of the face of the Man in the Moon, one wonders if this innocent phrase has a slightly more pointed meaning. It's possible, for Alex Moore was a singer with a sense of humour and of irony, as 'They May Not Be My Toes' indicates. More erotic, but still amusing, is 'Blue Bloomer Blues' (transcribed in *Screening The Blues* p.186). No doubt one needed a sense of humour in those days. Or good fortune.

That's what Hattie Hudson had, apparently: 'I got a gold horseshoe, gonna put it on my door, doggone my good luck soul,' she sang on a more exuberant recording. Her pianist may have been Willie Tyson, though she encourages a 'Mr. Jefferson' on this side of the record. In my opinion she is Hattie Burleson working under a pseudonym; or perhaps her maiden name. Singers from her 'stable' recorded for the same company, included Lillian Glinn, whose pianist was also Willie Tyson. Hattie's inclusion here serves to remind us that there were other Dallas blues traditions at the time, though the piano blues that centred on Texas Bill Day and Alex Moore forms a special genre of its own.

Notes to Magpie PY 4415, 1980

Holy Memphis
MEMPHIS AND THE DELTA

'Like Jerusalem in the Bible you could put a wall round it these days and call it "Holy Memphis". But we're hopin' that times'll get better and life'll come back to Beale,' said the pool-room operator Robert Henry as he looked out on Beale Street, almost empty of people in the full heat of the afternoon. Robert Henry, who had been living on Beale before the First World War, had seen generations of blues singers come and go. And go. The last generation seemed to burn itself out in the 1950s, to quit playing or to move north. They were the younger men; the older singers like Will Shade and Gus Cannon and Memphis Minnie and Bo Carter were too old, and most of them too ill, to move again. Like Robert Henry they waited and hoped that times would get better. The times were better in the years when Boss Crump ruled the city, for in the near half-century that Crump's word was law the blues flourished. It was odd that it did, for the tall and lean 'Boss', the Mayor of Memphis who did not smoke or drink or swear, who exercised a dictatorial authority and who ensured that a rigidly enforced poll-tax gave little opportunity for the forty-odd percent of residents of Memphis who were coloured to vote, would seem to have had little in common with the bluesmen and their world. But in fact he liked the music of the jug bands, employed them for dances and for the great annual picnics in the fairgrounds, and turned a blind eye to the brothels, the clubs, the joints and jukes that flourished in the underworld block between Hernando and Fourth on Beale.

It wasn't just the Crump administration that made Memphis a centre for blues singers but a multitude of related factors. Its strategic position as a railhead, as a major river port and as a centre of the cotton industry made Memphis a focal point for commerce with its catchment area extending into Tennessee, Arkansas and Mississippi. Sooner or later Negroes who had freed themselves of share-cropping serfdom, or who wished to escape being enmeshed in its net, made their way to Memphis for the longed-for opportunities offered by an urban centre.

So it was that only a few of the blues singers associated with Memphis – Will Shade for instance – actually came from the city. Some, like Furry Lewis, were raised there by parents who had migrated from adjacent States; others like Gus Cannon or Memphis Minnie, Bukka White or Jim Jackson, Willie Newbern or Noah Lewis came from Arkansas, Mississippi, Tennessee or Louisiana, to work in the city, to play music in the joints, to move out to the country in the picking season, sometimes to move back to rural grounds for a few years before drifting once more to Memphis. These were the men who were around when the recording companies opened up in the Peabody Hotel, hung the walls with blankets and proceeded to audition local talent for the few brief days of a historic 'session'. Scores were overlooked over the years as the reminiscences of the blues singers reveal; others participated as accompanists, a Dan Sane to a Frank Stokes, a Hosea Woods to a Gus Cannon. Or, like Bozo Nickerson and Jab Jones, Hattie Hart and Jennie Clayton, Lige Avery, Tee-wee Blackman and Will Batts, they were heard in the group sound of the most typical of Memphis creations between the wars, the jug band.

Guitarists, mandolin players, mouth harp-blowers, piano bluesmen, they played a greater range of instruments than the attention given to the guitarists would suggest, and came from a wider area than the Mississippi Delta that lay to the south with Clarksdale as its legendary capital. Singers have been classified according to their towns, counties or States of origin, but they might as readily be classified according to the kind of cotton they helped cultivate – the Benders, or bottomland cotton from the flooded bends of the Mississippi River, the Allenseed or the Peelers, all of which soon finding their way, like the singers, to Memphis. In the dark years of the Depression, Memphis gave itself a boost and inaugurated the Cotton Carnival with a four-day celebration in May 1931. The pageants rolled down Main below the imposing facades of Haverty's, Loews, Goldsmith's, Rhodes, and the Hotel Claridge – and off the main stem, on Beale, Negro Memphis rejoiced in the annual Cotton Pickers' Jubilee in the shadow of Pee-Wee's Place, The New Daisy, The Beale Street Palace and the Monarch.

The Monarch was where Sonny Butts and Benny Frenchy played years ago and the shade of the oldest generation of bluesmen still influenced the men that followed. And they in turn inspired and shaped the music of those that came later, who slowly made a new music out of the old and developed their own traditions. 'Pre-war' and 'post-war' in a city where music flourished even when recording did not is misleading though: Roosevelt Sykes, born in Helena, Arkansas in 1906, was a recording blues singer in the late Twenties; Sunnyland Slim, born in Vance, Mississippi, just a year later, had to wait until after the War before he could achieve a limited fame on record, and then at first through the reflected glory of being 'Doctor Clayton's Buddy'. Their tradition conditions their music. 'West Helena Blues', which Roosevelt Sykes sings is a song that he learned as a boy from the Arkansas blues pianist Jesse Bell; 'Going Back to Memphis' which Sunnyland Slim sings is clearly derived from Hambone Willie Newbern's 'Roll and Tumble Blues'.

Deeply affecting the music of those who succeeded him, the singer Robert Johnson has left an impression at first and secondhand on the music of a number of these artists. His own visits to Memphis were fleeting; Will Shade recalled his brief appearance overnight. But Roosevelt Sykes and others remembered him in Helena, Sunnyland Slim in Memphis. There is little doubt of his influence on Boyd Gilmore's 'Rambling on My Mind' even if it has been through the intermediary of Elmore James. And Elmore James himself, one of the most influential singers ever to work in Memphis acknowledged freely his enormous debt to Johnson in his use of the latter's walking bass and ringing treble. But he shaped it to a sound that was recognizably Elmore's, a sound that was born in Memphis and became the characteristic music of Chicago of the late Fifties, spearheaded by Elmore himself. Baby Face Turner's 'Gonna Let You Go' is clearly indebted to Elmore James in turn. Robert Johnson's more contemplative blues, played with a singing bottleneck, were imitated by Muddy Waters. A son of the Delta, his own early guitar playing is imitated almost note for note, perhaps by Turner, on Junior Brooks' 'She's a Little Girl' and Drifting Slim's 'Good Morning Baby'. Drifting Slim – Elmon Mickle – was born in Keo, Arkansas and was inspired as a young man by John Lee 'Sonny Boy' Williamson, the harmonica player whose name was used by another fine harp player who worked in the same region, Rice Miller. Mickle's own records and those of 'Crippled Red' Junior Brooks, Boyd Gilmore and Baby Face Turner were made at sessions in Little Rock, Arkansas. Shortly after, Junior Brooks died of a heart attack and the last generation of blues singers from the region was beginning to break up.

Another singer from Arkansas, Forrest City Joe Pugh, was also influenced by Sonny Boy Williamson, who had made the trip to

Chicago many years before and was killed there in 1948. He made his tribute, 'Memory of Sonny Boy', only a few years before his own death in a road accident in 1959. Two years before, the pianist Willie Love, one of the major personalities in the Memphis-centred region had also died, mourned by the people who enjoyed his original compositions and novel line in blues lyrics. Joe Willie Wilkins played guitar on his train-theme, 'Seventy-Four Blues' and Jimmy Cotton played the drums. Jimmy Cotton was a boy, twenty-four years his junior, born in 1935; a member of a younger generation still, with his sights on Chicago.

Ain't gonna raise no mo' cotton, I'll tell you
the reason why I says so, (repeat)
Well you don't get nothin' for your cotton and
your seed's so dog-gone low.

he sang in his own 'Cotton Crop Blues'. He was not prepared to stay around Memphis, and with Pat Hare, his guitarist on the record, he moved north to join Muddy Waters in Chicago. Elmon Mickle stayed on in Arkansas for a couple more years and then he, too, hit out for new territory, migrating to the West Coast. Elmore James had made a hit in Chicago where he died a year or two ago; the more obscure people like Houston Boines and Luther Huff were not heard of on record again. The one-man band Joe Hill Louis, followed the same path. Some were dead, others were gone and the Memphis blues of the Fifties, along with Boss Crump and his political machine, which by its very methods had somehow allowed it to thrive, were at an end.

Acknowledgements:
'Drifting Slim Discovered', edited by Simon Napier from reports by Frank Scott and Henry Vestine, *Blues Unlimited,* January 1967 pp 5–8.
'Memphis' by Mike Leadbitter. Discography 1950–1953, 'Collectors Classics No. 13' published by *Blues Unlimited,* 1966.

Notes to Blues Classics BC 15, 1968

Detroit Bound
DETROIT, MICHIGAN

Just fifty years ago the *Chicago Defender* for 7 October 1916 carried an editorial by Robert S. Abbott. Himself a Negro migrant from Georgia, he addressed his words to Negroes in the South. 'Have they stopped their Jim Crow cars? Can you buy a Pullman sleeper where you wish? Will they give you a square deal in court yet?' he asked. 'Once upon a time we permitted other people to think for us – today we are thinking and acting for ourselves with the result that our "friends" are alarmed at our progress. We'd like to oblige these unselfish (?) souls and remain slaves in the South, but to their section of the country we have said, as the song goes, "Good-bye, Dixie Land."'

His editorial was part of a concentrated campaign conducted by the Northern newspapers to draw Negroes from the South, and the opportunities for employment in the factories getting into production for the war effort provided the incentive. Many went to Chicago, Cleveland, Pittsburgh, and other major cities but a large number went to Detroit where the promise of a basic wage of $5 a day in Henry Ford's factories drew them like a magnet. Maybe they sang 'I'm goin' to Detroit, get myself a good job' rather than 'I hear you calling me' but the song was one which was shared by thousands in the years of Detroit's dramatic expansion. In 1910 the Negro population amounted to a mere 5,471 persons; eight years later it was in excess of 35,000. The National Urban League was invited to make a 'Survey of Negro Newcomers in Detroit, Michigan' and their study revealed that between twelve and fifteen thousand Negroes were crammed into the area bounded by Brady, Lafayette, Rivard and Beaubien Streets. Once, it housed much less than half

that number of white persons, but the houses were old and 'in very bad repair, many of them actual shanties. The rents on houses occupied by coloured people have had an estimated increase during the past eighteen months from 50 percent to as much as 350 percent in some cases.'

In spite of the pressure, more Negroes arrived and by 1926 the population had expanded to 80,000. The Mayor appointed a committee on race relations which reported that 'many of the dwellings in the St Antoine District are unsanitary beyond redemption'. On this the National Urban League commented in 1943 that 'these and other observations made in 1926 were no less true in 1941, as was revealed in the 7th Annual Report of the Detroit Housing Commission'. The situation became explosive as the influx of Negroes from the South, greater to Detroit than to any other Northern city, showed no sign of abating. In 1942 and 1943 a series of sporadic racial conflicts culminated on the night of Sunday–Monday 20 June 1943, in a number of fierce altercations. Twenty-four hours of cruel fighting and looting resulted in the deaths of 34 persons and the injury of 500 others. Of the 1,800 rioters under arrest, 1,300 were Negroes.

It was against this background of pressure, of economic strain brought about through exorbitant rents, of racial hostility occasioned by infiltration into white areas and competition at the assembly lines, that the Detroit school of blues singers evolved. Some, like Boogie Woogie Red, were raised in Detroit from early childhood, while others came to the city with their families in the Thirties. Though Chicago attracted a large proportion of Negroes from

Mississippi, the location of Detroit further to the East accounted for a more mixed origin in its Negro population. Some, like Eddie Kirkland came from Louisiana, others (like Little Son Willis) came from Alabama. So, Washboard Willie came from Georgia, while Mississippi was the birthplace of singers like Eddie Burns and John Lee Hooker. Sharing a confined environment once in Detroit, but originating from many different areas with their own musical traditions, the musicians who worked in the city produced a music which was hard, markedly rhythmic and forcefully exciting.

Though it would be difficult to define special characteristics that distinguish the music of the Detroit musicians from that of Chicago, the close partnerships of harmonica and electric guitar teams are characteristic. Often they play with strong piano blues and boogie players, who, from the days of Will Ezell and Charlie Spand through Big Maceo and Floyd Taylor to Boogie Woogie Red or Bob Thurman, have been a strong feature in Detroit's blues. Drums also feature prominently in Detroit; socking, hard-hitting and played by a Tom Whitehead or in primitive imitation by a Washboard Willie. The melodic line is generally carried by a harmonica player and a number of guitarists like Eddie Kirkland or Eddie Burns double on harmonica and can play the organ too, weaving in with the sax players who play a bigger part in Detroit blues than in that of Chicago. This complexity of instrumentation against steady-beat rhythms gave birth to a smoother, more sophisticated music where the instrumental lines were carried by vocal groups against similar rhythm backgrounds, and which borrowed freely from the gospel idioms which also form an important part of the Detroit musical scene. This was the Tamla-Motown 'sound' which was so successfully exploited in the Sixties and which

forms an essential part of the Negro music of Detroit. But it is an amalgam of many elements, not wholly blues; the hard-core blues of Detroit is tougher stuff – the music of the Club Caribe and Swann's Paradise Bar, the Apex Club and Club Basin – of the multitude of bars and joints which flourished in the two main Negro areas in the city.

Until 1960, when the bulldozers shovelled the joints off the map to make room for a broad Expressway, the main stem of Detroit's main Negro sector was Hastings Street – the Hastings Street of Charlie Spand and Blind Blake's 'Boogie' of close on forty years ago. Hastings, a string of low-level buildings festooned with cables and telephone wires, where the loan-sharks and dry cleaners, drug stores and chicken shacks rubbed shoulders with the clubs, was alive with music in the Forties and Fifties, the peak period of Detroit's blues. Here Joe van Battles had his record store, and here he recorded not only the better known names like John Lee Hooker but the one-off musicians from the sidewalks: One String Sam, wailing in African-sounding dissonance on a home-made instrument, Brother John Hairston proclaiming in his 'Alabama Bus' his relief at being up North whatever the pressures, or Detroit Count who did for Hastings Street what Willie Love did for Greenville's Nelson Street – recorded a gazeteer of its joints and bars: 'The Corner Bar . . . boy, that's a bad joint . . . Golden Bell across the street – that's the onliest place where, when you walk in, you have to shovel the sawdust off the floor before you can buy yourself a drink . . . Silver Grill . . . where you have to make the bartender and the owner drunk before you can get a drink . . . Wilson's, the longest bar in town . . . Cross the street, Jakes Bar . . . Garfield and Hastings, Mar's Bar, Hung-One Ranch – that's the onliest place you can fight and nobody run out – Willis Theatre . . . if you missed the picture fifty years ago you can see it at the Willis Theatre, right now showin' Rudolph Valentino – *The Lost World* . . . Joe's Tap Room, old folks home . . . Dixie Bar, one way out – never go in that joint . . . Leland and Hastings, Leland Bar . . . where the bartenders carry pistols . . . cross the street, Joe's Record Shop – he got everybody in there but a T-bone steak . . . Three Star Bar – call the fire department to put the band on the bandstand . . . here's a little joint better known as Brown's Bar . . .'

Brown's Bar was where Big Maceo held down the piano stool for many years; the Blue Heaven rocked to Eddie Kirkland's group; Porter Reed's Music Bar – 'anything can happen there' – and generally did. These were the places where the blues singers worked after hours when the joints opened up and the regular jobs closed down. Few Detroit singers were full-time professionals – when they made these recordings John Lee Hooker was working as a janitor for Comco Steel, Doctor Ross was employed in a General Motors Plant in Flint, Michigan, and Bobo Jenkins was a filling station attendant. Only John Lee Hooker 'made it' to become a big recording artist and ultimately to leave the blues world of Detroit behind him. The others have died, like Big Maceo and Sonny Boy Williamson, or disappeared like Jenkins or One-String Sam, or continue to play in the clubs like Eddie Kirkland or Washboard Willie.

Now the clubs are centred along Twelfth Street, a mile or two removed from Hastings Street but called 'the new Hastings' by the men who recall the earlier days. In character it is very similar, with jostling crowds on the sidewalks, posters and name-boards reaching out to catch the eye and Joe van Battles' Record Shop still a centre for musicians to exchange stories, seek engagements and hope for a recording session. They dream, of course, of making it, of a record which will get big distribution and air-time and which might free them of work in the automobile plants. In Detroit a quarter of the Negro males are employed as labourers and nearly thirty percent are operatives. A further twenty percent are service workers and only a minute proportion are employed in work at clerical level or above. The blues singers are similarly employed for the most part, and when they play at the Congo Lounge or the Caribbean Club they play for drinkers and dancers who work beside them during the day. In a sense there is something essentially amateur about the Detroit blues and there is none of the big name professionalism that marked the Chicago blues of Muddy Waters or Howling Wolf. It has retained the character of an urban folk music and it is perhaps for this reason that today it is more vitally alive than the declining music of Chicago. The success of the Detroit 'sound' in the singing of Mary Wells and Marvin Gaye, the performances of The Miracles or The Contours may threaten the future of the blues in Detroit. Undoubtedly the commercial forms of R & B, Detroit style, have received far more attention than the sorely neglected blues of the Motortown.

Notes to Blues Classics BC 12, 1963

On Maxwell Street
CHICAGO'S SOUTH SIDE

At 1330 on South Halsted Street there is a minor intersection. The corners are crowded with people and temporary stalls at any time, but especially on Sunday, for the narrow road that cuts across Halsted is Maxwell. Maxwell Street is at once a sad and an exciting place. The walls are blackened and the paint has peeled off the ill-fitting doors; garbage lies thick in the gutters and the narrow side alleys are littered with the refuse of years. To the west, the street loses its identity in the depressing anonymity of the bleak, poverty-struck roads that cross it; to the east it is an almost impassable confusion of market stalls that suddenly give way to a vast, horizonless plain of mud and rubble and debris where an Expressway will sweep southwards in the undated future. Amongst the rough-clad women who grope through the piles of discarded clothes and the tough, unsmiling men who pick their way through the wires, cables and electrical parts laid out haphazardly on the trestles – amongst the loiterers, the occasional sight-seers and the pickpockets – are the beggars, as many as are to be found in the shadows of the churches in a southern Italian town, or along the shrouded streets of an Arab Quarter. Beggars – but with one striking, exhilarating difference. These are not wheedling seekers after alms with cries of 'baksheesh' or 'Gawd Bless yer, guv', but proud men, creative artists, singers of the blues who accept the dimes and quarters as tokens of esteem for their playing and singing.

If the blues in general has tended to become more sophisticated in recent years Maxwell Street exists as a living storehouse of the folk blues, the blues of the rambling man. And in its few hundred yards is pic-tured the life story of the blues singer of the streets, from the children who stand wide-eyed close to the singers of their choice to the young men who are trying their luck and their talent on the critical audience of the market; from the tough music and manner of the street singer of many years to the fading abilities of the old men who have played in the street in all weathers for more years than they can count.

The introduction to the blues of Maxwell Street was salutary. Descending from the Halsted streetcar brought us within earshot of the powerful voice and thunderous guitar of Blind Arvella Gray who was shouting his blues to an unseen audience, tin cup on his chest and white stick held against a sewer vent on the sidewalk's edge so as to orientate himself. The first two fingers of his left hand were missing and his third finger was sheathed in a glass bottleneck which he slid up the strings of his old National steel guitar, picking and plucking rapidly with the case-hardened fingers of his right hand the while. A burly, muscular man he re-inforced the impression of great physical strength and fitness with the ferocity of his blues singing.

In contrast to Blind Gray were a number of groups of singers who lined the street in small bands, a lead singer and guitarist being supported by a washboard player, another guitarist, even a rough-hewn trumpeter. Seated on a couple of boxes on a street corner were two young blues singers who took turns to accompany each other. One was Maxwell Street Jimmy, who played a fast and highly rhythmic guitar in which the influence of John Lee Hooker could be heard, though he had much to give that was essentially his own, whilst his companion answered only to the name of King David – playing his harp with an ability that could well be the envy of many a better known harmonica-player, and singing in a gritty, deep voice at variance with his amiable features. Another nearby corner was occupied by a venerable singer three times King David's age, a veritable one-man band who had a harmonica on a frame round his neck and who pounded a cheap guitar on which a length of iron had been tied with a piece of string to act as a capo. Dressed in a royal blue jacket with gold epaulettes, the parade dress of some forgotten lodge which he had probably picked up on this self-same market, and in his shiny-peaked cap, Daddy Stovepipe was a diminutive but striking character who drew the attention of the passing crowd.

Above the sounds of the many groups of blues singers could be heard a more rocking beat and the volume of many voices singing verses and responses of gospel songs. In nearby Sangaman Street, within sight of the store-front 'Chapel of Hope', an impassioned jack-leg preacher was leading a choir: old and middle-aged men and women beating drums and tambourines and playing guitars. Amongst these could be heard the accomplished guitar-playing, with more than a shade of the blues in his phrasing, of a blind, straw-hatted man seated on a folding-stool: Blind James Brewer. Near him an earnest seventeen-year old boy named Froine, his lead boy, kept watchful eyes on him whilst he sang the words of the gospel songs. Like a number of other street guitarists on Maxwell, Blind James Brewer was playing, surprisingly, an electric guitar. The owners of the houses that lined the road hired out extensions from their light installations for a dollar a day to the performers below, and as the dimes clattered in the tin cups and plates it was not long before the cost of the hire was met.

The blues singers of Maxwell Street are many, and many are transitory figures, here today, hopping a freight train tomorrow. Amongst the best and most familiar figures on the Street are Blind Gray, Blind Brewer, King David and Daddy Stovepipe, and these are the singers who are featured on this documentary of one of the most colourful Negro streets in the United States.

At the time, Blind Gray was living in a tall apartment house on State Street which is already demolished. The ancient and treacherous unlit staircase led to the top of the building where in bare but tidy rooms Blind Gray lived, with the position of every item firmly fixed in his mind so that he could retain his independence. Born in 1906 in a small Texas township not far from Galveston, he was a member of a desperately poor family. When a small child he was set to work on a farm and when his mother died in childbirth in 1918 he left the large family and rambled from plantation to plantation. His early life was rough, tough and dissolute; he was, he admits, 'a roughneck all the way round'. He took every form of manual work, from raising tents for a circus to laying track on a section gang. For a time he peddled dope and in the worst years of the depression was not above sticking-up filling stations and even a bank for his money. An inveterate gambler, he experienced many changes of fortune, living easy when he was winning and working on the railroads, riding the freight trains when times were bad. Then on 13 September 1930 he returned to his woman's home in Peoria, Illinois, and knocked on the door. Waiting outside he struck a match on the glass of the window to light a cigarette. It was the last thing he ever saw, for his woman's lover blasted away at the reflection on the glass and Arvella Gray lost his sight and two fingers. Stumbling out into the street he tried to commit suicide in sheer despair but the police frustrated his attempt. After being unconscious for two weeks he resigned himself to his blindness and decided to learn to play the guitar so that he could earn a living by begging. For a few years it was a life of near starvation for he could not manage the fingering with his maimed hand but another blind guitarist showed him how to play in Sevastapol, tuning with a bottleneck on his finger. And so, for the past thirty years he has travelled through the Central States, playing and singing his blues and the songs that he learned in earlier years, the work songs he used to sing as a gandy-dancer on a section gang. Amongst these are the work song included here and the superb version of 'John Henry' which must be one of the most forceful on record. For Blind Gray singing endlessly on street corners, in Greyhound buses and streetcars, his blues are not neatly parcelled in complete compositions but are one, endless song, a continuous comment-ary on his life, spiced with an ironic humour and satirical appeals to 'Mister Percy' – the white man on the street. Recording a man with a stentorian voice and a guitar that can be heard above the rattle and clamour of Chicago's traffic presents many problems to which an echoing location added further difficulty. If these were not entirely over-come the essential dynamicism of Blind Gray's blues which so reflect the man has been preserved in these recordings.

Frequent companion to Blind Gray and by no means solely dedicated to gospel music, Blind James Brewer was present at the session and recorded a couple of numbers including 'I'm So Glad Good Whiskey's Back', a tribute to Peetie Wheatstraw whose influence he freely acknowledges. A few years younger than Blind Gray, James Brewer was born in a 'flag-stop' town in Mississippi and was almost totally blind from birth. He can see a little from the

corner of one eye and says: 'I never did think too much about my affliction; I've just been thankful for the sight that God gave me.' His incapacity kept him from many of the customary forms of Southern labour and there was little attention or assistance for a blind child. He had a yearning for a guitar and his father bought him one. Unable to play it he smashed it against a tree in a fit of anger – and immediately began to save up for another. His second guitar he traded for a shotgun, though it was pride of possession alone for he could not use the weapon. He could not leave music alone and with his third guitar determined to concentrate on playing blues and dance music for country suppers and gospel music from the church. Later he wandered slowly northwards, first to Memphis, then to St Louis. For some years he settled in East St Louis where he joined many blues singers and admired in particular William Bunch – Peetie Wheat-straw – who was celebrated for both his guitar and his piano playing. Later James Brewer moved to Chicago, where he readily found work in the store-front churches and by playing on the streets, sometimes in the company of Blind Gray. Living in Sangaman Street just off Maxwell he has found that his requirements are few, and most of his life is centred about his guitar and his music. Blind James Brewer punctuates his verses with spoken com-ments and he shares with Gray a sardonic sense of humour. In 'Good Whiskey' his flowing Mississippi style guitar playing is well exemplified.

King David appears to be in his late twenties or early thirties. A taciturn man, he is reluctant to talk about himself or to admit to any other name than that by which he is popularly known on Maxwell Street. He is proud of being 'the King', even if self-styled, and is a dramatic and moving blues harmonicist. Living with his large family he apparently obtains casual work in addition to playing blues, though it is clear that he lives mainly for his music. With eyes closed and fingers fluttering, cupping and muting over the small 'harp' he either alternates vocal and instrumental line in the manner of Sonny Boy Williamson or accompanies Maxwell Street Jimmy's singing. It had been the intention of Don Hill and Bjorn Englund, who recorded King David, to have him play with one of the several Maxwell Street groups but in spite of arrangements to this effect assembling the group proved impossible. Equally impossible was a joint recording of Jimmy and King David, for the former's mother refused to have 'sinful music' recorded in her home. Eventually King David was recorded solo in his own home in a session which fully demonstrated the remarkable ability of the street singer. For a man who has no accompaniment other than his own harmonica, King David sings blues verses of unusual length but the dovetailing of instrument and vocal set against the regular beat of his foot gives unity to his blues, of which 'Fannie Mae ('Don't Start Me To Talkin')' and 'Sugar Mama' are original examples.

Most elderly of the Market's entertainers is Daddy Stovepipe, the only one to have appeared previously on record. His real name is Johnny Watson but he had been known as Stovepipe for longer than he can recall. Stovepipe claims to have been born in 1870 though he is a singularly sprightly nonagenarian. Coming from Mobile, Alabama, he travelled throughout the South as an itinerant street singer, taking work as a field hand when he felt so inclined. In 1928 he was recorded with 'Whistling Pete' in Birmingham, Alabama, for Gennett and a couple of years later he made a number of sides in Memphis, Tennessee, for Vocalion and Bluebird, with his wife Sarah Watson, known as Mississippi Sarah. For a time they lived in Greenville, Mississippi, but in 1937 Sarah died and Stovepipe was on the road again. He went South to Mexico and worked along the Gulf Coast, playing with zydeco bands in Galveston and Houston. The man who made the exciting recordings of 'Sundown Blues' and 'Jail Cell Blues' some thirty years ago is now old, and the blues are almost forgotten. His recordings of 'South of the Border' and 'Monkey and the Baboon' give only a hint of his former abilities but the spirit is still present and the blue notes whine on the rusty guitar strings. It is easy to sentimentalize the blues, but the life of the blues singer is a hard rather than a romantic one. These recordings of the street entertainers of Maxwell Street Market, Chicago, are eloquent testimony to the remarkable way in which these rough, unlettered men have created a folk art form from the harsh, unlovely world in which they live.

Notes to Heritage HLP 1004, 1960

Arvella Gray was born Somerville, Texas, 8 January 1906, and died Chicago, 7 September 1980.
Daddy Stovepipe (Johnny Watson) was born Mobile, Alabama, 12 April 1867 and died, aged 96, Chicago, 1 November 1963.

Goin' to California
THE WEST COAST

Detroit's phenomenal growth as a result of the developing automobile industry was echoed on the West Coast during the Second World War with the rapid expansion of the defence factories. When the factories were open to Negro labour in the early Forties thousands of coloured families poured into California to start a migratory trend which has continued to the present day. The figures tell their own story. In 1930 there were 81,000 Negroes in California. During the next decade their numbers increased by half as much again and the 1940 census showed a Negro population of 124,000 in a total of six-and-a-half millions.

The war years saw a dramatic increase: over half a million Negroes on the Pacific Coast by 1950 and nearly all of them in California. Some moved into the Valley districts to work on the farms and to catch the seasonal harvests but by far the majority concentrated in the urban areas. Places like Bakersfield or Fresno took a small proportion of the incoming coloured population; most of them crowded into Los Angeles and San Francisco. A booming industry needed a labour force and for this, at least during the War, the incoming Negroes were fairly welcome. But not as neighbours. As always they found themselves densely concentrated in specific areas – Oakland in San Francisco or Watts in Los Angeles. These shabby, run-down districts soon suffered the same strains as those which had occurred in other cities which

had witnessed a similar pressure of coloured immigrants. The pressure built up within them to explode in the tragic holocaust of the Watts riots. But that was in the mid-Sixties at the end of a quarter of a century of expansion.

Where did the Negro emigrants come from? From 'all over', but especially from the Central South-west and Texas in particular. In spite of a movement into Texas from Louisiana and further east, Texas Negroes declined in number by some 40,000 in the Forties. Had Texas not itself been a State receiving large numbers of immigrants the figures would have been far higher, for Negroes left Dallas, Houston, Austin and San Antonio in their thousands for the West. And with them went the blues singers, often seeking the same jobs but finding a demand for their music. Unsettled and lonely in strange surroundings the newly arrived migrants hungered for the music and culture that reminded them of home, just as their earlier counterparts had done in the Northern cities. If there is any characteristic of the blues in California it lies in its Texas origins. Singer-guitarists like Lowell Fulson and Smokey Hogg had the Texas stamp in the pitch of their voices and their accents, and sometimes in the melodic arpeggois of their guitar playing. Clubs and bars opened, musicians and blues singers got together, and the California Blues, as indefinite a term as any of the others but as justifiable, was born.

Notes to Polydor 423 242, 1961

5
Stomp 'em Down

Illustration from *Radio Times*, August 1959

We were standing on Harrow-on-the-Hill station, my friend and I, waiting for the 'steam' to come in. We preferred to go home from school on the London North-Eastern steam train, rather than the 'electric' which was nowhere near as exciting. 'Do you like boogie-woogie?' he asked me suddenly. I remember being quite surprised by the question as it had not occurred to me that anyone would *not* like it among my friends. Boogie-woogie was the music which we grew up with; it was part of the routine of life, like Wall's ices in their cardboard prisms, or playing flicksies with cigarette cards, something that had been there since the world began. I don't know what I said in reply, but I do remember that *he* didn't like it – my introduction to criteria in blues, I suppose.

It stays in my mind, I think, because I always associated the 'steam' with boogie-woogie. One of the first records I owned, if not *the* first, was 'Honky Tonk Train Blues' by Meade Lux Lewis, on Parlophone R2187 backed by 'Barrelhouse' by Jess Stacy. I still have it, and the 'Barrelhouse' side is hardly worn. It had been issued in England in 1936 and there were quite a few other titles by Lewis on British labels that were still obtainable during the War. One was 'Yancey Special', but we had to wait until 1944 before Jimmy Yancey's 'Five O'Clock Blues', 'State Street Special' and 'Slow and Easy Blues', among others, were available in the HMV Swing Music series. By that time I had discovered that boogie-woogie, especially Jimmy Yancey's way of playing it, was a part of blues; when I first bought a record or two by Meade Lux Lewis they weren't a part of anything, not even Swing – they were just records that I liked, though none of them seemed to come up to 'Honky Tonk Train'.

I'm not sure when Red Nelson's 'Crying Mother Blues' and 'Streamline Train' was issued, but I rather think it was around 1943.

It had the finest piano playing I'd heard, by 'Cripple' Clarence Lofton; forty years later it is still one of my Desert Island Discs. A lot of my friends were playing boogie-woogie and mastering the bass figures was one of the competitive sports of the Forties. My performance in this was on a par with my performance in other sports – with the difference that I was interested in boogie. But we had no piano at home and I had no opportunity to practise. Besides, I met up with Pat Hawes, and he played such a thunderous, exciting boogie with a rock-steady left hand, that I knew I wouldn't be able to match it. I can picture him now, wearing his wellington boots as he played – he was a wartime 'Young Farmer' – lower lip dropped, broken tooth, red-faced, absolutely absorbed. (Only we said 'sent' in those days). He went on to play with the Crane River Jazz Band, but we kept in touch for several years. He played at a New Cross pub where I held a 21st birthday drinking spree, and even played when Val and I were married – only I don't think that many of the guests thought that his music was quite the right thing for a wedding. But it was; for *ours*, anyway.

More blues singers play piano than may be generally realized; Brownie McGhee for example, could play a very solid 'Hooking Cow at the Landing' on piano, though I don't think he ever recorded it. Edith Johnson, St Louis Jimmy, Victoria Spivey and Jimmy Rushing were among the vocalists who were normally only recorded singing blues, but who could play adequately when they wished, or could be persuaded to do so. On the other hand, Champion Jack Dupree, normally thought of as a heavy barrelhouse pianist, could play simple but effective guitar. He also played the piano in a hokum fashion, with his elbows or with his shoes, as an entertaining gimmick.

Some blues pianists have habits and tricks

that either do not get on record, or which have to be seen to be appreciated. Roosevelt Sykes, for example, plays 'Dog Finger Blues' in which a crooked 'pinky', 'dog', or fourth finger, is held up from the keyboard and then brought down in a syncopated fashion. Some pianists like to take the front out of the upright piano exposing the hammers. It affects the sound in a somewhat clattering, vibrating fashion but apparently they like it. The preference for this slight distortion of the pure sound and the minor vibration has very strong parallels with African practices where metal vibrators are put on stringed instruments or small chains attached to 'thumb pianos' to produce a similar vibrating, resonating effect.

The problem with pianos is that they can slip out of tune very easily, and in field recording one of the main difficulties is finding a piano that is in good condition. Often one can stand the slightly out-of-tune instrument when listening in person, but the flaws are painfully apparent on disc. Another problem is simply that the sound may resonate in a small, tight interior with reflected sound bouncing off hard surfaces producing slight echo effects. I recall the piano that Joe van Battle had in his back room at his music store on the 'new Hastings' of 12th Street, Detroit. It was cramped into a tiny space, but every passing bluesman would play a few runs, or a boogie bass on it. I recorded 'Boogie Woogie Red' on it while small children ran in and around the room playing a black version of 'Cowboys and Indians'. I recorded Floyd Taylor, too, a veteran Detroit pianist who could recapture the styles of different phases in the blues with great flair, and I planned to have a full session with him. He didn't turn up, and I lost contact with him. On West Lake in Chicago I encountered a middle-aged blues pianist who was literally carrying his piano with him; it was a small portable, but not

electric, instrument; a street piano. Again I hoped to record him, and again he failed to turn up; I presume that the scouts I discussed in 'Special Agents' often encountered similar reluctance to record. Sunnyland Slim was so dissatisfied with pianos being out of tune that he carried an electric instrument in the trunk of his car – but it didn't make a very agreeable sound, or match his somewhat harsh and powerful voice.

One of the appealing aspects of the way piano bluesmen approach their work is the way in which they gradually settle down to the instrument. Often they will sit at the piano as if uncertain whether to stay and try out a few phrases with the right hand, or a bass figure or two, before swinging into the blues. I can visualize Buster Pickens, with his cigarette between his second and third finger of his left hand, still playing the bass without dropping it; and Curtis Jones with a small stack of lemon halves on the piano top, sucking a half dry of juice, between each blues he sang. But if I were asked which blues pianist remains most vividly in my memory it was Georgia Talbert. Georgia never made a record, though I did record her with a small group of gospel singers. They were still at school – the Higgins High School at Clarksdale, Mississippi. Afterwards I asked her if she played any blues. In answer she proceeded to play an extraordinarily strong blues with a sonorous bass and simple but beautifully timed right hand. She was just fourteen. When I think of Hersal Thomas enthralling the South Side in Chicago with his piano playing when he was sixteen and just up from Texas, or of Louise Johnson playing 'By the Moon and Stars' in the company of Son House and Willie Brown, I think of Georgia Talbert. Twenty years later, when she would have been thirty-four, I asked around for her in Clarksdale. No one remembered her, but she remains permanently in *my* memory.

Piano Blues and Barrelhouse
RURAL AND URBAN PIANISTS

Late in 1923 the Gennett division of the Starr Piano Company issued a coupling by the vaudeville-styled singer, Edna Hicks, who was accompanied on the record by the pianist Lemuel Fowler. Edna Hicks came from New Orleans and she was the half-sister of the better-known Lizzie Miles. Though by no means all her recordings could be classed as blues, 'Satisfied Blues' on Gennett 5252 was a strong twelve-bar item which included many verses that were already traditional. Significantly, the label bore the subtitle 'A Barrel House Blues' – even at that early date in the recording of Negro music the term had associations that would appeal to the prospective purchaser. Lemuel Fowler's accompaniment was slow and powerful and included occasionally the walking bass figures that were to be popularized as 'boogie-woogie'. When he took his solo Edna Hicks cried out 'Rock, church, rock!' a reference which should not be lightly overlooked. The barrelhouse seems far removed from the church, but as Aaron T-Bone Walker said a number of years ago 'Of course the blues comes a lot from the church too. The first time I ever heard a boogie-woogie piano was the first time I went to church. That was the Holy Ghost Church in Dallas, Texas. That boogie-woogie was a kind of blues I guess . . .'

Boogie, blues and barrelhouse – the edges are not clearly defined if, in fact, any real distinctions can be made between them. Edna Hicks' record might not sound 'barrelhouse' any more than it might sound 'church' to the modern listener who would probably dismiss her recording for not being 'authentic blues' anyway. But he would be hard put to dismiss Lem Fowler's accompaniment, even if such a recording as

Mildred Bailey's 'Barrelhouse Music' could lay few claims to any justifications of the title. These are the labels we use to identify aspects of a large compass of music whose specific character has always remained elusive. Hugues Panassie, for instance, equated 'Barrelhouse' as a 'synonym for rough, spontaneous, uninhibited jazz' adding that 'in piano the style is harsh and strident, with great swing, played with a hard touch required to make itself heard above the bedlam going on around'. But the only example on piano that he cites – Pinetop Smith's 'Pinetop's Boogie Woogie' – is by no means harsh or strident and the touch is light. Though 'Barrelhouse' and 'Boogie-Woogie' rate separate entries in *Jazz Directory* this recording is also one of two which he uses to illustrate the latter theme.

A more thorough analysis of the musical and structural elements in blues piano was made by Rudi Blesh in 'Shining Trumpets'. He, too, found the definitions interchangeable however. Describing a 'parlor social' when discussing Sippie Wallace's 'Parlor Social De Luxe' he noted that it offered 'the musical entertainment of blues piano playing (boogie-woogie and barrelhouse) and the semi-ragtime party piano style'. Later he discussed barrelhouse more specifically as a 'qualitative category which includes a number of formal elements: primitive ragtime and ballad, the blues, and the special forms of piano-blues called boogie-woogie which may, in turn, be mixed with the others but, by itself, is a distinct formal and technical development'. One can sympathize with these and other writers in their dilemma; these pianistic styles cannot be easily defined yet they are indisputably within the realm of the blues. Blues pianists are vague themselves in the use of the terms, and understandably so, for they are primarily metaphoric. Marshall Stearns stated that 'there were a dozen or more separate regional styles . . . and thousands of bass figures for the left hand' – the latter comment a conspicuous exaggeration. Later he limited the problem, writing that 'the early boogie-woogie, honky-tonk, barrelhouse, house-rent party pianists worked out their style . . .' – using terms which were descriptive of places (honky-tonk and barrelhouse) and functions (boogie-woogie and house-rent party) to identify the music more by the purpose it served than the form it took. In this he followed common usage among blues pianists.

One cannot attempt precise definitions – in such a field they are almost impossible. Speak of a sonata or a symphony and one speaks of a particular form, one which imposes its structure on its treatment whether the result is good or indifferent. Speak of the blues and one may well speak of a form – of the familiar twelve-bar pattern, but one may also speak of less clear structures. The blues is as much a way of playing and feeling as it is a formal construction; without these indefinable but essential qualities the strictest application of a twelve-bar, three-line form fails to be the blues. Barrelhouse music, likewise, is more revealed by example than by description, and even boogie-woogie with its distinct form and technical development is not necessarily played with eight beats to the bar. Here then is a selection of recordings by pianists who, by their own identification of themselves, or by common agreement are the 'boogie, blues and barrelhouse' men. Their music offers its own definition.

If any measure of agreement exists among the writers, the musicians and the theoreticians of piano blues, it is that the barrelhouse character is represented in the meeting of influences on the music. Whether these are church rock, rough, spontaneous, uninhibited jazz, primitive ragtime and ballad, or honky-tonk and house-rent party – whether they are, therefore, in the nature of the music or the function that it performs, they are aspects which have given a special character to the blues. With the exception of the church rock association they are all linked with entertainment rather than with singular self-expression as we have come to regard the blues proper, and they are, without exception, forms in which group activity is important. Thus the associations with boogie-woogie and barrelhouse and the styles of piano blues which are loosely linked with these terms are of the dance, the hop, the 'struggle', the 'parlor social' or indeed, the service. Additionally, they seem to stretch back in time to the pre-blues forms which were performed for these functions and which subtly shaped the later music; one should not be surprised if a hint of the cakewalk appeared in barrelhouse.

It is, for example in the playing of Rufus Perryman (Speckled Red) one of the pianists we met in St Louis, among them Henry Brown and Roosevelt Sykes, who were all recorded for the first time within months of each other – in May, June and September 1929, respectively. Their recording careers span nearly four decades but Speckled Red, by far the oldest, was at the time already nearly forty years old with a long life of piano playing in the joints of the black belts of numerous States behind him. His ''Tain't Nobody's Business' is a venerable item in the blues tradition which looks back to the ragtime pre-blues era. It comprises a succession of couplets in which the second line is the title one, and is usually sung in sixteen-bar groups. Speckled Red sings and plays it with gusto and one can imagine that it may have been the sort of song that Paul

Seminole featured in the early days of the century. Paul Seminole was a ragtime–cum–blues pianist who was well known on the East Coast and whose playing first inspired the near-blind Speckled Red to try his hand at playing the piano. In spite of the fact that he was born in Louisiana and raised in Georgia, it was not until he settled in Detroit that Speckled Red started to play the piano in earnest – and when he did it was under the influence of the 'stride' piano man. But it must be realized, of course, that by 1910 such New Orleans piano players as Tony Jackson and Jelly-Roll Morton, who had brought with them their own brand of ragtime and blues, were already familiar figures in Chicago and New York, and the mobility of the early pianists must be borne in mind before any rash assumptions as to currents of influence are drawn.

Champion Jack Dupree, pianist from New Orleans and a score of years Speckled Red's junior, played 'You Got Me Way Down Here', a stomping hokum piece with a vamping bass figure. Its simplicity is deceptive for it relates to the very old levee song 'Coonjine Baby' which was known on the Mississippi River before the end of the nineteenth century. Undoubtedly the river was an important course for the musical currents which flowed more rapidly, it seems, than the Father of the Waters itself. There is much evidence to show that New Orleans jazz was influenced heavily by the publication of the *Red Book of Rags* and the many ragtime sheets published by John Stark and Son of Sedalia and St Louis and other music companies in Missouri and elsewhere. These centres were remarkable for the concentration of ragtime pianists which they supported in the Nineties and subsequent years, and the blues pianists were their logical successors.

Notes to Storyville SLP 183 an 187, 1966

Speckled Red was born Monroe, Louisiana, 23 October 1892 and died St Louis, Missouri, January 1973.

Tight Like That
GEORGIA TOM DORSEY

Outside the store-front churches in Chicago during the Thirties a tall, slender and rather shy man would often be seen, offering a sheaf of papers to the worshippers and the church leaders as they left after the services. Many would stop and for a humble 10¢ would purchase a broadsheet crudely printed on a hand-operated press on which would be the legend:

Just after Prayer in your Service have the choir sing this number:
TAKE MY HAND, PRECIOUS LORD
by THOMAS A. DORSEY

The man who issued the gospel songs from his own small publishing premises on East 40th Street, Chicago, was sincere, devout and a major influence in the development of gospel music in the Negro church during the second quarter of the century. Few who bought his sheets and sang his religious songs recalled that he was once the highly popular 'Race' artist Georgia Tom and the composer of 'Tight Like That'.

Thomas Dorsey was born at the turn of the century of middle-class Negro parents outside Atlanta, Georgia. He did not suffer the poverty that many of his race experienced who lived in that area, and by standards of Negro education had a satisfactory schooling. From childhood he could play the piano, and gifted with an accurate ear for various forms of music, he gained even in his teens a considerable local reputation as a pianist. Parental restrictions do not seem to have been severe and he was in demand to play ragtime pieces, stomps and blues at dance-halls, private functions and small gin palaces on Decatur Street and in the Negro sector of Atlanta. There he became known as

'Barrelhouse Tommy' during the years of the First World War, and by his ability and likeable personality he ousted 'Long Boy', 'Nome', and other admired barrelhouse pianists of the area and the day, from the better jobs. He gathered a small band together and would probably have been satisfied with the moderate if casual income that his playing brought him had he not fallen in love with an Atlanta girl. Contemplating marriage and his personal finances, he decided to obtain a job which would bring him a larger and regular wage. The demands of war had opened up many opportunities for Negroes and the great steel mills at Gary offered good incomes for steel workers. Barrelhouse Tommy Dorsey migrated North.

In spite of his height Dorsey was so sparely built that he weighed only a fraction over nine stone. He was sensitive of his build and boyish looks and was certain that he could cope with the heavy labour of the mills. By the time he had saved sufficient money to consider returning to Atlanta and his intended bride he had damaged his health with the work he had undertaken – and the girl had moved with her family to Alabama. He decided to remain in Chicago, and continued with his work as a labourer so that he might study music in the evenings at the Chicago College of Composition and Arrangement. He aspired to be a professional musician and he still sought out every opportunity to play with other pianists and musicians. He played blues and ballads but his mind was troubled, for he was attracted to the Negro Baptist church. 1921 was the year of the National Convention of Baptist Churches which was held in Chicago, and Tom Dorsey attended the services and listened to the impressive sermons of the celebrated Texas preacher, Reverend A. W. Nix. He became a member of the Pilgrim Baptist Church and sang and played the joyous gospel compositions of C. A. Tindley which were now becoming popular in the Negro churches more than fifteen years after their composer had first published them.

His increasing interest in the Pilgrim Baptist Church did not sway Dorsey from his intention to earn his living by playing and singing, and his chance eventually came when he was invited to join Will Walker's Whispering Syncopators, a jazz band which included the then little-known Les Hite and Lionel Hampton in its composition. The band proved popular and so did Tom Dorsey now known through his country origins, more frequently as 'Georgia Tom'. His $40 a week was not a fortune but it was earned less strenuously and more agreeably than his pay in the steel mills. The Whispering Syncopators were offered a tour but Georgia Tom did not wish to go with them, still preferring to continue his musical studies and attend his church. Fortunately he had been heard by the great blues singer Gertrude Ma Rainey. Homely and thick-set herself she liked to have young, slender, good-looking men to accompany her and she invited him to form a new group of 'Rabbit Foot Minstrels'. Tom chose Al Wynn on trombone, Eddie Pollock on saxophone, and King Oliver's young nephew Dave Nelson on trumpet. With Gabriel Washington on drums and himself on piano, he took care of the rhythm section. It was a successful group and throughout 1923 they worked in Chicago and subsequently through the mid-West and the Deep South, Tom no longer feeling it necessary to remain in Chicago.

His lessons in music over, he applied his knowledge of arrangement to the accompaniments of the band, and began to compose songs and blues for Ma Rainey and for other singers, one of his first, 'I Just Want a Daddy' being recorded early that year by Alice Carter. He was also composing gospel songs in the manner of C. A. Tindley and his first, 'If I Don't Get There', was published in the Gospel Pearl Hymn Book at the same time. It was followed by a gospel hymn with hillbilly overtones, 'We Will Meet Him in the Sweet Bye and Bye' which appeared in a special edition of the National Baptist Hymnal shortly after. When he returned to Chicago he devoted himself increasingly to the needs of the Church and married a girl he had met who was similarly inclined, but he remained in touch with blues singers, pianists and guitarists, playing for social occasions when required.

Then came a period of considerable distress for Tom Dorsey when his health began to deteriorate. His weight dropped and he was unable to work. His wife took a job working in a laundry and strived to support them both. It was then that he found solace in the Pilgrim Church and he concentrated his efforts on the composition of gospel songs, the occasional sale of which augmented the wage which his wife brought from the laundry. Eventually he recovered and when he was offered a post as talent scout and recording adviser for the Brunswick Record Company he was able to put the experience of the past to good effect.

As he did not record any gospel items in the Twenties at all, it seems probable that Thomas Dorsey had no intention of putting his own talents on record. The credit for persuading him to do so would appear to go either to his friend Tampa Red, or to his old associate Ma Rainey, if he is numbered amongst that curiously primitive group, the Tub Jug Washboard Band which accompanied her on the Paramount recordings of the summer of 1928. For a musician of his training and inclinations it would appear to be an odd recording debut, though he may have felt lost in the obscurity of such a band.

At all events it was Tampa Red who encouraged him to make the first recordings under his own name.

Hudson Whittaker also came from Atlanta and was about Dorsey's own age. In all probability they knew each other as children but Whittaker went to Florida and was raised in Tampa. When he finally came to Chicago in the mid-Twenties he was known as 'Tampa Red', his pink complexion accounting for the second part of his sobriquet. Tampa Red played an arpeggio style of guitar requiring rapid fingerwork and economic use of strummed chords. Wearing a glass bottleneck on the fourth finger of his left hand he made the treble strings whine when he stopped and slid them across the frets, producing a quality of sound that was peculiarly his own and instantly recognizable. He induced Georgia Tom to compose the melody to a lyric of his own and the resultant tune – perhaps a memory of one previously heard by the pianist – became one of the most famous vehicles for blues song compositions: 'Tight Like That'. They recorded the title for Vocalion in September 1928 and their fruitful partnership really began with its release. 'Tight Like That' was astonishingly successful and sales of the record were remarkable. The first royalty cheque netted $2,400 for the composers and the much recorded tune continued to be a money-spinner for a number of years. If Georgia Tom was not completely enticed from the church, the receipts from his first recordings were so considerable that he could not afford, with his limited means, to ignore them. He saw in them an eventual source of capital which would enable him to devote his time completely to the church and for the time being he capitulated to the demands of his rapidly expanding audience. For the blues enthusiast it was a happy decision.

Though their partnership only lasted four years 'Dorsey and Whittaker' were exceptionally prolific and they enjoyed a wide popularity. Frequently they recorded jointly as 'Tampa Red and Georgia Tom' but they would act as accompanists to each other when the recordings were issued under the name of either one. Together they accompanied such artists as Ma Rainey, Victoria Spivey, Jenny Pope, Madlyn Davies, Chippie Hill and Frankie Jaxon, but they also worked independently during this period and Georgia Tom was generally to be found as sole accompanist to Thelma Holmes who recorded as 'Kansas City Kitty'· He also recorded with Big Bill Broonzy as guitarist on many items including the accompaniments to Hannah May and Jane Lucas – the identities of whom still remain somewhat controversial. But it was in the company of Tampa Red that Dorsey made his most typical sides even if he is more audible as an accompanist on some of the titles on which Red was absent. Together they formed the nucleus of Tampa Red's Hokum Jug Band and of the original Hokum Boys. Later, Tom Dorsey continued the Hokum Boys with Broonzy and Frank Brasswell, but they changed in character in the process, losing something of the quality that made the early Paramount group so popular.

In fact, the precise nature of the appeal of any of Georgia Tom's talents remains somewhat elusive. He and Tampa Red, when they worked together, are artists who appeal to the wholehearted blues and Race devotee who has 'got under the skin' of the music. They are not rough, untutored folk blues artists and seldom do they sound powerful or dramatic. Many of their recordings were extremely sophisticated – sophisticated to the point of self-caricature. They deliberately exploited 'corny' vocal duets and routines, they sang without marked 'down home' accents though they were not above parody – and yet they remained firmly within the field of blues and Race music. But it was in this very plurality that their appeal for their audiences lay. For a pianist of his training, Tom remained extremely simple in his phrasing, seldom demonstrating any of the complexities of composition that his studies would have enabled him to use. Instead, he preferred a simple, stomp-time beat or syncopation in his left hand and light melodic but blues-based passages in his right-hand work. Only occasionally did a more flourishing or decorative run indicate his potential capability but these instances were enough to display his talent. His voice was a little deeper than Tampa's and showed more traces of country origins, though these were by no means pronounced. When the Hokum Band and the Hokum Boys sang and played, Georgia Tom would turn in a barrelhouse piano performance or Tampa Red would rasp a crude kazoo solo – to balance their tongue-in-cheek vocals sung or chanted in chorus. Even the name they gave to their groups – blatantly acknowledging that they were 'hokum' performers – defied blues conventions. In such ways they established their popularity with countless thousands of other Negroes who, like themselves, had come North during the Twenties from rural and Southern backgrounds. In their recordings were echoes of their country origins and reflections of their new city environment. Memories of country blues and country dance bands were linked to witty, sophisticated songs; barrelhouse piano and blues guitar were played by men with city voices and little of the 'yard-and-field-Negro' about them. To the 'new Negro' recently arrived from the South and desperately trying to be in tune with the faster life of the Northern city, and to the Southern Negro left at home, reluctant to let go of his folk beliefs yet anxious to be a part of the 'improving' Race, their records appealed alike.

During the few years of their recording together Georgia Tom and Tampa Red looked forward to the development of 'city blues' whilst casting uncondescending glances back to their folk origins. Tampa Red was to continue in later years and in the company of Big Maceo, Big Bill Broonzy, Willie Lacey, Ransom Knowling and many others, was to play a large part in the changing nature of the blues. But to Georgia Tom the downfall of their fortunes occasioned by the Depression, and the suffering that he witnessed amongst his associates and church members was a challenge that he felt he could only meet by wholehearted devotion to the church. 'How about you?' he asked those who would join him, and his last record told of 'Singing in my soul'. He was lost to blues but not to Race music, for he has continued to compose gospel songs for the past quarter of a century, in which field he is pre-eminent. Only recently Brother John Sellers recorded some of his gospel songs, written in 1959, for Monitor. But to recall the days of his career as a blues pianist is embarrassing for the tall, shy, Thomas A. Dorsey and all that remains of his place in the story of the music are the records that he made nearly thirty years ago. Last year, through the thoughtfulness of Brother John Sellers, I met him at a South Side store-front church, an impressive, dignified man. Since 1933 he has been president of the National Convention of Gospel Choirs and Choruses which he founded and which he has supplied with over 400 gospel songs. 'When a person is filled with troubles, this music makes his worries take wings and fly away,' he said at the Convention in Washington in 1960. He could have been talking of the blues.

Jazz Monthly, November 1961

The Honey Dripper

ROOSEVELT SYKES

'She's a copper-coloured woman, looks something like a Japanese . . .' run the words of a verse in Roosevelt Sykes' blues 'Miss Ida B'. The description could be applied to himself with his medium-toned, warm-hued skin and his oriental features. His broad, generous countenance and his expansive smiles close his eyes to slits and in repose he looks a little like Oliver Hardy – a comparison which Roosevelt, a keen cinema-goer, would not resent. In height he barely makes five feet, four inches, and these days his increasing girth is beginning to rival that of Jimmy Rushing. Even in early years he was stocky and inclined to be plump and it is easy to see why, in spite of his lack of height, Roosevelt Sykes was immediately recognizable when he came into a barrelhouse joint. And when he did the crowd parted, the pianist stepped down from the stool and Roosevelt was pressed into playing. Wherever he went, from his early teens, he was recognized and welcomed and throughout his long career as a blues singer and pianist he has enjoyed his modest fame and the unwavering acclaim of his audiences.

Talk to any blues pianist and the name of Roosevelt Sykes will come up within minutes; his fame in the blues world has been universal and unfluctuating over four decades. Perhaps this is why he is such a settled and well-adjusted man. In some ways he even lacks colour in the sense that spectacular deeds, an impulsive temper, a violent life and hard drinking make for good and repeatable stories about blues singers. Few stories are told about Roosevelt in the way that they are told about many lesser men, and indeed he has relatively few to tell himself. Other musicians just talk about his superb musicianship, his sympathetic accompaniments, his original blues compositions, his generosity and his good nature. Unlike most blues singers Roosevelt Sykes has led a happy, largely uneventful life, spent contentedly playing the music he loves to audiences that always want to hear him and always ask for more. It seems to have been that way always.

Roosevelt Sykes was born in Helena, Arkansas, in 1906 close to the Mississippi River. His parents moved to St Louis when he was only three years of age but his vacations were always spent with his grandfather on his farm some sixteen miles south of Helena. Even today Helena is still 'home' to Roosevelt and the area about the Arkansas town was the one in which his happiest days of his childhood were spent. In vacations, or when his mother brought him to stay with his grandfather, he did a little ploughing, 'not too much, I was too little, but I liked it,' he recalled to me nearly fifty years later. He chopped and picked cotton and whenever he could, as he got older, went into Helena to hear the blues pianists. Helena in the years during and after the First World War was a blues centre of considerable importance and Roosevelt remembers vividly the playing of a number of blues players who had a profound influence on his style. 'They was what you call real blues players, always be playin' the blues,' he said recalling in particular a 'real stomp-down blues playin' pianist' by the name of Jesse Bell. He recalls many others, and that in West Helena the bluesmen congregated at 'a place down there they call Dixie's Drug Store; 'most everybody hung around this corner. I think it was on Walnut and Missouri Streets'. It was the theme, as a matter of interest, of another blues pianist's composition 'The

Dixie Drug Store Down On Missouri Street' recorded by Arnold Wiley who also came from the area. That was in 1927, just a couple of years before Roosevelt himself made his first recordings.

In 1929 Roosevelt was twenty-three and already well-known as a blues pianist. He had learned to play the organ on a small home model that his grandfather owned, and at school the organ used to accompany morning prayers became the vehicle for some of his earliest blues playing to an audience: 'See, I used to play the organ at school for prayers and things, and when I got me the chance I used to play me some blues on that ole school organ, liven it up a bit. And when I gets to playin' the blues the kids all come runnin' round me like they was bees or somethin'. So people gets to say "he must be honey 'cause they all around him like bees" and so they call me the Honey Dripper on account of it.' Perhaps his honey-hued skin had a little to do with it too.

His association with Leothus 'Pork Chops' Green was a fruitful one and Green taught him a number of blues themes which he used when he first recorded for Okeh in June 1929. Having signed up with Okeh he was in some difficulty when approached by Paramount to record only a couple of months after. He decided to change his name for the session: 'At that time you could change around, sort of change your name and if you have a different tune why you could make recordings for different people. So I had a contract with Okeh and I did recordings for other companies under different names. One of my names when I was a kid was Dobby. They always called me Dobby, so my mother's name was Bragg so I used the name Dobby Bragg.' So the first titles in the present set were made: 'Single Tree Blues' and 'Fire Detective Blues'. The rural associations of 'Single Tree' clearly reflect Roosevelt's country connection, though it may be a composition of his own

or based on a traditional blues theme. The words 'Hit my woman with a single tree, you mighta heard her yellin' "Daddy, don'cha murder me"' reappeared just a month later in the Memphis Jug Band's 'I Whipped My Woman with a Single Tree' on Victor, and six years later in Leadbelly's 'Becky Deem, She Was a Gamblin' Gal'. A memory of the field and levee, the single tree was a wooden spar which linked the harnesses of a pair of animals in a working team. Many of Sykes' early recordings were autobiographical in content and 'Fire Detective', with its reference to insurance enquiries, is based on an actual incident as the specific detail suggests.

There has been some doubt cast on the identification of Dobby Bragg with Roosevelt Sykes and whilst there seems little reason to suspect that it is anyone else in the first Bragg sessions it must be admitted that the artist of the second session, from which '3, 6 and 9' and 'We Can Sell That Thing' are taken, sounds a lot less like Sykes. The talking accompaniment and even the tone of voice against the complex bass figures of the piano sound far more like Wesley Wallace on the admittedly slender evidence of No. 29, and I would suggest Wallace as a possible alternative identification. The growling passages on the other title are not particularly like Roosevelt's playing either, but the low-down material is characteristic of some of his more robust titles. '3, 6 and 9' is the 'numbers' combination in 'policy playing' for excreta and to a Negro audience an effective euphemism for a four-letter insult. Paramount apparently slightly bowdlerized the second title which, in spite of the label clearly should be 'we can *smell* that thing'. No doubt the discographical wrangle will continue.

Roosevelt Sykes' themes are often amusing twists on well-known basic ones and the story of the woman who 'come runnin' with a marriage licence' in her hand is a good example. Many of his compositions have become blues 'standards' and few are more famous than 'Highway 61 Blues' which was recorded a year-and-a-half before Jack Kelly's version and sparked off a number of variants by Curtis Jones, Big Joe Williams and others. As the blues, sung in a very simple, country style by Sykes, makes quite clear, the celebrated route for migrating Negroes runs through Memphis and St Louis.

Apart from his work as a solo performer, Roosevelt Sykes earned the admiration of his colleagues for his understanding playing as an accompanist. For an artist of his repute to play sympathetically in support of other singers without intruding or even dominating the proceedings demanded both feeling and restraint. Sykes makes an admirable accompanist for he never attempts to use another man's recordings as an opportunity to display his pianistic technique; instead he plays thoughtfully, with simple phrases behind the vocals that do not threaten to impair the vocal line, and with embellishments in the breaks that are in keeping with the theme of the blues. For this reason he was featured on literally many hundreds of recordings by blues artists as varied as Walter Davis, Alice Moore, Napoleon Fletcher, Oscar Carter, Washboard Sam, Kokomo Arnold, Jazz Gillum and Peetie Wheatstraw, amongst many others. Several of these were artists of his own finding, for early in his career Lester Melrose and Dave Kapp employed him as a talent scout to seek out likely artists to record. Some of the artists whom he accompanied in the early recordings, including some whose appearance on record was his own responsibility, are featured in the remaining tracks on this record.

First of the singers represented here is Edith Johnson, the widow of Jesse Johnson, who at that time was a noted impressario and talent scout in St Louis. Jesse and Edith owned the De Luxe Music Shop, a famous St Louis rendezvous for blues singers and Edith heard scores of them when she worked at the shop. Her husband was not enthusiastic about her recording her own blues but eventually she won him over. The present session, in September 1929, was the one which made her name. It took place, according to Mrs Johnson, in Indianapolis and she was accompanied by Roosevelt Sykes, Ike Rodgers, a trombonist who usually worked with pianist Henry Brown, and Baby James (or simply 'J'), a blues trumpet player with a considerable reputation in St Louis. James recorded little and the accompaniment to Edith Johnson affords a rare opportunity to hear this esteemed blues musician. With Sykes he plays a sensitive, understated but expressive obligato. Ike Rogers, with his tough and primitive trombone playing is the more suitable accompanist for Edith Johnson's other track, 'Good Chib Blues' with its cool threats of a woman who intends to get her way with her 'chib' or 'shiv' blade.

'Specks' McFadden had poor eyesight and the glasses he always wore gave him his nickname. One eye failed him completely and subsequently he wore one lens of his spectacles blacked out entirely, earning him the name on one record of 'Black Patch' McFadden. Intermittently over a period of eight or nine years Specks and Sykes worked together, travelling from St Louis southwards through several States and even to Texas. Always McFadden was called upon to sing two items, 'People People Blues' and 'Piggly Wiggly' ('Groceries on My Shelf'), each of which he recorded four times. His strangely high, but very blue voice was immediately recognizable and the words of his unusual blues known by everyone. Piggly Wiggly was the name of the first Supermarket chain in the United States in which all groceries could be obtained under one roof. With the complicated Negro sexual metaphors on the theme of food in mind – bread, jelly-roll, cabbage greens, yellow yams and so on – the witty implications of McFadden's joke of obtaining them all in one place greatly appealed.

Eighteen months later the memorable session which provides the items on the second side took place. Mary Johnson is in no way related to Edith Johnson; she was at one time married to the celebrated blues singer Lonnie Johnson and took his name, though she was born the daughter of Emma Williams in Yazoo City, Mississippi, in 1900 – or 1905, she has given both dates. At any rate, before she was twenty she was working as a singer in St Louis where her mother had brought her as a girl. When the present recordings were made she had just separated from her husband and was earning a living as a singer at Charlie Turpin's Jazzland club on Market Street. Her disillusion over her separation is clearly reflected in her 'Mary Johnson Blues' in which her name as the title makes its own point. Known as 'Signifying Mary' she had a determined delivery with no frills and she remained popular in St Louis for two decades. A few years ago, however, she suffered a paralytic stroke and when I met her in St Louis in 1960 she was living with her aged mother on relief.

Also in retirement today is St Louis Jimmy who suffered serious injuries in a car accident several years ago. Until then he had been continually active as a blues singer, his lean, economical style of half-sung, half-spoken verses marking him out as an individual artist. He was born James Oden in Nashville, Tennessee, in 1905 but was orphaned by the age of eight. He is reticent about the life he led in the next few years but by the age of fourteen he was working in a St Louis barber shop and listening to the blues singers who congregated there. He taught himself to play piano but felt he could not compete with pianists of the stature of

Sykes with whom he struck up a friendship that has lasted nearly four decades. He was a highly original blues composer and many of his compositions have become blues 'standards' which were always in demand when he and Roosevelt toured together. 'St Louis Jimmy and I worked together for some years, we travelled on a lot of one-nighters throughout the country, north, south – travelled through different towns, playin' one-nighters for different clubs and theatres.' It was early in this period that the present recordings were made in the company of the country violinist Curtis Mosby.

St Louis Jimmy Oden went on to record for many years but the other artists on the session were destined to remain in total obscurity, these sides being virtually all that is known about them. Matthew McClure, it seems, had a talking style, recited rather than sung, not too dissimilar to Oden's own, and ideally suited to the melancholy theme of 'Prison Blues'. Eithel Smith, like her better-known namesakes Trixie Smith and Ivy Smith, has a somewhat anonymous voice, clear and characteristically Race without the individuality of Edith or Mary Johnson. Her song 'Jelly Roll Mill' is a cheerfully bragging sexual fantasy placed squarely in the popular genre of the day to which Roosevelt Sykes plays a suitably light and slightly 'raggy' accompaniment.

That was thirty-three years ago. Today Roosevelt Sykes has left both St Louis of his formative years and the Chicago of the postwar period to live with his wife and children on the Mississippi coast at Gulfport. But he hasn't retired for the blues is his life.

Notes to Riverside RLP 8879, 1966

Mary Johnson died St Louis, *c*.1965.
St Louis Jimmy Oden died Chicago,
30 December 1977.
Roosevelt Sykes died New Orleans,
11 July 1983.

Devil's Son-in-Law
PEETIE WHEATSTRAW

'. . . I'm aseventhsonofaseventhsonbawnwithacauloverbotheyesandraisedonblackcatboneshighjohntheconquerorandgreasygreens – ' boasted the red-eyed Negro who pushes his cart into the ninth chapter of Ralph Ellison's *Invisible Man*, (Random House, 1947; Victor Gollancz, 1953). The stream of jives slows and the tough little character introduces himself: 'My name is Peter Wheatstraw, I'm the Devil's only son-in-law, so roll 'em!' Ralph Ellison, whose angry, confused but brilliant book gives a profound insight into the complex of Negro life in the United States, has recently turned to jazz criticism and has given a telling picture of Jimmy Rushing as he knew him when a boy. He may possibly have known the blues singer Peetie Wheatstraw also. If so, then he has a story that demands the telling, but in all probability he was more attracted by the picture conjured in his mind by the recordings of the man. Such a string of rapidly uttered syllables is hardly in keeping with the lazy verses of the singer on record, but even if he appears as a half-fictional character in *Invisible Man* he would also seem to be half-fact; the aggressive self-description seems to suit the type of man who could have made the discs.

Few blues singers are more fully represented on record than Peetie Wheatstraw; few blues singers are more obscure in proportion to their popularity and fame. Ironically, it was the circumstances of a cruel and untimely death that brought any information on the singer to light at all, when the barest details were given in a *Down Beat* obituary for 15 January 1942. If there was anything to be gained from this slight recognition by the jazz world and the musical press, it came too late to be of any benefit to Peetie Wheatstraw.

Peetie Wheatstraw was not his real name, though it was the name that always appeared on his recordings. He was born William Bunch, but with a flair perhaps for the dramatic and the curious, he styled himself with a traditional Negro folk name – not one as well-known as Stavin' Chain or Long John, John the Conqueror or Jack the Bear, but one that had well-rooted folk associations. At his death William Bunch was said to have been thirty-six; born in Little Rock, Arkansas, in 1905. But even this is disputed: Panassie gives his birthdate as 1894, the place, St Louis. From the admittedly doubtful evidence of his records the later date might be considered the more likely: those of 1930–31 have the voice of a young, even immature man, whilst the most recent items do not suggest the work of a man nearing fifty – but neither did Big Bill Broonzy's. Whether he was born in St Louis or not, Peetie Wheatstraw had close links with many singers from that city and spent most of his life there. Of the boyhood, the youth, the early manhood of the singer, nothing is to be found in print, though there must be many persons alive today who could fill in some of the details if called upon to do so. And of the decade during which he recorded fairly prolifically little more is to be learned about the man than is to be found in his recordings.

Not content with one sobriquet, William Bunch styled himself 'The Devil's Son-in-Law' and from his earliest recordings this additional title is beneath the name 'Peetie Wheatstraw'. Later, on the isolated recording he promoted himself to 'High Sheriff from Hell'. His debut on record was made in October 1930, when he made with one 'Neckbones' the item 'Tennessee Peaches Blues'. It is a provocative disc which raises a number of points of interest, for the accompaniment is highly reminiscent of Leroy Carr and Scrapper Blackwell, a possibility made all the more tantalizing by the close proximity of the recording block made by that team which concluded with 'Carried Water for the Elephant'. There are two singers, the mysterious Neckbones taking the first few stanzas until Peetie, singing on record for the first time, with energy but not quite in tune, breaks in on the vocal line and exchanges variants of the same verse to the conclusion of the disc. Who was Neckbones? Jessie Clayton perhaps, who made 'Neckbones Blues'. Certainly it is not Jennie Mae Clayton, Will Shade's wife who sang with the Memphis Jug Band, though the tune is the tune of her 'Bob Lee Junior Blues'.

Shortly after, Peetie began to record by himself and he appears as an individual personality. His early recordings have his own piano accompaniment, which gives support to the possibility that he came under Leroy Carr's influence. Though his early piano blues are fairly simply constructed and have a vamping left hand they have the mellow, but rolling quality that was characteristic of Carr's playing. Peetie's piano style is not sufficiently arbitrary to make it outstandingly recognizable, though its essentially 'blue' phrasing and mood is undeniable. As he developed, his playing became more imaginative and more emphatic, with greater variations in his bass figures and stronger, harder-hitting melodic improvisation in the treble. But he remained a pianist in the school of Leroy Carr as long as he continued to play his own accompaniments. By reputation, Peetie Wheatstraw was a greater guitarist than he was pianist. Talking to Big Bill Broonzy on the relative merits of various blues guitarists the present writer mentioned Peetie. Almost peremptorily, Broonzy replied: 'Man, that boy could get him a job playing guitar *anywhere*,'

setting the seal on any further discussion by placing him beyond dispute. Though the testimony of other blues singers lends support to his considerable reputation as a guitarist, little can be derived from his discs as a measure of his ability, for few if any can be stated with any certainty as having his own guitar accompaniment.

Until 1953 the name of Charlie Jordan (or as Decca would have it Charley Jordan) is closely coupled with that of Peetie Wheatstraw and he frequently provides the guitar accompaniment on Peetie's records, whilst the honours are returned on many of Charlie Jordan's own items. A comparison of discographies and matrices soon reveals the close relationship between the two men who undoubtedly travelled and worked together. In the Decca Race catalogue of the 7000 series is to be found the key to his partnership, where Jordan is stated as 'Peetie Wheatstraw's Brother'. Those who have attempted to unravel the intricacies of a blues singer's family tree will not be surprised by the difference of surname. According to Joe Lee Williams, Jordan came from 'Maribello', Arkansas – possibly Mabelville, a township close to Little Rock, which might lend support to the report that this was the birthplace of William Bunch.

Charlie Jordan lived for over twenty-five years in St Louis where he acted as a talent scout for the Decca and Vocalion companies and was probably instrumental in securing work for Peetie. During the Thirties Peetie also recorded as accompanist to Alice Moore, a St Louis singer, and was, in all likelihood, supported himself by J. C. Stoat – Jelly Joe Short – on one session, himself a St Louis man. Though Peetie and Charlie Jordan together and under their separate names recorded almost fifty items, Willie Bunch made fruitful partnerships with Kokomo Arnold, Lil Armstrong, and Lonnie Johnson, who each cut twenty or so more sides with him, and also with Casey Bill Weldon.

Bearing in mind the successful sessions with Lil Johnson, Barrelhouse Buck, and Bumble Bee Slim in addition to the very considerable body of recordings made under his own name and with the above mentioned artists, it is remarkable that Peetie Wheatstraw has been so neglected as a blues artist. It is difficult to trace any reference to his work in jazz literature published before his death, although he made in his own name more than 160 items and with his accompaniments included appears on well over 200 blues recordings. Familiarity with the recorded work of Peetie Wheatstraw may not substantiate his considerable reputation amongst other blues men of his ability as a guitarist but justifies his reputation as a blues pianist of importance if not in the top rank. Above all, his records reveal him as a blues singer of great individuality and quality.

As a vocalist Peetie Wheatstraw is instantly recognizable. He had a fairly deep voice, with a blurred enunciation and grainy texture; the voice of a blues singer who made no concessions to concepts of the vocal inside or outside the jazz field. He was not excessively rough or coarse in the manner of Tommy McClennan for example; he did not strain for effect or attempt to force his words by strong expression. Rather, Peetie Wheatstraw was an abundantly relaxed singer who seems to have performed without effort or self-conscious technique, casually eliding some syllables, dropping consonants, slurring his words through half-open lips; singing from deep in the chest rather than from the front of the mouth. But any impression of indolence, or idle neglect in his singing, was negated by the menacing undercurrent that runs throughout his work. In spite of his seemingly off-hand manner his words demand attention and an indefin-

able quality in his delivery insists that he is heard. He was a singer who sang from personal experience: though occasional items are credited to close associates, Charlie Jordan or St Louis Jimmy Oden, the majority of his blues are his own compositions and they bear the indisputable stamp of his authorship. The bitter years of the Depression were his maturing years and from his blues one learns something of the hard, unglamorous realities of the life of a Negro at that time.

Many of Peetie Wheatstraw's blues reflect the prevailing poverty of Negroes in the Thirties:

> *I have walked a lonesome road, till ma feet is*
> *   too sore to walk,   (repeat)*
> *I beg scraps from the people, oh well well, till*
> *   my tongue is too stiff to talk.*

> *Anybody can tell you people, ooh well that I*
> *   ain't no lazy man,   (repeat)*
> *But I'll guess I'll have to go to the Poorhouse,*
> *   mmm well well, and do the best I can.*
> *   'Road Tramp Blues'*

Others add to the extensive catalogue of railroad blues which owe their origin to the Northward and interstate migrations of Negroes seeking employment and better living conditions who hoboed their way on the great trunk lines:

> *Whoo-hoo, cain't you hear that C and A*
> *   whistle blow?   (repeat)*
> *Mama, she blow so lonesome baby, because I*
> *   want t' go.*

> *Eeeee-hmmmmm, few more days, few more*
> *   nights alone.   (repeat)*
> *Baby then I will pack my suitcase honey,*
> *   then I will be gone*
> *   'C and A Blues'*

Federal attempts to solve the serious problems of unemployment by the works projects of the Public Works Administration and similar bodies are illustrated from the personal angle of the man employed in them by such blues as 'Working on the Project', 'New Working on the Project', and '304 Blues', ('Lost My Job on the Project').

> *Working on the project with holes all in my*
> *   clothes,   (repeat)*
> *Trying to make a dime to keep the rent man*
> *   from putting me out doors.*
>
> *Working on the project with pay-day three or*
> *   four weeks away,   (repeat)*
> *Now how can you make things meet oh well*
> *   well when you can't get no pay?*
> *   'Working on the Project'*

There is little doubt that these and similar blues were drawn directly from personal experience, and the repercussions of the loss of his employment made of Willie Bunch a bitter and unhappy man.

> *When I was working I give you all of my*
> *   pay-roll,   (repeat)*
> *Now I am out of a job, oh well, you put me out*
> *   in the cold.*
>
> *When you have got money, you have got a lot*
> *   of friends,   (repeat)*
> *But when you get broke, oh well, your friend-*
> *   ship comes to an end.*
> *   'A Working Man's Blues'*

Rather cynically he permitted himself to indulge in occasional, ironic fancies which, by their very extravagance, underlined the true situation which featured so prominent-ly in his other blues.

> *I could just 'phone, anywhere in town,*
> *   (repeat)*
> *Mister Livingood wanted it, oh well well, and*
> *   they rush it on down.*
>
> *I had a butler just to fetch me my gin,*
> *   (repeat)*

> *Livin' seven days to the week, ooh well, but*
> *   now I'm livin' ten.*
>
> *On big parties, I got money on the floor,*
> *   (repeat)*
> *And leave it to the sweeper, and walk on out*
> *   the door.*
> *   'Mister Livingood'*

Such blues were no means of escapism, as Wheatstraw's intonation and manner of delivery emphasizes beyond any measure of doubt. More often than not his songs were essentially realistic; some display a certain unlikely optimism as, for example, when Peetie sings 'Oh when I get my bonus, things will be coming my way . . .' but generally there is little sign of self-delusion in his work. Instead he frequently offers advice which is summarized in the philosophy 'It pays to Look Out for Your-self', the belief that 'every tub stands on its own bottom'.

> *Every time the rooster crows for day,*
> *I get up early and meet the sun halfway,*
> *Well now it pays you to look out for yourself.*
>
> *When you get flat broke, ain't got a dime,*
> *Don't give up; it'll come in your time,*
> *So it pays you to look out for yourself.*
>
> *Your friends will stand by you before they get*
> *   up on top,*
> *When you need a favour, they will let you*
> *   drop,*
> *So now it pays you to look out for yourself.*
>
> *Make it the hard way the best you can,*
> *The dollars will start rollin'; they gotta roll in*
> *   your hand,*
> *Well now it pays you to look out for yourself.*

Violence in various forms appears in the work of numerous blues singers and that of Peetie Wheatstraw is no exception. Such items as 'Kidnappers Blues', 'Pocket Knife Blues' and 'Gangster's Blues' ('I'm gonna take you for an easy ride, drop you off on the riverside . . . I'm gonna bind your mouth so you can't talk, tie your feet so you can't walk . . .') are only a few of the many blues which reveal the background of brutality against which the blues was frequently created. Love, too, in Peetie's blues is always 'of the salty kind' as he sings in 'My Little Bit', and the sexual imagery that he employs is of a kind familiar to the blues collector though his use of it is, as always with him, highly original.

I want some sea-food mama, because I'm a
  sea-food man,   (repeat)
When I can't get my sea-food mama, oh well,
  I'll go to raisin' sand.

So bye-bye people, I hope this July will find
  you well,   (repeat)
Because this sea-food I'm talkin' about is rare
  as a bug in Hell.

Tough, even aggressive; uncomplaining and self-centred, Peetie's blues appealed to his coloured audience because they made no compromise. He sang in their language, he sang of his life which was their lives, he rose above his troubles and his difficulties by creating from them and in doing so was an inspiration to the lonely or the despairing Negro. If any blues deserve the term 'Race Blues' with no hint of any derogatory implications then his undoubtedly do, for he was addressing his own people alone and his blues was especially and wholly for them. Herein lies the clue to the neglect which he has suffered, for his work tends to appeal only to the 'hardened' collector who has allowed himself to be absorbed by the idiom. There is none of the driving impact of a Leadbelly in his work; none of the jazz-inclined phrasing of a Bessie Smith. Even the stark rawness of a Tommy McClennan which has a certain romantic appeal for some whose contact with the blues is slight,

is missing here, and there are none of the customary qualities associated with the singing of say, Jimmy Rushing, Joe Turner, even Big Bill Broonzy, which makes them more readily acceptable to the purely jazz-minded. Yet fundamentally, the heart of the blues lies within the recordings of such a singer as Peetie Wheatstraw, though it is more elusive there than in the singing of Blind Lemon Jefferson, for example, whose character is more obviously primitive.

Anecdotes there must be about Peetie Wheatstraw; in the life of a man who lived as richly as his recordings suggest there must be the material for a full biography, but none of this appears to have reached the printed page. One cannot even be certain of his physical appearance: the photograph that was reproduced in one of the few articles on this singer – Derrick Stewart-Baxter's in *Jazz Journal* some years ago – though signed 'The Devil's Son-in-Law' was emphatically denied as being a portrait of Peetie by Big Bill Broonzy to the present writer, and by Sam Price to the French blues collector Jacques Demetre. In this he appeared as light-skinned, round-headed and with long, flexible fingers. A small portrait appeared on the Race catalogue of the Decca 7000 series which portrays Peetie as dark-hued, long of feature and similar to Curley Weaver.

So important was Peetie Wheatstraw to the Negro audience for whom he sang that a number of other singers exploited their association with him; Charlie Jordan deriving some benefit from being 'Peetie Wheatstraw's Brother'; Robert Lee McCoy, a St Louis singer, making use of a youthful association by recording as 'Peetie's Boy'; Joe McCoy (no relation) undersigning himself as 'Peetie Wheatstraw's Buddy' and Floyd Council acknowledging the effectiveness of the relationship of similar titles, calling himself 'The Devil's

Daddy-In-Law'. Such reflected glory did little harm to Willie Bunch himself and the use of such names were, in themselves, marks of esteem.

Probably through the difficulties arising over union regulations Peetie did not record with his own piano accompaniment after 1938, and the Decca house pianists Sam Price and Lil Armstrong were chiefly responsible for the piano work on his later sides. On the whole, his work showed a slight decline in his later recordings, perhaps because the overlay of piano and voice could never be quite as distinctly personal to the man, when another artist was providing the instrumental accompaniment, where he himself had played his own piano blues for so long. These later recordings are still exceptional nonetheless. According to Big Bill Broonzy he continued to play both piano and guitar consistently through this period off the record, Peetie remaining an outstanding exponent of that unusual instrument, the nine-string guitar.

On 25 November 1941, Peetie Wheatstraw had his last recording date; a singularly ominous one which included 'Don't Put Yourself On the Spot' and 'Hearse Man Blues' amongst the items, and which concluded with his last words on record in 'Separation Day Blues'. Less than a month later, on 21 December, he was dead. Driving his automobile across a level crossing on the outskirts of St Louis his

vehicle was struck by an express passenger train and he was fatally injured. His nine-string guitar passed into the hands of blues singer Joe Lee Williams who still plays such an instrument. His brother Charlie Jordan continued to seek talent for the Decca company, though he himself no longer recorded. He, too, met a violent death when he was shot through the spine on 9th Street, St Louis, 1954. Other friends and associates of Peetie's have also passed on, amongst them Big Bill Broonzy, Big Maceo and, according to Will Shade, Casey Bill Weldon. Kokomo Arnold recently disappeared in Chicago – but there are others who could still tell us much about William Bunch: Lil Armstrong, Sam Price and Jonah Jones amongst them. 'Bring me flowers while I'm living,' Peetie sang at his last session:

> *Don't bring me flowers after I'm dead, a dead*
> *   man sure can't smell.   (repeat)*
> *And if I don't go to Heaven, I sure won't need*
> *   no flowers in Hell.*

Unhappily there were few flowers for Peetie when he was alive and true recognition, when it comes, will come too late to be of use to him. But when he sang, he sang for his whole people, and what he sang was the life-blood of blues and therefore of jazz. To know him better, even posthumously, is to know more about the music.

Jazz Monthly, May 1959

Bee's Back in Town
BUMBLE BEE SLIM

In the history of the blues the Thirties were years of change as the music moved from its folk origins in rural styles and the blues of the city emerged. In this period many singers who were born in the country but who matured in the Northern cities made their names. They recalled enough of the South in their blues songs to endear them to those of their race who lived there or who, like themselves, had recently moved North, yet their freshness of delivery and the aptness of their verses also appealed to the town-dwellers. Folk idiom and city slang coloured their songs, country guitarists and night spot pianists played together in the accompaniments, new names appeared on the record labels and in the mail order catalogues. The names themselves are worthy of study for the changing state of the blues as reflected in the sobriquets chosen by, or for, many of the singers. Some have an aggressive note, others have slyly sexual overtones. There was The Honey Dripper and Peanut the Kidnapper, Black Spider Dumpling and Black Ivory King, Peetie Wheatstraw the Devil's Son-in-Law and a host of other colourful and evocative pseudonyms by which the artists were often better known than by their own names. One of these was Amos Easton who was known to the great blues public of the day by the name of Bumble Bee Slim. Bumble Bee Slim was one of the best known and best loved blues singers of the Thirties. His recordings in those pre-long-player days numbered some 170 items, a prodigious number by any standard. During the years 1934–1936 a couple of new records by Bumble Bee Slim were appearing every month and his records on Bluebird, Vocalion or Decca were to be found in every Negro home. The secret of his success lay in the manner in which his blues reflected the common condition and predicament of his audience. In those trying years 'Running Bad Luck Blues' and 'Lost Confidence Blues' had sympathetic hearers who gained heart from 'Some Day Things Will be Better' and shared the pain of 'My Troubles'. The man on the 'job' welcomed 'Piney Woods Working Man', the numbers player 'Policy Dream Blues' and the helpless understood the significance of 'Fattening Frogs for Snakes'. This was Bumble Bee Slim's period of achievement but the memories of a hard life were always with him to give meaning to his blues.

Born in the country, in Georgia, on 7 May 1905, Amos Easton hardly knew his father. He was four years old when his father died and his mother, with six children on her hands, soon married again. Amos didn't get on very well with his step-father and as the family increased with another two children he found himself having to work hard in the fields when still barely of school age. Bumble Bee Slim takes up the story:

'It rocked on 'til I got to be about nine years old. Then I decided I was gonna learn to cut hair. I learned how to barber. So, at nine, I made my first attempt to run off . . . be my own man. That's what I always wanted anyway. So, I went off, set up a barber shop, had me parched peanuts (you know, down South they call them goobers). Anyway, I had my stand set up. "Let the kid cut your hair, come on, come on, that kid he's a good barber. He's good barber, go!" That went on 'til they found out where I was. My step-daddy was there with the mule, wagon, and tied me on and took me back.' When he could, Slim ran away from home again. This time he joined a circus that came through the district and as it was travelling he soon put a fair distance between himself and his family. It was two years before he returned home. He was now his own man, he felt, and independent. He tried a variety of jobs and in his early twenties got married. Whether it was because he treasured his independence too much or not, the marriage was not a success and within a year or two the couple had separated. The experience was a bitter one but it was one which found expression in a number of his blues. Since boyhood in the circus he had been making up songs, noting them and putting away his compositions for future use. He had little doubt about his eventual intention to make use of his blues compositions. Somewhere along the line he had started to play guitar – not well, but adequately enough to accompany himself at country functions. Lean years in the South finally made up his mind for him and he decided to try his luck in the North.

'I took off for Chicago, hoboin'. I had a little guitar swingin' on my back. This was right during the time the Scottsboro Boys were in a jam. I was hoppin' freights, and they arrested about a hundred hobos and I was one. I had a little boy along with me. I didn't know him, he just took along with me because I had the instrument, I guess. So, they pulled us off the freight and took us off to jail. This was in Tennessee. It was real hot. They set us out in front of the jail until it cooled off. So they had me play the guitar and I sang. The little boy was right there along with me. They started lining us up to go inside and I was right there in line because I was as guilty as anyone. They put me on the end of the line and the little boy was right behind me. They marched everybody else in and when they came to me the doorman stopped me and let everybody else go in. He told me: "well you take this little feller here and you hit the highway and don't ever take a freight again." I thanked him and said I wouldn't. So, we walked on down to the corner to a gas station. Some fellers drove up with a Model T. They had some moonshine and they said they were puttin' on a party that night. So, they took me and the kid way out in the country and we played pretty near all night. Next day they brought us back to the railroad track and we blinded a passenger train. Well, I promised the feller I wouldn't take another freight, so I blinded a passenger train . . .'

The passenger train took him to Cincinnati and from there he made his way to Indianapolis where he met Leroy Carr, the celebrated blues pianist and singer. Carr influenced Slim's singing style considerably and he struck up a warm friendship with him. When Carr died in 1935 Bumble Bee Slim wrote a blues about the tragic event which he recorded as 'Death of Leroy Carr' and on 'Last Respects' he paid another tribute to him. He pays one now with his version of Carr's famous blues 'In the Evening'. Indianapolis was a crossroads town where singers from many quarters and entertainers of all descriptions met and worked. Slim joined up with the Ringling Brothers Circus there and was soon on the road again, playing his guitar. Eventually he made it to Chicago.

Chicago is a vast, tough city and in the Depression years it was doubly so. With no friends and no one to advise him Slim had to 'scuffle', earning quarters playing in neighbourhood joints. He made the acquaintance of other singers and eventually met Lester Melrose who was seeking talent for the Paramount Record Company. In 1931 Bumble Bee Slim's name appeared on record – 'Chain Gang Bound' – for the first time, but his Paramount recordings did not sell well and are exceptionally rare today. The following year brought him his break when he brought his sackful of songs to Mayo Williams at his office on Lakeshore Drive. 'Ink' Williams was prepared to sign him up but insisted that Scrapper Blackwell, Carr's guitarist, should play the instrument and Slim should only sing. He cut four sides on 16 March and two the following day; happily, the second record that he made was a hit. It was 'B & O Blues' one of the best-known of railroad blues. Oddly enough, Slim explains 'I didn't know there was a B & O Railroad, I just imagined there was. So I wrote the B & O Blues . . . my baby's gone, she won't come back no more; she left this morning, she caught the B & O . . . well, I didn't know there was the B & O, really I didn't. A couple o' years later a box car was goin' along. I say to my manager "I noticed B & O just like the B & O on the record." He said, "yeah that's the B & O Railroad."'

The 'B & O Blues' was the first of many hits for Bumble Bee Slim and for this reason it is especially important to him, as his 'New B & O Blues' confirms. It inspired many other railroad blues by various blues singers – as well as some others of Slim's own writing. In the next few years he worked and recorded with many celebrated names in blues history: Jimmy Blythe, Big Bill Broonzy, Cripple Clarence Lofton, Memphis Minnie and Honey Hill, amongst them. He worked with Georgia White though he did not record with her, and with Peetie Wheatstraw with whom he made an amusing duet on record. But Slim was more ambitious and, hearing that new motion picture studios were opening in Los Angeles, he went there hoping that he might obtain work as a song-writer. He had other ideas in mind too and prepared plots and sequences

for movies. But his break in the movie industry didn't come and when Melrose sent him a contract to return to Chicago and record he signed it willingly. Mayo Williams considered Slim still contracted to him and the situation led to a stormy scene between the promoters. Somehow Slim convinced them that he could produce enough material to satisfy both men and their respective companies and he did – material which included many considerable hits including 'Meet Me in the Bottom' which he remade for this album.

Tired of the repetitious accompaniments of piano and guitar which had backed him on so many recordings Slim decided to move to the West Coast where he would get a change of music and musicians. His taste in blues and the musical accompaniment to it did not stand still – as his tributes to Joe Turner on 'Wee Baby Blues' and to Charles Brown in 'Drilling Blues' underline – but he was unable to get the sort of backing that he wanted. He hoped that he could complete his recording contract with Melrose using West Coast musicians but was not permitted to. The name of Bumble Bee Slim dropped out of the record lists; collectors wondered where he had gone and a number of attempts were made to find him. In 1950 he gained the interest of Art Rupe who recorded him for Speciality but the session was not a success. Rupe arranged for Slim to compose material for Percy Mayfield and for a short while he was back in the world of music. It was more than ten years later before he recorded again, and this collection of blues made when he was fifty-seven is the result. It shows a Bumble Bee Slim with a strong voice, new ideas in the blues and undiminished optimism backed up by the modern, up-to-date music that he liked.

Notes to Fontana 688 138, 1964

West Dallas Drag
JOE PULLUM AND ANDY BOY

It is the distance in time that seems to place the blues singers and pianists of the Thomas family quite apart from the pianists and singers of Houston and Galveston seaports. Their records were made a decade later, between 1934 and 1937, and in our perspective of blues history they seem to belong to quite a different age.

In a sense they do, for the blues and black society had both changed. Nevertheless, Andy Boy (Boy was his surname) and Rob Cooper were a few years older than Hersal Thomas, having been born around 1906. That Hersal, the child prodigy, was a highly influential pianist among his peers there is no doubt; even though he left Houston in his very early teens he had established a reputation there which remains still in the folk memory. Careful listening to Andy Boy's playing reveals hints of the connection between them; in spite of the themes that he sang and played with their somewhat more modern sound, Galveston-born Andy Boy was a pianist whose formative years were spent in the company of Hersal and his fellow pianists. Several of the latter, among them Scanlin Smith and Peg Leg Will, never recorded, and consequently we inevitably gain a somewhat incomplete view of the talent of the pianists of this time. Those we admire as principle exponents were not the only celebrated musicians in their day; Edgar Perry, for instance, was acclaimed as the outstanding pianist of the group who worked the seaports but he, too, was never to record.

We can only reconstruct the picture from shadowy recollections of pianists dead long ago and the demonstrations of the very few survivors, Edwin 'Buster' Pickens or Robert Shaw, who ran around with them and their fellow group who worked the Santa Fe railroad townships. Rob Cooper is almost the sole representative on record of the barrelhouse style of the pianists with their roots in the ragtime-derived pre-blues music of the early part of the century. His 'West Dallas Drag' with its stomping beat was a piece from a genre that included the 'first cousin to the Dozens' the 'Ma Grinder' and the 'Cows' which he recorded as 'Cows, See That Train Comin'. It was shared by many others; close affinities can be heard in the relatively recent recordings of Robert Shaw. Ragtime and barrelhouse elements are likewise to be heard in Andy Boy's accompaniments, which, though heavily flavoured with blues, have flourishes that led one writer long ago to speculate on his being Fats Waller under a pseudonymn.

If the evidence of their history and elements in their music point to overlap with the Thomas family and their generation, the fact remains that there are distinct and audible differences in approach and content which single out the Texas seaport artists. The Depression had a lot to do with this, and it is not easy to understand their work or their importance without some reference to the social changes that took place in Houston and Galveston at that time. For the Depression hit both great ports as it hit every other city in the early Thirties. Inevitably, blacks were hardest affected, being on the bottom rung of the economic ladder. 1934 saw a period of serious unrest, with strikes in Houston's textile industry, in the oil fields, and in the meat packing industry. The effect was the paralysis of the industries on which the seaports depended and which, somehow had more or less survived the worst of the deep Depression years. These effects were countered by a massive Public Works Administration programme for county road development, the building of a new parcel post station in Houston, and more than a million dollars of Federal Funds for improvements to the Ship Canal. Violence among the longshoremen caused several killings, but PWA was providing employment for over six hundred men of whom a high proportion were black.

Within a year or two, clearing house and port accounts showed extraordinary increases at a time of acute financial shortages elsewhere; the peculiarities of Houston's economic recovery, matched on the Gulf at Galveston, led to a revival of employment and of spirits. The rising prosperity filtered down to the working classes and the spirit of optimism was evident in the boisterous, rolling blues piano of Cooper and Boy, and the urbane singing of Joe Pullum. Pullum's success was indicated by his record sales and by the frequency of his appearances on radio station KTLC with his pianist, Preston Chase, known as Peachy. 'Pullum and Peachy' became household names, and it must have seemed strange to some that Andy Boy and Rob Cooper accompanied him on record. Part of Pullum's appeal lay in his unique, boyish, falsetto voice. It sounded new and yet it had the melancholy of the blues within it. But he was also popular for the wit of his references, now almost lost to us. One example, 'Careful Drivin' Mama', must suffice to illustrate it: in the mid-1930s transport was a major issue in Houston – non-stop flights to Atlanta commenced in 1930 and five years later the quantity of air traffic was causing concern. On the highways the density of automobiles was greater than anywhere else in the south. When Pullum sang 'I'm gonna buy me an aeroplane, make me a non-stop flight . . .' and 'she's a careful drivin' mama, parks in the same place all the time . . .' he was employing metaphors that were apt and smart because they were wholly contemporary. Parking in the same place was such an issue that the following year parking meters were introduced in Houston, which was soon making the unlikely claim of 'Parking Meter Capital of the World'.

Joe Pullum was conscious of modern taste; references to being 'out of style' occur in his blues while 'the blues with a feeling, you know what I mean, the blues with *class*' was peculiarly of the period. In contrast, Walter Washington, a barfly on the waterfront who had worked as a cowpuncher, was a tough, rough-voiced singer. His 'West Dallas Woman' like Cooper's 'Drag', referred to the main stem of Houston's Fourth Ward, but the tune he used was an old one, the probable source of Hart Wand's 1912 compostion 'The Dallas Blues'. If Pullum represented a new sophistication, Washington was a reminder of the Texas blues' earthier past; Andy Boy was poised between them. 'House Raid' was a typically knockabout piece which described a police break-in at Charlie Shiro's Galveston club – though Boy changed the venue when he sang somewhere else. It has links with Little Hat Jones' 'Hurry Blues' and probably comes from a traditional source, adapted as were his blues, with his unique use of idiom and imagery. There is sadness in Andy Boy's voice in his words: 'I've been a burnt child, you know a burnt child is afraid of fire; I got the evil blues, prejudicy on my mind; you can take my money, I know that's the thing you lack, but please don't mistreat me just because I'm black.' Perhaps he knew it was all drawing to a close when he cut his eight solo titles, and four with Washington, on 24 February 1937. 'I'm going down to the Gulf, watch the waves come in . . .' he sang on 'Church Street' dreaming of 'that good old seaport town, where we all had fun and stomped "The Grinder" down.'

With the entry of the United States into the Second World War everything changed. The group dispersed: Andy Boy made his way to Kansas City where he was last heard of in the 1950s, while Joe Pullum migrated to California. Rob Cooper disappeared after woman trouble, and Cowboy Washington was forgotten. Down on Houston's Mc-Kinney Street or Church Street in Galveston they don't stomp 'The Cows' or 'The Ma Grinder' any more.

Notes to Magpie PY 11815, 1979

Johnson Machine Gun
SUNNYLAND SLIM

Most blues collectors are aware of the remarkable concentration of singers in the Mississippi Delta region formed by the Mississippi and Yazoo rivers and it isn't necessary to list their names yet again. There is a belief, though, that these blues men were all guitarists: an idea which runs parallel with the assumption that the guitar is a country instrument whilst the piano belongs to the city. Like other generalizations there is some truth and a considerable inaccuracy in the belief. Guitarists would appear to be numerically greater but the roadhouses, the jukes and country saloons that played host to the blues generally sported pianos and blues pianists were to be found in any community. In addition, the country frame churches always attempted to model themselves on the larger ones of the towns and when they could afford it, installed harmoniums and parlour organs. It is true that there were probably fewer pianists in Mississippi than there were in Louisiana and East Texas where the piano traditions were widespread and important, but men like Friday Ford and Lee Green of an older generation, or Eddie Boyd and Otis Spann of a younger one, were typical of the blues pianists of rural Mississippi. And amongst them Albert Luandrew is as well-known as any.

Albert Luandrew was born in a tiny township, Vance, on 5 September 1907. Vance was just a collection of shacks and so small that the maps of a decade before do not hint of its existence. Lying about seventeen miles south-east of Clarksdale in the bottomlands between the Sunflower and Tallahatchie rivers, it was bisected by the border between Quitman and Tallahatchie counties: a sultry, sleepy, featureless landscape of cotton rows and little wood houses. Here Albert was raised in a limited world which centred around the production of cotton. As a child, like every other boy his own age in the district, he carried water, chopped the cotton of weeds, pulled cotton as the bolls ripened, and as he grew big enough, managed the mule teams and the big ploughs. His family had strong ties to the church and, showing a musical talent at an early age, he was encouraged to play the piano and the church organ. By the time he was fourteen he was playing the organ regularly for the church service – and the blues on the piano when he could steal the opportunities.

It wasn't long before Albert Luandrew got more than a local reputation and when the movie house at Lambert was looking for a pianist to provide the incidental music, the seventeen-year-old blues man filled the bill. The silent movies required variety of piano expression – he gave them slow blues for the sentimental bits and rolling piano in a boogie rhythm for the exciting chase scenes of the melodramas. But he picked up some popular tunes on the way and the experience stood him in good stead in later years. And they were full years. The mid- and late-Twenties saw him wandering throughout the Delta, down through the Lower Mississippi regions, across the river and into Arkansas, working the levee and sawmill camps in Louisiana. Around that time he picked up his nickname. He came from the Mississippi bottom of the Sunflower River, from the 'Sunny land' and in the customary manner they named him after the colloquial term for his home region. He was well over six foot, slender then, and tough. They called him Sunnyland Slim.

Sunnyland Slim was highly popular with

the women in the Louisiana joints to which Little Brother Montgomery introduced him after they met in the late Twenties. They have been close friends ever since. He was popular both for his build and his blues. His blues were rough and ready, strong and not too subtle. Sometimes his piano playing was erratic but it was always the blues and always memorable. Sometimes he played the slow blues like 'Sad and Lonesome' the type of blues they like 'back in '29 and '30', or 'Anna Lou' of which he says, talking about the conditions that inspired blues of this type:

'. . . that's back in the days of the cotton harvest, when the steamboats was runnin' regular. The people all had to cry and suffer for money; chop cotton all day from sun-up to sun-down. And when night time come they was glad of what they did. It's not like these days . . . no schoolin' . . .'

He used his talent to get away from the toil of the fields and moved to the towns – Helena and West Helena, West Memphis and Memphis. In Memphis, Tennessee, he found work as a pianist in the theatres along Beale and in the many clubs and bars of the Negro sector. Here he came in contact with many of the important blues singers of his day, listening to Bessie Smith at the Beale Street Palace, playing as accompanist to Ma Rainey and the blues guitarist Blind Blake.

In 1932, he recalls, he made some recordings for a travelling recording unit. Untraced today they were probably never released, or if they were, under a different and unidentified name. The Depression hit Sunnyland Slim as hard as it did other blues men and indeed all in the South. He found work where he could; labouring when necessary and playing when there was a demand. He found work playing in white clubs, and as an entertainer providing background music in a speakeasy . . . so the tougher years passed. Generally he came back to Memphis, to work with Buddy Doyle or Blind Boy Fuller when the celebrated guitarist visited the city. Ten years after his unknown recording session he moved to Chicago.

Settling in on the South Side of Chicago, Sunnyland Slim found work as a truck driver or spent periods in factories. But he had many friends and was soon playing in the clubs at nights, working with Lonnie Johnson and Peetie Wheatstraw; the latter, with his high falsetto yells, influencing him quite a bit. He met up again with an old partner from Memphis, 'Doctor' Clayton, and they were often together on dates between Clayton's spells of alcoholism and travelling. Eventually, after he had been in Chicago for five years Sunnyland recorded again in 1947, under the name of 'Doctor Clayton's Buddy'. Blind John Davis played piano on the session and Big Bill Broonzy accompanied him on guitar. A year or two later he recorded again, this time with Lonnie Johnson as guitarist and cut two of his own favourite numbers – 'Brown Skin Woman' and 'The Devil is a Busy Man'. The following year he made another of the blues with which he is especially associated – 'Johnson Machine Gun' with Muddy Waters. When making it again he remarked, 'I believe the gangsters liked that one' and sang:

I'm gonna buy me a Johnson Machine-gun
*   and a carload of explosion balls,   (repeat)*
And then I'm gonna be a walkin' cyclone baby
*   from Sagitaw to Niagara Falls.*

Please get my Johnson type-writer, and a
*   whole round belt of balls,   (repeat)*
I'm gonna free my no-good woman, she's
*   down at the State Penitentiary Walls.*

Now l'il girl I think the undertaker been
*   lookin' for you woman, and I've given him*
*   your height and size,   (repeat)*
If you don't be makin' whoopee with the
*   Devil this time tomorrow baby, God*
*   knows, you'll be surprised.*

Unobtrusively, Sunnyland Slim has made some eighty recordings since he moved to Chicago and some of the important ones he has remade here. He has also recorded tributes to some of his friends, cutting St Louis Jimmy Oden's 'Goin' Down Slow' and Roosevelt Sykes' 'Miss Ida B'. He has the blues pianist's special regard for a warmly remembered giant of the music, Leroy Carr and plays Carr's 'Prison Bound'.

To the blues of others and to his own compositions Sunnyland Slim brings his own brand of music – loud, declamatory, filling the room with his immense voice. He whoops and yells, sings falsettos with ear-splitting volume in person, presenting some problems at times in recording. And in the background he plays his knocked-out blues piano with its hard basses, or slow vamping chords against rolling tremolos, opening his numbers with a certain little phrase which has become as emphatically his trademark as his old friends Leroy Carr and Peetie Wheatstraw stamped their recordings with their own.

Recently Sunnyland Slim came to Europe on the 1964 Negro Folk Blues Festival but the circumstances of the tour hardly gave him a chance to show his potential. He has a big capacity – not least for whiskey, which flowed liberally down his throat during the course of this session of blues without frills. Now that he has returned he has moved to a suburb about forty miles out of Chicago, where, as he says 'I have a l'il ole hassle goin''. His 'hassle' is a restaurant-bar where he can provide Southern food and his own line in Southern piano blues. We wish him good luck in his new venture, knowing that however novel his plans may be his music will remain the same.

Notes to Storyville SLP 169, 1965

Worried Life
OTIS SPANN

In the opinion of many who know him and his music well, there is too little heard of Otis Spann. It is not the view of blues enthusiasts only; a number of blues singers have said as much in conversation with interviewers. In point of fact one can hear a good deal of Otis for he is accompanying pianist on the records of many currently popular blues singers but there is all too little of Otis by himself. Though his accompaniments are often hard-hitting and loud, fitting in with the general sound of the Chicago blues band, when he is playing by himself he is quieter and more contemplative. He has recorded relatively little alone and the present opportunity to hear him as blues singer and pianist in his own right is to be welcomed.

Outside of a tight Chicago blues circle, Otis Spann was little known half-a-dozen years ago. He was first heard of when Muddy Waters was invited to England in 1958 to sing at the Leeds Festival. He said that he was bringing his own piano player and it was some indication of the anonymity of the pianist at the time that there was speculation as to whether he was the son of the old boogie pianist Charlie Spand, and that his name was spelled 'Stann' in the official programme. But when he sat down at the piano and began to play on the day of his arrival, European blues enthusiasts realised that they were hearing a considerable, if unknown, talent. Otis Spann all but stole the show from Muddy Waters.

Otis Spann was born on 21 March 1930 in the small Mississippi town of Belzoni, deep in the Delta country. His parents were cotton farmers and he had to work in the fields at an early age. His background was characteristic of any Negro boy in that part of the South; Belzoni is a low-lying hot and humid small town with heavy, dense trees to supply some shade in the town itself; open and exposed to the burning sun in the neighbouring country. It is a strictly segregated town and the coloured citizens live a life apart from the white, meeting in the course of work but severely separate socially. Amenities for Negroes are very few and even today social life centres around the church for the religious and the juke for those not so inclined. Today, however, the juke is likely to have a brash and shiny juke box to provide the music, which features the latest 45rpm issues from Chicago – maybe even a Muddy Waters with Otis himself playing piano in the group. When Otis was a boy the juke entertainer was to be found sitting at the piano: the piano was a fixture but the entertainer was the man who at that moment had the piano stool. There was no lack of blues pianists to take over the chair; when one man got up another was ready to take his place. Much attention has been given to the Mississippi blues guitarists and rightly so, for theirs is a remarkable tradition. The interest that they have commanded has frequently diverted attention from the blues pianists of the State whose music and whose lives are no less interesting. Pianists like Sunnyland Slim or Eddie Boyd had careers which parallel that of Otis Spann, coming from similar rural districts in the Mississippi Delta and playing the same kind of Mississippi piano blues.

One of the pianists well-known and greatly admired in Belzoni was a man named Friday Ford. 'He was my daddy,' says Otis Spann with that casual disregard for the accuracy of family relations that so often confounds the notes of the blues historian. He was his 'daddy' in the sense that he was the father of the piano and the man who inspired Otis to play the instrument. When Otis was a small boy Friday Ford would take him on his knee and press his fingers on the keys. Gradually he came to a stage where he could pick out simple blues himself. Otis' father soon discovered that his son was following a blues player but was sympathetic enough to ask him if he would like a piano. Eventually he had one installed in the house and Otis waited for a chance to play. Unfortunately his mother was a strict church-woman and had no intention of letting Otis play anything but religious songs on the piano. When his parents went off on a Saturday shopping excursion however, Otis was able to sit down at the piano and pick out the blues.

When he was about twelve or thirteen Otis' mother died. His father was unable to maintain him as he would have wished and arranged for the boy to go to Chicago to stay with relatives. There he took a job as a house plasterer and followed this trade for some years. In the evenings he was soon listening to the bluesmen in the Chicago clubs and, when he could, sitting in to play the blues himself. When his half-brother Muddy Waters came to Chicago he renewed a family tie which has remained close and unbroken to the present day. And when Muddy Waters eventually formed his band, Otis was its first member.

Behind Muddy Waters, Otis Spann plays a rocking, loud piano blues on the hard-hitting, shouting numbers and a deep, rolling boogie on the slow blues. A band that will include such blues artists as Pat Hare or Jimmy Rodgers guitarists, Little Walter Jacobs or Jimmy Cotton harmonica players, Freddy Bellow on drums and in the earlier days, Big Crawford on bass could be relied upon to make tough, deafening music 'wailing the blues'. This was the basic band, with variations in instrumentation, which

held down the stand at Smitty's Corner on 35th and Indiana. Sitting on a low stand bedecked with booster flags for the Chicago White Sox, surrounded by amplifiers, a low fence and the densely packed crowd of listeners sitting at the circular tables, the Muddy Waters band made a truly formidable sound. Sooner or later the band would be standing. Muddy Waters would be shouting with his shoulders and hips jerking in time to the beat and in the background Otis would be 'laying them down'. But it *was* generally in the background and in the sheer volume of sound it was often difficult to hear the music that he was playing. That is why Otis has always been a favourite 'after-hours' pianist, for his fellow bluesmen know the quality of his work and always encourage him to play for them.

When he plays, Otis Spann sits three-quarters on to the piano, almost as if he were about to get up to leave. It is generally some time before he faces the instrument, and when he does he settles in with a concentration that is almost unbreakable. Contrary to his performances when he is playing with a band he is, in person alone, a very restrained and introverted blues singer. His piano work is deep and low-down, favouring the slow blues rather than the fast. He lays down grumbling, bass chords in the left hand and rolls complex, rippling phrases in the right which cascade down to the next verse of his blues. When he sings his eyes are shut and his words are spun out as if he is reluctant to let them go. Just as the Mississippi blues guitarists have stolen the attention from the pianists, so, too, have the Mississippi blues singers that use the harsh and declamatory style of singing stolen the thunder from the quieter singers. But there are many artists like Jimmy Reed or Robert Curtis Smith, for example, who sing in a style similar to Otis – lightly and wistfully. He has an unusual lisp in his speech and like many blues singers, from John Lee 'Sonny Boy' Williamson to John Lee Hooker who have a slight speech impediment, he uses it to marked, personal effect.

Muddy Waters' home is a blues centre in itself. Otis Spann lives in the same house with his wife whilst down in the basement St Louis Jimmy lived until recently. The associations between blues singers are close and there are hints of them in their work. There are echoes of the great blues pianist Big Maceo, whom Otis much admired, in his version of 'Worried Life Blues' and others of St Louis Jimmy in 'Goin' Down Slow'. On the 1963 American Folk Blues Festival which toured Europe. Otis Span met Victoria Spivey and doubtless heard her sing 'T.B. Blues'. He sings 'T.B. Blues' himself on the present occasion, but whilst the experienced listener will detect traces of Victoria's composition, this blues sung by Otis is indisputably his own version of a theme that has become traditional. A pianist who has worked and recorded with artists as varied and with the stature of Howling Wolf, Sonny Boy Williamson, Muddy Waters and Bo Diddley must have the whole blues tradition literally at his fingertips. And this, from the rocking figures of 'Spann's Boogie' to the sad, autobiographical verses of 'Riverside Blues', Otis Spann demonstrably has.

Notes to Storyville SLP 157, 1964

Otis Spann died Chicago, 24 April 1970.

6
Talking Blues

Illustration to "Blues '65" *Jazz*, Vol 4, No 7, July 1965

Talking blues, not *the* 'talking blues' that Chris Bouchillon recorded in the 1920s and many white singers from Woody Guthrie onwards have made a speciality over the years, but just talking about the blues – that seems to have occupied a lot of time in my life. A good deal of the talking has been in lectures and seminars; I first gave a talk on blues with a friend of mine, James Gribble, when we were still art students in our teens. We went to great pains to find examples, armed with Iain Lang's WPA Booklet, the *Background of the Blues* as our sourcebook. It went down well with our fellow students, I remember, and infuriated the teaching staff. It's hard to imagine how impassioned was the objection to the records that I used to play in lunch-times at art school; but they were real enough to lead to serious threats of expulsion from the Principal. I identified with the anarchic spirit of the blues singers that I believed was expressed in their lyrics, and went right on playing their records and talking about them.

There were talks about blues at 'Rhythm Clubs' in the Forties and Fifties; gatherings of jazz collectors in rented schoolrooms in South Harrow or Watford; a little piece of social history that may get forgotten, or may be written up as a thesis one day. There was even a Radio Rhythm Club, though the resident band was Harry Parry's and they certainly didn't play blues. Very occasionally in the 1940s Alan Lomax, or later, Max Jones, would give a talk on American folk song or on work songs, and I would avidly transcribe the stanzas from the broadcast programme. After much nagging at the BBC, I managed to secure an occasional blues talk for myself in the mid-1950s and continued, at intervals, to broadcast talks on Urban Blues (a decade before that became the title of Charles Keil's book), on Washboard Bands and similar themes. I had the satisfaction of playing the first records of Lightnin' Hopkins, and John Lee Hooker and Smoky Hogg on the radio – the Light programme, or sometimes the Third.

I went on talking blues for many years, at schools and University Students' Unions and occasional gatherings of folklorists and educationalists, carrying a black box with Paramounts, Okehs, Columbias and Victors in cardboard sleeves. The BBC used to apologize after my talks for the sound quality of my records – though I felt rather insulted as I was usually playing my mint copies. Record clubs were different: I think they rather liked the hiss and crackle, and hearing the voice of Blind Lemon piercing through it. There was an evangelical element in my talking about blues, I realize now, an urgent need to get the message across to as many people as I could in as many ways as I could. Like any enthusiast for a subject who feels passionately about it, and about its neglect, I wanted the blues to be recognized and enjoyed. And also, like any enthusiast who has been a sort of missionary, I felt a few pangs of regret when it *did* become widely accepted: not regret for the fact that it had, only regret that the passionate desire to convert now had no outlet.

Even today, I talk about blues occasionally, but now the context is different. Maybe it is to an academic audience, or to students who are studying blues as part of their degree course (*unthinkable*, once!), or to a conference. The conferences aren't generally blues gatherings though, but assemblies of folklorists or ethnomusicologists. Or, most frequently now, gatherings of writers and scholars interested in the study of popular music. Evangelizing again? Yes, I admit it.

There's another aspect of talking blues that has been important though, and it's the one that I am including here: talking to blues singers. The 'interview' with a blues singer is almost a cliché of blues publishing today; in fact most blues magazines are largely made up of interviews. The first inverviews with blues singers that I conducted were with Big Bill Broonzy; then later with Big Bill in the company of Brother John Sellers, Brownie McGhee and Sonny Terry, Jimmie Rushing – and many others eventually. Some of these early interviews I'm including here because they contain information that has seldom, if ever, got into print since, or which appears in the original form in these articles. Generally they are articles; before 1960 I never used a tape recorder for interviews and made copious notes instead.

I've explained in the Introduction to *Conversation with the Blues* the circumstances of recording in the field in 1960. I had with me a heavy recorder made by EMI for military and BBC use; it could not erase a tape once recorded, and playback was very difficult. But it was immensely rugged and the sound quality was extremely good. I found that most blues singers were curious about the machine, and often used it as a way of breaking the ice at the start of an interview session. It was also a way of talking about something other than blues – which could lead to general conversations that helped in filling in something of their local backgrounds. But the high humidity in Houston, coupled with the heat, melted the glue that fixed the recording meter and it fell into the machine. A few fruitless days were wasted while attempts were made to repair it. In that book I've told something of the hazards and the successes of interviewing, and I related some of the frustrations of field work in an article for *American Folk Music Occasional*. There were some incidents that were still rather indiscreet to narrate at that time – like the fact that Henry Brown was a 'number runner' in the policy racket, and was extremely embarrassed by the punters who were trying to place their numbers while he was being interviewed in the street, before going off to record. What he knew,

but the punters didn't, was that Charlie O'Brien who had discovered Henry, and brought me to see him was a lieutenant in the police. Or the row that Black Ace had with his wife that led him to sing with meaning and emphasis, well within her hearing, blues like 'Evil Woman' and 'No Good Woman'.

A lot of interviews, though, were made back here in England. A number of blues singers came to Europe as solo performers, often at the invitation of Chris Barber, who featured singers like Roosevelt Sykes or Champion Jack Dupree in concerts. In the Sixties there was the remarkable series of American Folk Blues Festivals organized by Horst Lippmann and Fritz Rau. With their elegant programmes, designed with taste and illustrated with excellent photographs, they set a standard for presentation which was quite new to jazz and blues concerts in Britain.

However improved the presentation was, the backstage hassle was much the same. One of the curious aspects of the blues concerts and festivals was the competitive desire on the part of blues writers to be backstage during the concerts rather than out in front. To conduct interviews – that was the idea; but generally it seemed to be an excuse for a booze-up, and not always with the musicians either. Blues writers for the new blues magazines pumped one blues singer or another for 'information', while others exchanged details of the going rates for 45rpm discs on Cobra or Goldband, or tried conning the despairing theatre attendants to let them in to another sanctum. I seldom enjoyed this aspect of the concerts; after all, the singers were there to perform and they needed us out there in front.

For my part, I preferred to interview singers in their hotel rooms, and invite them back to my home to meet a few friends and enjoy a more sociable evening. Blues singers in hotels were often really quite apprehensive, I realize now. They usually sat with the shades down – nightbirds all – and rang room service for a 'fifth' of Scotch. Room service soon learned what this meant, and also to put aside several bottles in their lobbies so that they could produce them when called for, whatever time of day or night, and charge two or three times the price for them. Among the Blues Festival singers there was a lot of fooling, but also quite a bit of jealousy and disagreement between the singers. Often this arose out of misunderstandings, and the pressure of being cooped together in coaches for long trips between one unknown European city and the next, equally unknown to them. Single performers fared better, though they were often lonely. I can recall only two who showed any curiosity about London: Brother John Sellers, who got to know a number of restaurants, clubs and shops on his own initiative; and Lowell Fulson, who enjoyed a morning walk in Hyde Park instead of breakfast and genuinely liked to visit some of London's buildings. But these were, by blues standards, more 'sophisti-cated' singers, and perhaps more capable of coping with the pressures of being alone in an alien city. Though even Josh White never ventured out of his hotel room on his own.

Collected at the hotel and driven to my home, or to Francis Smith's or some other enthusiast's, most blues singers welcomed the release from the claustrophobic surroundings of the concert tour. I recall Sonny Terry fast asleep among a pile of beer bottles, placed there as a joke by Brownie McGhee; Lightnin' Hopkins picking up an African hunter's two-string fiddle that I had collected in Nigeria and playing a blues on it; Jack Dupree attempting to ride Francis Smith's penny-farthing bicycle and settling for pushing it instead. Of course, there was, I suppose, an ulterior motive. I genuinely wanted the blues singers to visit an English home and feel welcome; but I also wanted to be talking blues with them some of the time. I don't think they minded; after all, it was what they knew best and felt most at ease talking about. The outcome of some of those conversations is the theme of this chapter.

Blues Backstage
WITH BIG BILL AND JOHN SELLERS

Though the rooms were centrally heated and warm by British standards, to Brother John Sellers his London apartment felt cold. Almost invariably when I called he was wrapped up in the covers and feeling keenly the damp chilliness of an English March. In the mornings his throat was sore and his voice croaked – discouraging for a singer! But as the day wore on and became warmer the mellowness of his talking voice would return. When, after picking him up at his apartment we brought Brother John to the Royal Festival Hall for the rehearsal, he was further discouraged by the bleakness of the empty building itself. As it happened, we were the first to arrive, the promoters having taken the precaution to advise everyone to be there early. Within a few minutes Big Bill Broonzy had arrived with Alex Korner but it was a long time before anyone else seemed to put in an appearance. The shutter slammed down at the artists' and staff's bar at that moment and remained firmly closed in spite of all entreaties. So Brother John and Big Bill were introduced to British catering – an aspect of life here that they learned to regret more than once.

With practised assurance Big Bill led the way to the changing rooms and carefully selected the one marked 'Conductor'. It was here that we settled down to talk and here that the singers made themselves at home in the vast unfriendliness of the empty Festival Hall.

It was possible now to see the two singers and listen to their conversation with a freedom that had scarcely been practicable at the Press reception. Between the older and the younger man there exists a closer bond than many in the audiences may have realized. It was Big Bill who supervized Brother John's first recording session, made for Victor a dozen years ago, and though there is always much good-natured banter and 'jiving' between the two men, the regard they share for each other's work is very real. This is not to say that they agree on all points; far from it. Their disputes about the relative merits of many singers are debated with spirit. Take the 'Frog Man'. He is a singer by the name of Clarence Henry, very much in the modern R & B vein who records for Argo and who is extremely popular amongst the younger Negroes. It may come as a surprise to many therefore to learn that it was Big Bill who brought the record with him from the States, and Brother John who winced at the singer. Clarence Henry has earned his name of the 'Frog Man' from his song 'Ain't got no Home' (Argo 5259) in which he declares 'I can sing like a maaan!' and proceeds to sing in a medium pitch, to follow this with the announcement 'I can sing like a girl!' Then he sings in a high falsetto before he finally follows with 'I can sing like a frooog!' and growls in a deep bass voice. To Brother John it was singing full of tricks without meaning or value; to Big Bill it was original and entertaining.

One of the lessons to be learned from the tour of these two men is that the blues does not easily fit into comfortable compartents, cut to size and made to measure. This has always been the fault of an overwhelming majority of British enthusiasts of jazz, in that they believe that the blues should be sung in a certain manner and expect all singers to conform to that style. One has to hear many hundreds of blues records before one fully appreciates that there are almost as many styles as there are singers and musicians, and to parcel them too neatly into separate categories is to do the individual artists great injustice. This attitude is of course the blight on jazz appreciation here, largely caused by the limitations imposed by recordings. But it is even more pronounced in the case of the blues, in which field there is still only a relatively small amount of recorded material available. This, it is true, is increasing, but great as they are, Big Bill, Blind Lemon Jefferson, Joe Turner and Jimmy Rushing only characterize very loosely certain particular aspects of the blues and there are whole fields that are virtually unrepresented and scores of truly important singers – the most obvious being Leroy Carr – who are completely unknown to the average British collector. This leads one to speculate on the effect that a singer like Carr might have on a British audience. Though there are in our skiffle groups literally scores of imitators of Leadbelly I have yet to hear one who has dared to sing in the manner of say, Peetie Wheatstraw or Big Boy Crudup. (Not that imitation is a virtue, but the whole British jazz movement is built on imitation and without it there would be no jazz here.)

So there, in the room marked Conductor it was possible to hear Big Bill and Brother John happily discussing the merits of the San Antonio singer Smoky Hogg and his fine recording of 'Too many Drivers at the Wheel' (Modern 20–532). While Big Bill laughed and told stories of staying at Smoky Hogg's home shortly after the latter had sent a small royalty to Bill for using his song ('He don't owe me *nothin*' now brother!' commented Bill meaningfully), John gave an impersonation of Hogg's style of delivery. These impersonations are one of the entertaining features of Brother John's conversation. He imitates the posturings of Elmore James, the flamboyant style of Gate-mouth Brown and the perpetual dance that Muddy Waters performs throughout his

singing and playing. The undulating movements, the knee flexings, finger snappings, head rolling that John unconsciously uses are those employed by many coloured singers when working in their clubs in Nashville or St Louis. Many of the mannerisms that some British listeners found irritating, were in fact mere token gestures that symbolized rather than repeated the powerful, often wild and almost uncontrolled bodily rhythms that a Negro singer naturally uses in the Deep South.

There was a violin lying on the table, left from a concert of a night or two before. It was a fine instrument with a rich, pure tone and it caught the eye of Big Bill Broonzy. 'I used to play one of them,' he announced as he picked it up. During the next few moments that violin played notes it will never play again and learned more about one aspect of music than any of its fellows in the string section will ever know. With his powerful fingers twisting, sliding and releasing strings Big Bill played pure alley fiddle, grinning broadly as the strangely remote sounds filled the room. This was the style of blues fiddle that occurs on the discs of Macon Ed, of the Georgia Pine Boy and Peg Leg Howell. It is a pity that Big Bill could not be persuaded to play the instrument at the concert to present an altogether new problem to the skiffle groups. Jazz . . . blues . . . violins?

From fiddle to guitar. Soon the whining blue notes, the intricate runs, the guitar rags and the familiar features that make Big Bill's guitar playing essentially his own, came flowing from the instrument and with them the exciting rhythms of another instrument. Jazz . . . blues . . . violins . . . and tamourbines? There were many shocked jazzmen when Brother John reached for the instrument of his long church experience. With ball of thumb and fingertips, with thigh and knee and elbow and palm he produced a bewildering variety of punching rhythms, more driving, more urgent, more vital than the combined efforts of whole rhythm sections in a multitude of European and white American bands – as was all too sadly demonstrated later that day. With the playing came the singing, spontaneously and naturally. From this was born the series of duets that brought to an exciting climax a score of concerts, and the repertoire was modelled on the songs that sprang to mind during those few minutes.

John was anxious to get on with the rehearsal. It had been his desire to arrive in England several days before so that he could practise with the bands that he was to work with. That he was advised not to do so, though on the grounds of the duration of his work permit, was an undoubted error as far as the first concert was concerned. Not for a moment was he in doubt as to what he wanted, but it was patently obvious that the band could not meet his requirements. So he stood out in front, singing with tremendous power and swing, before an acoustically defective microphone and an empty hall. Big Bill stood watching frowning. He did not want to rehearse. 'I never knows what I'm gonna play till I gets out there and starts playin' it,' he said.

After the brief run-through we left. A few hours later the first concert in a tour, the full import of which has yet to be appreciated, was due to begin. For me there were to be many other meetings with Big Bill and Brother John, but none was to make as deep an impression as the occasion when two great blues singers, one representing the living past, the other the flourishing present, prepared themselves for their first joint tour in Britain.

Music Mirror Vol 4, No 4, May 1957

Boss of the Whole Bunch
MANCE LIPSCOMB

'Just wait. We've got something for you to hear will set you back on your ears!' Exasperatingly, Mack McCormick and Chris Strachwitz would say very little else about their new-found 'discovery' but their ill-suppressed excitement was assurance enough that we were soon to hear something special. It was August 1960. A few weeks before, Chris and Mack had been on a search for songsters and blues singers in East Texas. A man named 'Peg Leg' at the Navasota railroad depot told them that the best guitar picker around was Mance Lipscomb, an opinion that was confirmed by others in the area. Their inquiries led them to Lipscomb's home and to the man himself as he returned from cutting grass on the State highway. Much of the music that Mance played for them that evening was recorded and issued on Arhoolie F 1001 'Mance Lipscomb – Texas Sharecropper and Songster'; the balance of the record was taped when Mack and Chris took my wife and me to visit him on 11 August.

We drove out from Houston west towards Sugar Land and the prison farms familiar to collectors of the famous Library of Congress penitentiary recordings made by the Lomaxes in the early Thirties; crossed the Brazos River at Richmond and struck north through the bottomlands towards Sealy and Bellville on the west bank of the river. The Santa Fe railroad runs between the road and river and in the flat, featureless and unlovely country, the long lines of the sad telegraph poles defined the route against a grey, lowering sky. From Bellville we crossed the muddy, yellow, sluggish waters of the Brazos again and through Hempstead reached the trim town of Navasota. Crossing the tracks we drove down an unmade road to a vague and nondescript area where scattered cabins loosely indicated the edge of town. Outside one we stopped, and a slender Negro man in his mid-sixties came to the door. With his aquiline features, his slightly arched nose, deeply hollowed cheeks beneath finely drawn cheekbones he had the expression of an Indian, an impression heightened by the gathering of lines at the corners of his experienced eyes like those of a veteran of a Blackfoot Sun Dance. Mance welcomed us with warm dignity and showed us into his two-room home.

It was a timber frame house of indeterminate age with featherboarded walls patched here and there with roofing felt 'brick veneer'. The front room, in spite of the pressure on space, was virtually empty of furniture except a wooden chair or two which stood on the bare floor. Years of scrubbing had worn away the softer wood of the floor planks and the hard knots stood out, polished like bosses. A thin partition divided the cabin and we were invited into the back room which served as living-room, bedroom and, with the aid of a screen, stove and a faucet, kitchen too. His wife Elenora, ample, maternal, made us welcome and smiled with pride as her husband began to run through a few phrases on Chris' Harmony guitar with the authority of a lifetime of playing and singing. In the ensuing hours, the promise of Mance's reputation was brilliantly justified as he talked of the singers he had known and the music traditions of the Negro sharecroppers of the Brazos Bottoms. His grandchildren crept in, sat on the bed and fell asleep: Mance, indestructible from years of playing at all-night country suppers, delved ever deeper into his memory to play a succession of jubilees, breakdowns, slow drags and blues. Elenora's eyes never left him, and no one heeded the procession of roaches which trooped endlessly across the walls and into the pockets of the working clothes which hung across one corner of the little room.

That was five years ago. 'Oh man,' sighed Mance, 'I just wish you people had come along twenty years ago; I was in my prime then.' Now, he explained, the young people didn't want to hear his old-time music. Now, too, his voice wasn't like it was and some of those songs he hadn't sung in many years. He spoke with quiet pride of his inexhaustible fund of songs and of his ability to play in any key; and proved his claims triumphantly. He has done so ever since. In the ensuing years Mance has gone far beyond the limited horizons of Navasota to play at concerts and colleges in folk festivals and coffee bar centres from coast to coast, bringing to an ever-widening audience the richness and variety of Texas Negro folk music. Many of his fellows might have been over-awed by the change of circumstances, or altered by a fame which has become national and then international. But Mance Lipscomb, with his innate dignity and remarkable character has met the challenge with equanimity. The cultural shock of the contrasts of wide acceptance and total appreciation has not affected him; on the contrary, he has been able to realize his full stature as an exceptional man and an outstanding creative talent.

Born in Brazos County on 9 April 1895, Mance Lipscomb was the son of a fiddle-player who had been born in slavery. When he was still a child of eleven he took his father's place in supporting his mother and her children, and for over forty years worked as a sharecropper on the blackland plantations. Most years he cleared little more than $100 and during the war years he did little better, farming on rented land. After a brief spell managing a farm he moved in 1956 to Houston to work for a lumber company. An accident caused by an overturning truck injured his eyes and spine and he was forced to return to Navasota. There he took a job cutting grass on the highways with a gang of three: 'I'm the boss of the whole bunch,' he told us. With his workman's compensation for his injury and the first royalty cheque he ever received for his music he put down the deposit on a three-quarter acre plot on the Washington highway out of Navasota. There he has built for himself a more substantial home in which to care for his ailing wife and his large family of grandchildren.

Throughout his active, hard and materially unrewarding life, Mance has augmented a minimal income by playing his guitar. Not by much – a dollar or two for playing all night in a country juke joint, but sufficient to keep him continually in practice and in voice. As, in this sense, a professional musician, he had a continual interest in the music that he heard around him and drew freely on the songs, the ballads, the dance tunes and blues which constituted the popular musical entertainment of the Brazos bottomlands. He was, and is, a 'songster'; in other words he did not restrict himself to a particular idiom as many blues singers have done but, coming from a generation of musicians who prided themselves on their versatility, embraced many forms, of which the blues was just one. Mance's life spans the history of blues and the formative years of his musical development are well rooted in the older traditions. At this point in time it is important to realize that this seventy-year-young man is a living embodiment, and genuinely one of the last great exponents of the Southern Negro folk song forms before the blues, and the mass media which popularized it, swept them aside. This of course is why his guitar-playing grandson, Frank Lipscomb emulates a popular blues idol, Jimmy Reed, for he is as much a part of his time as Mance Lipscomb is of his generation.

With this in mind, it is possible to appreciate to the full the range of Mance's repertoire and to get a better perspective on the dissemination of popular music and its cross fertilization with the folk forms. It is something of a shock to hear a Texas songster come up with a blues-intoned version of 'Shine On, Harvest Moon' but this sensational hit song, popularized by Jack Norworth and Nora Bayes in 'Follies of 1908' when Mance was a lad just beginning to maintain a family and to feel his way round the guitar, had a success which cut right across all notions of 'folk' or Negro music. It does in fact give an added dimension to the recollections of the early examples in Mance's repertoire which do properly fall into such categories. When he says 'Here's about the oldest number that I could recall back in the days when I was learnin' and heard people play – "Take Me Back",' we have a specific frame of reference in which to place these important yet now almost totally forgotten themes.

For the student of Negro song in its various aspects Mance Lipscomb's work is of special interest for its reveals many facets of the folk process. It is interesting to note for instance, how the song 'Little Brown Jug', which was first published nearly a century ago, has been modified to suit new circumstances. Mance's version has verses which have come from many sources with the 'some folks say a preacher won't steal' theme of the minstrel show, the rural detail of the broken wagon wheel, and the in-group racism of

Monkey sittin' on a pile of straw,
He was waggin' his eye at ole grandmaw.

with its cross-reference to 'You're Bound to Look Like a Monkey When You Grow Old'.

Other items are equally revealing, whether in the social implications of 'Mean Boss Man' or the widespread influence of certain spirituals like 'Nobody's Fault But Mine' and 'Motherless Children' which Mance plays in 'cross-note tuning', bottle-neck-style. The function as dance music of so much of his work is very evident in the echoes of buck-dances, 'cuttin' the pigeon-wing' and the 'buzzard lope' which are the basis of his highly rhythmic playing with its counter-melodies skilfully executed. It illumines, too, the dance elements in the boogie-woogie bass figures which he plays with such consummate skill on 'Blues in G'.

This serves to emphasize that Mance Lipscomb's music is first and foremost entertainment, to be enjoyed with the heart and the body rather than to be subjected to academic analysis, however much it is informative in this respect also.

It is the secret of his contentment in playing to coffee-house and folk club audiences, for, an old man now, he has the infinite satisfaction of passing on his heritage to a younger generation. For those of us who have been fortunate enough to know Mance Lipscomb and to hear him in person, the privilege is a rare and valued one; for all of us with whom he shares his music on record, the experience of hearing him is infinitely rewarding.

Notes to Arhoolie F1026, 1965

Mance Lipscomb died Navasota, Texas, 30 January 1976.

Back to Froggy Bottom
WHISTLING ALEX MOORE

'I just sit down, sing and play them, unaware to any knowledge or idea or thoughts of them until I sit down at the keyboard and begin playing and making them up on the piano.'

His own unassuming words explain the nature of his blues. He is a true original, a folk blues singer of the city who can sit at the piano and improvise endlessly piano themes and blues verses that are sometimes startling, sometimes comic, sometimes grim and very often, are pure poetry. Though his first recordings were made in 1929, barely a dozen items have appeared on record under his name, Alex Moore, but amongst these are some of the most profound, original and poetic blues that have ever been issued. When I first heard his records, a dozen years ago, I was attracted by their unique quality and hoped that I might one day meet the man whose memorable blues had so enriched the Columbia and Decca catalogues. After pursuing many false leads and encountering a number of setbacks I finally found him seated on the screened porch of a small bar situated scarcely a hundred yards from the street where he was born in North Dallas, Texas.

It was a sweltering, burning hot day and the sun beat down on the dusty, rubble-strewn, unmade roads of the Negro sector of Dallas. It was a district where no white people – except a policeman or a rent collector – were to be seen at any time, and the silent streets, the screened and shuttered fronts of buildings presented a formidable appearance. When I had overcome Alex Moore's bewilderment at being approached about his blues singing by a white man with an 'English accent', we strolled out into the street and considered where a piano might

be found. The notorious Central Tracks district which once housed the honky-tonks and chock-houses was now a vast stretch of red-brown rubble a matter of yards away: the bulldozers had arrived before us and had swept away the clapboard shacks to make room for a new Expressway. Chris Strachwitz who would be doing the recording, and my wife, joined us. We thought that Alex Moore might need time to practise and to think up ideas for blues, but he dismissed the suggestion with scorn. He played at different places in the district frequently and he had more blues in his mind than he could find time to play. But he did not own a piano; those that he played were generally out of tune and, somehow, we had to find one.

Together we walked towards the area that had once been Central Tracks and in a bar still standing nearby there was a good piano. A few moments were all that were necessary to prove that Alex Moore was a finer blues player than, on the evidence of his records, at any time in his life. But the bar had a regular blues band which was shortly to appear and though the owners were quite willing to let us record there, we felt that time was limited. We tried one place after another and as we walked and drove Alex Moore talked of the great singers of the past who had made Dallas one of the major centres of the blues: of Blind Lemon and Rambling Thomas, Blind Norris and Willie Reed . . . Sixty-one years of age, Alex Moore had spent his life in the blues world of Deep Elm and Central Tracks, Froggy Bottom and East Side. His conversation was the story of the blues. But to hear him sing and play . . . still no piano.

'Strictly For Colored Only' read a

warning notice on the blank wall of a large rough Negro hotel overlooking a vacant lot. Here Alex Moore had played for years and he and I went in. The big rooms were almost empty of furniture but in three of them pianos were standing. Alex sat down at each and started to play as one who had spent long hours at these same piano stools. He rolled a fierce boogie on one; shouted a hoarse, eccentric blues at another. His playing was superb, but the pianos were grossly out of tune. Disappointed, we left.

'You don't know of a music teacher in Dallas, do you Alex?' asked my wife suddenly.

'Madame Pratt!' he exclaimed, and cursed himself for not thinking of her before. So we drove around to Madame Pratt's Music School which was identified by a little sign on the grass in front of her house. It was not going to be an easy day: Madame Pratt was at the dentist a neighbour informed us, so we sat on the wall and waited until she came. To our relief she was delighted at the idea when Alex explained our reason for calling.

'She doesn't just play piano: she can play *any* instrument!' Alex whispered. It was no exaggeration: her house was crammed with instruments and on the walls were faded pictures of some of her past pupils – members of the Troy Floyd Band and that of Alphonso Trent. In a moment Alex Moore was at the keyboard and to the approval of Madame Pratt and our delight poured forth his blues . . .

Alexander Moore had boundless ideas. Betraying hardly a hint of any influence from other singers, he played with great variety and sang in a throaty, husky voice. A man rich in worldy wisdom he is yet a man curiously limited in his knowledge of the world. Only once in his life has he left Texas: most of his life has been spent in a small section of Dallas. So his blues reflect a very personal, singular view of life, and because

he is an eccentric man, his words are often unexpected and manifestly original. The immediate circumstances of his environment are reflected in 'Going Back to Froggy Bottom' or 'From North Dallas To The East Side', but his sharp eye and neat wit leads to such highly unconventional blues lines as 'Sack dress is all right but I'd rather see you in a pair of pants . . .'

Interspersed with his playing were reminiscences of playing at Minnie's Tea Room or of police raids in district chock-houses: memories that would lead him to new blues improvisations. He talked of the years when he had driven his horse and cart through the streets of Dallas: years when life was wild and cheap and money scarce – and broke into 'Black Eyed Peas and Hog Jowls'. Such blues as 'Rubber Tyred Hack' or 'Miss No-Good Weed' were spur-of-the-moment creations played and sung with feeling and pleasure in his own music. His bass figures were varied and intensely interesting and he took an off-beat pride in his sudden flashes of inventiveness and flurries of right-hand creations. Then he doubled back his lip and shrieked a piercing whistled blues by which he had gained his name of Whistling Alex Moore but which had in the past, as now, presented problems for recording.

It was after many hours, much perspiration and innumerable beer cans, that we finally turned on the cartwheel of a fan again and prepared to leave. Within a few hours we had to point the car South towards the steaming bayous of Houston, and so we left him to talk over his old times with Madame Pratt. We drove in silence, speculating on the bitterness of segregation, the apathy and disinterest of the public in the blues, the pressure of the business managers and the ironics of a music entertainment world that would permit a man of the original talent and stature of Alexander Herman Moore to scuffle through half a century, creating his blues from the viewpoint of a carter and hotel porter. We thought of him as he had described himself in his deep, husky voice, softly laughing between his phrases:

'Old Alexander . . . at the pianner . . . sober . . . lonesome . . . hard-headed . . . but good-natured . . .'

★ ★ ★ ★

Nine years were to pass before we were to meet again – in London, at the notorious Albert Hall. The piano was wheeled on, the acoustics were terrible, the amplification equipment a mess. Tempers were frayed and rival impresarios fumed in anger and frustration at the calamities that beset the beginning of the European tour of the American Blues Festival 1969. Throughout it all, as blues singers grumbled, or swore, or drank, or suffered interviewers, Alex Moore played quietly at the piano, still wearing the old raincoat and cloth cap which he had when he got off the plane. He'd scarcely ever been out of his home State, seldom even left Dallas, but had the philosophical poise of a man who has lived through the setbacks, frustrations and hard times of a lifetime. And they have certainly dogged him in his life as a junk man, hotel janitor and performer of casual jobs. For him, his piano playing has been his real life and blues his outlet, his release, his pleasure and his passion. 'I say the reason why I never got married is I always been married to my piano,' he explains in his thick, husky voice.

Seeing Alex Moore settle slowly to the piano, nodding slightly with head a fraction to one side, seated so that the left leg is angled away from the stool, one imagines that he is about to fall asleep over the keys. One is totally unprepared for the sudden onslaught that hammers the ivories in to the wood, that thunders out a boogie bass beneath fingers gnarled grey as old timber, that strikes out in outrageously unpredictable right-hand passages. Or for that

matter, for the piercing whistle as he cleaves the air with a shrieking blues, emitted from what appears to be a slot in his tongue; or for the unlikely lines and blues verse, couplets and doggerel, humming accompaniment and cries of delight, which issue from his lips:

So long as I have . . . skin on my head,
Scalp under my skin . . . brains under
my scalp . . .
I'm never gonna see that woman ag'in . . .!

He was in great form in Stuttgart when he recorded these items, 'stretching out' as he termed it; 'Ole Alex . . . playin' at the pianner . . . in boogie-woogie manner.' He produced new items like 'Flossie Mae' or 'Rock and Roll Bed Blues', improvised piano blues with adventurous flights of fancy in the treble, backed up by solid bass figures; roared into boogie solos. But he revived one old blues, a favourite which he recorded as far back as 1929, and again in 1937, the erotic, engaging 'New Blue Bloomer Blues'. And he indulged in reminiscences of far-off days, half a century ago, when he was a young man playing in the saloons and joints of Central Tracks in Dallas. That the memories are still clear is evidenced by the pictures he summons as he plays and talks, imitating the arguments as rival pianists claim the piano stool. Obviously those were the days when the blues was most alive and Alex Moore was in his prime. But the blues has continued to be his elixir; the secret of his long playing life and his continued creativity has been his total involvement in the blues. He has refused to lose himself in fading recollections of the past, but has drawn upon his long experience to create the vital music to be heard here. Let us hope he will long continue to do so.

Notes to Seventy Seven LA-12, 1960
and Arhoolie 1048, 1969

All Alone and Blue
LILLIAN GLINN

She was tall and neatly dressed in a well-cut, conservative suit. Composed and friendly, she sat with her hands loosely clasped in her lap, a gentle smile on her dark brown features and her eyes magnified by her glasses. Lillian Glinn looked exactly what she was, a stalwart in her community and a devout member of her church. A decade ago I had obtained a lead which enabled me to make contact with her at her California home, but it took many letters and several phone calls before she agreed to meet me, just once, in August 1970. When she spoke, in her full, warm voice, it was just possible to imagine her as the singer who recorded over forty years before under her unmarried name. She recalled her career as a theatre blues singer with great difficulty and considerable reluctance.

It was all so long ago, she explained, when she 'was in The World'. For two-score years she had been in 'The Other World', devoted to her church, and now, close on seventy, she did not wish to recall her few years of sinful life. Lillian Glinn was born in a small town some thirty-odd miles from Dallas, early in the century; she did not know her birth date but it may have been 1902. In her early twenties she moved to Dallas where she was heard singing at a neighbourhood church by the much respected, though little-recorded, Texas singer Hattie Burleson. Through Hattie she was introduced to Ella B. Moore, the celebrated owner of the Park Theatre on Central Tracks, and the two women coaxed her into singing blues and vaudeville songs.

She was an instant success when she appeared at the Park, and was compared, locally that is, with Bessie Smith. Other Texas singers like Maggie Jones and Lonnie Johnson sang with her and became her friends; the pianist Willie Tyson became her regular accompanist.

It was R. T. Ashford, who was responsible for getting Blind Lemon Jefferson on record, who got her a contract with Columbia, and it was he, as her manager, who was shrewd enough to ensure that she was singing in New Orleans or Atlanta when the recording unit visited those cities. Popular and dependable, she composed new songs with relative ease, and some assistance from Hattie Burleson. But by her last session she was becoming disillusioned with show business and tired of touring. She quit, returned to the church and forgot her worldly career.

In spite of the brevity of her professional life as a blues singer, Lillian Glinn was undoubtedly one of the finest on record. Many better known singers, like Sara Martin, Mamie Smith or the youthful Lizzie Miles, had thin voices. But hers was a strong contralto, ideal for projecting on stage without losing blues coloration, as is evident from her first hit record, 'Doggin' Me'. She sang the title phrase with trombone-like glissandi, carrying the audience with her by elongating it in performance. Though 'All Alone' or 'Come Home' were lyrically undistinguished with their sigh/cry, true/blue rhymes and standard imagery, many of her blues were original in structure and attack. She concluded each stanza of 'Where Have All the Black Men Gone' by repeating the line, allowing the sombre and slow theme to get a relaxed treatment from the excellent New Orleans band. On 'All the Week' she introduced a refrain couplet which gave variety, though, like any other vaudeville blues singer, she had her 'standard' treatment which appears on 'All Alone', 'Lost Letter' and 'Best Friend'. But on this item she introduces a slight reprise phrase in the first line of each stanza: 'I know I ain't good lookin', ain't got no long black hair – no curly hair . . .', her voice rising on the last syllables.

Though she seldom invented totally original blues verses, she had a gift for restructuring them; so, on 'Best Friend' a lover is warned 'you better be careful, or you'll reap what you sow'. She declares that her 'daddy's love is like a hydrant, he turns it off and on', and that 'men are like streetcars, runnin' all over town'. Sometimes there is an engaging inconsistency: 'I'm going over to Japan, get a Chinaman to chop my wood' or 'they caused me to walk till my feet was thin as a dime'.

Typically, a Lillian Glinn blues song was addressed at other women, offering warnings about the unreliability of men, or advice on how to keep a lover, sung with a swaggering confidence. Black men were more reliable than 'yellow' men, 'brownskin' men were generally better.

> . . . a brownskin man will sweep you right off
> your feet.
> If you don't believe just what I say
> Just get him to shake the shivaree –
> That's why I say a brownskin man's all right
> with me.

she sang on another hit item. It called for an unusual response from Barbecue Bob who, on record, sang 'I'm like Miss Lillian, like Miss Lillian, I mean Miss Glinn you see . . . she says a "brownskin man's all right with me".'

Though she had her mannerisms, such as a habit of splitting a vowel: 'I met a man one day-hay . . .' – Lillian's singing was free of contrived artifice. Instead it was forthright and direct, relieved sometimes by half-spoken, half-sung recitative passages in the 'preaching blues' style, and more rarely, as on 'Front Door Woman' or 'All the Week', by a hummed stanza. Some of her songs are aggressively sexual, like 'Wobble It Daddy' with its routine door-key image, or 'Packing House' which opens with the startling lines:

> A bucket of blood, a butcher's knife is all I crave,
> (repeat)
> Let me work in your packing house daddy, while
> I am your slave.

The use of thinly-veiled double meaning is most effective on 'Shake It Down' which at the outset purports to be a dance but soon dismisses the pretence. Sung with tremendous assurance, in broad, sweeping phrases that lead to a half-spoken verse and a stomping conclusion it is undoubtedly one of her finest recordings. But for me she reached her peak in the splendid 'Atlanta Blues', with its light swing, open delivery and excellent rapport between singer and instrumentalists. She evidently delighted in the wide-open city, but it was in Atlanta, at the TOBAs 81 Theatre right there on Decatur Street, that she resolved to give up professional blues singing and return to the church. Decatur Street as she knew it has long gone, the old black strip with its joints, saloons, brothels and theatres swept away in a clearance programme. 'I don't regret my time in The World,' she said, for it was through these brief years that she discovered what her way in life would be. Fortunately for us, though Lillian Glinn would hardly agree, 'Mister Ashford' made sure that the wayward young woman, who had them shrieking for more at the Park and the 81 Theatres, was recorded by Columbia's travelling unit four decades ago.

Notes to VJM VLP 31, 1978

Scufflin' Boogie

HENRY BROWN

St Louis City lies west of the Mississippi River, its main thoroughfares running east-west from the waterfront. The principal Negro areas lie in the older parts of the City close to Downtown St Louis and from Washington north, Lucas, Delmar, Franklin, Cole, Carr, Biddle, O'Fallon and Cass run parallel to each other – streets whose names are familiar from the words and titles of many blues that have been recorded by the innumerable blues singers and musicians who lived and worked in the densely populated area. A mile and a half from the river there is a large open triangle on Franklin where a number of roads meet and where the rectilinear monotony of the street planning is broken. It is a crowded, bustling forum where coloured children dart around the knots of laughing, chattering people in the hot, dusty street. Less than a block away on Easton lives a legendary figure in the story of blues piano, Henry Brown. To find him in this maze of streets would require the skill of a detective – and did, for his whereabouts were traced by Charlie O'Brien of the Police Department, a few years ago. Charlie and I again went in search of him, finally interrupting him in a game of pool in a joint on the corner of Easton and Garrison.

A tall, loose-limbed man in shirt-sleeves and a white jockey cap, Henry Brown emerged blinking in the sunlight. His sad-eyed, even truculent features brightened suddenly and generously as we talked of the days, more than thirty years before, when he first recorded his piano blues for the Paramount label. To our relief and pleasure he still played and was willing to do so there and then. Around the corner on North Garrison, a tiny hairdressing salon and beauty parlour owned by one Pinkey Boxx,

included in the furniture a small piano, and it was to this that Henry Brown led us. Pinkey Boxx by way of introduction rolled off a rough-and-ready 'Early In The Morning Blues' herself before letting Henry take the stool. A few exploratory phrases and Henry Brown settled into 'Deep Morgan Blues' and 'Henry Brown Blues' with all the confidence and authority of his recordings of these titles made in 1929. It was an historic occasion and though I had only portable equipment with me, this recording of 'Henry Brown Blues' made in Pinkey Boxx's beauty parlour is included in the present album. It soon became evident that Brown had more ideas for solo blues than have been issued under his name in the past, and that the passing years had matured rather than in anyway impaired his playing. Though he has only earned a casual living from playing blues at various times and has had to depend on other employment for much of his life, though he has not been able to afford a piano of his own, Henry Brown has always been in demand to play at house parties and in neighbourhood joints and so the blues has remained very much a part of him.

Having lived in St Louis for so long he looks upon the city as his native home, but Henry Brown was born in Troy, Tenneesse, in 1906, moving to St Louis when he was twelve years old. He was raised in Deep Morgan, the stretch of Delmar Boulevard that runs to the river and whose rather lurid history the City hoped to forget along with the change of name. For a year or two he attended the Del-Lin School and received an elementary formal education. But it was the education in the blues, offered by the innumerable pianists in the local saloons and joints that interested him more. In particular he was impressed by the playing of a rough and unrecorded blues pianist by the name of 'Blackmouth' and it was he who had the strongest influence on his style of playing. At sixteen he was playing regularly in bars and at rent parties and shortly after he made a firm friendship with a man a few years his senior, Ike Rodgers, who played rough 'gut-bucket' trombone with a variety of tin cans, liquor glasses and other mutes of his own devising. Their friendship lasted until Rodgers' death in 1941 and throughout the years they played together, sometimes alone, sometimes in the company of Lawrence Casey a guitarist, or Earle Bindley on drums. Amongst the many places where they worked, the 905 Club, the Blue Flame, Jim's Place on 23rd and Market, and particularly Katie Red's in East Louis, are outstanding in his memory. At many of these they accompanied Mary Johnson, Little Alice Moore, Robert Peebles and other blues singers from the district.

When times were good and money was freely spent Henry Brown was able to live on his earnings from his playing, but generally he had day work of various kinds. For four years he worked in a dairy and followed this with work in a laundry, steaming and pressing clothes. In the worst years of the Depression he and Ike Rodgers worked together on WPA projects, labouring in a road construction gang and cutting stone in a rock quarry. In 1941, the year of Ike's death, Henry was drafted into the Army. Fortunately his talent as a pianist was quickly recognized and he toured the camps as far as Texas and Florida playing with a four-piece band. In 1945 he was released from service but still continued to play, generally with three or four other pieces which would include the prematurely bald Lawrence Casey known as Papa Egg-Shell or Papa Slick-Head – to whom his 'Papa Slick Head' is dedicated – or his old friend Henry Townsend. Roosevelt Sykes, St Louis Jimmy, Blind Teddy Darby – these and may other blues singers who have centred in St Louis have been his friends and associates for many years, and though to the blues collecting world he was 'obscure' or 'forgotten', around Franklin, Lucas or Biddle he is a well-known figure. In recent years Henry Brown has worked with the Edwin Brothers Shoe Company on Washington Avenue – and played piano there too, so it is not surprising to find that far from being out of practice Henry Brown plays his simple, contemplative blues piano better than ever before.

Apart from a few recordings of long ago he has never had an opportunity before to express himself fully on record. A taciturn man, he communicates more eloquently in his music than in his taut speech, as his subtle playing on 'Got It and Cain't Quit It' or 'My Blues Is In The Bottle' indicates. In 'Blues for Charlies O'Brien' he acknowledges his indebtedness to the interest of the detective – and slyly jokes about the Police Squad. His inexorable left-hand boogie figures are powerfully demonstrated in 'Scufflin' Boogie' whilst he plays his 'Handy-man Blues' to an unexpected tango rhythm. These and the remaining titles should help to bring Henry Brown the recognition he deserves as a blues pianist of the first importance.

Notes to Seventy-Seven LA-12-4, 1960

Henry Brown died St Louis, Missouri, 28 June 1981.

Crying the Blues

SLEEPY JOHN ESTES

Close on twenty years ago the Jazz Appreciation Society managed to persuade the English Brunswick record company to issue a selection of rare jazz and blues recordings from Decca masters. None seemed rarer nor more strange to unaccustomed ears than the coupling on Brunswick 03562, 'Drop Down Mama' and 'Married Woman Blues' a 'Vocal Blues with Guitar & Harp Accompaniment' by 'Sleepy' John Estes. The broken voice, the wailing accompaniment, which one commentator observed was 'a harmonica, not a harp', and the compulsive rhythm which produced vague references to Africa all confounded criticism. The twelve-bar blues had been accepted as a traditional pattern, the three-line standard verse accepted as the traditional blues stanza. But at the time when Bunk Johnson was talking of playing the 'twenty-four bar blues', here was issued a blues from a decade before which was on a loose twenty-four-measure structure and sung in verse and refrain of a quite a-typical form:

> Some of these women sure do make me tired,
> Got a handful of 'give me', a mouthful of
>   'much obliged'.
> Well mama, don't allow me to fool around all
>   night long,
> I may look like I'm crazy but poor John do
>   know right from wrong'.

This was unconventional enough in terms of the blues convention but it was sung in a fragmented, crying voice and the lines were so split up, the words enjambed and others elided that it sounded more like

> Some-a these wimmin – sho do
> Make me tire' – gotta
> handfulla 'gimme' mouthfulla –

> much oblige' well mama
> don' 'llow me to – fo-ool –
> roun' all ni-ight long . . .
> I may look lak I'm craz' – but
> Po' John do know – right from wrong.

We called Sleepy John Estes' way of playing and singing the blues "crying the blues" because he did really cry when he was singing work songs or some blues,' said Broonzy. (*Big Bill Blues*, Cassell 1955, p82–83). Crying the blues undoubtedly described Estes' way of singing, and though some of the titles that Big Bill quoted were not associated with Sleepy John's records they could have been in his repertoire, and anyway 'My Mother Don't Allow Me To Stay Out All Night Long' was quite clearly 'Drop Down Mama'. Bill told an engaging story of Estes as a track-lining boss and concluded: 'John Estes is just about eighty-seven years old now because I was nineteen years old then and all of this happened between 1912 and 1915. I would run off home just to work under John Estes' singing and he would let me sing with him some time. In 1922 I met him in Chicago where he was singing the blues.'

If he were alive in the 1960s he was a nonagenarian it would seem. Yet there were rumours – a hint from Will Shade in Memphis; a comment from Memphis Slim. Big Joe Williams provided the real clue and acting upon it David Blumenthal from Chicago, who was engaged in filming a documentary under the title *Citizen South, Citizen North* found him and photographed him in his broken-down sharecropper's home on the outskirts of Brownsville, Tennessee. Back in Chicago, Blumenthal reported his discovery to Bob Koester of Delmark

Records who brought him North to appear at one or two concerts. Estes proved to be in fine fettle and playing as well as ever he had on his records of thirty years before. His companion of forty years, the rotund and amiable Hammie Nixon whose very existence had been the subject of some discographical dispute in the past, came with him to act as his guide and companion. John was now totally blind but he was a tough man in his early days and a resilient one still. Moreover he was at the time still in his fifties: two-score years younger than any justifiable estimates would have made him.

John Adam Estes was born in Lowry County, Tennessee, near the town of Ripley, the son of a tenant farmer, on 25 January 1904. He was one of some sixteen children all of whom worked on their father's plot as they became old enough to do so. In 1915 the Estes family moved to Brownsville where, at a school on Winfield Lane, John Adam got a rudimentary education. Like his brothers he worked on his father's share but was more inclined to follow his musical leanings, playing his father's guitar whenever he could. He was still little more than a boy when he was struck in the eye with a stone during a friendly game of baseball. Though he did not lose the sight immediately his vision was seriously impaired and he turned more to music than to other work, probably partly as a result of the accident. His father died about 1920 and with his restraining influence no longer present, John Adam turned to his music as a means of making a living.

'I used to hear a lot about him, John Adam,' Hammie Nixon told, 'and I was just a kid, living out on my parent's home near Ripley. Then he comes in at one of those old country suppers and I was blowin' my harp. I'd been playing harp since I don't know when, just a kid on up. And he heard me playing and he asks me would I like to go and play my harp for him? So I told him yes, but I had to ask my mama first because I was just young, see. So he comes back to my mama's house with me, but she didn't want me to go you know. Anyhow he says like he would look after me and provide for me and so forth so she let me go. And we been together ever since.' John awoke to laugh at the end of the story and agree – he proved the aptness of his nickname to everyone's satisfaction by falling asleep whenever the occasion presented itself.

It was 1927 and Hammie was just twelve years old. The following year the man and boy went to Memphis, Tennessee, where they met many of the famous bluesmen of the day. Estes teamed up with Yank Rachel, another singer from his own locality who played mandolin. Rachel was acting as a talent scout and secured Sleepy John's first recording date. There in Memphis, on 24 September 1929, he made his first title, 'The Girl I Love She Got Long Curly Hair', which he made again just thirty-five years later for this collection. A few scattered dates followed but the Depression forced their return to Brownsville for a couple of years. Then in 1931 John and Hammie decided to try their luck in Chicago where eventually they met Mayo Williams who arranged their celebrated recordings for the Decca 7000 series. These items are exceptionally rare today and for many years they have been outstanding collectors' items. For this reason a number of Estes' most original creations have been recorded again for this collection, and they demonstrated amongst other things his extraordinary memory. No prompting was necessary to stir his recollections: a title given and he would launch into the song with Hammie's moaning harmonica backing him up at every phrase. So it is possible to hear again such classics of the 1937 sessions as 'Airplane Blues' or the haunting 'Vernita Blues' about the woman who, at the time of the original recording was 'givin' lots of trouble'. Another masterpiece from these exceptional sessions is 'Needmore Blues' which demonstrates in this recreation the remarkable musical sympathy between the two men and their control of the subtle rhythm changes. Theirs is a sense of rhythm which holds together such a slow and disturbing blues as 'Easin' Back to Tennessee'. Originally made in 1938 a comparison of the two versions shows that the suspense created by the timing, the pauses in the melodic line and the apparent near-disintegration are essentially a part of the composition – a folk invention of great originality. Soon after, Hammie and John did 'ease back to Tennessee' and for nearly a quarter of a century were sure that they had been forgotten, unaware of their distant admirers throughout two continents. Happily their obscurity was eventually ended and the present recordings were made in England and Denmark when they made their triumphant tour in the autumn of 1964. Then their fans saw the legends brought to life, heard in person Sleepy John's strange singing with its sudden barks and unexpected power, wondered at the interweaving of voice and instruments, laughed at Hammie's delight in his own 'jug' blowing on a whiskey bottle. For those who had been able to decipher the admittedly difficult enunciation of John's blues their recordings had added meaning; here was a blues singer who had experienced all that he sang, whose every verse had immediate reference to the hardships and drama of his own life and who had recreated the world of a Negro in Brownsville, Tennessee, through the medium of the folk blues.

★　★　★　★

Listening to Sleepy John Estes for the first time can be hard going for those unacquainted with his early records. He has a curiously broken voice which seems always at the point of disintegration. It doesn't fall apart, though, but leaves the listener in a tense state of anticipation. Though Estes has a ribald, earthy sense of humour in conversation this doesn't come over in his records, which are nearly always extremely sad and poignant. Though one expects blues singers to create blues from their own experience, some draw upon the repertoires of others more extensively than they do the events of their own lives. Not so Estes, who sings almost exclusively about himself and the people that he has known intimately, the events in his own experience and that of the people who lived in his own very circumscribed world. His world is that of Brownsville, Tennessee, and it is the township, the minor incidents in the lives of the people, which assume large proportions because of their isolation, which figure prominently in his records.

> *Now Mis' Clark is a lawyer, his young*
> *   brother is too,*
> *When you bound to get hot, he'll tell you what*
> *   to do,*
> *   Boys y'know I like Mis' Clark, yes he*
> *   really is my friend,*
> *   He says If I just stay out of the grave he'll*
> *   see that I won't go round the bend.*
> *He lawyers for the rich, he lawyers for the*
> *   poor,*
> *He don't try to rob nobody, just brings them*
> *   round to the door,*
> *   Boys you know I like Mis' Clark etc.*
> *Now Mis' Clark is a good lawyer, he's good as*
> *   I have seen,*
> *He's the first man that proved that water runs*
> *   upstream,*
> *   Boys you know I like Mis' Clark etc.*

The words are from 'Lawyer Clark Blues' made by Estes in Chicago in 1941 (Bluebird 8871) and they illustrate many aspects of his approach to his blues. I know of no other blues by any singer which is devoted to the subject of a single professional man – hardly any so much as mention a lawyer at all, but here Estes made his own tribute to a man who had helped him in one or two minor 'scrapes'. This is unusual enough, but so, too, is the verse form, for though it is sung to a twelve-bar blues tune the structure of the blues is rather different, with a couplet verse and repeated couplet refrain. This is a form which Estes particularly likes and perhaps links to the country dance tunes which he sometimes plays still and which once formed quite an important part of his music. The blues shows also Estes ability to use very direct statements like 'He lawyers for the rich, he lawyers for the poor' with a striking image like 'He's the first man that proved that water runs upstream' which is as effective a way of saying that Lawyer Clark could defend a man successfully when the odds seemed impossible as any one could wish for.

Uncannily, Sleepy John Estes remembers with clarity all his recordings and can sing these blues again when called upon to do so. But though he appears to compose his blues carefully and to learn them, he is also capable of improvising verses with unusual skill and originality. His performances are always surprising because of the topicality of his songs and at any session he is almost certain to make up a blues about the people present. And all the time, when he is working with him, Hammie Nixon, who anticipates his every thought, plays a sympathetic harmonica accompaniment to his words.

Hammie Nixon (or Nix, as he was often called on the labels – Nickerson sometimes, too) played harmonica on 'Fire Department

Blues', one of the many Estes' descriptions of an incident, in this case the burning down of a house in the street where 'Marthy Hardin' lived:

> *Now I'm gonna call the Fire Department for*
> *my house is burnin' down.   (repeat)*
> *You know that musta be li'l, Marthy Hardin'*
> *what lives on the north side of town.*
> *When you see the Chief, please clear the street,*
> *(repeat)*
> *'Cause you know he's goin' down to save li'l,*
> *Marthy Hardin's home for me.*
> *Now I wrote li'l Marthy a letter, five days it*
> *returned back to me,   (repeat)*
> *You know li'l Marthy's house done burned*
> *down; she done moved on Bradford Street.*

★　★　★　★

All Sleepy John Estes' blues are basically autobiographical and at the sessions a few minutes' talk about incidents long past would remind him of a blues. But as Bob Koester wryly observed: 'he's got material enough to be singing about this trip for a year.' His inventiveness never flagged and, somewhat embarrassingly for those concerned, but entirely in keeping with the man who had composed blues about friends over the past forty years, he sang of Karl Knudsen in 'Denmark Blues' and myself in 'You Stayed Away Too Long'. 'I'm playin' the guitar – I believe it belongs to Paul's wife,' he sang. It did, and it bears the scratches of the finger-picks to prove it.

Notes to Storyville SLP 172, 1965
and *Jazz Beat*, September 1966

Sleepy John Estes died Brownsville, Tennessee, 5 June 1977.

Gonna Pick No More Cotton

JOHN HENRY BARBEE

It was a Thursday, 8 September, and the year 1938. A lean, bespectacled and serious-looking Negro recorded his 'Six Weeks Old Blues' and shortly after, it was issued on Vocalion 04417, backed by 'God Knows I Can't Help It', a verse-and-refrain fast blues with words that seemed to go far back in the blues tradition. The record was a preliminary issue to test public reaction to the new singer and it sold well enough to cause the company to invite the singer back to Chicago to record again. But by this time he had disappeared and the name of John Henry Barbee became a lonely entry in the discographies and the single record a treasured rarity in a few comprehensive blues collections.

The blues bass-player Willie Dixon was mainly responsible for the return of John Henry Barbee. He has continued in recent years to seek out new blues talent and has always interested himself in any news of singers unknown to him. One of his younger supporters sang him a blues that he had learned from an ice-cream vendor who sang to the children who gathered about his South Side stall. Stories of the 'old man' sounded interesting and Willie was impressed when he heard him sing and play. A short while later, following the rediscovery of Sleepy John Estes and a number of singers from his region, the name of John Henry Barbee was mentioned and Willie Dixon brought him from his virtual retirement.

The blues map is undergoing change as recent research has brought new information to light and the two or three centres of blues concentration that the field of recording units had implied are not now so simply defined. Many of the recordings made in Memphis, for example, were of singers not only from Tennessee but from Mississippi,

Arkansas and elsewhere too. In Tennessee itself Memphis was by no means the only town of blues interest: now the map is dotted with important place names – important at any rate in the cartography of the blues: Jackson, Brownsville, Ripley and so on. Ripley was the home of the harmonica player Noah Lewis and of the pianist Lee Brown. Brownsville was the home of Estes and his own harmonica player Hammie Nixon, and the home also of the guitarist-singer Son Bonds. But the townships were close enough to be on the blues-playing circuit of all these artists and, so, too, was Henning, a few miles south of Ripley on the 51 Highway to Memphis, where John Henry Barbee was born on 14 November 1905.

In this rural community the Tucker family – John's parents – were farmers and his early life followed the now familiar pattern of working in the fields as a child at tasks almost too demanding for his years. At this time he wasn't known as John Henry Barbee – that was to come later. His real name is William George Tucker and even when he began to be known as a blues singer and guitarist at local country suppers he was still using his given name. His repertoire ranged beyond the blues to embrace the broader Negro folk tradition – minstrel and work songs which he picked up from other players he added to his ever-increasing stock of songs. One that especially appealed to him was the old ballad 'John Henry' which he learned to play in the old traditional way, with a bottleneck or knife slid against the reverberating strings, giving them a singing sound. It became a sort of signature tune, a ballad by which he was particularly known and in the way that folk singers collect sobriquets that become more lasting than their own names, he was soon known by his song – as 'John Henry'.

During the Depression years and the bleak decade of the Thirties John Henry, now a spare and small but tough man in his late twenties and going thirty, travelled widely through the South. In lean times he worked as a field hand but he found that he could earn money adequate enough for his needs by begging in the streets of the small Mississippi, Alabama and Arkansas townships. Throughout these years he made many associations with other blues singers – local ones like Sleepy John Estes and others like Big Joe Williams who liked a similar wandering life. For a while he teamed up with Big Joe and they worked side by side in the cotton rows and the barrelhouses. Then in Memphis he met Sunnyland Slim and for a time they formed a guitar-and-piano team working the joints in the Mississippi Delta. Back in Tennessee he met up with the youthful Sonny Boy Williamson – John Lee Williamson, the 'first' Sonny Boy, at least on record – and the two men worked together off and on for three years. John Henry was getting pretty well known in blues circles.

He was living across the Mississippi River in Luxora, Arkansas, when he got an invitation to record for Vocalion in the early Fall of 1938. He made the trip to Chicago and recorded four titles, two of which were issued. Then he went back home: home to a tragedy in his personal life. In his absence another man whom he refers to rather ominously as 'Mister Charlie' (Mister Charlie is a common Negro term for an anonymous white man) made love to his woman. John Henry returned to find them in bed together and with the rough, peremptory means of settling such affairs he got a shotgun and shot him.

Believing he had killed the man John Henry slipped away and hid in a swamp.

For a long time he led a desperate life, close to starvation for he was terrified of being discovered and tried for murder. Eventually, when he felt it safe to emerge he did so, quietly and under an assumed name. When he was asked to give a complete name for his first record and not just his nickname of John Henry he said 'Barbee'. 'I couldn't just leave it as John Henry could I?' he explained to me, 'so I thought up Barbee. Just made it up by myself.' It was a good name and it was the name he answered to from then on. William Henry Tucker he left back in the swamp along the Mississippi.

John Henry Barbee moved to Chicago. Unknown to him there had been attempts to find him to record again but he missed the chance and did not dare to seek out further opportunities to record, still fearing recognition. Also unknown to him, 'Mister Charlie' survived the gunshot wound having received the charge in the leg, living on until 1949. Eventually John Henry heard of the fate of his late rival and breathed easier but by that time he was living permanently in Chicago having done a variety of jobs. He worked for some time as a presser in a laundry and more recently as an ice-cream salesman – the employment which led to his rediscovery.

Though he had withdrawn from active blues singing, John Henry had never given up the guitar, or his singing, or his interest in the blues. His superb country style of blues playing was virtually unimpaired and though the years had taken a little of the edge off his voice, its musical qualities were still far above the ordinary. John Henry needed no time to practise and in the short period of his return to active singing he proved to be immensely popular. He joined the 1964 American Negro Folk Blues Festival for its European tour – a festival which included such celebrated names as Lightnin' Hopkins, Howlin' Wolf and Sleepy John Estes – as an almost unknown artist to the vast majority of his audiences. He immediately endeared himself to his listeners by his unassuming artistry, his splendid musicianship and his quiet dignity.

Unhappily, John Henry was a sick man on the tour. He had a pain in his back which he thought was caused by strain when lifting his suitcase, and was often in acute discomfort. In spite of his great pain he insisted on playing at the concerts and hoped to stay with the show to its conclusion. In England a doctor diagnosed a dangerously malignant growth and he was flown back to the United States with little expectation to live. It was a tragic end to his briefly renewed career but John Henry was happy to have been on the tour, happy to discover that he had so many friends in countries that were entirely new to him.

Since his rediscovery John Henry had recorded barely a couple of tunes and so it is of especial importance that these recordings were made on his European tour. They reveal the breadth of his taste and the inventiveness of his playing, as neither his few previous recordings nor his brief tour appearances had been able to do. Some of his blues, like 'I Ain't Gonna Pick No More Cotton' and 'Miss Nellie Gray' were auto-biographical, whilst others, like 'That's All Right' or 'Dust My Broom' are the compositions of other singers – in these instances, Arthur Crudup and Elmore James – to which he brought his own extremely personal interpretations. His fine bottleneck guitar technique is to be heard on 'John Henry' or the slow blues 'I Heard My Baby' on which the rattling of the glass against the frets is clearly audible. In his later years he was influenced by the playing of Big Bill Broonzy and echoes of his technique are to be detected on 'Tell Me Baby' though the long recitatives are entirely his own. Whether he was reinterpreting old blues or singing his own lyric creations, John Henry Barbee stamped every performance with his own special quality of blues artistry.

John Henry will never record again. On his return to the United States he bought himself a car, the first he had ever owned. A week later he was involved in an accident and a man was run over and fatally injured. John Henry was jailed and was unable to contact his friends. No one went bond for him and he died there, of cancer, on 4 November 1964.

Notes to Storyville SLP 171, 1965

The Black Ace

B. K. TURNER

*I am the Black Ace, I'm the boss card in your
hand,*
*I am the Black Ace, I'm the boss card in your
hand,*
*But I'll play for you mama, if you please let
me be your man.*

These were the words that listeners to the
regular blues programmes relayed from
Station KFJZ out of Fort Worth in the late
Thirties would hear as the programme was
introduced. At that time the name of the
Black Ace was a familiar one in the home of
both Negroes and white persons living in
the city and in the surrounding country.
'They started to call me the Black Ace when
I put out the "Black Ace Blues" in 1937,' the
singer recalled when we recorded him some
twenty-three years later, in the summer of
1960. 'When I was broadcasting they had
me play that for a theme song all the time.
Folks didn't know who I was and when they
commenced to announce me over the radio
as the Black Ace, folks just called me Black
Ace. But that's not my real name. My name
is Babe Kyro Lemon Turner. I don't know
why they named me like that. I throwed the
"Lemon" away and just used the initials of
Babe Kyro – B. K. Turner. Never did use
the "Lemon" and the "L". Fact is my wife
never knowed what my full name was until
just now.' It is as 'Ace' that B. K. Turner
is known today and the name is neatly
embroidered on the fresh white linen of his
shirt.

In the summer of 1960 Ace was living in a
small, compact house, in the suburbs of Fort
Worth. He was working, as he still works,
in a photographic studio in the city and his
steel guitar with which he had once earned
his name was gathering dust in the attic.

Working in the Don Juarez Studio 'shootin'
movies and makin' all kinds of pictures,'
watching the television in the evenings in
his neat home, sitting out on the porch with
its modern metal chairs or watching baseball at the weekends, his life was relatively
comfortably ordered, and the blues were
forgotten. But his life has not always been as
secure in the past and like most other blues
singers, Ace came from the country. He was
born in 1905 at 'a little ole place they called
Hughes Springs, Texas – oh, about seven
miles this side of Louisiana. I stayed at home
with my daddy on the farm down there;
stayed on the farm all my life until I was
about thirty years old'. His work on the
farm was hard and the profits were low;
there was little enough time for recreation
and not too much money for entertainment.
But his brother had an improvised guitar
made from a 'guitar neck which had some
wires on' and on this crude instrument he
learned as a child to play elementary guitar
styles. He had a good voice and in his youth
sang in church choirs. He learned a little
music: 'doh-re-me-fah-so-la-te-doh and
such as that, and teach it to other young
people.' When Babe Turner, as he was
known, became about twenty-two years of
age he was able to purchase for himself an
old guitar; not a good instrument but one on
which he could play the blues that came to
his head when he worked on the farm.

It was the Depression that changed Babe
Turner's way of living, for his father's farm
was hit by the accumulative effect of dropping prices and rapidly diminishing markets.
Soon it ceased to support the family and, as
so many others had done throughout the
country, the family broke up in the search
for other employment. Ace made his way to

Shreveport, Louisiana. It was a fortunate and fateful decision for it was there that he met the blues singer Oscar Woods, then about thirty-five years old, and in his prime. Though some five years his junior Babe Turner – now Buck Turner, or 'B. K.' and Buddy Woods became close friends. Woods played guitar, but in a different style from that in which B. K. was playing at the time. He had a steel Hawaiian guitar laid across his knees which he picked with a bottleneck as he sang his blues. Though he was a taciturn and singular man and known as 'The Lone Wolf' he readily teamed with the young Texan, playing together at joints, and particularly at house parties. The house parties were as much a feature of Southern life as the more widely publicized 'rent parties' of the cities of Chicago and New York, and an evening's playing would bring B. K. Turner $1.50 – more than he could earn for a day's regular work, if indeed he could have found it.

Playing with Buddy Woods, he had an opportunity to watch the older man's unusual style and the technique suited him perfectly. He rapidly assimilated and improved upon it, buying himself a National steel-bodied Hawaiian guitar with a thick-square-sectioned neck. At first he played this with a bottleneck in the traditional manner of the knife and bottleneck blues guitarists, but soon saw the possibilities of extending the range of the instrument by using a small medicine bottle to stop the strings at the frets. Holding this in the left hand and picking the strings finger-pick style but with the guitar placed horizontally, he could block whole chords in 'Sevastapol', tuning or stop individual notes by using both the sides and corners of the bottle. In this way he could play the open strings in a range of keys; and as he developed he devised a number of original tunings and unusual rhythmic patterns. How effectively is brilliantly demonstrated in the instrumental solo 'Bad Times Stomp' or in the accompaniment of such a blues as 'Fore Day Creep'.

As conditions became better in the later Thirties, Buck Turner found himself in great demand. He travelled in Louisiana, Oklahoma and Texas and finally settled in Fort Worth. A talent scout heard him playing and this resulted in the six sides for Decca, rare collectors' items now, on which his fame amongst the blues enthusiasts outside his home country depended. Amongst these were 'Black Ace', 'Lowing Heifer' and 'Santa Claus Blues', of which two were remade for this collection. In 1936 the Kimber Brothers approached him to play on Station KFJZ and for that station and for others in Texas and Oklahoma he played intermittently until 1941. During this time he made a number of titles for Vocalion in Fort Worth in 1938, but although one coupling has been reported as having been released obscurely on Melotone under the name of Buck Turner, the others were not pressed. But if a wider fame eluded him through recording, he was offered a small role in the film *Blood of Jesus* in which he played and sang. 'Then after that I was doin' pretty good when Uncle Sam told me to come on, "Let's go fight". And that broke up the musical career and I quit then, 1943.'

Returning from the services, Ace was faced with the problem of securing new work. He tried numerous jobs – 'What kind of work?' he exclaimed, 'Man, I done everything!' He was married, had a son and times were tough. 1949 found him and his wife plucking cotton bolls in the cotton patch. 'We went out to try to pick some cotton, me and my wife. I think we could pick, oh, about 300lb. Well, that kept us eatin'.'

When the cotton-picking season was over Ace secured a job as a janitor at the Fort Worth airport which he held for more than five years until he was laid off in 1955. That year he found himself picking cotton again and the future seemed as bleak as ever. 'We didn't pick enough cotton to keep my car – and they took the car away from me. I'd bought me new set of tyres and they took the car away from me, tyres and all. Finance Company took it. I believe they call it "Security". . . well, it must have been security! The car was worth $1200!' Out of work, he tracked the streets looking for a job and applied regularly at the Employment Office. 'Then the man sent me to this Don Juarez studio to work there a day, two days out of every week. And the man liked my work and he give me a regular job. So I been workin' there ever since.'

Working regularly at last and spending some of his earnings on his own photographic equipment, Ace had settled into a new routine of life at the age of fifty. In the evenings he sometimes whiled away a few hours with his friends at a wooden, white-painted clapboard juke called 'The Lucky Strike'. It was indeed a lucky strike that a chance remark led to his 'discovery' at his rendezvous, but when we visited him to record him, he was reluctant to play or sing. The blues seemed to belong to a past which had been riddled with changing fortunes and it seemed to him that no one would be interested in, or would recall, his old-style blues. The humming of his recorded tunes and the repetition of the words of blues that he had recorded more than twenty years before convinced him that there were people who still admired his way of playing the blues. His wife brought the old steel guitar which had been his constant companion before the War and he handled it a little strangely. Rather shyly and awkwardly he picked up a small glass flask and started to play. In moments the years seemed to slip away and the whining, singing notes of the blues rose above the humming of the whirling fan in the stifling heat of an August night. Ten days later, we returned to record a Black Ace whose abilities and whose originality as a blues singer were as great as when he first earned his name. His blues reflect his environment and his past life – from the necessity to seek work, to the symbolism of the Santa Fe Line, or the simple pleasures afforded by the local joints. Amongst a wide variety of blues and blues forms he includes 'Farther Along', a Texas spiritual that once was collected by Hally Wood at Reverend Palmer's Church in East Austin, Texas, but of which this may be the first authentic recording.

Of the few exponents of the flat Hawaiian guitar blues style who have been recorded, Oscar Woods is dead, and Kokomo Arnold – whom Black Ace resembles – has long since retired with no desire to play or sing again. These recordings of a great blues singer have the added importance that they may well be the last to be made of a style of blues which has all but vanished.

Notes to Arhoolie F1003, 1961

Black Ace died Fort Worth, Texas, 7 November 1972.

Key to the Highway
BROWNIE MCGHEE

'Once I went to the New York School of Music – I always reckon there's something new to learn in your playin' – so I went right along there with my old Gibson guitar . . . I says to the feller, told him I wanted to learn, to improve my guitar playin'. Well he started right back here .`. .`; a spatulate finger stopped the first fret on the top E string. 'Started me off on E, F, G, A . . . I said "Hell man, I want to learn what I can add to this to make my guitar playin' good",' a rapid arpeggio followed in demonstration. 'He says "Git you on outa here man! What you doin' likin' to wastin' my time. I cain't teach you nothin' less'n you start right from the beginning. I can't teach you to play anything more to that. What you playin' there right now ain't writ. It ain't in the book . . ."!' Brownie McGhee grinned delightedly and played a superb blues sequence to amplify his point. And it is just as well that the instructor at the School of Music did dissuade his would-be pupil, for in spite of the many years that he has spent in the relatively sophisticated surroundings of New York his unorthodox folk guitar playing has been unharmed. Not that he is ignorant of musical theory: far from it. 'Augmented chords? Sure I use them . . . in some of the stuff I'm writing now. But you don't use them much in the blues. See here, I can't play this kinda stuff on record. People would think ole Brownie's gone commercial. Besides I don't want to. But I *can* play them. You gotta know these things, you understand?'

When a son was born to George McGhee he entered the date and the name, Walter Brown McGhee, in the fly-leaf of the family Bible in accordance with the old rural tradition. Unfortunately, the Bible was subsequently burned in a minor conflagration and Walter Brown – 'Brownie' – was never certain of the year of his birth though he gave the date as 30 November 1914. It was not until this year that he learned from the official records that the year of his birth was 1915. George McGhee was a labouring man who worked at times on the river levee as a 'wheeler' and at times as a farmer working a holding at Kingsport, Tennessee. He lived mostly in Knoxville and it was here that his son Brownie was born and raised. When he had time on his hands he amused himself and his family playing guitar and singing country folk songs and spirituals. At harvest time he would play for corn shuckings and country parties. Brownie's Uncle, John Evans, also played at such functions. He played a hillbilly style fiddle, for the similarities between the white and Negro music styles in the hill districts were marked. It was Uncle John Evans who made for Brownie his first instrument – a banjo fashioned from a marshmallow tin with an arm made from a length of seasoned poplar. It was an effective instrument and had five strings, and on this a very youthful Brownie learned the rudiments of his music.

In 1918 Brownie's brother, Granville Henley McGhee, was born, and shortly after, Brownie was struck down by poliomyelitis which permanently affected the growth of his right leg. Unable to play as freely as some of the other children, he amused himself by learning to play the guitar and the piano, on which he became proficient at an early age. He attended school at Lenoir City, Tennessee, and, possessing a good voice, sang at school functions in West Tennessee and Virginia. A confident and fluent speaker even at that age he spoke for his school in inter-school debates and even made the trip to Nashville at one time for this purpose. The Solomon Temple Baptist Church at Lenoir gave him further opportunities to develop his musical talents and he sang, played guitar and piano for the church – and he operated the foot-pump organ. After reaching the 8th Grade at the School in Lenoir where he had been eventually appointed 'Superintendent', Brownie attended school for a year-and-a-half at Maryville, Tennessee. Here he was also able to play his guitar and piano and continued to sing at the Sanctified Church. At the weekends and during vacations he wandered around the district and played at summer resorts, swimming pools and the Smoky Mountain Hotel. The folks on holiday were clearly attracted to the light-skinned, lame little Negro boy who was so gifted on the guitar and who sang so well, and Brownie found that playing the resorts was quite lucrative. He had adapted a 'jazz-horn' – a long kazoo – into a home-made instrument of saxophone shape which he was able to hold under his arm and play whilst he accompanied himself on the guitar, and no doubt the novel idea attracted attention.

When Brownie McGhee left school he had decided on his future career and he had already a good deal of experience as an entertainer behind him. He played at picnics and carnivals; joined the medicine shows as guitarist and singer to attract attention to the wares that the 'doctors' were selling. For a while he worked with the Mighty Hagg Carnival and later with one of the companies of the Rabbit Foot Minstrels, sharing the bill with a character by the name of Jailhouse. He was only a boy in his early teens 'talkin' big, but I didn't know the *meanin'* of what I was sayin',' but he was rapidly getting himself known. He played at roadhouses and jukes, tough joints where a boy

of his age was an unexpected visitor, for his only thought was for the music that he was playing and the opportunities that he could obtain to entertain. Working far too hard to exercise strict parental control, his father was scarcely aware that his son was thumbing his way along the highways from township to township, picking up with casual folk singers and vagrants who introduced him to new districts. 'Man, I ran wild! I didn't see no danger in it. If it was somewhere I could play, I didn't think about nothing else. I'd just go along the highway with my guitar over my shoulder, thumbing my way. An' when I got tired of thumbing in one direction, well, I'd just go 'cross the road and thumb my way back! Sometimes I'd cross the State line three, maybe four times in a day. Up and down the roads, Virginia, Tennessee, North Carolina . . . that was my education,' explained Brownie.

At this time he was playing a Spanish guitar, finger style. 'But I figured I'd better learn to use the picks. My fingers were a mess. I reckoned that if I was goin' to play professional I gotta be able to play *all* the time. When you're professional you gotta play when you feel like it and play when you don't, so I went home to study the picks.' It took him nearly a year to re-learn the playing of his guitar using a thumb-pick and finger picks on his index and second fingers, but it was then that he developed the style that he has retained to the present day. 'Don't know that it has a *name*; I call it jukin'.' Maintaining a strong bass rhythm with his thumb he finger picks rapid arpeggios that produce a counter-melody. Much of this is the result of dexterous chord-fingering with the left hand, for Brownie's chords that 'ain't writ' are not so much new chords as unusual chord shapes of his own invention. 'I don't reckon to waste a finger,' he says, 'because that finger could be working.' And by evolving new chord shapes and great digital independence he can finger a full chord with say, thumb, third and fourth fingers and still permit his first and second fingers to stop the strings in a rapid succession of notes, thus producing the complicated but essentially 'blue' instrumental passages that are the despair of those who try to imitate him. But all this did not evolve instantly. It is the result of years of concentrated practice and determination, the foundations of which were laid during the period of intensive study of the picking style, 1933–4. Apart from entertaining, singing the blues and playing them on his guitar, he continued to play piano and to sing with a gospel quartette the 'Golden Voices' with whom he worked in Kingsport, Tennessee.

The Thirties were pretty lean years, but Brownie made a good living through Tennessee and the Carolinas, if a somewhat precarious one. Lame, and therefore more vulnerable to attack, he built for himself something of a facade of toughness, though the life that he had led had educated him well in the ways of men. Trading on their superstitions he slept, when he had to sleep out, in graveyards where he knew he was free from molestation. Settling for a few years in Knoxville he established for himself – 'a little racket, y'know? Just don't care to talk about that.' His address was simply 'Brownie's Alley, all the boys knew my place. Blues singer come in town an' he was cold broke, the boys tell him to go to Brownie's Alley, an' I'd put him up till he got lucky. Then mebbe he'd go, an' somebody else would come along, guitar pickers, something like that. That's how we got along.' In those days Brownie ran two juke bands which played local engagements at roadhouses, jukes and parties. The personnel varied according to the singers and musicians who were presently living in

Knoxville or staying awhile in Brownie's Alley, but the instrumentation was generally two guitars, a string bass, harmonica perhaps, and two washboards – 'one on the belly, one on the horse' – in other words, one washboard played on the lap, whilst the other player used two instruments strapped to a structure similar to a sawing horse which he straddled as he played. One of the washboard players was Leroy Dallas, famed today as a blues singer and guitarist. Another was Robert Young, known as 'Washboard Slim'. Sometimes Jordan Webb sat in on harmonica when he was in town – and it was Jordan Webb who was at least partly instrumental in getting Brownie on record.

In the late Thirties Brownie was on the move again, playing in the streets of one township or another. Sometimes he worked in the company towns but their system of payment by credit notes which could only be tendered in the company stores hardly appealed to him. He pushed on to Asheville, North Carolina, where he met up with one Peg Leg who played two harmonicas at once – one with his nose and one with his mouth. Then east again to Winston Salem, North Carolina. Winston Salem was a tobacco town centred around the firm of Reynolds, manufacturers of Camel cigarettes. The factories employed girl operatives and Brownie worked out for himself a circuit of the factories outside which he played when the girls finished work. 'Man, it was pay-day every night if you work' it right! Mebbe a girl take you up, feed you a good meal, too.' But Winston Salem had a law against begging. One day a policeman quietly warned Brownie to get out of town. He got out, but came back in the evening and 'got caught – run me in the hoosegow.' Though he talked himself out of an enforced vacation he knew that the police were serious. Jordan Webb lived in the town and Brownie spent the night at his home, but he was being 'run out of town' and he knew that he had to leave the following morning. Webb, though a stonemason by trade, was a veritable one-man band and brilliant harmonica player and he elected to go with Brownie. The next day Brownie bid goodbye to the tough neighbourhoods of the 11th Street Bottom, the 'Pond' and the corners of Fourth and Vine, and Seventh and Patterson which had paid off so well, and commenced a three-week hitch-hike to Greensboro, stopping off at villages on the way.

Beating their way east from Greensboro along the Southern railroad they reached Burlington where they met up with a washboard player by the name of George Washington. With sandy-coloured hair and pinkish complexion he was known as 'Oh Red'. Red introduced Brownie to a guitarist whose reputation extended far beyond the immediate area: Blind Boy Fuller, and his harp-player Sonny Terry. It was an historic meeting, though at this time Brownie had no thought of teaming with Sonny, who was working and living with Fuller. Oh Red was able to get Brownie an introduction to meet J. B. Long, the owner of a large department store in Durham who was Fuller's manager and who had strong connections with the Columbia and Okeh companies and who, as mayor of a nearby township, was quite an important local figure. Long was clearly more impressed with Brownie's playing than Fuller admitted to be – for the latter was somewhat grudging in his comments – and arranged for Brownie to go to Chicago to record. 'He offered me $500 to go, somethin' like that. Man, that much money! And I'd've gone for the trip to Chicago alone!' So on 6 August 1940, with Oh Red and Jordan Webb to accompany him, Brownie cut his first record: 'Picking My Tomatoes', together with three other titles, and the following day cut eight

others. It was a fine debut and established Brownie immediately as an outstanding blues singer and guitarist, though he was not yet twenty-five.

Brownie's guitar was a cheap model Gibson, possibly a Kalamazoo made under the name of Stewart. But within a short while he was playing another instrument: Blind Boy Fuller's heavy steel-bodied National. Fuller had died and his guitar passed into Brownie's hands. On 23 May 1941 he cut 'The Death of Blind Boy Fuller', playing that very instrument. In his blues he declared that he was 'carrying his business on' but it was J. B. Long who had the idea of billing Brownie as 'Blind Boy Fuller No. 2', a sobriquet which he had much cause to regret. 'I didn't want to be a second Fuller. I was Brownie McGhee and I *wanted* to be Brownie McGhee,' he recalled, still with some indignation.

A few months later, in October, a riotous car-load of Carolina blues singers made its way to Chicago, including Jordan Webb, Sonny Terry, Robert 'Washboard Slim' Young with his board hung with cowbells and gadgets, George 'Oh Red' Washington with *his* board and the forks that he played it with, Buddy Moss and Brownie McGhee complete with their guitars. In the lively sessions that followed they cut sides with various combinations: Brownie accompanied by one harmonica or another, or both; harmonica duets; one washboard or the other and finally, to close the session, Buddy Moss stepped in to play second guitar on 'Swing Soldier, Swing' with both Young and Washington on boards. Brownie by the way, returned the honours by playing *piano* on Buddy's 'Joy Rag' and certain other titles. It was Buddy Moss who drew Brownie's attention to the little name that appeared under the title of the tune – the 'composer credit' – and he explained that royalties were being paid for this. All this was new to Brownie who had not expected that royalties were to be paid as well as the session fee; the name that appeared under some of his titles and many of Fuller's was J. B. Long. 'But I don't bear no grudge man, that's how you learn. An' he got me on record so I didn't complain. But Buddy, he told me a lot of things like that.'

From the proceeds of his first records Brownie bought himself a new guitar, a Gibson J.200, the largest that they made. A huge instrument with an hour-glass body and flourishing ebony bridge, it had a spliced back and a metal rod that passed through the neck to a clamp at the top which could be used to correct any warp or fault arising in the course of use. He has it today, but now he has an amplifier attached. The full, round tone of the Gibson and its great volume proved to be assets for Brownie during the ensuing few years. Recording was at a standstill during the war and Brownie found himself often working on the streets again. But now it was on the streets of New York. He had decided to make his home in New York with a view to making money, but he had to work hard and his jobs as an entertainer were many and varied. Now he was usually to be found in the company of Sonny Terry who had first come to New York in December 1938, and who had also made the City his home. The two men worked and lived with the great Huddie Ledbetter, and Brownie secured cabaret and club engagements, advertising them by playing in the streets. Now he met other blues artists and folk singers, including Big Bill Broonzy and Pete Seeger, and appeared on various dates with them. But he still found time to sing with the Spiritual Keys on Sunday in church.

Late in 1944 he secured a recording contract with Savoy and a little over a year later made his recordings for Alert. These were for issue almost exclusively in the South and proved to be exceedingly popular. He liked

to back a 'standard' with an 'original', for he was shrewd enough to realize that the standard would sell his new blues composition and he would draw royalties on the latter. His fame began to increase rapidly and on the strength of his gathering reputation he opened on 125th Street, New York, 'Brownie McGhee's Home of the Blues', which he ran for some three years as a school for blues guitarists. His first pupil was Alec Stewart 'but he didn't study enough; didn't come more than three times a week'. It was a brave venture and gave a start to such singers and guitarists as Lewis 'Jelly Belly' Hayes and an opportunity for many youngsters to learn something of the blues. Here his record collection came in useful. Brownie had long collected the records of early singers such as Texas Alexander, Blind Lemon Jefferson, and Teddy Edwards one of whose songs became 'Barbecue any old Time' – and although many of the records were destroyed in Knoxville during Brownie's absence he added to the remainder with care. His was a business venture though he was primarily interested in promoting young singers, and he kept his books meticulously, with the result that he had developed a prodigious memory for the activities of singers that he knew.

Until the formation for recording purposes of Dan Burley's 'Skiffle' Boys, Brownie had never heard the term 'skiffle' used and its choice had indeed been arbitrary. On these memorable recordings for Circle his brother Granville also played. Granville had previously played drums and had been called 'Sticks' in recognition of the fact, but during his war service he learned to play the guitar and developed the habit of writing the name of every foreign place that he visited on the body of the instrument. It soon became a record of his travels – and 'Globetrotter' McGhee was the inevitable change of name.

For a while in 1947 Brownie worked for a

vendor of voodoo charms and philtres, an unusual assignment which he marked by recording 'Secret Mojo Blues' for Disc. In the ensuing years his Alert and Savoy recordings were fighting each other for places on the market and the name of Brownie McGhee was becoming almost too well known. 'Man they'd get sick of Brownie McGhee' he reasoned, and began to record under pseudonyms: as the Tennessee Gabriel for Circle; as Spider Sam for Atlantic; as Big Tom Collins with Champion Jack Dupree on piano for King; as Henry Johnson for Decca, accompanied by a white group; and as Blind Boy Williams for Jade, on which session he played piano whilst brother Granville played guitar. The seal was set on his career with the issue of 'My Fault' on Savoy 5551, which he cut with Lonnie Scott on piano and Hal Singer on tenor. Curiously, there was much opposition to his making the track but Brownie, for whom the song had particular meaning, was determined to make it. It proved an outstanding success. 'For twelve weeks my record was on the top of the *Billboard* list; it gave me the greatest kick ever. Wherever I went there was "My Fault" by Brownie McGhee . . . it was just wonderful you know?'

Champion Jack Dupree, Melvin Merritt and Van Walls frequently accompanied Brownie on piano when recording, but in his work, as an artist, he was ever more in the company of Sonny Terry, for their long association made them extremely sympathetic to each other's ideas and styles. In 1950 they formed with singer Coyal McMahon a group called the 'Folkmasters'. As Coyal did not play an instrument – bar the maracas – he was nominal leader, but his trained voice did not suit the group ideally. In spite of the success of their 'Get on Board' album for Folkways they obtained relatively few engagements and they were forced to disband. Brownie accepted the minor failure

philosophically for he was now recording for innumerable companies and was providing the accompaniment for such singers as Bobby Harris, Bessie Griffin, Buddy Lucas and Ethel Davenport, to mention only a few. He was to be heard in the company of the late Ralph Willis on such labels as Abbey, Prestige, Jubilee and Signal and with the great Blind Gary Davis, for whom he has the most profound admiration, on Continental.

In 1950 he married his charming and attractive wife Ruth and began to raise his family of three children: two daughters, Vediazella and Vilhemina (called 'Bonnie' – a contraction of 'Brownie'); and his son George Walter. Regular employment was necessary with his added responsibilities, which fortunately came with a speaking and playing part in Langston Hughes' 'Simply Heavenly' in which he played the part of 'Git-fiddle'. Followed by an opportunity to play the background music to the documentary film *The Roosevelt Story* in which Canada Lee spoke the narration, and a three-year engagement with Sonny Terry in the Broadway production of *Cat on a Hot Tin Roof*. Recently he provided the music for Kazan's film production *Face in the Crowd* and in recognition Andy Griffin made him a present of the Martin guitar which he now plays.

These days Brownie McGhee appears on television, at concerts and folk song festivals, in schools, in clubs and cabarets – travelling up, down and across the country. Sometimes he works with Blind Gary Davis, Guy Carawan or Pete Seeger; at other times he plays in Negro blues clubs where the tough music of Little Junior Parker or Little Walter Jacobs on harps, Champion Jack Dupree or Sunnyland Slim on piano, provides fitting accompaniment. For the past four years he has had Bob Gaddy as frequent accompanist on piano, but though they do not always work together his true partnership is with his companion of nearly a score of years, Sonny Terry. Together they have evolved a perfect relationship, a harmony that is as manifest in their friendship as in their playing. Sonny plays the harmonica 'crossed' in the manner of Jordan Webb and other folk players; holding his harp upside down, with the treble to the left, he plays an A harmonica when Brownie with guitar tuned '4/40 – concert pitch' plays in E. When Brownie plays in A, Sonny plays his D harmonica, producing the strange blue harmonies that are such a feature of their work together. Sonny frequently leads, for he sings fairly straight in his rich grainy voice, whilst Brownie harmonizes an improvised vocal counterpoint. His own voice has been softened but not sweetened in the years and has greatly increased in range. At times, as in his version of Fuller's 'Lost Lover Blues', he sings full and deep, and it is Sonny who sings an octave higher. Because it gives a certain 'edge' to the music, Sonny likes him to use a capo on the first fret, but Brownie has no need of the capo. 'If I can't play a piece in every key, I won't meddle with it,' he declares, which

means in fact that he can play any tune in his repertoire in any key. His versatility extends to witty interpretations of the style of Gary Davis or Big Bill Broonzy, and few records demonstrate his remarkable skill; none his consummate ease and relaxation as he plays with fingers that barely brush the strings. In his pocket he carries a length of brass tubing cut and slit with a hacksaw until it fitted his little finger, and with it he plays the whinning, moaning guitar blues of the bottleneck style – but this he has yet to put on record, for he is too self-critical. 'I've never made a record which I really liked; never made one I couldn't find faults in. But I'll keep right on trying.' Those collectors who are familiar with his recordings may argue with Brownie's own estimation of his worth – he considers himself a 'damn good entertainer' but does not think of himself as a musician. In experience as a blues singer Brownie is a veteran, but in years he is still relatively young. The blues are in his fingers, his voice, his thoughts and his life. And whilst Brownie is with us to play and sing, the blues are in safe keeping.

Jazz Monthly, August 1958

Lonesome Bedroom
CURTIS JONES

In the appreciation of any art form it is customary to categorize the artists by style, period or technique. Such categories can be arbitrary and artificial but they aid comparison, give indications of affinities of expression and reveal the existence of schools of thought and creation. A minor art like the blues still lends itself to such classification and we talk, too glibly at times, of 'the country blues', or of 'city blues', 'classic blues', the 'Mississippi blues'. Some blues singers fall easily into such groups but Curtis Jones defies any such simple definition. He is the bluesman's blues singer. All that he plays and sings is blues, but it cannot be lightly asserted that he represents the blues of Texas, where he was born, or of the West where he worked for some years. His is not merely 'Chicago blues', though he lived there for a quarter of a century. And how does one type a blues singer who has made Paris, France, his home?

A little less than medium height and slightly stooped, Curtis Jones has a stocky build and deceptively broad shoulders which hint at the strength that he can summon in his playing. His dark features are creased now where early photographs showed dimples and the corners of his eyes are drawn. A wisp of a moustache and slight goatee beard are greying and his hair, always immaculately ridged, is showing signs of his age. There is something of the Plains Indian in his features which have at times a similar inscrutability. Then he breaks into a soft laugh and talks quietly in his grainy, unemotional voice. There is nothing sensational about Curtis Jones. He has no outgoing, extrovert personality and has none of the exaggerated mannerisms of the professional entertainer. He is modest, makes no attempt to impress and talks with unassuming candour of his experiences. As he talks one realizes that the blues is his whole life, and because he has lived along with the blues the changes of style that one comes to associate with period or place all have relevance to one phase or another of his career.

Curtis was born in a farming community in the small town of Naples. Texas, on the Louisiana border on 18 August 1906. His parents had lived in the district all their lives and were very poor, hardworking sharecroppers. When Curtis was six years old his mother Agnes Logan died but Willie Jones, his father, kept the family together and continued to work the land. Curtis started to work in the fields at the age of eight and came in contact with adult migrant workers. Many of these sang the field work songs that were the primitive form of the blues and some played guitar or harmonica. Curtis himself tried 'scratching' the guitar (as he calls it) at that early age and soon acquired considerable skill. He was to give up the guitar for the piano only a few years later, and although he eventually became a prolific recording artist he never recorded playing his first instrument. The blues that he sang were those which reflected his immediate world. Now, recording with guitar for the first time, he sings 'Red River Blues' about the great river that divides Louisiana and Texas, in a pure country tradition which he has almost unwittingly preserved in this form for almost fifty years.

When he was ten years old Curtis Jones moved to Dallas. His prematurely adult life was extremely hard for him and the years of scuffling he treats lightly now. 'Skid Row is in your town,' he says meaning that he was virtually 'on the skids' wherever he went in

those early years. It is the theme of his other
blues on which he plays guitar, 'Skid Row'.
In Dallas he gave up the guitar for the organ
and the piano, at first playing in a style which
clearly derived from his guitar technique
and then, as he learned more about his new
instrument, developing a piano technique of
his own. He sang and played at joints in the
city and in the Negro resorts that lay outside
the city limits. In his late teens he met up
with the important Dallas blues pianist
Whistling Alex Moore who was also known
as 'Papa Chittlins'. He sometimes sang
whilst Alex Moore played and has a distinct
recollection of recording with him about
1924 although the records were apparently
not released. Alex Moore remained in Dallas
where he was still living and playing when I
met him in 1960, but Curtis, a few years his
junior, was unsettled. It was the bootlegging
era and Curtis was caught up in it. He ran a
little bootlegging venture of his own but the
police caught up with him and he spent
forty-seven days in jail. When he came out
he was told in no uncertain terms that he
could 'shake the dust of Dallas off his feet'.
Curtis hopped a freight train and cut out for
Wichita.

The next couple of years found him singing and playing in a bewildering succession
of locations and townships as he beat his way
to Newton Kansas, Topeka, and ultimately
Kansas City. In Kansas City he hit the real
nightlife of a wide-open town in a hard-
drinking era. 'Alley Bound Blues' is a cameo
of his life at that time. He worked 'off the
Twist' at 1314 Harlem, and met up with a
multitude of blues singers and musicians
who thronged the subway at 18th and Vine.
Engagements at Nates' on 12th and Lydia,
at the Panama on 18th followed, and the end
of 1931 found him on the move again.

'They were mostly good-time houses I
was playing at, because I wasn't good
enough for the joints,' explained Curtis

Jones with a fine emphasis on the nature of
the places where he worked, 'I was learning all the time.' He struck out West to
areas where the Negro communities were
extremely small and where he was greatly
welcome as a blues singer – Cheyenne and
Laramie in Wyoming, Reno in Nevada. In
Cheyenne he met up with a company of the
Georgia Strollers minstrel show. It was a
lucky encounter for they needed a pianist
and for the next nine months he toured with
them, playing at a different town every
night. Through the small townships of
Wyoming, North Dakota, South Dakota
they toured and played, finally reaching
Fremont, Nebraska, where they played the
Empress Theatre. He had enjoyed the spell
on the road but it was hard and taxing work.
Now just forty-five miles from Omaha, he
teamed up with a girl to work a double act
for a while in that city. But he had itching
feet and by Christmas he was back in Kansas
City where he played for a spell before trying his luck in the joints of Oklahoma City.
There he stayed at the Little M and M Hotel
– the one for coloured – and sang in a number of the spots in the lively mid-West
town. He had ideas of reaching Dallas and
when the weather was warm enough and he
could stand the exposure of riding the freight
cars, he hopped a train to Texas.

Dallas proved to be an uneasy stop, for
though Curtis' record was not a particularly
bad one, he was remembered. Texakarna
and Shreveport followed, and after a while
playing at Stiffly and Willie's joint on Main
Street, Shreveport, he hoboed across Louisiana to Baton Rouge. This part of Texas
and Louisiana is blues piano country and
Curtis had plenty of competition. By now
though, he could hold his own with the best
of them and found himself a good job as a
pianist at the Anchorage in West Baton
Rouge. The workers in the area were largely
employed on sugar cane plantations and

they made a tough, enthusiastic audience, crap-shooters to a man. Curtis heard of a big crap game running at a joint on the outskirts of town on the North side. But he was a newcomer to the area and someone 'put the finger' on him to the police. He was taken to the jail, innocent bystander though he had been, stripped and given twenty-five licks of the lash. 'Don't let the sun go down on you, buddy,' the police told him. 'Hell!' says Curtis, 'it was six o'clock already!' All the same he wisely took their advice and caught the next freight train for New Orleans.

In New Orleans Curtis Jones secured a good job working as pianist in a club owned by a noted local politician. He settled down for a while with his wife Lula Stigers until he decided to follow the many other bluesmen who had gone North to Chicago. 1936 saw the worst of the Depression over and Curtis in Chicago. For him conditions there were much better than those that he had often experienced and he was determined to make the city his home.

He gathered a few musicians to his side – trumpet player Lawrence Hall, tenor sax player Jasper Edwards and Bob Harris on drums. With his group he obtained good work in South Side joints and his unique piano soon attracted the attention of Lester Melrose who offered him a contract with Vocalion. So his recording career started in September 1937, but unhappily his wife Lula did not stay with him to see it through. 'Lonesome Bedroom Blues' was the result of her leaving, and perhaps because it was so heartfelt it was an outstanding seller in the Vocalion Race List.

In the next few years Curtis Jones' name was known to every Negro area through his highly popular blues recordings. Many of his blues like 'Highway 51' or 'Bull and Cow Blues' were celebrated items with other blues singers and he was greatly re-spected for his husky, sincere singing and unusually personal way of playing. His piano style was economical but deceptively simple. Big Bill Broonzy was under the impression that no one could play with Curtis because of his original phrasing, although in fact two guitarists who themselves derived much from Broonzy accompanied Curtis frequently. Willie B. James was one of them, and the other, 'Hot Box' Johnson, was his regular guitarist for a long time. Hopson 'Hot Box' Johnson eventually gave up the blues and the guitar for the church and is today a preacher in Chicago. Freddy Flynn, the drummer, sometimes accompanied him, and his later records also featured the harmonica of Jazz Gillum. He did not record with his band however as such groups were not greatly to Melrose's liking at that time. On club dates he liked a band with him, or at least a rhythm group, and on the present session he had the sort of group that he liked to back him up on some items.

The War brought the virtual end of Curits' recording career for almost twenty years with the exception of a single, un-promising date in 1952. To the blues-buying public he was largely forgotten although he had spates when he worked with his band at Chicago clubs. In the leaner years he scuffled back on Skid Row again until the times became less hard. He did not forsake the blues, for the blues was the music that he knew. Sometimes his playing looked back to the long blues tradition behind him, as 'Curtis Jones Boogie' for example, cast in a traditional blues-boogie pattern. But he also moved with the times and the post-war blues idioms are an essential part of his music too. He pays tribute to one of the most important of the blues singers who emerged in the post-war years and who died just before the present record was made, Elmore James, with that singer's famous 'Dust My Broom' played in a powerful boogie version. Another figure of the more modern blues scene, Joe Liggins, is remembered with a refreshing and original interpretation of his well-known 'Honey-dripper' whilst he even remodels Percy Mayfield's 'Please Send Me Someone to Love' into a blues version.

When the French blues authority Jacques Demetre found Curtis Jones in the summer of 1959 after a tip from Sunnyland Slim, he was living in miserable circumstances in one room of a shabby hotel at 3953 South Michigan. If the conditions were wretched, Curtis retained his personal dignity and optimism, looking forward to a brighter day in the future. It took courage for him to leave even this setting in the Chicago that he knew well to try his luck in another country on another continent where he was totally unknown. Stranger though he might be, he decided to take the risk for he was at least no stranger to travel. In 1962 at the age of fifty-six Curtis Jones commenced a new life in France, his optimism and his creative faculties undiminished. There, an ageing man, he creates exciting music which delights the young generation (for whom he named his new boogie with its latin-styled rhythm) with a rocking 'Shake It Baby', or charms them with his first attempts at a new language with 'Syl Voo Play Blues'.

Notes to Decca LK 4587, 1964

Curtis Jones died Munich, Germany, 11 September 1971

A Rollin' Mind
CHAMPION JACK DUPREE

Home Coming Midnight Ramble
featuring New Orleans own
JACK DUPREE
King of the Junkers, direct from the
World Famous
COTTON CLUB,
Indianapolis, Indiana
In a Midnite Ramble at the
LINCOLN THEATRE
Washington Ave, & Feret Street
Sat, Nite, August 2nd 1941
Doors open at 11.30 pm
featuring in person, Jessie Edward, King of
Electric guitar players Ruth Dupree, 1940
Queen of New York World's Fair Jitter Bugs
KING DUPREE recording star of
Angola Angola Blues, the Junkers
many others
A hip-swinging chorus of Brown Skin
Sweethearts and many other acts including
the Comedians Convention with Pee Wee,
King Kubs, the Algiers Terror, and
Jack Dupree, King of the Blues.
Admission – 21¢
pay at the door

Jack Dupree was just thirty-one years of age. In the space of a couple of years he had been playing piano and singing his blues professionally, and now the city that had given him small attention when he had returned there frequently as a hobo, was welcoming him as Jack Dupree, King of the Blues. Still a comparatively young man, he had behind him a lifetime of hard experience which enabled him to meet the change in his fortunes with humour and philosophical acceptance. 'Sometimes I've been up, sometimes I've been down . . . don't make no difference. I've never worried about tomorrow if I've got enough to eat for today,' he says, explaining his capacity to take the good times with the bad. But as Jack Dupree talks on in sober, matter-of-

fact tones that contrast with the extrovert nature of his 'act', one cannot but remark that he has had more than his share of hard times.

The youngest of five children, Jack Dupree was born in a house in the 'Irish Channel' of New Orleans, on 4 July 1910. His parents kept a grocery store where they sold, amongst many other commodities, fuel oil for kerosene lamps. One night when Jack was barely a year old, one of the large oil containers exploded. The circumstances were never satisfactorily explained but the flaming oil pouring from the cans made the house a holocaust within minutes. Shortly after the start of the fire the first floor fell in and Jack's parents were consumed in the flames. Somehow he was thrown clear and a fireman rescued the coloured child and brought him from the burning building to safety. 'Whenever I goes to New Orleans that old fireman still reminds me that if it wasn't for him I wouldn't be here at all.' The elder children could not care for Jack and he was sent to the Colored Waifs' Home for Boys where he was raised from infancy.

'That was my onliest home – didn't have no other. I sure was lonely. Come Christmas all the other children would have presents but there weren't none for me. Every Saturday I'd look at the board where some of the other kids would have letters and parcels and things, but there never was anything for Jack Dupree. One time though, one of the wardens there he said to me "How come you don't have any presents or money to buy candy for you on the board?" I told him nobody left me none. And after that he always left me a little money on the board for me to buy – y'know, peppermint candy an' things, jus' kids' stuff. But I sure did appreciate that, and I do now.' Jack's brothers and sisters were leading their own lives and, being older than he, had little to do with him. One brother, George Dupree, went North to Chicago where he was a detective for some twenty years. Another, Victor, worked in a hospital whilst his sisters Dora and Bernadette married and settled down. At the age of fourteen Jack left the Colored Waifs' Home and attempted to join one of his sisters, 'but her husband and me, we didn't get on so well, so I quit and just played in the streets. When night time come I'd just curl up where I could, maybe on a grating where it was warm, and go to sleep.' There followed a dark and miserable period for the fourteen-year-old boy, who begged and snatched what he could to eat. He made friends with a boy of his own age and together they played in the French Quarter.

'When he'd go home to bed I wouldn't say nothin', but one day he asked me where I lived. I told him no place. So Richard asked his mama if I could come home with him. She says "one more child won't make no diff'rence if you just take it as it comes" and she looked after me. Her name was Olivia Gardner and she was the only mother I ever knew. Her husband worked on the railroad and looked after all of us kids. He died a few years ago but the old lady is still alive and I go to see her whenever I'm back in New Orleans. I last saw Richard about four years past.'

Such money as Jack brought in was largely obtained by begging and from tips. He had shown an ability for singing in the Colored Waifs' Home and he would stand in the corner of one of the many dives on Franklin or Rampart Street singing for coins. Though really too young to be admitted, he was able to get by with his singing provided he kept out of the way. 'Seems I always sang the blues; can't remember when I first heard

them. There was many good blues singers in those joints – there was Little Butch I remember. He used to sing that 'How Long Blues' but it was Leroy Carr who eventually made the record. Little Butch didn't make no records. I'm telling you, those were really low-down joints, none of them guys ever sang in the dictier places and they never made no records. There was a good blues singer we used to call "Rabbie", and there was Ruby Gules who used to sing the blues and played good piano. He's in Chicago now.'

Jack Dupree would wander from one joint to another, singing with, and learning from, the barrelhouse pianists who worked them. Of these, the man who particularly appealed to him was a rough and powerful pianist know in the tough red-light district as 'Drive-'em-Down', – 'he didn't have no other name that I knew of.' Standing in his corner, singing his blues in his youngster's voice, Jack Dupree watched and studied the older man's style and learned from him such blues-ballads as 'Stackolee'. Drive-'em-Down lived on Poydras Street and played in many of the local barrelhouse joints such as Del Peas on Franklin Street – 'man, that was some hole-in-the-wall'. Another rough and low place was run by 'Sam the Wine Man' and situated on Rampart Street. 'He used to sell that "Splo" and that "Sneaky Pete" wine. That's where I learned that the drink'll really get you. That's why I don't touch nothing but a glass of beer or maybe a glass of whiskey before I start playing.' Tony's Place on Saratoga and Gravier was another favourite rendezvous of the longshoremen and railroad men who made up the majority of the customers at the barrelhouses where Jack learned his blues. In these and other joints other pianists also worked, amongst them Willie Hall, 'Red' Toots, Bill Fugus and a 'great girl pianist, Margaret Bush who played real barrelhouse music at the Cotton

Club on Rampart Street'. Of the better known New Orleans pianists Jack Dupree knew nothing; his world was a tougher, rougher one than even they experienced and of the blues pianists that he knew, nothing has been written and he may himself be the only source of information.

On Sundays in New Orleans Jack would board the 'wagons' advertising dance functions and sing with the rougher Negro jazz bands who still worked in the city after the close of Storyville. Amongst those he recalls particularly were the bands of Kid Rena, Papa Celestin and Chris Kelly and he is emphatic in his praise of those men in their best years. Living and working in a tough neighbourhood had its disadvantages; 'stay a little too long, get yourself in a fight and you liable to get yourself killed,' he comments drily. His years in the Waifs' Home and on the streets had taught him to fend for himself in spite of his diminutive size and he found himself visiting ever more frequently Kid Green's Boxing School on Rampart Street. It was a school of roughhouse fighting, perhaps not over-attentive to the finer aspects of the gentle art, but it gave Jack a source of income. He joined Kid Green's team of boxers on an irregular basis and prepared to take on all comers in the lightweight class, at 9 stone 12 lbs. Boxing became his job. Often he would cross over to Algiers to fight with the tough neighbourhood boys from that Quarter; at other times he would travel in the State and sometimes outside Louisiana, wherever he was required to fight. Sometimes it was at the Golden Gloves – a proper ring; other times he would fight in gymnasiums, clubs and society rooms, baseball parks and basketball arenas. 'Didn't make much money – $40 for six rounds; $90 if you went ten. But it kept me in food and clothes and I could take a bit back for Mrs Gardner.'

There were periods of inactivity and dur-ing these Jack Dupree would wander out of the State, hoboing his way up the Illinois Central line. In this way he found himself at the age of seventeen as far north as Chicago. Whenever he went he would rapidly seek out the blues singers and the piano players, naturally gravitating to those with whom he had some kinship. So it was that he met Pinetop Smith in Chicago, who was only a few years older than himself. Clarence Smith, he states, was called 'Pinetop' not so much for his height, which was admittedly above average, but for his red hair. He had a friend, Fisher, who was a little older, who also played slow blues and boogie piano and who shared the characteristic of red hair. Pinetop and Fisher roomed together and were often to be seen in each other's company. When he had hoboed to Chicago, Jack Dupree was to be found with them. Fisher ran a Club on Indiana Avenue, where he himself would play piano and where Pinetop Smith would also play. Unfortunately Fisher's temper would occasionally get the better of him and over a small altercation with a customer he got into a fight and pulled a razor, leaving the patron with his features expertly and swiftly slashed. The man ran from the club and Fisher turned to the piano where he played a while before Pinetop Smith took over. A short while after, the door swung open, a gun was pulled and the red-haired Pinetop was shot through the back of the head as he sat at the piano; slaughtered, according to Jack Dupree who claims to have been present, in mistake for the similarly coiffed Fisher. Such vendettas and sudden murders were not uncommon in this environment, explains Jack: 'Once I saw a guy get into an argument over a two-dollar bet when he was playing dice. The other fellow went back, and got him a shot-gun; came back and shoved it clean down his throat and pulled the trigger – "bam!" Killed him for two dollars!'

Times were especially hard in the mid-Thirties and boxing promotions were fewer. Jack hoboed his way up the IC line again, dropping off the train when he saw the approaching 'railroad bulls'. On one such occasion he begged a bag of biscuits and retired to the woods to eat them. It was then that he saw a stiff, motionless figure, a white boy who was close to death from starvation. 'He just about crawled to me, and he ate all them biscuits from my hand – jest like a dawg,' recalled Jack shaking his head with wonderment still at the memory. The two hobos became good friends and bummed around the States together for the next three years, returning on occasion to New Orleans. On one occasion Jack and his companion – Wilford Le Shay – spied an orange grove from the box car in which they were riding, and they dropped off the car to stock themselves up with fruit from the orchard before continuing their way to Detroit. The owner had different plans and set a trained police dog on them. They separated but the dog caught Wilford and held him until his owner came. Jack had a good start and made for open country, finally hiding in long grass. He thought he had escaped but the sniffing of the hound was soon too close for comfort. 'Here I am!' he shouted in surrender to the dog and sprang up for the animal to see him. He still laughs at the incident: 'Well, the man says, "I'm gonna take you to the judge". And he did. The judge sentenced us to sixty days. We didn't mind, we weren't really goin' no place anyways. So they locked us up in the County jail. After the second day the warder says "Would you boys like to look after the boiler-house?" We told him yes, and we moved our cots down by the boiler. Man, we could go out to the grocery store or to a movie any time we liked! We were real sorry when them sixty days was up!' The incident stands out as comic relief in a tough story of bumming,

begging and sleeping in the jungles.

Jack's boxing career continued intermittently until 1940, when he fought his last bout. In 107 professional bouts he had been knocked out only twice, and he had a succession of triumphs to his credit, one of the last being the occasion when he knocked out Battling Bozo in the tenth round. It was not his last fight, but he was beginning to lose interest in being battered about the face and head. When he lost to Bob Montgomery on points by referee's decision he felt he had battled enough and resolved to quit the ring. He decided he would try his luck in New York.

There was one way to get to New York for Jack Dupree – as a hobo. By stages he bummed his way north and he eventually made Indiana. On the outskirts of Indianapolis a railroad detective spotted him and was determined to make a 'kill'. When Jack dropped from the fast-moving freight train the 'bull' dropped from it too, and with a gap between them too small for comfort Jack ran down the track until he was able to make a break for the cover of the slums of the city. In the warren of streets he lost his pursuer, but it was now dark, wet and cold. He decided to investigate some of his old haunts. Jack Dupree was no stranger to Indianapolis; he had known the town when Leroy Carr was in his prime and had lived in the great singer's company for quite a while. 'He was sure some ugly man . . . he was real ugly, but he could play a mess of blues.' Now, however, Carr was dead and times had changed. Some of his old blues companions, Scrapper Blackwell and Little Bill Gaither among them, were still around and Jack readily settled in to the blues world of the city. Soon he was holding down the piano chair at C. Ferguson's Cotton Club where Carr himself had once been the star pianist. He forgot New York.

Press clippings from the column 'In the Groove' written by Elizabeth Brizentre-Taft 'alias Ye Scribe' and from the writings of other reporters to the Indianapolis papers, tell the story of Jack Dupree's rapid growth in stature as pianist, blues singer and entertainer. From the compliments paid initially to 'a new pianist, unknown to me' the notices change to a page-wide spread with photographs of Jack and a number of entertainers under a banner headline:

DUPREE'S FLOOR SHOW CLICKS
at Cotton Club
Popular Singer–Comedian is the tops.

A born entertainer who had previously suffered from too few opportunities to express himself, Jack Dupree was in his element. His many years of boxing had made him swift and light on his feet and, like many boxers, he was an accomplished dancer. The days when he had hung around Silas Green's premises on Rampart Street and when he had taught the girls of Bessie Smith's last troupe the steps of his own brand of sand dance and shimmy, now stood him in good stead. He danced, clowned, rolled his barrelhouse boogie and shouted his blues to the sweating, dancing throng at the Club. He gathered a good company of dancers and entertainers, singers and blues artists about him, changing the bill but remaining at the solid blues core himself. Noted Elizabeth Taft on the Cotton Club a little later:

'Lillie Mae breakin' the house down and Jack Dupree settling himself down in strict Dupree style . . .' and again: 'the show at the Cotton Club continues to pack them in.' Later Jack was joined by a fat, jovial comedienne with a ripe sense of humour and a gift for timing which matched perfectly his own. He had mastered a technique of talking blues and racy commentaries whilst rolling his boogie patterns at the piano and Ophelia Hoy's own lack of inhibitions, her ample proportions and Jack's small stature and expressive grimacing and eyebrow-raising

brought the house down. 'Ophelia Hoy and Jack Dupree are better than Butterbeans and Susie with all their years behind them,' ran one enthusiastic report. For his Master of Ceremonies, Jack employed a 'snakehips' dancer – a master at Jack's own dancing speciality – named George 'Rubberlegs' Williams. He was an excellent entertainer though Jack was unable to confirm whether he was the George Williams who had partnered Bessie Brown fifteen years before or the Rubberlegs Williams who recorded a few years after, for Savoy.

One of Jack Dupree's outstanding performers was the late 'Queen of the Jitterbugs' at the New York World's Fair, whom he married, Ruth Dupree. She was a sensational dancer as well as being most attractive and added to the show's appeal. Two years after he had commenced at the Cotton Club the reporters still commented on a show that did not get stale: 'S'funny how Jack Dupree always manages to bring the house down on Sunday night . . .' Jack Dupree's fame spread and brought him in the summer of 1940 a recording session in Chicago on which he was accompanied by his favourite bass player from Indianapolis, Wilson Swain and, on 'Gamblin' Man Blues' at least, guitarist Scrapper Blackwell. These recordings, issued on Okeh as by 'Champion' Jack Dupree, established him as a blues pianist of exceptional power and a singer of feeling and distinction. The subjects were scarcely those to be expected from a club entertainer, 'Warehouse Man Blues' dealing with the attempts to counter dietary deficiencies by the supply of grapefruit juice, 'Angola Blues' being devoted to the notorious Louisiana prison and 'Chain Gang Blues' being in similar vein. But such items as 'Black Woman Swing' and 'Cabbage Greens' revealed him in a less serious if no less earthy mood.

In January the following year Dupree was

again in the recording studios for a couple of sessions, the second producing the 'Dupree Shake Dance' which is a classic of its kind. Other titles were devoted to social evils, including 'My Cabin Inn' with its fierce bass figures, 'Weed Head Woman' and 'Junker Blues'. The latter items, dealing with drug addiction, have a subject frequently recurrent in Dupree's repertoire. They are there with a reason – two of his nephews died from drug taking, and their deaths and the fate of many other persons he has known in the grim world in which he has circulated have induced him to state, without moralizing, the dangers and the miseries of their effects.

Recordings featuring Dupree brought considerable custom to the Cotton Club and earned for the singer many out of town dates with his company. A one-night stand in Kokomo was typical:

SPRING DANCE
featuring JACK DUPREE,
KING OF THE BLUES
and his Bluebird (*sic*) Recording Orchestra
Direct from the Cotton Club, Indianapolis
Dance 9 until
Thel's Casino, Kokomo, Indiana
15 March 1941
Admission 35¢

Jack Dupree was riding high and he made a triumphant appearance at the Lincoln Theatre, New Orleans, in August. But the pressures of war had their effect on the night life even of the coloured wards of Indianapolis. 'Indianapolis went down . . . you had to close up at eleven o'clock.' One more session in Chicago for Okeh and Jack found his career temporarily suspended. He was called up for war service and drafted into the US Navy. A specialist in Creole gumbo when the ingredients were at hand, and at cooking in gallon cans over fires beside the railroad tracks when they were not, he was

taken on as a cook. From then until his release in 1945 he served in the Pacific theatre of war, eventually finding himself in Guam where there was more than enough action even for a man with experiences as hard as those that he had known.

During the course of the War Jack was sadly bereaved by the death of his wife Ruth, and when the War was over he had no desire to return to Indiana. Instead he settled in New York where he had made one or two records already on brief spells of leave. A further source of distress for him was the discovery through a coincidence, that his son who had been raised by his mother-in-law had got into trouble with a juvenile street gang and was now in reform school. Fortunately he managed to clear his son who is now serving with the regular US Army in Germany, to the pride of his father.

In the immediate post-war years his fortunes rose and fell. A series of recordings for Joe Davis on the label of this name brought him again before the public, demonstrating that his abilities as blues and barrelhouse pianist were unimpaired. On these his spoken passages iterated against a stop chorus or repeated rhythmic phrase became a feature which is now a hallmark of his style, and though a certain monotony of tune tends to creep into a number of these items, such recordings as 'Gin Mill Sal' and 'Johnson Street Boogie Woogie' are outstanding. Recordings did not provide a staple income and Jack moved from club to club, taking on semi-permanent bookings or acting as relief pianist as circumstances demanded. In this way he played at such clubs and centres as the Ringside Ball, the Spotlight on 52nd Street and the Italian Frank de Carlo's Mayfair Club in 125th Street. Regular employment was necessitated by his marriage in 1948 to Lucille Dalton, a registered nurse, and the subsequent growth of his family. His children now include his sons William Jack and Kelvin, and his daughters Ann Lucille, Julie Ann and Rose Mary – who has followed the unusual profession of mortician. Lucille Dupree has shown considerable and lively interest in her husband's work, and since 1955 has written most of the new compositions that he has recorded.

On a great many recording sessions Jack Dupree has worked with Brownie McGhee and Sonny Terry, being accompanied by them and acting as accompanist in turn. The association, starting in earnest in 1950, resulted in many outstanding recordings, some of which have become widely successful, including the Apollo releases of 'I'm Gonna Find You Someday', by 'Jack Du Pree and his Bucket Busters' according to the Apollo publicity sheets, and 'The Deacon's Party' which Apollo were moved to announce was 'Sweeping the Nation . . . by Jack Dupree – Original Blues Singer and Comedian de Luxe'. On these the piano was played by Wilbert 'Big Chief' Ellis, and Jack returned to his role of singer and entertainer. Subsequent records featured varying techniques and extension of subject-matter, including amongst them 'Tongue-Tied Blues' and 'Harelip Blues'. These titles have been commented upon as being caricatures of Southern or West Indian dialect, and have also been criticized for being humorous at the expense of persons physically afflicted. But no such intents were in his mind, he claims. 'I get the ideas for my records and my numbers from people I know and things I experience. It's people's lives I'm singin' about. There ain't nothin' funny in being tongue-tied. I got that idea from a tongue-tied man, and I sure feel sorry for him. *That ain't funny . . .* '

'I've got a rollin' mind . . . ' says Jack of his liking for travel. Although he has settled in New York he has frequently left to go on tour – one such trip in 1954 brought him to Detroit, where he found on point duty his old hobo companion Wilford Le Shay, now a policeman. The passing of the years in no way impaired their relationship and Jack was a welcome guest at Wilford's home. In 1958 he toured with Nappy Brown on an extensive trip through the States, and on his return accepted a two-week engagement offered by Big L. Price, Lloyd Price's brother, who runs the Celebrity Club on Sunrise Highway, Freeport, Long Island. The two-week engagement lasted forty-six weeks, and was only suspended when, at the invitation of 'Jazzshows' and Harold Davison Limited, he arrived in England and we were able to witness and hear at first hand the blues artistry of Champion Jack Dupree.

And it is an artistry that goes back to the roots of jazz, and yet in many ways is timeless. When he sits – or stands – at the piano and the left hand rolls its indomitable bass figures; when he leans back and hollers his blues, shuts his eyes and moans or utters his falsetto cries like a reincarnated Peetie Wheatstraw, the squabbles and disputes and categories and pigeonholes of jazz seem suddenly arbitrary and useless. Such moving, exhilarating, disturbing music and singing is a gauntlet thrown in the face of all petty argument and academic theory. Champion Jack Dupree's music stems from the barrelhouse of a New Orleans that now scarcely exists, but his blues at one and the same time is immediate, captivating, thoroughly of the present day. As he sings and plays, one is at once transported far back into jazz history and projected into the tumbling world of modern Harlem.

Superficially he seems two men: the near-diamond zircon in his ear, the tinselled tie, the long, orange drape jacket and peg-top trousers match the ogling, the bawdy lyrics, the bass figures that are fantastically produced from an elbow stomping on the keys and the passages played with the knuckles and the back of the hand; the frowning, thoughtful answers to questions, the readiness to discuss people and places as much as the music, link with the troubled, earnest meaningful blues that spring from a life of great experience. But he is truly one: an irrepressible entertainer genuinely interested in his audience; sober, introspective blues singer with a sincere belief in the subjects about which he sings. Roman Catholic, attending Mass not infrequently; cheerful shouter of 'The Dozens' and the 'Duck Yas Yas', Jack Dupree feels and expresses the tragi-comedy of life as he has known it.

Though he is one of the most 'adjusted' of musicians, Jack is by no means a rich man. His recent home on West 186th Street has been condemned and with his wife and family he is now living in Brooklyn. He is not worried about the future, nor is he particularly interested in making a large income as long as he can provide for his dependants. Apart from his family, his love is for his music: for singing and playing the blues and entertaining his audiences. All that he hopes for is their appreciation, because, he says: 'when people appreciate what you do, it's medicine to your soul.'

Jazz Monthly, January 1960

The Original Sonny Boy
ALEX RICE MILLER

Reappraisals in history seem to come in fifty-year cycles. A decade ago it was late Victorianism, then Fin-de-Siècle arts. Now we are in the midst of a reassessment of the period immediately preceding and during the First World War. So the time will come when our own present period of the middle 1960s will come under review, perhaps a half-century from now. And if that is the case, and it surely will be, some social observer will no doubt reflect upon the Teen-Age Age: the period when the adolescents of society have come in for remorseless criticism and comment, commercial exploitation and voluntary separation. Doubtless, too, he will note that this is not a phenomenon peculiar to one country or society – that it is one that is common to social systems remarkably at variance with each other, in communist and capitalist, egalitarian and totalitarian societies alike. Perhaps he might, with hindsight, see in this the seeds of a social revolution which we at the present are yet to experience, but be that as it may – and it belongs to the world of politics rather than, perhaps, of music – he may well consider the significance in this period, so attuned to a teen-age myth, of the direct appeal of veteran men, Negroes from the repressed section of a trans-oceanic society, many of them as old or older than the century, to vast numbers of young people in Europe. This sociological curiosity – and it is not a small one – may well indicate a bond in similarities of conditions; of otherwise entirely differing groups who have the common need for freedom from an outdated notion of social structure. There may be other reasons – but the fact remains, that the ageing blues singers of the United States have been welcomed with unprecedented affection and enthusiasm by those whose elders have generally cast a disapproving eye and ear to the blues music of a large number of artists who, if they share nothing else in common, are at least their close contemporaries.

In this connection the popularity of Sonny Boy Williamson is still exceptional. A tall but stooped, dark-skinned, grey-haired black man, born in the Mississippi Delta before the beginning of the twentieth century, he would seem on this bare evidence to have little in common with his youngest and most enthusiastic supporters. But any barriers of culture or years are broken down when Sonny Boy begins to play. His harmonica speaks a language of our time, tortured, wailing, crying – and strangely beautiful. The effect of his playing is powerfully human and its appeal penetrates national and racial frontiers. His artistry, therefore, forges the link between himself and his newly won audiences but, clearly, he also enjoins them with his personality. There is an engagingly extrovert streak in his make-up; it is not his whole being, which in some respects is oddly withdrawn, but it does manifest itself in his bearing and his dress. Amused by the comparisons made concerning his features – they summon the associations of an elderly roué with a fastidious taste in dry wines – he has played up to them. Now he affects an eccentric suit, harlequin divided in grey and black, the sobriety of the colour making almost logical the arbitrary division of the suit in its different cloths. With it he sports kid gloves and rolled umbrella, and wears a 'bowler' or derby hat. Showmanship? Of course. Unnecessary? Absolutely. If his playing were poor it would in no way disguise it;

brilliant as it often is, his affectations can make it no better.

So is all this unwarranted superficiality? Probably, but it is essentially part of the man, and deep down may be a part of his personal magnetism. So is his conversation. Sometimes it is difficult to get him going as he perches himself on the edge of a table, nodding his head, watching you with heavy lidded eyes. But once he is going, nothing stops him and fact and fancy merge in the flow of his reminiscences real and imagined. He improvises as he talks and one must accept it for it is his sheer capacity for extension of his ideas, for his avoidance of cliché that one admires in his playing, and really it is all one.

Maddening of course, for the would-be historian who hopes to fill in a little more of the blues story. For Sonny Boy is seldom consistent with the details: the theme runs roughly the same, like one of his blues, but it lends itself to fabrication and embroidering and he seldom misses the opportunity. On the notes to Storyville SLP 158, I attempted to pick a way through the mass of conflicting detail and trace the main path of his life. In doing so I quoted his passport, which gives as his birth-date the highly doubtful one of 7 April 1909; in a subsequent talk he admitted to 5 December 1897 the date implied in his 'Story of Sonny Boy Williamson'. But when all is said and done it probably matters little; what does matter is his music.

A subtle form of blues it is. Listen for instance, to 'Movin' Down the River'. This is an impressionist blues composition, a floating drifting improvisation: 'I'm just cruisin'' he says. The river is the Rhine and it impressed Sonny Boy as he followed its course by train through the undulating landscape of the Black Forest. 'I been . . . I been . . . cruisin' down the River Rhine . . .' he sings softly, alternating the words with short bursts on his harmonica. Slowly the beat begins to generate more of a rocking, train-like motion and the snapping of his fingers like the rattle of the points gives a pronounced syncopation to the piece. Or again, take 'When the Lights Went Out' in which his strongly tapping foot establishes a firm, solid beat allowing him to take extraordinary liberties with his instrument, playing across the beat or in chuntering, rapidly repeated short phrases which suddenly give place to a sustained, drawn-out note.

It isn't often that one gets an opportunity to hear Sonny Boy as an accompanist but this is afforded by an unusual item, 'Same Girl' in which he and Memphis Slim playing piano, take alternate vocal verses and exchange roles as accompanists. It is, incidentally, an amusing item in which both singers invent a situation where they are in love with the same woman. 'I guess you gotta have 'em on a co-operation plan,' sings Memphis Slim, recalling a Bessie and Clara Smith duet on the same theme of decades ago. This composition by Sonny Boy is out of the general run of blues of the present day and, indeed, most of his blues have this quality of originality. Not too many blues singers make the use they could of current images, but he brings an immediacy to 'Sonny Boy's Girl Friends' with the words:

> Some time I sit down at the television, see
>   pictures of all kinds,
> But I never saw in that picture, darlin' girl of
>   mine,
> I wonder, wonder what happened to my
>   telephone,
> Every time I call that number I can't find none
>   of these girls at home.

Behind him Memphis Slim plays simple but effective piano, imitating Sonny's own use of short notes, whilst on 'Movin' Out' he builds up the strength of the piano to the conclusion of the piece with a steady walking bass. An even more pronounced rhythm backing is provided for Sonny Boy's versatile harp playing on 'Chicago Bounce'. An aptly titled instrumental, this is a swinger in true Chicago fashion with Memphis Slim playing a Jimmy Yancey bass figure and Matthew Murphy giving more than a hint of Elmore James in the opening bars of his solo before launching into one of his expert filigree passages, whilst Billie Stepney gives the unshakeable rhythm foundation of the drummers from the Windy City.

However well he has been appreciated in Europe, when we hear such an item played with its medium-blues tempo and its captivating swing we know that the cities about the Great Lakes – Milwaukee, Detroit or Chicago are Sonny Boy's true home, spiritually and musically. But his two long tours that have taken him throughout Europe to Scandinavia and Poland and included a three-month stay in England have been happy and rewarding experiences for Sonny Boy Williamson as he sings 'On My Way Back Home'.

*This time, Sonny Boy Williamson's is on his
   way back home . . .
Sonny Boy is on his way back home,
Sonny Boy is on his way back home,
Over in Germany, God knows, I strictly had
   my fun.*

*But I'm leavin' goin' back to the States,
Boy I really had my fun, and I got my kicks,
I met some nice, nice peoples and everybody
   was Okay . . . Okay . . . Okay . . .
   Okay . . . , you know it? . . . you'se
   Okay . . .*

*Billie Stepney is on the drums and M. T.
   Murphy is playin' my guitar,
Make me feel so good a thousand miles away
   from my home and folks,
But I'm leavin', I'm leavin' kind peoples, I
   enjoyed myself everywhere.*

*I enjoyed myself since I been over here,
I hope you be – return to me to come back here,*

*I received all letters, I received all cards,
But the way I'm goin' I know it goin' break
   my heart.
'Cause I'm goin', I know it gonna break my
   heart,
I got to go peoples, I know it gonna break my
   heart,
Meets so many kind peoples, it hurt for me to
   part.*

★   ★   ★   ★

Seeing him poised on the back of a chair or hovering over a microphone, Sonny Boy Williamson reminded you of a buzzard. He had the same mocking grimace and the same, cool eyes with their sleepy lids that had seen so much and told so little. Sonny Boy was something of an enigma; one of his own making perhaps but just as puzzling nonetheless. His age, the details of his life, even his name, remained uncertain and now that he is dead will no doubt continue to provoke argument. But about his harmonica playing and his strange singing there was no question: Sonny Boy was an original with a highly personal means of expression within the blues idiom and an artist of real stature.

'I'm the only Sonny Boy; I'm *the* Sonny Boy; there ain't no other one but me,' he used to say, amusing himself with the repetition but meaning every word just the same. Blues collectors who knew the records and the reputation of John Lee 'Sonny Boy' Williamson were sceptical. The younger man, who was born in Tennessee about 1912 and who was murdered in Chicago in 1948 after a decade of recording, was a very popular and greatly influential singer and harp player; what could be more likely than another singer, an embittered man perhaps, should capitalize on his fame? So went the argument but the ageing Sonny Boy persisted: it was he that had been copied, his name that had been taken but it was John Lee who

was first to get on records that were commercially issued.

What was the truth? Unfortunately in his
last years Sonny Boy wove a mesh of confusion about himself in a tragi-comic endeav-
our to establish his reputation. He needn't
have bothered, for his reputation as an artist
was unassailed and he had his sincere
admirers in two continents. But he did
bother because it meant a lot to him and in
attempting any posthumous biography one
has to take into account his continued
striving for recognition of his story. His
birthplace was Glendora in Tallahatchie
County. Glendora lies about thirty miles
south-east of Clarksdale on the Black Bayou
and in Sonny Boy's day was little more than
a few frame houses. It has grown little with
the years and is today a sultry, sleepy little
township with its Negro area 'across the
tracks' of the Southern railroad. It's blues
country and Sonny Boy, born and raised in
the heart of it took the blues as a part of his
life. The details of his life, or at least his
childhood, still remain obscure though.
About his childhood Sonny Boy would say
nothing. The memory was clearly painful to
him, seems to have been tied up in some
way with the loss of his parents, and once
when I pressed him a little unkindly he said
'I had it tough you know, in them days, and
I just don't like to call it to mind.'

From this one can infer what one may,
although probably the inferences are not too
hard to make. 'You know, he was real evil a
long while ago,' one blues singer who had
known him for years told me, and in spite of
his reticence one knew this to be true. In his
sixties Sonny Boy could still be tough and
mean when he wanted. He always carried a
hip flask of whiskey and drank from it continually with some effect on his temper. In
some ways he completed the popular image
of the romantic, ornery, hard-drinking,
rough-speaking, creative blues singer – the
coloured counterpart of a latter-day cowboy
in dime-novel mould. This was the true
Sonny Boy Williamson – or at least, part of
him. But there was also the other side of the
man, the less easily comprehensible: the
veteran juke-joint bluesman who assumed
with ease and unconscious dignity the role
of an ambassador for the blues in countries
where he shared neither colour nor tradition
nor in many instances even language. Late
in his life Sonny Boy was brought by distant
admirers who knew of him only from his
records – these recordings – to Europe to tour
and to bring his blues. He was a remarkable
success as a musician and as a personality
and whilst losing nothing of the more formidable elements in his make-up, he endeared himself to his audiences and won new
adherents to the blues. Strangely enough he
looked the part: the features of a French
diplomat, the distinction of D'Annunzio –
and a certain Mephistopholean wickedness
in the eyes which was not at variance with
the European tradition of schemers, mani-
pulators and men of letters. Yet he was no
man of letters; he was a man of the blues,
and if it seemed at times that he was a person
of great potential whom fate had overlooked
in the circumstances of a boy born in a
Mississippi sharecropper's home, it was also
evident that the world would have been the
poorer for the loss of a blues player of
originality and distinction.

In action Sonny Boy unfolded slowly. He
did not give away all his secrets either in
conversation or music. Instead, when he
played he built up the tension of his phrasing
with logical development. One had to listen
for quite a while as he progressed from short
bursts, single notes, punctuated phrases to
filigree patterns of complexity and richness.
His large, calloused lips enfolded the cheap
harps that he played and he seemed to mould
the notes through the long fingers of his
cupped hands. He would utter the words of

his blues from the side of his mouth, slipping the harp between his lips as he finished a vocal phrase so that the melody was sustained on the instrument. When he sang his voice was husky, sometimes almost gutteral, at other times near a whisper. And through everything he sang and played, his impeccable sense of timing pervaded. Sonny Boy's rhythmic sense was uncanny, developed in a way that was rare even among blues singers. He would shift his weight on to one foot to leave the other free to tap and to rotate and his stooped figure would be poised like a bird of prey. Then he would rock, gently, this way and that, generating a subtle, compelling swing. His long, dry fingers would snap with whipcracks on the ball of his thumb, he would click his tongue in syncopation and, when he developed a microphone technique, would tap the mouth-piece in explosive timing. Sometimes he would place the harp between his lips and manipulate it without the use of his hands, snapping his fingers instead to a cracking rhythm. A complete master of his instrument he would indulge in a little showmanship, too, playing a small harp from inside his mouth, placing one end in his mouth like a cigar, or blowing simultaneously through his nose and his mouth two harmonicas at once. Then he would laugh cunningly, raise his eyebrows, close his eyes and wail a forceful, overblowing chorus. He had to be seen as well as heard, at least to enjoy his playing to the full.

It was through non-visual media that he made a wider name for himself after many years of playing in the Mississippi Delta, down to Texas and in Arkansas, however, when in 1938 he was asked to perform on the *King Biscuit Show*. The show was put out by the Interstate Grocery Company, being broadcast every day at 12.45 pm on Station KFFA from Helena, Arkansas. The show provided him with intermittent employ-

ment for many years: he worked on it fairly regularly from 1941 through 1948 and it became known as *Sonny Boy's Cornmeal and King Biscuit Show*. It seems possible that the 'Sonny Boy' tag was applied for the show, and his contemporaries in Arkansas knew him as Willie Williams – or Williamson. But further north in St Louis and Chicago his fellow blues singers insist that his name was Willie Miller – called, as a pun and perhaps as a result of the grocery association, 'Rice Miller'. In 1945 Sonny Boy met Mattie Jones and he married her three years later. They lived variously in Arkansas and Mississippi where in Little Rock and Belzoni respectively Sonny boy continued to broadcast early in the Fifties. Then in 1951, three years after the death of his popular namesake in Chicago, he appeared on record. He was at his peak in the South and the records that he cut in Jackson, Mississippi, in the company of Dave Campbell or Clarence Lonnie on piano, Joe Willie Wilkins on guitar, Clifton Givens on improvised bass and a drummer whom he recalled only as 'Frock' (or 'Frog'), were unsurpassed in his career. Down home blues in the post-war idiom, they range from the wistful 'Mighty Long Time' (on which, incidentally, Sonny Boy also plays guitar) to the rocking exuberance of 'Pontiac Blues'.

Until 1954 Sonny Boy Williamson remained in the South but his reputation was now widespread and he was engaged for many one-night stands and tours. Some of his associates had already gone North – Elmore James and B. B. King amongst them – and in 1954 he took a group, which included the pianist Willie Love, to Detroit. The following year he moved North, to settle with his wife in Milwaukee, Wisconsin. The late Fifties were spent in working in East St Louis, Chicago and Milwaukee and then, to his delight, and perhaps a little to his bewilderment though he never showed it,

he was invited to appear with Horst Lippmann's American Folk Blues Festival to
tour Germany, France, Holland, Denmark,
Sweden and Great Britain. Unquestionably
he was the outstanding success of the show
as the reviews of the European blues critics
in various countries are evidence. In
England, in particular, he was both popular
and very contented. When the rest of the
company returned to the States Sonny Boy
stayed on, first to tour in Poland with Memphis Slim and then to return to England, to
tour on his own. In the phenomenon of the
English 'beat' clubs, which have no preten-
tions to blues purism or folkiness, Sonny
Boy felt completely himself. The disparity
of ages of the sexagenarian harp player and
his teen-age beat accompanists never struck
him as incongruous and he was very anxious
to return to England to live. British formal
attire amused him and he had a two-tone
harlequin suit in black and charcoal grey
made in an English tailor's and with rolled
umbrella, bowler (derby) hat and kid gloves,
indulged in the gentle humour of the more
obvious incongruity of an American Negro
blues singer dressed like a city financier.

In spite of his late fame Sonny Boy did
not hit the 'folk blues' circuit in the States
and though he was on the 1964 European
tour he returned to the clubs and juke joints
where he had spent his whole life working.
When Chris Strachwitz visited him in
Helena, Arkansas, in early May of 1965 he
was working the joints and still playing on
the *King Biscuit Show* as he had a quarter of a
century before. Hardly anyone believed his
story that he had been touring European concert halls – for to his audiences in the Helena
jukes he was still the hard-drinking, hard-
living bluesman. They were to miss him
when he died a few weeks later on 26 May
1965, and unknown to them he is mourned
by friends in half-a-dozen countries.

Notes to Storyville SLP 158, 1964
and Blues Classics BC 9, 1965

Hoochie Coochie Man
MUDDY WATERS

On the edge of the ancient iron bed in his small, weathered farm house an old Negro man sat in wonder, his keen eyes deep-set in the dark and leathery features, never leaving for an instant the well-built, neatly dressed figure of the son whom he had not seen for thirty-five years. As his son talked and gestured, speaking with accents that told of his Mississippi origins but bearing himself with the confidence of a man who has been many years in Chicago and successful in his field, there were tears both of pride and distress in his eyes. And the man in his early forties who sat opposite him studying the features of the father that he scarcely knew and the bare walls, the simple furniture, the faded photographs and the few belongings that were his home, shared his sorrow that the bitter poverty of the pre-Depression years had forced them apart for so long until this day in the summer of 1958 when father and son met as strangers.

Outside, a knot of coloured children were gathered excitedly about the two sleek Cadillacs and the long station wagon whose extravagant lines and rich fittings the layer of Mississippi dust could not hide. A few yards away some of the older men sucked their pipes, talked of old Ollie Morganfield and his son who had arrived from the North with his entourage in these expensive automobiles which were of a type that seldom stopped in the tiny township of Rollingfork. At times they would look back at the vehicles and read again the name printed on the banners on their sides: the name that the returning prodigal had been given by his playmates in this very spot nearly four decades ago:

MUDDY WATERS

Muddy Waters, christened McKinley Morganfield, was born to Ollie Morganfield and his wife Berta Jones on 4 April 1915. Times were hard, they were desperately poor and Ollie, living by sharecropping could scarcely make enough to feed them. Children might mean eventual help on the scrap of plantation which he worked and McKinley, the second son, eventually had six brothers and five sisters – of whom all but two of the sisters are still living. But at this time the growing family was an added burden and Berta's mother, Della Jones, raised the boy from the age of a few months. When he was three years old his mother died and Ollie Morganfield felt himself unable to look after him at the little shack where the steps from the back porch were lapped by the sluggish waters of the Deer Creek. So at the age of three, McKinley Morganfield, already nicknamed 'Muddy' by the children that played with him by the creek, was taken up-State by his grandmother to Clarksdale.

In Clarksdale, Muddy Waters had the characteristic childhood of a small Negro boy in a poor Mississippi community. He had a rudimentary education, but when he was old enough and big enough to work in the fields during the peak periods in the cotton-producing year he was expected to labour alongside the men. Sometimes he was taken South to Rollingfork in Sharkey County to spend a while with his father, but as he became older and able to undertake more work on the Coahoma County plantations his visits became fewer. It was not a life entirely without recreation however, and during the slack season he had time enough to relax. His father had sung the blues and played his own guitar accompaniment and the blues was a part of Muddy's early life. It was the music of his people, of his friends and elders, and it was as natural to him as the desire to eat that he should want to learn to play and sing the blues. Like most Negro children of his age, he first learned to play on a home-made instrument but soon he was able to obtain a guitar for himself. Two childhood friends played guitar with him, Sonny Simms and Scott Bowhandle. They were a few years his senior and he learned to play most of all by listening to them and copying their fingering and chords. Like many other children in that community he also learned to play the har- monica – the mouth-harp – and the ringing sounds of the instrument may have helped him to shape his own individual style of playing the guitar, for soon he had developed his own characteristics and no longer played or sang in the manner of Simms and Bow- handle. Scott Bowhandle eventually gave up playing the guitar but Muddy did not lose touch with him; today Scott lives on West 13th Street with Muddy's aunt.

In the Clarksdale district there were some singers of outstanding ability who played guitar with a dexterity that earned them more than a local reputation. Though they played in the 'jukes' Muddy went to hear them whenever he could and learned a great deal from watching them play and hearing them sing. Amongst these were Charley Patton and Son House, both of whom had recorded for Paramount. Son House record- ed his 'Mississippi County Farm Blues' and 'Clarksdale Moan' back in 1931 when Muddy first heard him. He came from a plantation a few miles east of Clarksdale and, now in his sixties, is still living and working there. He played the characteristic 'bottle- neck' style of the Northern Mississippi region. A bottle would be broken at the neck and the glass neck annealed in flame until the rough edges were smooth. This would be slipped over the little finger and when the strings were picked – in particular the top 'E' string – the touch of the bottle

neck at the frets would send a singing, whining tone. Sonny House was particularly adept at this and the style matched his voice to perfection but, in the opinion of Muddy Waters who heard him at every available opportunity, he did not record to advantage.

Amongst the most impressive singers and guitarists using this particular style was Robert Johnson who worked the jukes in the Clarksdale area. He was a 'nice lookin'' man; brownskin, sort of medium height and got "good" hair,' recalled Muddy. 'He always had his guitar with him whenever I saw him; don't know what sort of work he did. He was the kind of guy you watched to get ideas from.' Muddy watched intently and to good effect, assimilating some of the qualities of Johnson's technique with such skill that the story got around – spread perhaps, unwittingly by Alan Lomax – that he was Johnson's nephew, although in fact they were quite unrelated. Robert Johnson was a restless man, however, and eventually he moved on, beating his way South to Louisiana and Texas where he recorded some of his most celebrated blues.

A few years later the folk song authority and collector Alan Lomax came to Clarks- dale looking for Robert Johnson and original folk talent amongst the Negro blues singers of the Delta. He did not find Johnson, who, it was said, had been poisoned by his mis- tress in the San Antonio district in Texas; but he did find Muddy Waters. McKinley Morganfield was working in a field, chop- ping cotton and singing to himself when Alan Lomax, acting on the advice of local people who knew a good blues singer when they heard one, sought him out. He was up- right, well-built and dark-skinned and he hollered his field cries in a rich, strong voice. 'I was always hollerin',' he recalled to me, explaining 'I was always singing "I Can't Be Satisfied". That was the first thing that I recorded, and I was always singin' it, because mebbe I didn't exactly know it but I jes' didn't like the way things were down there.' Alan Lomax talked to him and after hearing him sing to his own guitar accompaniment, encouraged him to record two blues under the titles 'Country Blues' and 'I Be's Troubled' for the Music Division of the Archives of the Library of Congress. His voice was deep and inexpressibly sad, and his words were echoed in the moans of the guitar strings as he brushed them with a length of brass tubing that he wore on his fourth finger of his left hand. The strange country blues were almost unique examples in the Archives collection for many years, a source of surprise to many who heard them. But few were as surprised as Muddy Waters. 'I really heard myself for the first time. I'd never heard my voice. I used to sing; used to sing just how I felt, 'cause that's the way we always sang in Mississippi. But when Mr Lomax played me the record I thought, man, this boy can sing the blues. And I was surprised because I didn't know I sang like that.'

Lomax went on and Muddy Waters was left behind. He was much encouraged though, and accepted the invitations to play at dances and jukes with alacrity. There was always more money and more time to play on Saturday nights. 'I used to play any old place – jukes, anywhere. For Saturday Night Fish Fry's, you know what I mean? Everybody fry up fish and have one hell of a ball. Yeah, jus' call it Saturday Night Fish Fry – Louis Jordan made a record called that.' Muddy worked hard at these boisterous, rowdy functions. 'Man, I'd play for a whole night, workin' till sunrise for fifty cents and a sandwich, and be glad of it. And they really made you work. They liked the blues; the real lowdown blues, all night long. That's the way you learn though.'

Muddy learned from working and he learned from other singers. But he learned from recordings too: recordings that he heard in the taverns, the roadhouses that lined the highways on the outskirts of the towns and in the homes of his friends. They impressed themselves deeply on his memory; so firmly in fact that although he had not heard them for more than twenty years, he could remember the words of Blind Blake's 'Detroit Bound', of Texas Alexander's 'Corn Bread Blues' and Blind Lemon Jefferson's 'Matchbox Blues' without difficulty and without prompting. He was happy to recall them for 'they were the real blues men, the old times. Of course I was too late in Chicago to hear them, but I knew their records. Blind Lemon, he was great. He didn't do much for me, you understan'? He wasn't my style, but he was a great singer. And guitarist.'

So Muddy's reputation spread as he played the blues more and more in public. His singing and playing were popular with the country cotton 'croppers who wanted to hear nothing but the blues. 'The blues is in my blood, you know? I can't play, can't sing nothin' else. And I don't want to, 'cause the blues is for me. It's like a shoe,' explains Muddy. 'You take a number seven shoe you sure can't wear a size four. You wear the one that fits. The blues fit me.'

Though he played guitar in accompaniment to his own singing, he secured his first 'professional' engagement as a harp player. A touring company of 'Silas Green's from New Orleans' the most famous of the Minstrel Carnival shows still active, hit town and Muddy joined the troupe as harmonica accompanist to other singers. He managed to get opportunities to play the guitar and sing the blues himself with the company as he became established. It was a short stint, however, and Muddy was soon back in Clarksdale and still 'Couldn't be satisfied'. Alan Lomax's visit had unsettled him and Negroes who had gone North came home with stories of greater prosperity, good jobs and good wages and lives that were not spent in constant servility. In 1943 Muddy Waters made tracks for Chicago.

With factories working at top pressure in the drive for maximum output occasioned by the national war-time Emergency, there were opportunities for employment for virtually everyone. Roosevelt's signature to the Executive Order 8802 in 1941 guarded against discriminatory practices and Negro employees were sought in many occupations. Muddy Waters signed on as a worker in a paper mill in Chicago and was soon making a decent living wage. Many of his fellow workers were Negroes up from the South like himself and he soon met others who played and sang at parties and social functions after hours. Here in Chicago, Muddy made the acquaintance of many older blues men, amongst them Tampa Red, Johnny Temple, Sonny Boy Williamson, Jazz Gillum – 'haven't seen Jazz in ten years now' – Memphis Slim, Big Maceo Merriwether and the man for whom he had the greatest admiration and respect, the late lamented Big Bill Broonzy who introduced him to other singers and helped him to settle down in the startlingly alien environment of Chicago. Not that Muddy was entirely without connections in Chicago, for his complex family tree accounted for the presence in the City of a number of relatives who had made the trip North at an earlier date. Amongst them was Joe Brant, son of Muddy's maternal grandmother Della Jones and therefore his uncle. Uncle Joe Brant was interested in Muddy's work as a singer and guitarist, but though he was a Mississippi man of the older generation his comparatively long experience in the North had made him fully alive to developing trends in the blues, and in 1945 he bought Muddy his first electric guitar. The new sounds that he could obtain from the instrument by applying his traditional blues technique of rapid arpeggios and bottleneck style appealed to Muddy and he rejoiced in the amplified volume that he could obtain on the bass strings when he desired a strong rhythm or on the treble strings when he played solo passages. He still hollered the blues in his tough but deeply-felt style, but the new instrument opened up great possibilities for him.

Another relative who was a child of only thirteen years of age when Muddy came to Chicago, was his own half-brother Otis Spann. Young Otis had come with his family from Jackson, Mississippi, to Chicago at the age of nine in 1939 but he, too, had a family background that was rooted in the blues tradition. At an early age Otis began to learn to play blues on the piano and he learned much from listening to Memphis Slim, Little Brother Montgomery and Roosevelt Sykes at parties, and when he was old enough to enter them, in South Side clubs. But it was Big Maceo who had the greatest influence upon him and he has absorbed many qualities of Maceo's in the mid-Forties and took every opportunity to sit beside him and listen to the rolling blues that his powerful fingers created. Merriwether took an instant liking to him and coached him, teaching him his driving bass figures. 'You ain't got to be like Sykes, you ain't got to be like me; you gotta be yourself. You got to carve your own style,' Maceo always advised, but though Otis heeded the advice well and developed qualities that are essentially his own, the influence of the great blues man on the impressionable boy was a lasting one. Maceo often played at 'Silvio's' the blues club where Tampa Red, his almost inseperable companion, Big Bill, Sonny Boy Williamson and many other blues men worked. This was the club where Muddy's reputation in Chicago was really established and the coloured people on the South Side paid good money to hear him play. He had left his job at the paper mill and later worked for a firm that manufactured radio parts; later still, he took up truck driving.

As Muddy's reputation grew he was noticed by an executive of the Aristocratic label, who found that he was not committed to a record company. He wasted no time but sent for Muddy immediately to record a couple of titles for the company. But Muddy was on the road, driving a truck for a venetian blind firm and he was hard to trace. It was heavy work but comparitively easy as far as the hours were concerned: if he had one or two heavy loads and long distances to go on one day he could be sure of a light day's work the following morning. Just where Muddy was at the time, no one seemed to know, but a friend of his, Antra Bolton, to whom he is eternally grateful, took it on himself to find Muddy in the vast maze of Chicago streets and finally succeeded in intercepting the blues singer's lorry. He delivered his message without wastage of words, and they exchanged vehicles, Muddy to drive as fast as possible to the recording studios whilst Antra Bolton cheerfully volunteered to finish delivering his load for him. So he came to enregister his first commercial titles, 'Gipsy Woman' and 'Little Anna Mae', in the company of the bass player Crawford and pianist Sunnyland Slim – Albert Luandrew. Shortly after, he accompanied Sunnyland Slim on guitar when Luandrew recorded two blues under his own name, and at the same session had the happy idea of re-recording his Library of Congress items under new titles, 'I Be Troubled' becoming 'I Feel Like Going Home', and 'I Can't Be Satisfied' being the new title for his original 'Country Blues'. His 'sliding style' of guitar playing with his strong voice give a wide range of tonal quality on these sides and his exultant cries, his glottal stops that punctuate his vocal phrases, were redolent of his Mississippi origins, even though several years had passed since he had left his home State. His records appealed immediately to the 'new' Chicago Negroes who, like the singer himself, had their roots in the Deep South. Aristocrat quickly realised that they had on their books a great Southern blues singer whose work was nonetheless of the present, and they signed him exclusively. When Aristocrat was absorbed by Chess, Muddy Waters was signed up with the new company.

In September 1946 McKinley Morganfield, it appears, cut three sides for the Columbia company; perhaps he was not 'ready', perhaps Columbia did not consider his material good sales proposition: whatever the reason they remain unissued. But Aristocrat made no such mistake and Muddy Waters' records sold widely in the South as well as in Chicago. In 1950 he made some fourteen tracks with Crawford backing him on bass on a number of them, and acting in a supporting role himself on a number of others. Guitarist Leroy Foster accompanied him once or twice and he played second guitar on Foster's 'Locked Out Boogie' and 'Shady Grove Blues', whilst he made a similarly reciprocal set of four sides with pianist and blues singer Little Johnny early the following year. With his 'Blues Combo' which included Sunnyland Slim on piano, he accompanied the veteran singer St Louis Jimmy – James Oden – on his impressive 'Florida Hurricane'.

'Rollin' Stone' and 'Walkin' Blues' were the last sides that Muddy Waters was to make as a virtual soloist (Crawford played discreet bass in the background) and these were the first sides that were to be issued on the Chess label. The bass string emphasizes the pronounced beat whilst Muddy picks the strings in a strangely insistent rhythm which conveys a feeling of restlessness eminently fitting to the theme of 'Walking

Blues'. He repeats fragments of the lines as he sings, filling in the breaks not only on his guitar but with broken vocal phrases, qualities that still recall the singing of Robert Johnson. This is still the Mississippi blues but Muddy's style was changing somewhat and he enjoyed the backing of other instrumentalists: the blues piano of Sunnyland Slim and the shrill, swinging harmonica of Little Walter Jacobs. Slim – Luandrew – came from Mississippi, Walter Jacobs from Alexander, Louisiana, but like the Texas born Big Maceo or the harmonica player Sonny Boy Williamson from Jackson, Tennessee, they had developed a forceful 'shouting' music that implied the influence of the noise and tempo of city life on the contemplative Southern blues. A perfect relationship of musical voices between Muddy's electric guitar and Little Walter's harp – not infrequently an electric model also – soon developed and for five years the two blues musicians worked in close harmony: 'He's the greatest harp player in the world – I'm telling you!' Less well known has been the lasting blues partnership with the Negro guitarist Jimmy Rogers, which has been inadequately represented on record but which has endured some thirteen years; and with Sonny Boy Williamson, drummer Freddy Bellow, and the faithful Crawford, until his death three years ago. Chess issued his records with discriminate economy and without flooding the market. He was soon able to give up factory work and truck driving and sing the blues professionally.

Southern Negroes who bought the records of Muddy Waters wanted to see and hear the man in person and from the early Fifties he commenced a series of tours which have continued until the present day. Generally the tours took place in the late Summer – early Fall, when the crops have been gathered and there is money to be spent. Muddy would take a group which would include Little Walter on harmonica, Jimmy Rogers on second guitar, and a pianist and drummer or bass player would make up the company which toured in a group of three automobiles, one a station wagon that would take the equipment and instruments. Sometimes they would stay a week or so in one place but more frequently they would make a series of one-night stands, beating their way through Tennessee, Alabama, Georgia, Florida, Louisiana and back North through Mississippi if their outward route could not be retraced. Muddy did not care to play in Mississippi for the people were poor and the money scarce; perhaps, too, he had bitter memories of the time when he was working for 35¢ a day. In the dance halls, the theatres, the barns and jukes, the show-places, sumptuous or makeshift, where they performed, the audiences were rough, tough and wildly enthusiastic. Muddy's virile Southern blues with their kicking beat and intense emotional impact stirred an exciting, even violent response in his listeners: the kind of response that spurs him to his best efforts. Then his hips would begin to shake, his fingers vibrate their tremolos from the strings; his head would be thrown back, his eyes would close tight and he would holler his words, shout his sentences and break up his phrases with joyful whoops and falsetto cries. Behind him his group would rock their fierce blues, the guitar and piano exchanging boogie rhythms and the drums socking a pronounced, pounding off-beat.

Big Maceo died in 1953 but his mantle was taken up by his pupil of half-a-dozen years, Otis Spann. Muddy Waters realized that in his half-brother he had found a great pianist, a pianist whom he insists is today the finest player of the blues though he concedes that Little Brother Montgomery may be more versatile. 'But Otis has got that rollin' left hand, he's got the blues in his fingers. And he's the Ace card in *my* hand. Man, when he plays, he works!' said Muddy in appreciation of Spann's great abilities. Otis sits three-quarters on to the piano, his right shoulder raised, his head inclined to the left as if he were straining to catch every note he plays. He sits to the left of centre and his right hand stretches out to the treble when he rolls out a phrase in contrast to the deep bass figures that characterize his work. The muscles of his face are constantly moving, his otherwise placid features are screwed up with the very intensity of his own playing and as he produces a cascade of falling notes from beneath his thick but incredibly nimble fingers his whole body trembles in sympathy. His approach is the exact pianistic counterpart of Muddy's own blues and the impassioned harp-playing of Little Walter. From 1953 Otis Spann has been Muddy's permanent accompanist and inseparable companion on their Southern tours. The reception that they have had has been universally enthusiastic south of the Mason-Dixon Line but never more than in Alabama. 'I *like* Alabama. People there, they *feel* the blues and that makes me feel good. They come from miles around to hear us and if we get less than six-seven-eight hundred people believe me, that's a bad house! And it ain't cheap to hear Muddy Waters! They pay two-three dollars a time to come in; mebbe they don't eat the next day, but, man, the place is really jumpin'! Some of them come up afterwards, y'know? Bring a jug of corn and we have a good time, sing all night. I like Alabama – big places like Birmingham, Bessemer, Montgomery, Mobile and all the little places way out, like Enterprise. It's all the same, they *know* the blues.'

Always an agitated singer, Muddy found that playing the guitar tended to hinder him when he sang, for he works with his whole body and sometimes he could not put all the expression that he wished into his singing when he was playing too. 'When I sing the blues, when I'm singing the *real* blues, I'm singing what I feel. Some people maybe want to laugh; maybe I don't talk so good and they don't understand y'know? But when we sing the blues, when I sing the blues it comes from the heart. From right here in your soul, an' if you singing what you really feel it comes out all over. It ain't just what you saying, it pours out of you. Sweat runnin' down your face.' So Muddy put aside his guitar early in 1955 and for more than two years did not play it at all. His band was his instrument and he sang unhampered, stamping, hollering, his whole body jerking in sheer physical expression of his blues. He would double up, clench his fists, straighten with a spring like a flickknife, leap in the air, arch his back and literally punch out his words whilst the perspiration poured down his face and soaked through his clothing. This is the blues as Muddy expresses it; the blues of today: 'Some singers they's cool. You know, they sing the words: "I'm broke and hungry blee-blah-doo". They sing the words but it don't mean nothin'. They too *nice* to sweat! But Howling Wolf now, he *works*. He puts everything he's got into his blues. And when he's finished, man, he's sweatin'! Feel my shirt, it's soaked ain't it? When Wolf finishes his jacket's like my shirt! He's a big man and he's a real blues singer. And B. B. King! He's the next man, I'm telling *you*! He's what I *call* a blues singer; when he sings, his veins on his neck they're right out here! And he's sweatin'! Big Bill, he used to sweat; Little Walter, he sweats; Otis, he's sweatin' now! When you sing the blues you sing with every part of you and you put all you got to give into it.'

Around him Muddy Waters has gathered a group of blues musicians with the same powerful conception of blues singing and playing as himself: Pat Hare from Arkansas, his lead guitarist: 'He's a real tough baby, and when he's liquored up, man he can really play!' James Cotton, his harmonica player who plays in a manner similar to that of Little Walter; Marcus Johnson, who can play any saxophone and is especially fond of the baritone and alto saxes; Francey Clay, his swinging drummer and, of course, Otis Spann, who not only plays piano but can turn in a fine blues on guitar. He has his eye too on Little Junior Wells, his harmonica player on the 'Mannish Boy' session: 'He's still young. I've known him since he was *that* high; used to be what you call his 'guardian'; take him in the clubs when he's too young to go by himself.' And Otis Rush, a blues guitarist 'coming up!' With such men he plays every night at Smitty's Corner on 35th and Indiana, except Wednesdays when he plays at a big dance hall in Gary. They accompany him on tour, too, when he again plays the guitar. Five days in Palm Beach; a

week in Los Angeles – 'the joint's really jumpin' when me and Guitar Slim get together in L.A.' – a week in Detroit with John Lee Hooker, and between them the numerous one-night stands for the mill-workers of Bessemer, the longshoremen of Mobile, the factory hands of Houston and the populace of countless Southern town-ships and communities.

When Muddy Waters came to England his rocking blues and electric guitar were meat that proved too strong for many stomachs even though he was in fact playing under a self-imposed restraint. 'I only half-did 'I'm a Man' then,' he said, after the most uninhibited performance of his stay – at a club session. But the blues is not reserved, nor does it benefit from restraint or the imposition of precepts of 'good taste'. When Muddy Waters works he sweats. That is why for a few million Negroes he is a real blues man, a big man, a 'Hoochie-Coochie Man'.

Jazz Monthly, January 1959

Muddy Waters died Chicago, 30 April 1983.

Blues at Sunrise
IVORY JOE HUNTER

'They don't appreciate jazz and rhythm and blues, and rock and roll here in England you know,' said Ivory Joe. I opened my mouth to protest out of a vague and rather rare sense of patriotism. 'Well, now you know yourself that they appreciate this type of music much better in France,' he continued, 'that's where jazz criticism really started, over there in France. In England – they don't like it too much. I'm really keen on going to France.'

I knew what he meant; rhythm and blues of the sort that Ivory Joe Hunter likes to sing and play is not appreciated here in England to any great extent, and he was quite right, there is a larger market and a bigger audience in France. In fact, the jazz audience by and large in England is very happy hearing its own jazz bands and many an orchestra and jazz band from the States has played to poor houses. We have not too much to be proud about in this respect and my mild protest was never uttered.

Ivory Joe Hunter is not the English idea of a jazz man, or of a blues man, and it is true that his work often wavers between the ballad and R & B. He is a highly popular singer and pianist in the States and in con-siderable demand, and however purist one's ideas may be there is no gainsaying that an essential part of the music as a whole has a poor audience in this country. But Joe Hunter was happy at the interest displayed by a number of genuine enthusiasts and was generous in his time and trouble when talking to interviewing writers.

He is a huge man, generous in every way. His voice can have great volume and his gestures are expansive, broad, emphatic. He stresses a point with a sweep of the arms and seems to hold his words in place with hand extended, palm down, fingers widespread. He is a lively talker and his knowledge of music is wide; his knowledge of jazz takes in the New Orleans musicians and the modern-ists without the barriers that we are so inclined in our detachment to create.

Ivory Joe Hunter was born in Kirbyville, Texas, in Jasper County near Louisiana. His family was musically inclined; his mother a spiritual singer, his father a blues guitarist. As a child he was determined to be in the entertainment business and taught himself to play piano 'by ear'. He had a few lessons from piano 'professors' but for the most part he learned by hard experience in a school which had no fixed location – he played in carnivals and circuses, travelling on the road with touring shows. 'Some people are kind of ashamed of their past lives but I'm really proud of mine. I mean I'm proud of where I came from and what I did and where I come up to . . . because these fellows that come up now they expect to be paid big money and they haven't had to work for it. But I really had to work for my place, and I had it hard, real hard.'

Ivory Joe talked at length of the life he had led in Texas in the late Twenties and early Thirties when times were very tough and he had nearly starved in periods when jobs were scarce and money was too. He worked in most of the Texas coastal towns with many of the pianists and blues singers that later became famous – though some of them retained local reputations only and never broke into a wider field of entertainment.

Ivory Joe was perfectly frank: 'I quit playing to coloured clubs exclusively after about 1932. You see I really worked at my piano until I could play in the white places where they could pay better. They only wanted good musicians and if you wanted that kind of pay – something to live on – you either had to work for it or you didn't get it. Well, eventually I got a job with a guy in Houston and worked there for several years. I learned to play popular ballads and so on – up to then I'd only been playing the blues. First piece I learned was taught me by my brother – 'You brought a New Kind of Love to Me'. Well in 1932 I needed money real bad, and I was good enough, so that's how I started on the road to success.'

The road to success eventually led Ivory Joe Hunter to the West Coast where he joined up with another Texas pianist Charles Brown, and the guitarist Johnny Moore. With Eddie Williams on bass they recorded in Los Angeles in 1945, Ivory Joe's first titles. They were, significantly enough, 'Blues at Sunrise' and 'You Taught Me to Love'. The combination of blues item and popular ballad in a sense set the direction of his subsequent recordings and, incidentally, of his career. His next record was with a neat little band which included the excellent Pee Wee Crayton – Connie Curtis Crayton – on guitar and 'Seventh Street Boogie' was the first of many boogie numbers that Ivory Joe was to record. After working with Johnny Moore's Three Blazers he had his own band and became a popular attraction on the West Coast, playing first in Los Angeles and later in San Francisco.

In 1947 he went to New York where he commenced a long contract with King Records. On a tour later that year he recorded a number of sides in Nashville, Tennessee, and with a fine group that included Tyree Glenn on trombone, Russell Procope on alto, Oscar Pettiford on bass, and Sonny Greer on drums, he had a particularly successful session in December that year in Cincinatti, Ohio. This was a group that remained fairly intact, and returning to the West Coast they continued to work to-

gether. Ray Nance the violinist and Ellington side-man joined them and he is to be heard on a session made in Los Angeles with Ivory Joe in February of 1949. Johnny Hodges was another important musician who teamed up with Joe Hunter; and the trumpeter Taft Jordan, who is undoubtedly another contender for the 'underrated musician' stakes, played on a brief session in New York in October that year for MGM, when Ivory Joe's contract with King finally ceased.

It is a very remarkable musician who can begin in such unpromising surroundings as Ivory Joe Hunter and who can eventually become as esteeemed as he is amongst the swinging jazz musicians, who tend on the whole to live slightly apart from those whose background was the world of the blues. Today, Ivory Joe is a much sought after musician and his appearance at a club commands a fee which enables him to live very comfortably and to enjoy some of the things which were totally denied him in early years. He considers, and has a right to do so, that he deserves this: 'for when they're paying me now, they're paying for the life I had and the way I came up. They're paying me for my hard training and my experience,' he says. He is a shrewd man and a warm-hearted one. He lives in the city and New York is now his home. But he hankers after the country and his greatest pleasures are to go shooting with his dogs or to go fishing in the Louisiana bayous and streams. Today he is able to maintain for himself a summer house near Monroe, Louisiana, where he can return to the type of country he knew as a child and as a young man and indulge in the simple pleasures that are not accessible to him in the Northern city.

We are very apt to judge musicians as they appear on the stage, on the television show or on record and to make our judgements sweepingly and with little regard for the many problems musical, economic, social and domestic that face any jazz or blues musician who lives by his playing.

Perhaps it isn't only the music that we sometimes fail to appreciate. I wonder if Ivory Joe Hunter will find it different in France?

Jazz News, November 1961

Ivory Joe Hunter died *c.* 1977.

Santa Fe Train

EDWIN BUSTER PICKENS

. . . You know I heard the Santa Fe blow one morning . . . It cried like a child – that engine was shootin' up steam . . . an' I talked with the conductor – the brakesman, in the caboose – and –

He said: Where ya goin' boy?

I said: I'm goin' to Cowswitch.

He said: I don't 'llow nobody to ride this train.

I said: Boss, I'm hungry.
What can you do?

I said: I can fiddle a l'il bit.

He said: All right go on . . . and fiddle . . . how–how do you do that?

I said: I do it on the pi-anno.

He said: All right – but you ain't got no piano . . .
That's right . . . but if I catch the Santa Fe, I'm gonna find one.

He said: I'll let you ride . . .

All right . . . then she blowed . . . Number 1435 – *Mountain Jack* . . . so he let me ride . . . but it was another stop there . . . and I quit 'er. And I met ole Robertson there . . . he was 'n old-time piano-player, and the saw-mills had rode him out.

him out.

He said: Son, take my place . . .

I said: I will.

He said: What'cha come in here on . . .?

I said: On the Santa Fe . . . ain't but one road . . .

He said: How did you get by the brakes-man?
I told him who I was.
Who *is* you?

I said: Well I ain't much, but I try to say what I can do.
Well whatcha go tell him . . . watcha do when you tell him?
Well, I say: looka here! I says: I'm just here trying to ketch this train. He says: I don't want you to ride my train! I says: I know

it's against the law to do that, it's – I'm on my way! . . . He says to me he says Get on – and ride! Where ya goin? Cowswitch!

That's where they make real saw – lumber. Change shifts – one shift goin' and one barrelhouse . . . in the sawmill . . . Brakeman said he wanna barrelhouse too, but he didn't have time, he was on the train.

I says: I'm on here too. So when you off there, come by and see me sometime!

He says: I will . . .

'Santa Fe Train' is a fragment of Edwin 'Buster' Pickens' autobiography. The story it tells – of begging a ride on a Santa Fe freight train, of meeting one of the veteran, unrecorded blues singers of the Texas barrel-house circuit and taking over from him at the sawmill town of Cowswitch – is one that has been repeated countless times in his life. Buster Pickens is a barrelhouse pianist who has played the sawmills, the turpentine camps and the oil 'boom' towns since his childhood. He has outlasted most of his contemporaries in their tough and often dangerous life and can lay good claim to be virtually the last of the sawmill pianists. This is partly due to his relative youth, for Ed Pickens was born in Hempstead, Texas, in 1915, though he was barely into his teens before he was making a living by playing the blues. Many of the bluesmen with whom he worked and who accepted him as an equal were twice his age when he com-menced his career in the late Twenties, but others, younger men, died before they were thirty from the effects of hard liquor, hard living and 'exposure' as he terms it. Riding the blinds through the chill night on fast-moving 'rattlers' after working in the hot and crowded barrelhouse took the life of many a pianist. Pickens recalled the advice of an 'old-time piano player, a notable pianist named Foster, who was never mentioned' who 'used to lecture me all the time. He'd say, "look son, whatever you do, when you play them places, I don't care whether it's the middle of July or August, you get a coat and put it on if you go out in the air." So I been doin' that ever since.'

'Exposure' conditioned the course of his life to some extent. He had opportunities to play in the travelling shows and circuses but generally refused them in favour of the mill camps and townships. 'I worked for a show back in the Thirties,' he explained. 'Temporarily – I never did fool with that show business too much. I didn't like it. Too much exposure out there in those tent shows. But I did a spell, back in the days of Sugarfoot Green.' With the closing of many of the barrelhouses in recent years and the extent of the curfew in Texas counties he has been obliged to take on other work. Only a few days before this record was made he had finished a tour with Doctor Sugar's Medicine Show, for although the medicine shows have virtually disappeared elsewhere, they are still to be found in Texas. In Texas the blues will die hard; today it still thrives and tough blues singers, pianists and guitarists of the order of Buster Pickens can still make a living even if, at times, 'it can be pretty rugged here'.

Nevertheless the great days of Texas blues were in the Twenties, when Pickens began to play for a living, and in the Thirties when he was one of scores of blues pianists whose fame went before them from town, to camp, to flagstop, to chock-house and honkytonk. These were the days when such pianists as Son Becky and Pinetop Burks, Andy Boy and Black Boy Shine were enjoying big local reputations, though if it had not been for a freak chance recording, they might never have been known outside Texas. Others, like Pickens himself, remained unrecorded though no less well known: the reminiscences of Texas Negroes are peppered with the names of fine blues artists which will never appear in the discographies. Buster Pickens knew them and worked with them, changed places with them in the never-ceasing blues entertainment of the barrelhouse joints. His blues are of the same order: his boogie basses, slow and fast, of the same character.

'Listen everybody . . . back in the late Twenties, early Thirties . . . when the blues touched a man's heart . . . whatever trouble he had, these blues solved his problems . . . even those tears soon dried up behind these blues . . .' he says when introducing 'Backdoor Blues', a version of the theme that he had heard Elzadie Robinson sing. He plays it slowly, sings in the husky, relaxed, sad tones that characterize the Texas blues and his fingers explore the keys unhurriedly. For this album Pickens recalled a number of the blues that were famous in past years, paying tribute in his essentially personal interpretations to the singing and playing of his companions: Hattie Burleson and 'Jim Nappy'; Joe Pullum and 'Hattie Green'. Slow and medium paced blues of this type; boogie instrumentals such as his 'She Caught the L & N' here authentically document the country blues piano of the Texas barrelhouses where the form originated. 'One shift goin' and one barrelhouse' – one shift working in the forests or in the sawmill and the other shift spending its time and money in the chock-joint on the site: drinking, talking, dancing, slow-dragging, singing and playing the blues. Sometimes, however, the music was faster and it was frequently rough. Appropriately, the second side opens with 'The Ma Grinder':

'I learned to play a number that was famous at that time which was known as

'The Dirty Dozens'. That was the openin'-up number of the house; we opened up with that number. Then we had another which was called 'The Ma Grinder' – that was "the first cousin to the Dozens". Well that number originated right in the barrelhouse. It was limited to that kind of life – in other words you couldn't carry it any further than just the barrelhouse. That was far as you *could* carry it; because it was a pretty rotten song, you know what I mean? So it wouldn't fit just anywhere, but it sure worked in the barrelhouse!' This is probably the first time that the famous but notorious Texas song has appeared on record.

If any aspect of the music is strongly featured in his playing it is that of the rail-road blues. 'Santa Fe Train', 'Rock Island Blues', 'She Caught the L & N', 'Mountain Jack' and 'Santa Fe Blues' are all train themes though they differ one from another. This is to be expected, for the life of the barrelhouse pianist in the vast state of Texas is strongly influenced by the railroads which link the centres. These are not necessarily the townships like Silsbee and Kilgore and Longview where Pickens would often play, but small, virtually unmapped railheads for the mill towns like Cowswitch and Raccoon Bend – well-known to the bluesmen if unrecognised by the Texas Almanac. Fittingly this album of Buster Pickens begins and ends with the Santa Fe, as did his 'territory'.

This is the first record that has appeared under Edwin Pickens' name, though it is not his sole recording. (He was playing with Leon Benton's Busy Bees when ' they accompanied Pickens' old acquaintance, the celebrated Texas Alexander, on his last record, 'Crossroads Blues'.) This has given him the opportunity to show some facets of his ability and it is to be hoped that others will follow. He is a stocky man with a deep speaking voice and a relaxed, easy manner of expressing himself. He dresses neatly in ageing clothes, his black suit, his bow tie and the quiff at his otherwise shaven forehead together proclaiming to those in the jukes that he is a pianist, not a mill–hand. Times are a little hard for him, but he takes opportunities as they come, hoping that one day the barrelhouses will be wide open again and that he can reply once more to the question 'Where ya going?'

'Cowswitch!'

Notes to Heritage 1008, 1960

Buster Pickens was shot and killed in an argument over a quarter, Houston, Texas, 24 November 1964.

7
Sittin' Here
Thinkin'

Illustration to "The Blues" *Jazz Monthly* Special Number, Vol 11, No 7, September 1965

How does one explain the interest in blues music in Europe? In Europe the picture's not the same as it is in the United States. You can't go to hear a blues singer or jazz musician just when you feel like it. There are a certain number of clubs where they play, but they can obviously only get to a very small audience. If you are an enthusiast, you really *are* an enthusiast, you try to find out as much about the music which fascinates you as you can; people who sing the music and so on. You also have to depend heavily on records and once you start collecting the records, you start finding out who's on the records; once you do that you get curious about who else they worked with, so you build up a kind of framework of knowledge and information which compensates for the lack of live music down the road.

Though there's nothing quite like listening to a blues singer in person, in a club or on his house porch especially, for me as for most enthusiasts, those records have been the raw material of our experience. Records compensate, too, for some of the things that you can miss from live entertainment, enabling you to bring the moment back and relive it, think about it. A lot of my life has just been spent 'sittin' here thinkin'' and listening to records. Of course you can listen, or only half-listen, and let the music wash over you. Or you can sing along, out loud or in your mind, with the singer and somehow participate with him as you listen. No one has done any research so far as I'm aware, on what we think we hear when we listen to blues, or what kind of pleasure we get out of doing so, or what it does for us, or how it does it. It's a fascinating subject in itself, and when most of the field-work has been done and all those biographies safely logged, I hope some day someone will do it.

After all, blues like all music, is both art and communication; we really know little about either aspect of its role though we do know quite a lot about blues as history, blues as personalities and blues as a social phenomenon. It so happens that all those aspects interest me a lot and I have over the past thirty years published a great deal on them. But I would still like to see more on the aesthetic of blues, more simply about the blues as *music* than I've seen in print. Whoever does that will have to get a lot of his material off the record too.

Much of my own writing has arisen from speculations on the records I've had: thoughts about where the singer may have come from, enquiries into the meaning of the terms that he uses, ideas about the influences and associations he has had. It has been a combination of hunches and theories, library hunting and research, interviews – and more 'sittin' here thinkin''. For someone fairly new to the blues, even for someone who has been listening to blues for ten years, a great deal of that speculation and its outcome is quite unknown. When the first blues discographies were being compiled there was remarkably little hard material to go on, and a great deal of listening, and yes, guesswork, had to make up for the lack of it. When there were no books to depend on and some very sketchy listings of records culled from old catalogues provided almost the only information on what a singer had done, or where he was, or when he lived, bending your ear to the speaker on the gramophone became an important activity.

Recalling the days when a few friends would cluster with me around a wind-up portable gramophone, furiously sharpening thorn needles on an Imhoff sandpaper strip meanwhile, seems like summoning up another life. We enjoyed arguing about the transcription of lyrics, or the straining after the fragmented syllables on a damaged record that was part of the experience. But I'm sure that such pleasures are shared by groups of enthusiasts in much the same way today, even if the records are long-play albums and the equipment made in Japan.

I'm aware that those friendly battles that were fought out long ago, and the exchanges of letters and hypotheses have no meaning now when the evidence that was being brought to an issue was eventually accepted as fact. For quite a few years I used to run a column in *Jazz Monthly* called 'Screening the Blues' – subsequently used as a title for a book that came out of some similar speculations – which was a platform for ideas about recordings, questions about pseudonyms, explanations of terms, comparisons of matrix sequences, suggestions as to musicians' identities and the like. I advanced a lot of theories myself and gave an airing to others; seen today, when most have been absorbed into *Blues and Gospel Records* or a similar work, they seem infinitely distant, if not irrelevant. But this book of items on blues off the record would not be representative if it didn't include something of that kind. So I have chosen a piece that I wrote on just three letters – the prefix JAX which signified a location recording, and the reasons why I felt that hitherto the letters had been incorrectly interpreted. After that it was received information; there was no more discussion on JAX and one more fragment of the blues jigsaw slipped into place. But who, looking at a completed jigsaw puzzle, remembers the frustrations of finding the right piece to fill in a single shape in the whole game?

I still like speculating today. There are a great many unanswered questions in the blues, and a lot of problems to be solved in blues history. Not all the clues are to be found in blues recordings, but some of them are. And some of them *might* be: what may be leads may also be misleading. Some recent speculations on singers about whom little or nothing is known beyond their records, are included here.

These, of course, are thoughts about individual singers and the blues that they sing; there are larger issues about the blues which also lead to speculation, of which the future of the blues is the most important. I wrote about its possible future in 1965 and now that nearly twenty years have passed it is interesting to look back from 'the future' to reconsider those observations. Do my thoughts then seem justified now? At the time I could see no 'real future'; I did not expect young blacks to take up the blues and I did not feel that it would gain wider acceptance in the middle class black milieu. Going back to Memphis and Mississippi a couple of years ago, I was surprised to find that there were young black blues singers around, and that blues still had some vitality in the State of its probable origin. Yet, reluctantly, I feel that while the process of decline has been slowed up, the blues will be spoken of more in the past than the present tense by the end of the century. By that time even the long-play reissue records will, in all probability, be a rarity.

What the future holds for me, as for anyone, is anybody's guess, but I do know that as long as I'm around I'll still be gaining a great deal of my pleasure from blues off the record, and doubtless I'll go on 'sittin' here thinkin'' about it.

The Jax Matrices
LOCATION SPECULATION

From Sweden, Bjorn Englund writes:

'The information in *Screening the Blues* (January) that Wesley Wallace is from Jacksonville is very interesting, for one *Minnie Wallace* recorded twelve titles for Vocalion in that very town in 1935, though only four were ever issued:

JAX 113-2	'The Cockeyed World'	Vo 03106
JAX 114-1	'Field Mouse Stomp'	—
JAX 115	'Let's All Do That Thing'	Vo 03145
JAX 148	'Pick 'em Up and Put 'em Down'	—

One of the unissued titles is 'Farish Street Stomp' (*sic!*) Is there any connection?'

By his reference to 'Farish Street Stomp' Bjorn Englund no doubt had in mind Little Brother Montgomery's 'Farish Street Jive' and that it was Little Brother who gave to Francis Smith the information that *a* Wesley Wallace came from Jacksonville. Bjorn also would presumably imply that there may exist some relationship between Minnie Wallace and Wesley Wallace on the basis (a) of surnames and (b) of Jacksonville associations. Minnie Wallace, however, recorded a few titles in 1929 in Memphis, Tennessee, for Victor. It is not inconceivable that in subsequent years she might have moved to Jacksonville, but the point must be borne in mind. Secondly, and this is the crux of the matter, do the letters JAX stand for 'Jacksonville' – or for somewhere else? What is the basis for the assumption that in fact this is a prefix to indicate a Florida recording location? This has bothered me for a few years and I have raised it once or twice with Derek Coller and other discographers. This seems an opportune time to consider the evidence.

JAX has for me now, incurable romantic that I am, memories of numerous jukes, bars and points where I have drunk the brand of beer of this name in Mississippi, Louisiana and Texas. The link is tenuous to say the least but I still associate JAX with Mississippi . . . Once, the JAX prefix to the Leroy Carter items mistakenly published in *Jazz Directory* as by Leroy Carr, gave rise to the theory that Leroy Carr was a Florida singer; even that his part-imitator Bumble Bee Slim came from that State too. This has been clarified but it is a warning of the importance that can be laid on a few letters. So we must proceed with caution.

In 'Discomania' – Walter Allen's excellent and lamented column in *Jazz Journal* – No. 64, he discussed the subject of Matrix Blocks. In this he established that the American Record Corporation – ARC – had studios in Los Angeles in 1933 indicated by the prefix LA. (LA-1 to LA-2371) which lasted until 1940 when these were supplanted by studios in Hollywood where the series was indicated by the prefix H (H-1 being 13 September 1940). The prefix DAL indicate the Dallas, Texas, studios used from September 1935–March 1941; the prefix FW the Fort Worth studios used from September 1934 to November 1936; the MEM prefix for the Memphis studios used in June/July 1939; and the SA prefix for the San Antonio location used for recordings from 1934 until 1938. The remainder he entered as *probable* locations implied by the prefixes, as follows: AUG for Augusta, Georgia; B for Birmingham, Alabama; HAT for Hattiesburg, Mississippi; HS for Hot Springs, Arkansas; SC for South Carolina; SL for St Louis – and 'JAX 100 – probably Jacksonville; Florida; October 1935'. Walter Allen, it may be stressed, suggests Jacksonville as a probability only, but one which repeats an opinion held when *Jazz Directory* Volume 2 was being compiled in the days when many a blues collector was still in the cradle.

My first serious doubts about the Jacksonville location theory arose when, quite a few years ago, Jim Davis loaned me a record by one Isaiah Nettles, and drew my attention to this very fine singer. Sung in a shrill voice, it was nonetheless unmistakably Mississippi in character and the guitar style was related to that of known Mississippi singers. One title was 'So Cold in China', the other was 'Mississippi Moan'. Moreover the artist was credited under the name of The Mississippi Moaner. The evidence of a Mississippi origin seemed obviously overwhelming and it occurred to me then that the matrix prefix JAX might have referred to Jackson, Mississippi, not Jacksonville, Florida. But without sufficient evidence to substantiate the theory at the time I kept to the customary usage and entered the latter as the recording location.

Through the courtesy of Helene Chmura, Derek Coller and Bert Whyatt, I have access now to the full matrix listing of the JAX SERIES of items recorded, both issued and unissued. These were made between 10 October 1935 and 22 October 1935 and examination of the files reveals many interesting points. First, however, I must refer back to Bjorn Englund's comment on Minnie Wallace. She recorded, as stated above, in Memphis, Tennessee, and therefore, if Jacksonville was not the location of the JAX recordings, Jackson, Tennessee, might have an equal claim to that of Jackson, Mississippi. Some support to this may be found in the fact that some seventeen titles were recorded by the Farmer Sisters who were apparently known, or self-styled, as The Tennessee Harmony Girls. One of their two issued records includes 'Little Home in Tennessee' (Vo 03104) as a further argument. But the unissued titles include 'Goin' Back to Texas' and 'Beautiful Texas' (JAX 127/8), 'Louisiana Moon' (JAX 111),

and 'Mississippi Valley Blues' (JAX 112). Though the fact that the only 'blues' – this could be a white group – refers to Mississippi is probably cancelled out by the references to Louisiana and Texas, the Tennessee title is also weaker as evidence in consequence. For the rest, nothing seems to bear out a reference to Jackson, Tennessee, unless one considers Minnie Wallace's unissued 'Jackson Stomp' (JAX 152) as being a Tennessee reference. I am of the opinion that the stomp is named after the Mississippi city, for the previous item is the one Bjorn mentioned – 'Farish Street Stomp' (JAX 151) – and Farish Street is one of the main Negro thoroughfares in Jackson, Mississippi. Little Brother Montgomery told me in Chicago that he had lived for a number of years in Jackson, Mississippi, and that his own 'Farish Street Jive' was indeed named after the street where he so often played.

What other evidence is to be found in the files? The Nations Brothers recorded 'Magnolia One-Step' (JAX 134); Mississippi is known as the Magnolia State and the magnolia is the State flower. That importance is, even now, attached to this is to be found, for example, in the paper place settings at cafe tables, giving the waiting patron something with which to amuse himself; a map of the United States emblems – and State flowers. The Nations Brothers also recorded 'Lincoln County Blues' (JAX 137). Lincoln County is not the county in which Jackson lies, but it is situated just a county away, due south on Highway 51. Lincoln County might well be the link for Blind Mack who made ten tempting titles though only one coupling was apparently issued. One of the sides, which I believe remains unissued, was 'Rochelle Blues'. Rochelle is not in Mississippi but in Louisiana, but for a blues singer travelling from Rochelle the route is clear: Highway 84 via Vicksburg to Brookhaven, Lincoln County and north to Jackson on

Highway 51.

Of the remainder, the two titles by the 'Delta Twins' may not be relevant but their own name is relevant enough to Mississippi. Another group, the Freeny Harmonizers included 'Roll on, Mississippi, Roll On' (JAX 204) amongst their half-dozen titles. Are all these references trivial? Too circumstantial? Perhaps in themselves and separately, they are, but together they seem to add up to a pretty convincing argument – even if Minnie Wallace did make a 'Cincinnati Blues' (JAX 116) and Isaiah Nettles made a 'Chicago Blues' (JAX 203). This is the sum total of references to specific places in the JAX SERIES; the recordings however, may reveal others. One thing is certain, Jacksonville, Florida, is never so much as hinted at.

Just one more point. On 22 October 1935 the last recordings of this eventful dozen days were made. They were four titles on JAX 212–215 made by Harry Chatmon – the brother of Sam Chatmon – Lonnie Chatmon, Bo Carter and other members of the family. Chris Strachwitz met him on his trip through the South in the summer of 1960 before we met in Memphis. For Harry Chatmon *still* lives in Jackson, Mississippi . . .

Jazz Monthly, April 1961

Got Cut All To Pieces

BESSIE TUCKER AND IDA MAY MACK

This collection brings together the voices of two of the finest country women singers known to us on record; 'on record' because women singers who were not on the vaude-ville circuit were recorded in very small numbers before the War. There is good reason for issuing them together for they shared two recording sessions on 29 and 30 August 1928 in Memphis, and the same accompanist, K. D. Johnson. Though both women came from Texas, at that time Victor had not set up recording facilities or their field units in Dallas, so they were brought to Memphis to record. How did Victor know of them? The question arises because they were the first Texas singers to be recorded by their units. It seems possible to me that they came to Memphis with another obscure Texas singer, Charlie Kyle, who was recorded on the same field trip, but their selection still seems unlikely in view of their anonymity.

Anonymous they certainly are; years of enquiries have revealed no data of substance on either singer, and close scrutiny of telephone directories and street census details for Dallas in the late Twenties has not led to a single lead. In 1960 when I discovered and interviewed Whistling Alex Moore, I asked him about the two women. He chuckled and shook his head, saying 'They're tough cookies, don't mess with them.' His use of the present tense made me think they were still around, but repeated questioning got no further information than 'Bessie did time in the pen'. This seemed firm enough, but Alex was otherwise extremely vague about both women and I rather suspect that he had heard their records and drawn his own con-clusions. A dozen years later he could not recall either name.

We know what they looked like from the Victor 'Race' catalogue illustrations repro-duced on the cover of this album, which shows the portraits of two pretty young women whose slight features hardly match their earthy voices. Ida May Mack had, it seems, a fair complexion, slightly buck teeth, and bobbed hair held in place with a fashionable bandeau; a soft line of draperies surrounds her neck. Bessie Tucker's features are more white than black, her lips thinnish, her skin light and her eyes alert. (Strange that two of the toughest voices in blues come from light-skinned, rather 'white' featured people: Bessie Tucker and Charley Patton.) Her long hair (or wig) is also held by a scarf or bandeau and she appears to have a lace-topped dress. All of which seems surprising when one hears them singing. Of the two, Ida May Mack is the lesser singer; a fraction less forceful, more deadpan in tech-nique using less ornamentation in her hand-ling of the words. But it is this simplified delivery, coupled with her strength of voice, which makes her blues convincing; there's little or no conscious artistry in her shaping of each blues and this gives them authen-ticity. Textually they are less interesting than Bessie Tucker's: she seems obsessed with abandonment and being jilted; in terms of theme 'When You Lose Your Daddy', 'Wrong Doin' Daddy' and 'Goodbye Rider' are virtually one blues. The thematic simi-larity is sustained in 'Elm Street Blues' even if the location has shifted from Beale Street in Memphis (on 'Wrong Doin') to 'Ellum' and Main in Dallas, and both 'Mr Moore Blues' and 'Mr Forty-Nine Blues' are not noticeably different in content, apart from their address to the two named men.

Unfortunately, it seems unlikely that 'Mr

Moore' was Alex Moore, though the suspicion remains. Mr Forty-Nine, however, is certainly K. D. Johnson, who is addressed by this title: 'play it for me Forty-Nine'. Tent shows in the plains were sometimes known as 'Forty-Nine shows', a term which may go back to the days of the Gold Rush when entertainment for the California miners was provided by travelling companies working under canvas. So it seems likely that K. D. Johnson was primarily a tent show pianist, which might account for the obscurity of this interesting and individual player. Occasionally his slightly 'under wraps' playing, controlled it seems, to accommodate the singers, is released, as in the lightly romping solo on 'Mr Forty-Nine Blues'. I suspect that he was more ragtime pianist than blues pianist in general, but that he may have listened to the few James P. Johnson accompaniments to Bessie Smith that had been issued up to that time, including the highly successful 'Backwater Blues', of which there is more than an echo on 'When You Lose Your Daddy'.

Two Ida May Mack items remained unissued, including the intriguingly titled 'Country Spaces'. She was not recorded when in August and October 1929 the Victor field unit recorded Bessie Tucker in Dallas. Bessie Tucker's combined titles tell a fuller story than do Ida May Mack's. She was a deep-voiced, tough singer whose accents have a rural Texas blacklands ring in her pronunciation of 'agree' as 'ogree', and 'thing' as 'thang'. Like Ida's, her rhyme schemes are artless: 'mind' rhymes with 'mind'; 'me' rhymes with 'me', or with 'Santa Fe', day/stay/away or behave/grave are used more than once, suggesting a singer who had not worked up more sophisticated stanzas for the stage. In spite of her Dallas references, Bessie Tucker may not have been known to the professional entertainers there. She was not recalled by either Sam

Price or Lillian Glinn, both of whom were very familiar with Ella B. Moore's Theatre and the Central Tracks cabarets of that time.

Bessie Tucker may well have been in the 'pen', as 'Penitentiary' (though she calls it 'Penritenshu' in her most ominous of blues) implies. 'Got Cut All To Pieces' has a violent theme, but such blues as 'Black Name Moan' and 'Key To The Bushes' shows a definite awareness of the prison farm. Both items are in fact, penitentiary farm work songs of the 'Captain captain' type. Few other singers on commercial records used such songs, though Texas Alexander, no stranger to the chain gang, was one who did. In her other blues Bessie Tucker makes frequent reference to the railroads, especially the Fort Worth and Denver and the Santa Fe, both of which served Fort Worth, and the Missouri-Kansas-Texas (the Katy) which paralleled the Santa Fe and served Dallas. Even the 'Dummy', the traditional term for a logging company train, provides the theme for one item sung to a slow version of the 'Tight Like That/Boot That Thing' melody.

Elusive though they are, perhaps through their impressive, formidable blues, we gain clues as to the personalities of these two women. I suspect that they were blues-singing street-walkers who never performed in the Park Theatre but sang with the brothel pianists between turning tricks. This would account for the pretty features, the preferred light skins, the fashionable hair styles and latest cut in dresses, and for the subjects of their blues. Was Bessie Tucker who had been 'in such a-trouble for the last few days' the woman who left Ida May Mack 'broken hearted, really worried in mind' over their pimp, K. D. Johnson? It's all speculation of course, but their convincing, insistent blues invite it. I doubt if we'll ever know their real identities, but at least we have their records.

Notes to Magpie PY 4408, 1978

Snatch It and Grab It
WALTER BUDDY BOY HAWKINS

Although serious field-work in blues research has been conducted for well over a score of years there are many gaps that remain to be closed. Walter Hawkins is a case in point – hardly a thing is known about him even though his recordings have been of considerable interest to blues enthusiasts for many years. It has been stated on more than one occasion that he came from Blythesville, Arkansas, but as far as I am aware no field research has been undertaken in that area to check the assertion. In view of the large numbers of blues enthusiasts who have beaten the highways south from Memphis to the Mississippi Delta it is surprising that none have chosen to go into the virgin territory that lies in the opposite direction. Blythesville is a small community in Mississippi County, Arkansas, which is situated in a lakes region at the extreme north-east of the State which nips into Missouri and Tennessee. It lies about sixty miles north of Memphis and was linked to it by railroad connections. Whether it turns out that Hawkins was from this interesting region or not, it is certainly an area which deserves local study.

As it happens, Hawkins does not mention Blythesville on his records, but he does mention Jackson, Mississippi, several times on 'A Rag Blues' stating that the piece comes from there. On 'Snatch It Back Blues' he says: 'Listen here people, these my blues I brought 'em all the way from Birmingham.' If he did not come from either city he does show some awareness of them. There are some elements in his singing, particularly the rather strident, barking tone that he employs, that do suggest a link with other Alabama singers, though such speculations are highly subjective.

One aspect of his blues that may be significant is his reference to railroads. Though trains are a common theme in both blues and gospel song, working on the tracks is not. There are a few recordings by blues singers which are clearly related to work song – some by Texas Alexander (Matchbox Bluesmasters MSE 206) have already been discussed, and 'Working on the Railroad' belongs to this small class. It is somewhat more descriptive: 'when you hear the captain call "You men, let's move that rail".' He gives as an explanation: 'my black woman she needs the money, that's why I work so hard; if I don't keep on rollin' she'll have another black man in my yard.' Of course, it is possible that he may have projected himself into the situation but it is also reasonable to consider that the blues was directly related to his own experience. Railroad engines figure in 'Number Three Blues': 'I say I flagged Number Four mama, she kept on wheelin' by; I couldn't do anything, partner, but fold my little arms and cry.' And again: 'Here comes Number Three with her headlight turned down; I believe to my soul she's Alabama bound.' Though the verses of 'Snatch It Back' are somewhat more conventional: 'I'm gonna lay my head mama down on some railroad track; so when that train come along I'm gonna snatch it back' and 'I can get more jet black women than that Southern freight train can hold', he does use railroad imagery. To this we might add his frequent reference to himself as 'Buddy Boy' and to his equally frequent use of 'Partner' as a rhetorical form of address. Both terms were common among hobos in the 1920s, when asking the name of origins of fellow 'vags' and 'bos' was not encouraged. In this light his use of the phrase on 'Awful Fix Blues' . . . 'I just strolled in your town; If I ask you for a favour please don't turn me down' has added significance.

If Buddy Boy Hawkins had been a youthful hobo, and had worked on the railroad as a casual itinerant labourer, he would have been in a position to have picked up a variety of songs and instrumental pieces from other bums on the road. Apart from his blues which, in the case of 'Jailhouse Fire' in particular, were quite original, he also played a number of ragtime dances and songs from the vaudeville and tent shows. In the latter category are 'How Come Mama Blues', a country version of a popular vaudeville song, 'How Come You Do Me Like You Do?' which had been recorded by Edith Wilson, Trixie Smith with the Original Memphis Five and by many other singers and groups. 'Snatch It and Grab It' is of this genre and is of the same tune family as Henry Thomas' 'Fishing Blues' among many other songs of similar type. It seems likely that Hawkins was himself an entertainer, possibly on the medicine shows, where 'Voice Throwing Blues' would have been a good crowd-fetching act. Like the Charlie McCarthy show, there is something incongruous about ventriloquism on radio or on record, for the trick is only really effective in live performance. Voice throwing in particular, which requires an illusion of projection of the voice beyond the proximity of a ventriloquist and his dummy, has to be experienced in person. Hawkins however, used a reedy, nasal second 'voice' which can be produced with the lips parted and tongue movement alone; it is skilfully alternated with his natural singing voice on an old standard, 'Hesitating Blues'.

Evidently Buddy Boy Hawkins was a guitarist of considerable accomplishment, whose instrumental command and use of harmonic structures far in advance of most rural black musicians has been the subject of analysis by Jerome Epstein. In his playing, Epstein detects classical Flamenco techniques, and he suggests that Hawkins picked them up in Europe during the First World War. It's possible, though black troops were in the front line, and not on the Spanish border. More likely he picked up the Spanish sequences heard clearly on 'A Rag Blues' from Mexicans in Texas as did Little Hat Jones. But whatever his sources, Buddy Boy Hawkins was a major figure in black country music.

Notes to Matchbox Bluesmaster
MSE 202, 1981

Poor Boy Blues

BO WEAVIL JACKSON

In the documentation of the rural blues Bo Weavil Jackson remains as a rather enigmatic figure. He recorded only twice, making half-a-dozen titles at each session, with a couple of takes issued of his 'Jefferson County Blues'. The sessions appear to have been only a few weeks apart, perhaps even less, and after 30 September 1926 he seems to have slipped back into the obscurity from whence he came.

According to the record salesman Harry Charles, who was interviewed forty years later by Gayle Dean Wardlow, he was found 'in the streets takin' up nickels'. Charles, who was part owner of the E. E. Forbes Piano Company in Birmingham, Alabama, recalled that Jackson's first name was James. It may well have been, but it may also have been Sam, for it was as Sam Butler that he recorded for Vocalion. Following a practice employed by musicians like George Thomas, or later, Roosevelt Sykes, he might have used his mother's name for his recordings for a rival company. It was as Bo Weavil Jackson that he recorded first for Paramount, and this is likely to have been the name by which he was known, even though promoters had a penchant for giving their artists colourful sobriquets. This is suggested by 'Devil and My Brown', a title which was then unissued. On it he sang in a blues version several verses of the 'Ballad of the Boll Weevil', which may well have been the tune by which he was known in Alabama. We can assume an origin in that state partly from the fact that Harry Charles found him there, partly because Birmingham is situated in Jefferson County, and partly from some stylistic features in his work – even though Paramount referred to him as coming 'down from the Carolinas'.

Bo Weavil Jackson may have been playing for coins in the street but he seems to have been a very accomplished guitarist, and a singer who was well aware of the recordings of other blues artists. 'Devil and My Brown', for instance, is derived from a Tom Delaney composition, 'Down Home Blues', with its 'Hey Lawdy Mama' tune, adapted to the 'Boll Weevil' theme mentioned above. It seems that he was a synthesizer of various sources who moulded the songs that he heard as well as the blues and spirituals of recording singers to his own, individual way of singing and playing.

Some of Bo Weavil Jackson's blues clearly derive from traditional sources and are important in the identification of the currents of standard themes that run through early blues. His first title for Paramount is a case in point; commencing with an eight-bar theme, 'Pistol Blues' is a version of 'Crow Jane', a blues which is frequently associated with the Carolinas and which therefore appeared to give some support to the possibility that he had come from that region. But it is also well-known elsewhere as 'Red River Blues' and even, with only a slight change of tune, as 'How Long, How Long Blues'. Jeff Todd Titon in *Early Downhome Blues (p 169)* considers it as the core theme of a blues 'tune family' which also includes 'Key to the Highway' and 'Slidin' Delta'. Though this is an aspect that clearly needs more research, Bo Weavil Jackson's 'Pistol Blues' is one of the earliest recordings of the theme. Half-way through, however, he changes the tune and moves to another form which may be representative of an early stage in the blues, a sixteen-bar, *aaa-b* sequence.

Another blues which is of verifiable early

date is 'Poor Boy Blues' which is played by Jackson with beautiful slide guitar. At least as early as 1910 it was being played this way, as Howard Odum and Guy Johnson noted when they published it the following year. The 'knife instrumental' as they called it, was 'regularly associated with several songs' of which 'Po' Boy Long Ways From Home' was one. Other versions include Blind Willie McTell's 'Travelin' Blues', Barbecue Bob's 'Poor Boy A Long Ways From Home' and Banjo Joe (Gus Cannon's) similarly titled piece.

Two takes exist of 'Jefferson County' which give a good indication how a folk blues singer associates certain blues stanzas with an overall theme, but changes their order or introduces new ones. Also sung to a slide guitar accompaniment with some fine bass runs, the versions include several references to Birmingham and Alabama. Another comparison may be made between the issued Paramount version of 'You Can't Keep No Brown' and the alternative, unissued recording of the blues. Here again a few core themes or phrases are the unifying elements but each version is treated virtually

as a new song. The latter seems to have been influenced to some extent by Blind Lemon Jefferson, whose guitar runs and closing coda he interprets rather than copies.

Textually, Bo Weavil Jackson's lyrics are interesting as examples of sequential narrative. Certain of his verses occur in the records of 'classic' women singers, particularly Bessie Smith and Ma Rainey and the latter singer would appear to have been an influence on his vocal style. Although his voice is strident and pitched fairly high, he uses an intonation and delivery that is close to Rainey's, particularly on 'Why Do You Moan?'. Generally his playing is more adventurous on his blues and he uses slide guitar in a church moaning style on gospel items. An early recording of the 'Saints' as a solo piece is of interest, though he seems to have introduced a phrase from it in 'Heaven Is My View' which varies slightly from the usual tune. But this may have been deliberate: it would have been in keeping with the approach of a very individual artist who clearly liked to juxtapose and interweave melodies and accompaniments from different sources.

Notes to Matchbox Bluesmaster
MSE 203, 1983

The Future of the Blues
LOOKING BACK AT LOOKING FORWARD

The blues, as a folk music of the American Negro, is essentially a twentieth-century art form. Though speculations on its origin in slavery or in the popular music of the nineteenth century, or even in the music of Africa, imported and adapted to changing needs, are made frequently, there seems no doubt that the blues in the forms that we now recognize did not exist much before 1900. Probably its origins, even the reasons why it came about, are lost for good, but it is still possible at this point in time to hear in personal performance most of its phases and styles. This situation cannot last much longer, and there is every argument for the sort of grant and sponsorship of study of the blues that has been accorded researchers in the beginnings of New Orleans jazz over the past decade. This is unlikely to happen, and it seems a part of the total story of the blues that it will not happen. As an art form – or art forms – jazz music has developed more or less concurrently with the blues and has been continually fed and revitalized by it. It was the blues that sparked jazz into life, that separated it from the music of the street parade or the ragtime pianist. And if there is any common factor that unites the widely divergent forms of jazz that have originated, flourished and in some instances already died during the past half century, it is the continued stimulation of the blues. How he plays the blues, his instrumental adaptation of the vocal blues, is still the criterion by which a jazz musician of almost any school is evaluated.

If jazz has depended on the blues for one of its essential qualities, the opposite is not the case. The blues has been influenced very little by jazz; few blues singers are aware of jazz musicians and their music, except as important figures who have made their way in a predominantly white world. Louis Armstrong and Count Basie will be known, and their music enjoyed, and they typify, along with much more blues-orientated musicians like Ray Charles, the achievements of a select few of the Negro race. But if jazz had never existed the blues would have flourished very well without it.

Until recently the blues had not significantly broken across the colour barrier; it was self-sufficient music which had real relevance to a segregated minority group and was interesting to a select few outside that group as a social curiosity, and to the jazz historian. The jazz historian generally acknowledged the influence and importance of blues in jazz, and always gave at least passing reference to the folk music form. It was, however, considered from the standpoint of jazz, and thus the form and the musical characteristics played a far greater part in these references than any understanding why the blues singer exists or why he chooses this idiom to express what he has to say. The content of blues – its reason for being – was of little importance to the appreciation of jazz.

Blues as a music of itself with its own message and its own values has received little critical favour, but the form did gain a wider audience and one which broke into a sphere outside of jazz with the appearance of Leadbelly. The Lomax's oft-retold discovery of the singer had a great influence on the folk music world, and incidentally confined the blues in a new strait-jacket. For now the blues was accepted as part of the body of Negro folk song, and conversely Leadbelly's highly personalized adaptations of an extraordinarily wide range of song were somehow established as the criterion by which all blues singers could be measured. His unique personality and unrivalled repertoire conveniently encompassed in one man the range of musical forms which, on the one hand, might be said to have been the folk influences on jazz and, on the other, could represent the Negro's contribution to American folk song as a whole. Unwittingly perhaps, he helped to shape a view of Negro song and therefore of blues which remains in the jazz field and has largely conditioned thinking in the folk field to the present day, some thirty years after his first appearance in New York.

Within the past decade the blues has suddenly spread its influence outside the artificial but definite confines of a racial group to become a significant force in the shaping of popular music. The dramatic changes in popular music which were occasioned by the advent of Rock 'n' Roll and Rhythm 'n' Blues have not been welcomed by the academics, the students of jazz or folk music. Views on such forms of popular music in which the blues is powerfully evident, range from despair at the degeneration of musical values, to the scorn of the specialized blues magazines at the imitation of the authentic article. Both have some basis in fact but the inescapable truth is that a vigorous folk music has broken out of racial confines to have an all-pervading, worldwide significance; profoundly and irrevocably changing popular culture. The reasons are manifold and could perhaps be equated with the new militancy of the American Negro, the moves towards enfranchisement and equality, and the self-conscious awareness of the Negro element in society by the liberal whites. It is also very much a part of the great social change that has taken place with the emergence of a recognizable teenage culture. It is an unlovely thought that social divisions may be necessary to society,

but as class structure becomes less defined and as deliberate attempts to break down racial segregation are becoming effective, a horizontal section has been sliced through Western society which divides the teenagers from the adults. They may feel resentment at an adult society that cuts them off, but it is a separation to which they willingly contribute and express in clothes, morals and behaviour patterns of their own. The blues, a totally twentieth-century art form of a similarly separate section of society, has had a topical relevance and, in its most recent forms, an aggressive blatancy that has won immediate sympathy in the new and youthful pop culture. That this is bolstered by mass media and the machinery of advertising and commercial exploitation of young entertainers, does not in any way affect the relevance of the music to them, at least for the time being. The changing dictates of fashion and the continual desire for the novel and the 'new sound' means that the blues is being devoured at an extraordinary rate. An examination of the compositions of the British 'beat' groups and their influences from blues sources over the past three years would reveal a rapid consumption of styles and group sounds which have taken a quarter of a century of evolution in Negro America.

The blues, from the point of view of the jazz world, is an influence of a musical form on a more significant music; from the folk view it is part of a body of Negro folk song which has become corrupted and commercialized in recent years; from the standpoint of popular music it has become a vital influence on the development of 'beat' music and to a great extent on current popular forms as a whole, to be superseded no doubt before long by still newer developments.

And what of the blues in Negro society, from which it originates and of which it has been an essential part of its creative culture in this century? It depends to a large extent on what one means by blues. It was stated earlier that it is possible to hear most phases and forms contemporaneously. This is broadly true, given the determination and the opportunity. If blues originated in work song it is possible to hear the last gasps of group work song in certain of the Southern penitentiaries; if its roots were in the field hollers and solo work songs, there are still cotton fields in Mississippi and Texas where they are sung. If the blues was a part of the Negro song tradition there are still veteran songsters who can sing the tunes that were to be heard at the turn of the century, who can draw on the experience of country suppers and medicine shows and the folk themes of latter-day rural communities. A Mance Lipscomb, or a Mississippi John Hurt, a Furry Lewis or a Bill Jackson can still be heard reminiscing about the music of fifty years ago and recalling the songs that were once prevalent in Negro families and functions. If the blues is the music of the singer who expresses himself in this vehicle exclusively, it is possible to hear old men, of once near legendary fame, singing the blues that they habitually played in the Twenties and Thirties; men like Sleepy John Estes and Bukka White, Son House and Skip James, Big Joe Williams and Fred McDowell. The blues of the Northern cities, rather than that of the Southern States which these figures largely represent, may be heard in the forms that emerged during and after the Second World War from the singing and playing of Jazz Gillum, Eddie Boyd, Memphis Slim, or until his death last year, Sonny Boy Williamson No. 2. The post-War blues in its toughest forms, as exemplified by Muddy Waters or Howling Wolf, is still sung by these men; in its Southern forms still played by Lightnin' Hopkins and Lightnin' Slim.

On the face of it, therefore, the blues are healthy enough, and the survival of all these singers of varying types can be credited to a virile tradition. Add to these the barrel-house pianists like Speckled Red and Whistling Alex Moore, the non-playing singers like Bumble Bee Slim, or the jazz-blues singers like Joe Turner and Jimmy Rushing, and the lists seem never-ending. Only the 'classic blues' of the Twenties seem to have died, with just a few lone figures like Victoria Spivey and Hannah Sylvester still around occasionally to sing the tale. But examination of the singers listed or any counterpart lists that might be drawn up soon reveals that even the youngest of them are around fifty years of age; the oldest are over seventy. It also soon becomes clear that with the exception of the 'post-War singers' they are 're-discovered' artists. In other words, that we can hear them now is entirely due to the specific efforts of a small number of dedicated enthusiasts who, in a variety of eventful trips, have sought out and found old forgotten musicians whose records they have admired from the distance of a thousand miles and perhaps thirty-odd years.

During the past five years or so, the number of old blues singers who have been found and recorded again is quite remarkable. The results have been of varying quality – tragic in the instance of, say, Peg Leg Howell; revelatory in the case of John Hurt. Some singers have preserved intact their music of three decades ago; others have been 'working on it' and there are hopes of future recordings. With others it is different. Arthur Petties, Freddie Spruell, Romeo Nelson, Doug Suggs – these are only a few of the blues singers known on record and in discographies to blues enthusiasts, whose rediscovery has not been followed by recording sessions, for they have forgotten all they knew, and hear with disbelief the records they made as young men. Time has passed them by and with it the changing pattern of Negro society – their old-time blues have no meaning in modern Chicago (where all these men live), and little for them either. With the encouragement and help of their discoverers, singers like Son House, Skip James and others have recaptured their old abilities. Some, like Scrapper Blackwell, never did. Only a few had the determination to turn angrily on their discoverers for interfering with their lives, like Kokomo Arnold for instance, who has steadfastly refused to have anything to do with playing again. For others has come disappointment as legal wrangles and jealous arguments between would-be managers have been over their heads: John Hurt has gone back to Mississippi.

In the main, the discovery of the older singers has been part of a great awakening of interest in the blues, and the devoted collectors who have sought them and found them have done so out of a love for their music. It has not always been paralleled by an understanding of their relation to their previous environment or the cultural shock that comes of transplantation and entry into the world of folk song festivals and coffee houses. Blues singers may sing about chain gangs and violence, drugs and sex, but they surprise when they suit action to the words. That Big Joe Williams has twice been jailed for knifings since rediscovery has not been publicized in the blues field; that many singers on visits to Europe have taken the apparently non-segregated parties at face value to the embarrassment of unwary girls and the pain of the artists alike is similarly evaded. For the blues singer who has been rediscovered has a role to play: he is a museum piece, an ambassador for his race, and a justification of the recognition of the blues that a select group of admirers have afforded. He must play to the unwritten rules: Bukka White has been called an 'Uncle Tom' by some critics in unguarded moments, and a garrulous old man by others – because he still remembers the rules of life

in Memphis and Hannibal, Mississippi, where he has been dwelling all these years. An ex-con from Parchman Farm, he can't forget them easily.

To the Negro world at large, this new interest in the folk blues means little. Though Muddy Waters still sings at Peppers Lounge, and Howling Wolf at Silvio's in Chicago, they are 'old men' to the younger singers and to the younger listeners. Already their audiences are ex-migrants who 'came up' at the same time as the singers themselves during the War years. Their children, if they like the blues at all, may admire the singing of Magic Sam or Buddy Guy; more often they will worship popular music idols whose links with the blues at best are tenuous.

It is one of the many popular romantic fictions about the blues that whilst there is social injustice, segregation and discrimination, whilst in fact there are reasons to sing the blues, the blues will continue. That there is a need for a catalyst of the emotions, for an aggressive outlet in musical form is probably true, but there is no special reason why the blues should perform this function. The great rise in popularity of the gospel song probably reflects this need and it may well assume the part the blues have played with the added advantage of having God on its side. It is a long time since the blues has had much to say about social conditions, low wages, high rents, unemployment; and as a vehicle for direct racial protest it has seldom been important. Anger and frustration may well be canalized into sexual themes which form the major proportion of blues, but it does not need the blues to express sexual or amatory subjects. Popular song can do this just as well and it is only the license that the blues enjoys which currently makes it more suitable for this purpose.

For the younger Negro there are connotations of discrimination in the nature of the blues itself; he recognizes it as a part of a past which he would rather forget: the blues are not embraced by CORE or the NAACP, the Black Muslims or any other active or militant group, and insofar as he wants to make his way in a world that is integrated, he does not want to take the blues with him. The future of the blues does not seem to rest with the younger generation. The discovery of a Short Stuff Macon, aged thirty and singing the old style blues, only points up the anachronism.

The future of the blues hardly lies with the jazz world which is fearful enough of its own future and never had a significant relevance to the blues. It cannot reside in the artificially propagated circumstances of the folk song revival which is still directed backwards to the formative stages of the country blues. It is unlikely to have any future in the pop music of the western world for all its present influence, for this is too ephemeral, too subject to new influences and fashions to last. In spite of the fervent belief that the future of the blues is in their hands, it is equally unlikely that it will survive through the imitations of the young white college copyists, the 'urban blues singers', whose relation to blues is that of the 'trad' jazz band to the music of New Orleans: sterile and derivative. The bleak prospect is that the blues has probably no real future; that, folk music that it is, it served its purpose and flourished whilst it had meaning in the Negro community. At the end of the century it may well be seen as an important cultural phenomenon – and someone will commence a systematic study of it, too late.

New Contact, Autumn 1966

Acknowledgements

During the past three decades I have been indebted to many magazine editors and people involved in the record industry who have invited me to write for them. This book, in fact, is indirectly the outcome of an idea of one of them, Karl Emil Knudsen of Storyville Records. I had written a number of notes for his 'Portraits in Blues' series which comprised European recordings of visiting blues singers. He suggested that the notes might be compiled into a booklet and though problems arose which prevented our doing so, the present collection stemmed from it, and includes some of those 'Profiles'.

That was in the late Sixties. By then I had been writing pieces on blues for more than fifteen years, commencing with articles for Sinclair Traill and Tom Cundall's *Jazz Journal*. Tom was also responsible for my writing for *Music Mirror*, later edited by Jack Higgins, which provided a 'platform' for my blues researches. Albert McCarthy gave me the opportunity to write longer articles for *Jazz Monthly* (later, *Jazz and Blues*) which were hazily discussed with other contributors at the unofficial *Monthly* office, Long's Wine Bar in Soho. Before meeting them in New York, I corresponded with Martin Williams and Nat Hentoff who invited me to write for the long-lamented *Jazz Review*. Jazz magazines had a struggle to establish roots in the States, but Pauline Rivelli's *Jazz* did establish itself, for a while. (My article 'Good morning, Gentlemen' in *Jazz* provoked the most violent reaction I've ever had to a piece of writing.) Eventually the magazine conceded to current taste and became *Jazz and Pop*. Then there were articles for *Jazz Beat*, edited by Derek Kells and Simon Meares, for Tessa Goldsmith's *New Contact*, and Jim and Amy McNeal's *Living Blues*. Some too, for Simon Napier, Mike Ledbitter and later, Mike Rowe and the *Blues Unlimited* team, though in this instance none are reprinted here as they have already appeared in book form.

It was as a graphic designer of record sleeves that I first did free-lance work for record companies. My designs for Peter Gammond and Ray Turner at Decca, for London and other labels, as well as the odd item for Carlo Cramer's Esquire label, had to be in 'two colours, black and white, line' in those days; when photographs and glossy sleeves were adopted my illustrative approach went out. Then there were jacket designs for jazz books, and line illustrations for John Underwood at the *Radio Times*. The first sleeve note I wrote was for J. R. T. Davies' Ristic issue of Blind Blake; many others followed, particularly for Fred Burkhardt of Dutch Philips and Riverside, for whom I co-ordinated the Philips Classic Jazzmasters series.

As a result of my extended field trip in the United States in 1960, Chris Strachwitz, who accompanied Val and myself in the South, issued a number of our recordings on his new label, Arhoolie. His subsidiary, Blues Classics, also called for liner notes. Some of the recordings we made in the States were issued by Tony Standish on his limited edition Heritage label, and by Doug Dobell on 77 Records. I was grateful for their faith in the Blues Research and Recording Project which Robert M. W. Dixon devised to provide funds for the sessions. More notes followed, for Terry Brown and the 'Folk Blues USA' series on Fontana, for Mike Vernon at Decca and his own Blue Horizon, and for David Howells at CBS. By the early Seventies I needed a respite, but eventually Steve Lane at the VJM team, and John R. T. Davies, Norman Stevens and the Fountain label asked for a note or two. So did Bruce Bastin of Flyright, including a few for Francis Smith's pioneering 'The Piano Blues' series on Magpie. Recently I've had a great deal of pleasure doing sleeve notes for Johnny Parth and Wolf Records and for Gef Lucena's Matchbox Bluesmaster series.

All these editors and record people wouldn't be in such a marginal field if they didn't love the music. I am in their debt for the opportunity to reprint some of those writings here, and my warmest thanks go to them. In a few instances some of those old friends are sadly no longer with us, and others I have been unable to trace. My sincere apologies to anyone whom I may have inadvertently overlooked or whose permission to reprint I wasn't able to obtain; I ask to be excused – for good times' sake! Finally, I owe a special debt of gratitude to Liz Thomson who coped with the scores of magazines and record sleeves, and advised on what should go in and what should be omitted; and to Kathleen Morley-Clarke who undertook the daunting task of editing the material.

Paul Oliver
Oxfordshire, 1984

Index